EUROPE'S
ANGRY
MUSLIMS

EUROPE'S ANGRY MUSLIMS

The Revolt of the Second Generation

ROBERT S. LEIKEN

OXFORD
UNIVERSITY PRESS

Oxford University Press, Inc., publishes works that further
Oxford University's objective of excellence
in research, scholarship, and education.

Oxford   New York
Auckland   Cape Town   Dar es Salaam   Hong Kong   Karachi
Kuala Lumpur   Madrid   Melbourne   Mexico City   Nairobi
New Delhi   Shanghai   Taipei   Toronto

With offices in
Argentina   Austria   Brazil   Chile   Czech Republic   France   Greece
Guatemala   Hungary   Italy   Japan   Poland   Portugal   Singapore
South Korea   Switzerland   Thailand   Turkey   Ukraine   Vietnam

Published by Oxford University Press, Inc.
198 Madison Avenue, New York, NY 10016

www.oup.com

Oxford is a registered trademark of Oxford University Press

Library of Congress Cataloging-in-Publication Data
A CIP record is available from the Library of Congress

ISBN 9780195328974

9 8 7 6 5 4 3 2 1

Printed in the United States of America
on acid-free paper

TO KATE

CONTENTS

PROLOGUE

THE STRATFORD CHILDREN

Outside the mosque on Stratford Street hangs a sign that reads "the Muslim Assosiation [*sic*] Mahdrasah." I encounter similar evidence of a foreign-born, first-generation leadership outside all the mosques I visit on Beeston Hill, the home of the bombers who terrorized the London subway system. The bombers had attended this fundamentalist mosque.

As I stand gazing at the maladroit sign, the door flies open and out streams a troop of tiny worshippers. They crowd the steps we stand on, faces lifted to me. I am among schoolchildren. Aged five and upwards, boys only, they tell me they come weekdays two hours each afternoon. But if the children here, as in Yeats's poem, "learn to 'be neat in everything,'" they decidedly are not here to "to cipher and to sing / To study-reading books and histories. . . . In the best modern way." No sums are conned in this place, and music is heard only in the profane Sufi mosque up on Hardy Street. The second generation is at Stratford Street to memorize the ancient Qur'an in Arabic, not a word of which they understand.

But hang on! During the day these kids go to public schools, like Hillside Day School, where the leader of the bombers, Mohammed Sidique Khan, was a teaching assistant. In the public schools there are girls and a medley of nationalities—Sikhs, Hindus, and Afro-Caribbeans. But the test scores and graduation rates of the Pakistani children trail those of other minorities.

Here at the Stratford Street *madrasah*, the teacher has mastered Arabic, not merely memorizing the lovely cadences but understanding their meaning. His pupils, however, some of them as young as four, learn only the sonorous sounds. As I await their imam, the students are friendly and curious, telling me their ages and their course of study, looking up at me in wonder. "Ah-Merry-Ka? Where is that?" It is so fun to have an exotic stranger appearing at the mosque door, like a visitor from Mars.

But there are hard looks fixed on me from the elderly men in pale green *salwar kameez*, standing apart from a group of veiled women. All seem to share a hostility the children have not yet learned. It even took the affable Sidique Khan a long time to acquire it.

The youngsters crowd around; their jeans, in accord with Salafi custom, are rolled above the ankle. They are eager to chat with this friendly alien. Until a menacing man approaches. He has been conferring darkly with the other, older men, who are all glaring at me from across the street. The scowling man, who won't look me in the face, announces fiercely that I am "standing on private property," and with his clenched jaw he thrusts himself forward and commands me to "move off." I step off the footstep on to the sidewalk. "Sure, what's the problem?" "Don't speak to these children!" "Okay, but what's wrong with doing that?" "You could be a pedophile." "I am a scholar. I was waiting for the imam." "The imam speaks no English; he speaks only Arabic." "With whom may I speak?" "Speak with men." "Could I talk with those men across the street?" "Those men don't want to talk with you."

Who am I? I am a connoisseur of slums. During a decade spent as an unlikely, and clandestine, revolutionary organizer in Mexico, I shared a fourth-floor walk-up in a bleak Mexico City proletarian housing project where electricity was a sometime thing. I spent weekends in the sole second-story room of the home of an "advanced worker" in a shanty-town outside an industrial park in Morelos. After that, I was a civil rights organizer in white Fields Corner, Dorchester, as blacks moved in during Boston's racial tensions in the 1970s. I got used to menacing stares. I knew South Boston when angry whites threw stones at school buses carrying Roxbury's blacks into neighborhood schools. During the 1980s I walked the sulking slums of Managua and Contra camps in Honduras. I spent days in territories occupied by Salvadoran guerrillas, and in Guatemalan villages terrorized by death squads. But rarely would I as an American encounter the kind of hostility that awaited me on Beeston Hill.

TRAVEL ADVISORY

In the 1970s I went, a sprig of the 1960s, to Latin America in search of Revolution—and found it in shantytowns, slums, Indian villages, peasant movements, union halls, classrooms, campus protests, and "liberated territories" where I became an improbable underground propagandist and organizer. I had second thoughts when I got to know some of the Revolution's many victims in Sandinista Nicaragua. Telling their story in Washington led to elections that produced the unprecedented peaceful deposition of a despotic regime.

But I would find myself, with the Cold War behind, like Tennyson's aged Ulysses by a "still hearth . . . among barren crags. . . . Made weak by time and fate. . . ."

How dull it is to pause, to make an end,
To rust unburnished, not to shine in use!

So I opted to explore yet one more mysterious world, bringing to it what I have "seen and known; cities of men / And manners, climates, councils, governments."[1] This time, the enterprise would be confined to the collection of data and to reportage and analysis.

My story here is of terrorists and rioters, of tribes and immigrants, of fathers and sons, of alien mentors ("Outsiders") and their second-generation pupils ("Insiders"), and of Islam in its copious, sometimes rivalrous, manifestations. What follows aspires to analysis, to decompose seeming wholes into constituent parts, to break down molecules into atoms and atoms into particles. For those occasions when the constituent elements may be unfamiliar, the reader may wish to consult the glossary.

To try to relate the tale of Muslim anger in each European country would hazard a volume too massive for the general reader and yet too shallow for the specialist. Hoping to interest both, I chose to focus on the three European countries with the most Muslims—Britain, France, and Germany. Each country has its own set of circumstances and responses, thus making possible a comparative approach. Because the jihadis who were responsible for the March 2003 Madrid train bombings were first-generation, not second-generation, immigrants,

Spain receives only passing attention, as I explain in the User's Guide (chapter 4).

Among Britain, France, and Germany, this study pays most attention to the United Kingdom, which I often place in pointed contrast to France. Indeed, the Island Nation and the Hexagon here form opposite poles, in terms both of policy and peril: France's professed assimilation and Britain's studied communalism; the former's relative success in banishing jihadism and the latter's chronic accommodation to it. The two immigration-cum-security regimes occupy different ends of a range within which the rest of Western Europe, including Germany, can be said to fall. Germany receives less attention than those antipodes, in part because Germany had not, as of this writing, suffered a major terror attack that could serve, as in the cases of Britain and France, as material for analysis. But the reader of the Germany section will receive sufficient alarming detail to prepare him or her should that eventuality befall.

We travel initially to France in part one, and the opening chapter tells the story of Khaled Kelkal, our first European postmigrant jihadi and the author of attacks on French trains in 1995. His tale presents the classic case of the Muslim victim of discrimination, of "Islamophobia," who evolves into an extremist.

But France did not go on to host a sequence of Islamist jihadis—a fate reserved for Britain—as our analysis of its widely misunderstood "riots" in chapters 2 and 3 will show these had little to do with Islamism or jihad. In the course of refuting alarmist stereotypes, those chapters introduce the predicament of Europe's second-generation Muslims in its knotty complexity. (The term "second generation" refers literally to the progeny of those who immigrated into Europe, or the "first generation." These offspring were socialized in the new country, by virtue of birth or entry as children. As the scholarly literature does, I will use the term "second generation" loosely to embrace, as the occasion merits, the third generation, and the entire set of postmigrants.)

Part two, "Guides for the Perplexed," first offers "A User's Guide" that may serve as orientation for the reader who wishes to travel further. This necessary background places "the second generation" in a broader context and defines and contextualizes jihad, Islamism, immigration, and other terms and issues. It is important to understand these matters so as to avoid the puzzlements and pitfalls and the siren songs the reader is likely to encounter. As he ventures ahead, he may wish to consult that travel manual to supplement the glossary.

Chapter 5, "The Outside," chronicles "the Muslim Awakening," the sundry origins, in the Middle East and South Asia, of the "single narrative" that has fired European Muslim radicalization. The Inside is the focus of chapter 6, "The Unwanted," which traces the routes, expectations, and destinies of European Muslim immigrants, their reception by host governments and communities, and the plight of their children. Chapter 7, "Angles of Aggregation," describes the basic approaches of the three major European Muslim host countries: France, Germany, and Britain.

Part three, "In Britain," is the most comprehensive section of the book, for reasons that will become apparent. "Ghost Towns" takes the reader to Mirpur, Pakistan, and to its "home away from home," Beeston in West Yorkshire, the stamping grounds of the London bombers. One ghost town is Outside in Pakistan, another is Inside in England, and the two joined in ways both outlandish and customary. "Cousins" then looks at those ways—at the anthropology of the Muslim migration to Britain and how it shaped postmigrant conditions and outcomes.

"Lords of Londonistan" opens a window on the Outsiders within the Inside, the alien exponents of a radical Islamist discourse who made London their worldwide megaphone, one loudly heard and heeded in Beeston. The "Life and Loves of a Suicide Bomber" is the story of the lead bomber, of Mohammed Sidique Khan, a counterpoint to that of Khaled Kelkal. Because Khan knew so many of the leaders, cells, groups, and institutions of radical Islam in Britain, because he was an Insider in two ways, his story serves as a touchstone and paradigm.

Part four, "In Germany," comprises two chapters. The first is "Germany's Hot Summer," which depicts the terrorist threats to Germany from Germans trained in Pakistani and Afghani bases and the reaction in Germany to them. The chapter discusses the pronounced role of converts, such as Eric Breininger, in the German jihad, pointing out the similarities between second-generation "reversion" and radical conversion. Converts like Breininger, convicts like Khalid Kelkal, and community organizers like Sidique Khan form our three European jihadi "ideal types."

The second Germany chapter draws attention to the country's unwanted and angry young Turks, and to their impact on Germany's handling of immigration, terrorism, and even its own identity. It points out their emerging role in the Taliban and al Qaeda's newest strategic phase—retaliatory jihad—and its European theater strategy to discourage and deter NATO's already reluctant war partners. Jihad has bloomed among German and Turk postmigrants thanks not only to palpable inequity on the Inside but an unexpected and circuitous intervention from the Outside. The latter has placed Germany somewhere between France and Britain in terms of policy and peril.

I firmly believe there are many policy lessons to be drawn from the material I present and analyze, but to endeavor to "take away" from this study the "best practices" in European antiterrorism will risk flattening the world whose irregular terrain I have explored and trivializing the task of developing antiterrorist strategy and tactics. My final chapter, "Figures in the Carpet," does identify some patterns in what we will have observed together, but it also warns against reaching for similarities and analogies, against homogenizing the varieties of Europe's angry Muslim experience.

The angry repercussions of Muslim postmigrancy need not take the form of jihad or even of Islamic militancy. There was doubtless plenty of anger in the French 2005 riots, but, as I will show, there was little Islamism. Conflating rioters with Islamists, folk Muslims with fundamentalist Muslims, pietists with jihadis, or immigrants with their children is the method of strategic incoherence—"in the night all cats are black." A generation ago, criticizing America's failure to distinguish nationalism from communism, or among versions of national communism, the prominent French realist and antitotalitarian Raymond Aron noted that "the essence of the art of politics is discrimination."[2] Drawing distinctions, as the epigraph to the User's Guide suggests, can be the beginning of knowledge.

PART ONE

IN FRANCE

EUROPE'S FIRST
ANGRY MUSLIM

*J'ai pas fait des études pour charger des camions. ("I didn't study
just to end up loading trucks.")*

—Khaled Kelkal, October 3, 1992

In 1995, the twenty-four-year-old French Algerian Khaled Kelkal
was tracked down and then killed in a French police manhunt
that ended in a dramatic televised shootout. Kelkal was the leader
of a Lyon cell of the Armed Islamic Group, the Groupe Islamique
Armé (GIA) implicated in a wave of bombings and assassinations that
had shocked and terrified residents of Paris and three provincial
cities.[1] Though hundreds of would-be jihadis before him had left
their European homes to fight in Afghanistan and Bosnia, Kelkal was
the first European Muslim fighter to target Western Europe, and his
was the maiden joint venture between aliens (Outsiders) and second-
generation immigrants (Insiders). The first postmigrant jihadi to attack his European home, Kelkal was a homegrown terrorist ahead of
his time.

THE GIA IN FRANCE

In the early 1990s, political and religious strife in Algeria, with its geographic and colonial ties to France, extruded GIA militants to Europe, especially Paris. After voiding an Islamist victory in the first round of legislative elections in December 1991, the Algerian army declared a state of emergency in January 1992 and canceled the second round, which the Front Islamique du Salut (FIS; Islamic Salvation Front), a loose confederation of Islamists and Salafis, was widely expected to win. (If you are unfamiliar with these terms and names, you may wish to consult the glossary and, for a more comprehensive exegesis, see chapter 4, the User's Guide.) The military intervention caused the FIS to split, expelling jihadi factions that were bent on revenging the stolen victory. Of those factions, the most important was the Groupe Islamique Armé, or the GIA. The GIA was composed mainly of young, urban poor, and it affixed returnees from the Afghan jihad to the bitterest elements of the FIS. The result was, according to Gilles Kepel, a "jihadist-salafist movement of extraordinary brutality."[2] In the time between the Afghan war and al Qaeda's 1998 bombing of U.S. embassies in Africa, the GIA was the vanguard and the cynosure of violent jihad.

The GIA's jihad was not global but national; it focused on the "near enemy" in Algeria not on the Western imperialist "far enemy." France's colonization of Algeria had been far more thorough than, say, Britain's of India. Annexed Algeria was made an official department of the Hexagon; hence, Algeria was considered not merely a colonial possession but an integral part of the Republic. In the Algerian war of independence (1954–1962), the National Liberation Front (FLN) had expelled the French administration, but it had, in the view of the Islamist FIS, retained the colonists' profane culture. The Islamist FIS regarded the postcolonial lay regime as insufficiently independent and revolutionary thanks precisely to its secularity, its *laïcité*. French refusal to isolate the FLN regime after it canceled the elections confirmed for the FIS that the revolutionary regime had become the puppet of the colonialists.

Even before the 1992 military takeover, FIS student activists and other Islamists created the Algerian Fraternity in France, the Fraternité Algérienne en France (FAF). Then after the coup the FAF and other militants who found refuge in France helped to set up "solidarity networks" among the Algerian population of both recent immigrants and postmigrants clustered in *banlieues* (outer "inner cities") around France's major cities.[3] The FAF was able to gain sympathy and then small operational footholds among French Muslim youth associations. Typically, hardened veterans of the GIA controlled these networks.[4] Whereas the FAF saw France merely as a safe haven and a megaphone to influence events at home, the GIA jihadis wanted outside logistical support for violence at home.[5] They often operated in a nether region inhabited by legal and illegal immigrants. For example, what French police dubbed the "Chalabi network," named after its leader Mohamed Chalabi, blended legitimate businesses with petty crime and document forgery, much like the Madrid bombers would do a decade later. In this case, recruitment, logistics, and procurement were for the Algerian conflict, not, at first, aimed at France itself.

Along with funding and logistical support for the Algerian jihad, the Chalabi group conducted recruitment among young postmigrant men (one vehicle: a "youth club" offering ski vacations and assistance on homework assignments). The scope of the Chalabi network's operatives was apparent in their eventual arrests, with 138 charged and held for an average of fourteen months. Because there were only twenty-four convictions (some overturned on appeal), the case was cited by some as an example of overzealous prosecution.[6] However Jean-François Clair of the Direction de la Surveillance du Territoire (DST), the domestic security agency, assured me that French security forces regarded the destruction of the Chalabi group as critical to their defense against the GIA.[7]

In retaliation for French support of the Algerian government and perhaps in a vain attempt to deter the crackdown on their support networks, the GIA began targeting French interests and citizens. These targets, moreover, possessed symbolic value in the war against the Algerian rulers whom the jihadis dubbed "the sons of France." Attacking France would demonstrate that the jihadis were better placed to defend the rights and honor of the Algerians than the regime, even though it had come to power in an anticolonial insurgency.

In December 1994, nearly seven years before 9/11, with al Qaeda little more than a rumor, the GIA hijacked a French airliner in Algiers with the intention of crashing it into the Eiffel Tower. The plot was thwarted midway by French Special Forces who stormed the plane during a fuel stop in Marseilles. Undeterred, months later the GIA began attacking the French railway system in what was the first successful jihad against Europe itself, the first to involve the European Muslim second generation, and the first joint venture between alien Outsiders and alienated Insider postmigrants. In response to the initial bloody attacks on the Paris Metro in the summer of 1995, French authorities cracked down with mass arrests in the metropolis. That roundup in Paris would force the GIA to withdraw from the capital to the provincial cities of Lille in the north and Lyon in the west. Investigators for the subsequent Chalabi trial found "that the dismantling . . . forced the 'center' Algerians to turn later to Khaled Kelkal."[8]

ENTER KHALED KELKAL

Khaled was brought as a toddler from Algeria to a suburb of Lyon in 1973.[9] That was when his first-generation parents were united under "family reunification" policies that were becoming typical in Europe (see chapter 6).[10] The Kelkals raised a brood of twelve in an immigrant banlieue of Lyon called Vaulx-en-Velin, where three-quarters of the residents resided along the barge canal on the western outskirts of France's second-largest city in bleak, chockablock five-story public housing units, or *cités*, much like those we will encounter in the slums of Paris when we consider the 2005 riots. However, a decade earlier, in 1995, the year of Kelkal's terror spree, nearly half of the Vaulx population was, like Kelkal himself, under twenty-four, and the employment rate for those under that age reached nearly 25 percent.[11] Petty crime would land the adolescent in jail where the Insider Khaled began his radicalization under the influence of an Arab mentor, an Outsider.

Kelkal was released from a second prison term in October 1992, just when, as it happened, the German researcher Dietmar Loch was conducting fieldwork for a book on North African youth in the ex-convict's hometown.[12] Loch's serendipitous interview with Kelkal, three years before his bombing binge, opens a window onto the twenty-one-year-old's passage from crime to Islamism and then to jihad. As a first-person, contemporaneous autobiographical account from a radicalizing subject, it is unique. The interview, first published as an obscure academic dissertation, was republished in full in the original French after the promising student turned petty criminal turned jihadi became France's most wanted.[13] Kelkal's type of downward mobility would become a prominent postmigrant path to extremism.

Our subject's family did not practice the strict and sectarian Islam its notorious child came to embrace, but rather a "private and discrete" form of folk or Sufi Islam.[14] Once, when the unruly Khaled fell behind in secondary school, his father gave him "a good spanking." From then on Khaled applied himself so well that, unlike his brothers, who earned only vocational diplomas, he could enter an academic *lycée* (high school) where he performed at the baccalaureate level in chemistry. Kelkal told Loch, his German interviewer: "It was a top rated high school. You had to reach a good level to enter. Freshman year, in [the last year of secondary school] I was fine. We [me and a friend] were at the top of the class, laughing all the way. We were sane, cool. But further on, no. . . ."

As the only Arab in the magnet school, he became the odd boy out. He told the German sociologist, "They never had an Arab in their class and they told me openly: 'You are the only Arab . . . '" At school, the crucial institution for immigrant integration, Kelkal became a prime exhibit of France's all-or-nothing assimilation policy, one that, unlike the American, really does aspire to be a "melting pot," boiling away the residues of cultural identity that subsist in the U.S. model. "I had the ability to succeed," Kelkal remembered ruefully, "but I had no place because they insisted on total integration. It was impossible to forget my culture, eat pork. I couldn't do it. And when they got to know me, they would say, 'You are an exception.' Even if I talked, even if I had a good relationship with my classmates, it wasn't natural."

At his elite school, Khaled felt not only out of place but also under suspicion. "Once, an adding machine disappeared from the classroom. Though I had done nothing, I had to be the thief, since I was the only Arab. It bothered me to think everyone must be thinking it was me. They looked at me funny. I said to myself: What I am doing here?" This was the social and psychic foundation of a descent into burglary, prison, and finally terror, but it began with truancy: "I lost my pride and had to put my personality aside. I couldn't do it, I couldn't find my place. . . . So, I started to skip class, once, twice."

The lapses became habitual, and Kelkal stopped school altogether and now crossed swords with his family, incurring shame as well as guilt.

My mother, and the whole family, blamed me. I felt totally cut off from my family. . . . [B]ecause of that I went down the wrong way. I also left my home for a little bit because my mother blamed me: "how have you come to this point and now you don't want to go to school anymore!" For me, because my mother constantly reminded me, I knew that I was in the wrong. That was why I left, because I knew that I was in the wrong.

The feelings of guilt and shame associated with family disapproval and censure will turn up again as we encounter other angry Muslim Insiders, particularly Mohammed Sidique Khan. In many instances of European Muslim radicalization, a family rupture will precede or accompany the conversion to radical Islam. That will be the pattern followed by Khan and many other "reverts" to radical Islam. In fact, radicalization rarely involves a "reversion" to an Islam once practiced and then abandoned. Typically, what is involved is not a reversion but a conversion—to a dogmatic, sectarian, and fundamentalist Islam that has little in common with the folk or Sufi Islam of the father.

Even before he left school, Khaled's truancy took him to the street, where neighborhood solidarity would supplant the forfeited family bond. "In the afternoon, everyone went to school, but I didn't have anything to do. And I started getting around, making acquaintances. They're good people. Even if a guy's a thief, we don't question a guy when he arrives. When he's a friend, he's a friend." Much like, as we will see, Sidique Khan, Khaled, known as "Mr. Smiley," was of a sunny, friendly disposition.[15] His new friends steered him to a new calling: "The guys told me there's a lot of good stuff lying around [at school]. It [theft] becomes a habit; it clicks in."

Resentment of racial prejudice was only a part of the complex explanation for his turn to burglary that Kelkal advanced to his German interviewer. Need was a factor. He told Loch that in his hometown of Vaulx-en-Velin "70 percent of people are into stealing because their parents cannot afford to buy things when there are six children. When you steal, you feel free."[16] His father and eldest brother (who also later landed in prison) had both lost their manufacturing jobs, sharing the fate of immigrants all over Northwest Europe who were originally hired in the "miracle" years and then cashiered as the region deindustrialized (see chapter 6).[17] Kelkal was among countless jobless Muslim youth drawn to gangs and petty crime, activities which then buttress negative images among the native-born, leading to "Islamophobia," which in

Portrait of Khaled Kelkal, drawn on December 20, 2005.
© Rama Neko; used by permission.

turn nourishes Muslim feelings of exclusion in a mutually reinforcing downward spiral of alienation from which Islamism, often encountered in prison, may seem to offer deliverance.

But along with emotional and economic distress, with estrangement from family and country, the future jihadi offered another explanation for his fall, one that we can call political, or prepolitical: "I had to count on myself, obligated to steal. But it was above all a question of vengeance. You want violence, so we give you violence." Kelkal's reminiscences followed two terms with militant Muslim cellmates who furnished him an ideology and a narrative, a framework, for his previous actions. We cannot know how much credence to afford to Khaled's posterior political explanations, but what is more important to us was his mind-set when he offered them in 1992, in the process of his radicalization.

Rather than capitulate to the French, the Algerian immigrant and his comrades vowed to punish their oppressors, an eye for eye, in order to

"create [their] own system."[18] At twenty-one talking with Loch, Khalid
was a petty thief but also a politicized born-again Muslim.

In another premonition he told the German researcher, "When you
stole, you felt free because it was a game. Until they catch me, it's me
who's winning. It's a game: you lose or you win. . . . If there were cops
behind me, I sped up so they weren't there anymore. It was a delirium, a
game, and we were good at it." The ecstasy of escape, of eluding the cops,
may have returned later when Kelkal would exhaust the nation's police
at the end of his jihadi version of a Bonnie and Clyde chase.

The Kelkal who throws a retrospective light on his past is the young
man who emerged from two stays in his adopted country's prisons,
known even then as disproportionately Muslim. What was less recognized then, but quite well known today, is the role prison experience
can have in Islamization and radicalization.[19] Islamization, often a first
step toward radicalization, happened in Khaled's first prison stay. The
eighteen-year-old Lyonnais was arrested for car theft and released after
four months. He told Loch that prior to jail he did not "know how to
write and read Arabic. When I got to prison, I said to myself: I must not
waste my time. There was a Muslim Brother with us. . . . I learned Arabic
fast." In jail, he enjoyed being in "a tight-knit group." And in Islam he
experienced "a great opening of the spirit."[20] Khaled now saw himself
as "neither Arab nor French, but a Muslim."[21]

FROM ISLAMISM TO JIHAD

Members of the Society of Muslim Brothers had begun arriving in
France in the 1960s, fleeing repressive secular regimes in Egypt, Syria,
and Tunisia, or simply pursuing graduate studies (usually in medicine,
engineering, or natural sciences). Though the Brotherhood was a seed-
bed of Islamic revivalist anti-imperialism, by the 1970s, most of its radicals had abandoned the society to form violent jihadi organizations (see
chapter 5). Meanwhile, in Europe, the Brothers found a sanctuary in
which to mold militants in anticipation of political openings in the
home countries to which they expected to return to campaign for
Islamic rule. Thus, for a generation, Brotherhood recruitment in France
centered on visiting students and exiles, not immigrants or their offspring. After the formation of its French offshoot in 1983, when it did

begin to recruit French Muslims, the group drew upon students and the upper middle classes. Its French incarnation, the Union of French Islamic Organizations (UOIF), never attracted workers, and still less (as we will see in the next chapter) slum dwellers like Kelkal. That is one reason for the group's essentially conservative, even aristocratic, character.[22] And despite claims to the contrary, the Muslim Brothers hardly aspired to convert Europe to Islam.[23] The UOIF accepted Muslims' minority status and on that basis sought to think through the implications of being Muslim in a non-Muslim society. From the beginning, it emphasized respecting the host society's laws and claiming rights accruing to a religious minority.[24] At the time that Kelkal came under the influence of the Brotherhood, its French incarnation, the UOIF, had become a player in French politics, thanks mainly to the headscarf controversy (see chapter 2) then brewing in the country's pronouncedly secular public schools, such as the one in which Khaled felt so isolated.

Kelkal told Loch that on this first prison stay, he had "regained the religion" while learning Arabic under the tutelage of the Muslim Brother. He began going to the mosque every Friday and "when I watched cassettes, when the scholars spoke, there was no place any longer for doubt. . . . Everything had its reason. Everything had meaning." This was a religious conversion—like other radicals, he did not "revert" to his father's folk Islam but embraced a new faith. If his conversion to an activist political Islam was not in itself a radicalization, Islamism, nonetheless, afforded his downward mobility a frame of reference, gave his descent a "narrative." Innocuous in themselves, little more than embracing a born-again fundamentalism, these were the first steps in Khaled's radicalization process, the embrace of the unquestioning certainty that often underlies totalitarian ideologies.

But they were faltering steps. Out of jail, Kelkal fell off the wagon, stopped praying and fasting, and resumed his criminal calling. "Where did I end up? In prison." Indeed, several months after his release, Khaled was arrested for driving stolen cars into store windows and stealing luxury goods. He was convicted and again imprisoned, this time from July 27, 1990, to July 27, 1992.[25]

The second, longer, visit to the penitentiary revived his piety but, more importantly, placed him firmly on the radicalization track. This time his cellmate, though Khaled does not mention this to Loch, was not a political Islamist but a jihadi named Khelif B. who was "close to the

GIA," for whom he proselytized in the jails.[26] It was during this second term in prison that Kelkal, in a course to be traveled again in Europe's prisons, turned to radical Islam.[27]

It was two months after Kelkal's second prison release that Loch interviewed the ex-convict as part of the sociologist's survey of Lyon's immigrant youth. For the benefit of the German scholar, Kelkal portrayed his delinquency as a result of inequity and "racism." Those living "in the chic zones . . . have jobs. . . . Their sons are well off. The son gets his diploma and the father buys him a car and his license. He has everything he wants. Me, I am twenty-one years old, I don't even have my license. I have nothing."[28] The high school dropout held the state to blame for legitimizing this inequity: "The judges, society, they don't know that it's their [own] fault. If they had only looked at what was happening in these neighborhoods, there wouldn't be all this delinquency,"[29] and he warns of a new, younger generation of postmigrant youth as a "powder keg" and "in the process of becoming gangsters."[30]

This interview took place shortly after riots in a nearby neighborhood. Though Loch's subject notes that he had "responded" to his own circumstances "with individual violence,"

> over in *Mas du Taureau* . . . it was a group. . . . The [police] murder only set them off. The jobless were trying to say: "Stop. Think about us. You may be living the high life in town, but look around and see what is happening in the inner city, the poverty, the drugs." There are fourteen- to fifteen-year-olds, stealing big cars to harass society and the police. . . . It is only after the riots that [the authorities] began to understand.

More than a decade before the great riots of 2005, which were particularly furious in Lyon, Khaled, in this politicized account of his motives, was conceiving the riot as a form of social protest. They were becoming almost routine in French slums, and were usually, as here and in 2005, sparked by the killing of a second-generation male by the police.

But in his account it was not only destitution and depravation that Kelkal earmarked as the cause but also institutionalized racism—directed at him as "an Arab."

> Let me tell you a story. I was in court. Two guys are brought in for burglary. Neither had a previous conviction. The French guy had

broken into a house and hit a woman. The Arab had only tried to break in. . . . The judge gave the French guy two months. The Arab—he had not even broken down the door—got eighteen months."

Kelkal's conclusion was clear: "The justice system is no friend of ours. There is justice at two different velocities. The guys from Vaulx-en-Velin that are caught are guaranteed a year and a half more than the others. . . . What is called justice is injustice."

This sort of injustice was, of course, not sociology for Kelkal, something on which he ruminates from afar, like the riots "over in *Mas du Taureau.*" No, the political was personal. "Me, personally, I have no rights. Me, right now, me on the street. Somebody attacks me. I defend myself. That guy is in the right. I'm the one who's at fault, . . . seeing as how I've already been in jail. Even if a mob of skinheads attacks me and I legitimately defend myself." And the personal was political. Kelkal sees not only racist groups but also the state itself and society aligned against him, bringing him onto the political terrain: "I was interested in politics. I followed politics, but it's all bullshit. I was interested what was happening in Vaulx-en-Velin. But I saw that for the mayor, it was all image, all protecting his image."

But jail turned Kelkal, the future terrorist, into a kind of social activist:

When I see a dude from my neighborhood using drugs, I deal with him forcibly. I lock him in the cellar, bring him food and water. The desire for drugs must pass, even if he has to suffer. I was in jail with a dude who used drugs. For a year I spoke to him of religion. . . . I told him you have to stop hanging out with drug pushers. If you hang with them, you will relapse. . . . He never uses drugs anymore. We know how to help each other. When you help, feelings are established. At the end I can say: he, he's my brother.

As he tells it, Kelkal had become a kind of drug counselor. Both of the other notorious European postmigrant jihadis, Sidique Khan and Mohammed Bouyeri—the ritual murderer of the Dutch filmmaker Theo van Gogh—were social workers who focused on drug rehabilitation, though in a more formal sense than Kelkal. In all three instances, it was their religiosity that inspired their work against drug abuse, because their newfound militant Islam made recovery a spiritual event.

And the Islam that each of the three embraced was belligerently sectarian. Adopting the first-person plural, Kelkal makes it clear to Loch that, despite popular misconceptions, "we have nothing to do with Iran." He regards Shiites as false Muslims, belonging to a sect "created by a Jew" in order "to infiltrate the Arabs." "It is all in the Qur'an." And, in another illustration of the maxim that "a little knowledge is a dangerous thing," the former chemistry student tells the German sociologist that "NASA's leading authority" and "the leading Japanese scientists" have all "certified" that "the Qur'an is the voice of God." On cassettes he rented "every three of four days" he hears these truths from "the greatest scholars of Islam." And "when the greatest scholars certify, you can no longer doubt." (We shall encounter again the impact of such "scholars" in the chapter titled "The Lords of Londonistan.")

When he uttered these verities to Loch, the radicalizing Kelkal, newly released from jail, was frequenting the Bilal mosque in Vaulx-en-Velin, a facility affiliated with the Faith and Practice movement, the French branch of the Islamist missionary movement, Tablighi Jama'at (TJ).[31] Gilles Kepel, a French scholar of the Islamic and Arab world, wrote that TJ played a "decisive role in reaffirming an Islamic identity among the Muslim population of France," as its promulgation of Islam responded "quite adequately to the needs of the less educated . . . preach[ing] an Islam that [was] simple to understand and practice" to those who "suffer from a great loss of identity."[32] As described in the User's Guide, TJ's missionary Islam is apolitical, but it frequently serves as an antechamber to Holy War. As we shall see in chapters 9 and 12, a number of terrorist plotters made contact with jihadi organizations at TJ mosques and that may well have been Kelkal's case. In a 2005 report, the DST, the French domestic security agency, would call attention to TJ "canvassing tough neighborhoods in large cities" especially in Paris and "the suburbs of Lyon, the hometown of several Islamists implicated in various cases linked to terrorism."[33] The agency's veteran deputy director, Jean-François Clair, would tell me in 2002 that upwards of three-quarters of France's radical Islamists were linked to the TJ movement.[34] Thanks to the "passive complicity between the mujahideen and the authorities in Tabligh centers," the 2005 DST report would depict "Tabligh mosques" as "settings just right for recruiters looking for militants prepared for violent action."[35]

But apparently it is in Algeria in 1993, not long after talking with Loch, that the Lyonnais militant consummates his transition from Islamism to jihadism. He had told the German scholar that "the one thing I want to do is get out of France, forever." "Where would I go? Back home, to Algeria. I have no place here. All an employer has to do is find out that you were in prison. If there is something missing in the workplace, I'm going to be charged."

To Algeria he went, and found there, if not a home, a mission. While visiting family in Mostaghanem, his natal village, Kelkal made direct contact with the GIA.[36] A decade later Madrid bombers would take a similar radicalization route in their Moroccan hometown of Tetuan.[37] Kelkal wanted to join the GIA resistance movement "in the region of Mostaghanem, where one of his uncles was a senior Islamist militant. But he was told he would be more useful in France."[38] Mohammed Sidique Khan, as we shall see, also returned to his ancestral homeland to wage jihad and was similarly instructed, as were many British Pakistani jihadi wannabes, that he would be more useful in Europe. Theirs were particularly striking elucidations of a hard lesson taught to many estranged postmigrants: their ancestral countries were not home either.

Back in Lyon, Khaled began to model himself on the terrorist guer-rillas in Algeria. The cassettes he revered now were jihadi videos. Inspired by them, Kelkal drilled in the hills surrounding Lyon with his childhood friend Karim Koussa, who had gone to Pakistan to fight the Soviets and was recruited there by the GIA.[39] Not many years later, Sidique Khan and his fellow London bombers would rehearse on West Yorkshire hills by mimicking similar videos in games of paintball.

Khaled's terrorist career began in earnest in the summer of 1995. On July 11, Kelkal and his friend Koussa assassinated the Algerian militant Abdelkader Sahraoui, a cofounder of the Islamist FIS, which had pub-licly censured GIA violence in France.[40] Two weeks later, Kelkal placed a bomb at the busy Left Bank Saint-Michel metro station.[41] The explo-sives detonated gas canisters filled with nails and bolts, leaving eight dead and over a hundred wounded.[42]

On August 26, 1995, police found Kelkal's fingerprints on a very large unexploded bomb on a track north of Lyon for the high-speed TGV train (Train à Grande Vitesse).[43] That discovery made Kelkal the "most wanted man in France." A manhunt followed, involving eight hundred police officers and soldiers. After tracking Kelkal for three days in the forests outside of Lyon, the searchers found and shot him dead.[44] French television aired the final shootout in which viewers could hear gendarmes

shouting, "Finish him off!"[45] The next frame showed a sharpshooter kick-
ing Khaled's body to confirm his death.[46] The airing provoked riots
around France, including the burning of cars in Khaled's banlieue.[47] In
France's Muslim slums, Kelkal, who made filmmaker Jean-Luc Godard's
Breathless postmodern protagonist seem meek and mindful, became for
some a new kind of avant-garde antihero.

Among Khaled's belongings, investigators found the phone number of
the GIA's Rachid Ramda, an Algerian national who had been granted asylum in the United Kingdom in 1992.[48] The French accused him of being
the "banker, logistics chief and the mastermind" of the attacks orchestrated
by Kelkal and his group.[49] Clair, the DST deputy director, explained to me
that the GIA newspaper *al Ansar* furnished operational directions from
London to Paris in code.[50] The French requested his extradition, but British
courts refused the request for ten years, citing concerns that Ramda would
be subjected to torture while awaiting trial.[51] That accusation, even as London was hosting dozens of prominent GIA and other jihadis, infuriated
French officials who then christened the city "Londonistan." After a decade
of strained cross-channel relations, Ramda was extradited in December
2005, and in March 2006 Ramda was convicted and sentenced in Paris to
ten years' imprisonment for his involvement in Kelkal's attacks.[52]

If Khaled Kelkal was a harbinger, he was also an outlier. Over the next
decade the union of alien jihadi with alienated postmigrant, of Outsider
with Insider, would become rare in France compared to Britain. Partly
as a consequence of its early, one might say premature, onset in France,
that country was to offer a less propitious legal and security environment
for such a movement. Armed with custom-made antiterrorist judge-
prosecutors, courts, and police, an inquisitorial trial system, and a state-
friendly public, French authorities were able to prevent the outbreak of
"two, three, many" Kelkals, the common conjunction of alien Outsiders
with alienated postmigrants. But if Islamic terrorism was not to convulse
France, another form of postmigrant anger would.

A FRENCH INTIFADA?

God gave Noah the rainbow sign
No more water, the fire next time!

—Epigraph to James Baldwin's *The Fire Next Time* (1963)

O ver a span of five months beginning in late October 2005, France was convulsed first by an uprising of the second generation in its immigrant ghettos, where cars burned like autumn leaves, and then by a springtide of very different protest from very different quarters. However, Islamism was not a protagonist in France's autumn's unrest, and it was altogether absent in the spring marches. In events that nearly unhinged the country, Islamism was the dog that did not bark.

Paris was not "Londonistan," where jihadi bombs had exploded months earlier. That was not the outcome anticipated by media reports, best-selling exposés, and government investigations depicting the Islamization of French ghettoes and their schools. In the years prior to the fall riots, the government had stepped up surveillance of mosques and banned the wearing of the veil in public schools. The alarming reports and the stern government reaction, alongside the sheer number of French Muslims—the largest in absolute and relative terms in Europe—created the general impression, inside and outside of France, of a rising radical Islam.

That is why a number of French and overseas commentators viewed the stone-throwing riots of autumn 2005 in the Muslim slums as a

"French intifada" or a "Palestinian-style intifada" or a "permanent" intifada and seasoned their columns with "speculative reports that 'hidden
hands'—meaning Islamic radical groups such as [al Qaeda]—are orches-
trating the violence."[1] "The rioting by Muslim youth that began October 27 in France to calls of 'Allahu Akbar' may be a turning point in
European history," intoned the prominent neoconservative Middle East
expert Daniel Pipes.

But if the episode constituted a "new French Revolution," as Pipes
declared, it was a revolution that dashed his own expectations.[2] One
portentous blog, www.brusselsjournal.com, labored to demonstrate that
Islamists had inspired and directed the riots. But all the blog could cite
were impressionistic opinion pieces and two hysterical reports, a loud
but lonely recycled screed from the conservative London *Spectator* and
the rants of a sole French police officer.[3]

Pascal Mailhos, the Director General of the domestic intelligence service Renseignements Généraux (RG), told *Le Monde* that "radical
Islamists had no part in the violence."[4] The RG, which dates back to
Napoleon I's secret police, embeds agents in communities throughout
the country. Five years earlier, its agents were ordered to concentrate on
the immigrant housing projects, or *cités*, where petty crime and Islamist
radicalism was reportedly rife. But the chief of the Paris RG told me that
of the three thousand rioters arrested in and near Paris that fall, there was
"not one known as belonging to an Islamist crowd and we monitor
them quite closely."[5]

As for jihadis in particular, Jean-François Clair, the deputy director
and chief operating officer of the Direction de la Surveillance du Territoire (DST), recounted to me how, at the very moment when cars started
burning, his agents were poised to arrest two jihadis preparing to leave
for Iraq. Postponing the collar till the ghettos quieted down, the security
agency maintained surveillance on the militants. The agents recorded the
jihadis bemoaning the riots: "Now the cops, may Allah rain down curses
on them, are everywhere." As Alain Bauer of France's National Crime
Watch (l'Observation National de la Délinquance) told *Le Figaro* a week
into the uprising, "The radical Islamist prefers to see calm return to be
able to act quietly."[6]

Both Clair of the DST and Mailhos of the RG related that, on the
other hand, local Islamists had tried unsuccessfully to quell the riots.
Indeed the principal Islamist organization, the Muslim Brotherhood–led

Union of French Islamic Organizations (UOIF), issued a *fatwa* denouncing the behavior of the rioters while deploring the conditions in the slums.[7] Europe's leading Islamist intellectual, Tariq Ramadan, an Islamist bogeyman for foreign observers, went further. He condemned "the adolescent stupidity" of the rioters who "destroy a fragile economic tissue and burn the very vehicles that carry their relatives. Some of these arsonists were victims of a social system before becoming small-time hoods who profit from the situation."[8] Likewise, Christophe Bertossi, an Islam and immigration specialist at the French Institute of International Relations, pointed out: "The youngsters who were involved in the riots do not even practice Islam. They don't read the Koran, they don't go to mosques."[9]

Weeks after the uprising, surveying the damage, I frequently found defiance recorded on walls—"fuck the police"[10] and "fuck the informants"—but not a single *surah* (Qur'anic verse) or crescent scrawled on the graffiti-choked ramparts of the pallid, lonesome housing projects, the cités that hover by the terminus of French cities like colonnades of ghosts, next to overgrown, weed-infested lawns, rotting sewers, and vacant strip malls. Islamists like the leaders of the UOIF attempted, when they dared venture into these *banlieues*, to mediate between the rioters and the authorities. They were rebuffed *sans cérémonie* by the former, a rebuff punctuated often by a distinctly unbrotherly cannonade of rocks.

In three and a half weeks of violence, the organized sector of the largest Muslim cohort in Europe failed to burn a car, fire a shot, or pitch a rock. Then, four months later, at demonstrations that drew millions into lengthy marches, strikes, and mass meetings, in long afternoons spent with the protesters, I found nary an Islamic poster, leaflet, or banner. In events that convulsed contemporary France, which were indeed a "turning point" of a kind, militant Muslims, who fired the ready imagination of so many strident, categorical commentators, were conspicuous for their absence. In an epoch of riots and protests, the European country with the greatest Muslim presence, "the Islamist menace" thought to be gathering "while Europe sleeps," itself slept. [11]

Had we all been exaggerating "Europe's angry Muslims?"[12] Or is France not the rule when it comes to radical Islam but the exception? Are "European Muslims" only the Muslims of individual countries, with a range of "anger" that varies with local political culture, Muslim provenance, and perhaps the entire history of both the sender country and the receiver country?

If we should not now expect the crescent to supplant the *fleur de lys*, the bookend events of the autumn and the following spring did unveil a France facing a different sort of danger. After the riots, an RG report found that the "state [had been] preoccupied above all with the rise of radical Islam and religious terrorism" but had "neglected the complex problem of the *banlieues*."[13]

Neoconservative pundits such as Mark Steyn enjoyed schadenfreude at the plight of President Jacques Chirac's government that allegedly had

> led the opposition to the Iraq war out of fear of how his Muslim population would react. This fear is a big part of why France portrays itself as America's counterweight and why it criticizes Israel at every turn and coddled the terrorist Yasser Arafat right up to his death. . . . The notion that Texas neocon arrogance was responsible for frosting up trans-Atlantic relations was always preposterous. . . . Unlike America's Europhiles, France's Arab street correctly identified Chirac's opposition to the Iraq war for what it was: a sign of weakness.[14]

In an editorial entitled "Intifada in France," the *New York Sun* vouchsafed that it was "a barely kept secret that Mr. Chirac led the opposition to the Iraq war out of fear of how his Muslim population would react. This fear is a big part of why France portrays itself as America's counterweight and why it criticizes Israel at every turn."[15] And a commentator in the Canadian *National Post,* dropped the e-word: "In elite French society, the enemy was clearly identified: not Islamism or Islamofascism, not the stewing mobs in the Paris suburbs, not Saddam Hussein, not al-Qaeda, but the British and U.S. troops in Iraq."[16]

But can these "I-told-you-sos" all be chalked up merely to neoconservative grudges deriving from the French obstruction of George W. Bush's sprint to war in Iraq, to the resentment that served up "Freedom Fries" in the United States? But one who had devoted attention to events in France in the preceding months and years had ample reason to assume that radical Islamism was at work here. Our observer had been treated to two deeply disturbing government reports documenting Muslim youth extremism, to monthly tabulations of attacks on women and Jews by Muslim youths, to Muslim demonstrations on behalf of the Palestinians, and to a French media obsessed by the contest between veiled Muslim girls and the secular French state. From this reporting, it was most reasonable to draw the conclusion that Islamic extremism was boiling in the banlieues.

PERVERSE PRELUDES

Starting in the autumn of 2000, France endured an outbreak of anti-Semitism rivaled only by the German occupation during World War II or the notorious Dreyfus case a half-century earlier. However, this time the overwhelming majority (80 percent) of the incidents came not from the fascist right but from Muslim youth.[17] The reporting of the Interior Ministry (considered by Jewish organizations grossly to underestimate the severity of the outbreak) showed that anti-Semitic incidents from September to October 2000 soared from a dozen to 418 and that violent acts leapt from zero to 102.[18]

Why such a sharp rise that autumn? Late September 2000 saw the outbreak of the second Palestinian intifada. From that period until mid-2003, desecrations of Jewish cemeteries and synagogues, threats against or attacks on men wearing yarmulkes, and other anti-Semitic abuses would continue to chase events occurring outside France: 9/11, Israel's Operation Defensive Shield in the West Bank (April 2002), and the U.S. invasion of Iraq. But from September 2003 and through 2004 anti-Semitic incidents occurred at a very high steady state, with spikes unrelated to outside events. The 2004 report of the National Human Rights Advisory Center (Centre Nationale Consultative des Droites de l'Homme; CNCDH) indicated that the perpetrators were predominantly from the "*quartiers sensibles*" of the often largely Muslim banlieues.[19] Increasingly, the phrase "*jeunes issus de l'immigration*" ("immigrant youth") could be found in media reports that documented anti-Semitic violence. Meanwhile *Le Figaro* correspondent Marie-Estelle Pech and the 2001 film *La Squale* were presenting horrifying accounts of gang rape of unveiled women in the banlieues. One of Pech's pieces told of a certain "Sarah D." who summoned up the courage needed to send the several young men who raped her to jail. Her life was subsequently made almost unlivable by her male neighbors.[20]

In 2002, *Lost Territories of the Republic* was published, a stirring collection of tales out of ghetto schools, recounting male Muslim adolescent abuse of "uncovered" (i.e., unveiled) Muslim girls and Jews.[21] The book reportedly "made a deep impression on French president Jacques Chirac."[22] It certainly fed the swelling debate about *le voile* (the veil) that had been roiling France for more than a decade, in part because the veil, or *hijab*, was often worn by women in the ghettos to protect them from the sort of abuse that Pech, *La Squale,* and *Lost Territories* depicted as widespread and typical.

The covering of women is not explicitly commanded in the Qur'an. There is mention of the need to erect a "curtain" between women and men and for Muhammad's wives to draw the long, flowing garment known as a *jilbab* around them to prevent "molestation."[23] Veiling was instituted in certain patriarchal Muslim societies shortly after the Prophet's time, but in some places it had been practiced long before Muhammad arrived. In some places it was simply expedient (to keep dust and sand out) and in others, veiling was a vestige from Jewish tradition. Veiling became a source of contention during the Western colonization of Muslim countries, but it receded as those countries sought to modernize under nationalist secular regimes. The practice then reemerged and intensified with the Islamization movements of the latter twentieth century.

In contemporary France, the contested article could vary from a "flimsy chiffon or expensive silk" *foulard* or hijab, at the crown of the head to "a heavy folded black scarf made of thick fabric" covering the entire face.[24] Is the scarf an item of personal identity chosen by, as it were, headstrong women or the imposition on submissive ones by domineering "bearded ones"? Is it donned as a simple act of faith, or as a barrier to staring eyes? In many cases, the headscarf expresses the second-generation defiance of parents' more relaxed old country ways with which we will grow familiar.[25]

The item acquired nationwide significance on October 4, 1989, when the principal of a *lycée* (secondary school) expelled three students for wearing headscarves. Had the event occurred a year earlier, it probably would not have gained the prominence it did in the Islamist *annus mirabilis* of 1989—the year of jihad triumph in Afghanistan, the Rushdie Affair in Britain, the birth of the Islamic Salvation Front (FIS) in Algeria, and the emergence of Islamic militants on international magazine covers, often in the form of veiled women.

The conjunction of domestic and foreign challenges, of events inside and outside the Hexagon, converted the local incident into the national "headscarf affair."[26] When the matter reached France's supreme administrative court, the State Council ruled that the headscarf did not violate the country's sacred principle of *laïcité* (secularism) in public schools as long as the Muslim garment was not worn in order to proselytize. Then the first of several executive branch decrees left it to the discretion of school principals, historically powerful and respected figures, to determine whether a given scarf was an item of faith or of propaganda.

Those decisions were to prove just the beginning of a national imbroglio. Soon students, teachers and their unions, school officials, human rights organizations, mayors, congressmen, domestic and international eminences (such as the King of Morocco), and, of course, the media were enmeshed in a dispute that would seethe for a decade and a half, involving more expulsions and more protests, strikes in support of embattled principals or punished pupils, court opinions, rulings, and appeals, executive branch decrees, parliamentary reports, a government "scarf mediator," dress codes, public debates, academic studies, state and private commissions and proposals, fevered disputes over the meaning of laïcité, semiotic disquisitions, extended media coverage, zealous Islamist and feminist groups, indignant teachers, belligerent students, and, more often than not, bemused parents.

Though centered on the school, the dispute brought in train all the issues and proposed solutions regarding the massive, contentious presence of Muslims in France. Between 1989 and 2002, there were to be four attempts to establish an organization that would serve as the official representative of Muslims in France, an interlocutor with the French government that could voice representative opinion on religious concerns (dietary rules, holidays, grave sites, pilgrimages, the appointment of imams and chaplains, headscarves, and so forth). The hope was to institutionalize French Islam and diminish the influence of "garage mosques," which were held to be the source of anti-Semitism, abuse of women, radical proclivities, and terrorism.

The first three attempts foundered over *fitna,* the diversity and discord among Muslim groups. The fourth survives but is still beset by the same heterogeneity. All of the efforts assumed that the way to represent Muslims was through their mosques, though most French Muslims do not attend services regularly, and many are scarcely more observant than France's lapsed Catholic majority. Then there was the multiplicity of Muslim national origins: Algerian, Moroccan, Turk, Tunisian, West African, among others, each with their own national allegiances, embassies, mosques, networks, and federations. Forming other levels of discord was Islamic doctrinal and ideological diversity—from Sufi traditionalists to Salafist fundamentalists, from apolitical to political to insurrectionary (see the User's Guide).

None of these obstacles deterred hard-charging Interior Minister Nicolas Sarkozy from attempting to midwife a representative body of Muslims where his predecessors had failed. In April 2003, the newly formed Conseil Français du Culte Musulman (French Council of the Muslim Faith; CFCM) held its first elections in some one thousand mosques. The federation associated with Morocco (the National Federation of French Muslims; FNMF) and that promoted by the Muslim Brotherhood–led UOIF emerged as the top vote getters.

The formation of the CFCM was one phalanx of the French government's strategy to diffuse what it saw as a crisis created by radical, separatist "garage mosques." The other was to pass a law banning the veil. Six days after the second round of CFCM voting, the UOIF held its annual meeting. The UOIF was the single truly Islamist federation, and the one most demonstrative on behalf of the headscarf; indeed it owed its national prominence to its outspoken defense of the expelled girls in 1989. Sarkozy was the first French minister to attend the annual meeting, fully aware that the UOIF represented the most adversarial of the otherwise rather tame constituents of the CFCM. If Sarkozy could beard the lion in his den, it would represent a major personal victory and a clear signal that the French policy was working. In the preceding weeks, Prime Minister Jean-Pierre Raffarin and a swelling chorus across the political spectrum had endorsed a headscarf ban.[27] What would his interior minister have to say and how would he be heard?

The mood on the evening of April 19, 2003, was celebratory and congenial as Sarkozy entered the cavernous hall in Le Bourget as UOIF Secretary-General Fouad Alaoui was extolling his organization's strong election showing. The building, in the Parisian region of Seine-Saint-Denis, once an airport hangar, was now lined with stands selling books, videotapes, CDs, and Mecca-Cola. In attendance were several thousand Muslim men and women, many in Islamic garb; amid them, radical youth would show their disenchantment with the organization's conciliatory policies at this and future annual meetings.[28]

But if Alaoui had to worry about alienating radicals, Sarkozy nursed similar worries concerning Jean-Marie Le Pen's Islamophobic National Front. Le Pen's party had shocked the country, just a year earlier on April 21, 2002, by gaining the second round of the presidential election by edging out the Socialist party candidate, Lionel Jospin. Now himself a rising presidential aspirant, Sarkozy later would explain that his speech at Le Bourget had been a "reply to April 21st." Was it then to appease Le Pen–leaning voters that the interior minister punctuated his hitherto conciliatory remarks by rebuking Muslim women for refusing to remove their veils for national identity card photos? Sarkozy remonstrated that there could not be "a different law" for Muslim women or for Muslim federations.[29]

Now it was the UOIF leaders' turn to be shocked . . . and outraged. Sarkozy, contrary to customary procedure, had not shown his speech to his hosts beforehand. One of them would fly off the handle, comparing the demand that women remove headscarves for official photographs to Nazi laws requiring Jews to wear yellow stars. The crowd was in an uproar; jeers, boos, and whistles drowned out the remainder of Sarkozy's speech.[30]

The rumpus drew headlines in all the major newspapers, turning the hitherto unnoticed Le Bourget meeting thenceforth into an annual news event. Moreover, though Sarkozy's speech had not mentioned schools, the coverage was quick to conclude that the interior minister "had launched a new headscarf war" and had "put his foot on the veil."[31] *Le Monde* would editorialize six months later that the jeering of Sarkozy at Le Bourget had led the French media to spotlight the headscarf and French politicians to raise the stakes.[32]

Among the many ironies in this tale, the very man who started the bandwagon rolling towards the school headscarf ban was singular in Chirac's cabinet, and quite rare among French politicians of any stripe, for his opposition to such a ban and for supporting "positive discrimination" (affirmative action in American jargon).[33] For their part, the supporters of the headscarf ban in Chirac and Sarkozy's Union for a Popular Movement (UMP) saw a ban as a way of neutralizing Le Pen, besides supporting hard-pressed teachers, reinforcing fraying laïcité and stigmatizing the Left's embrace of multiculturalism. Moreover, the ban offered the additional attraction of maybe taking the wind out of the insurgent interior minister's presidential sails for opposing a measure that Chirac, still angling for another term, had endorsed.[34]

In July, President Chirac formed a commission to advise him on the wisdom of legislating a ban of le voile. By that summer of 2003 the tumult was such that "almost anything about Islam that surfaced . . . made the newspapers."[35] Factor in that season's record heat wave, in which air conditioners failed and hundreds died of heat prostration, and it came as no surprise that news of women-only hours in swimming pools, a measure promoted by Muslim groups, would lead to protests, demonstrations, passionate municipal council meetings, and the declaration by the Minister of Sports that such practices were "a deep challenge to the value of our country and our sports."[36]

Temperatures cooled in September but the coverage did not; each of the three chief national dailies was running an average of two headscarf stories a day.[37] So unsurprisingly, when schools reopened, a furor erupted over the expulsion of two veiled girls, the daughters of a Jewish father and a Muslim, but unveiled, mother. They did not approve of their children's refusal to remove, even during gym class, scarves that covered "the ears, the neck and half the forehead" (i.e., not merely the tolerable "light scarf behind the head").[38] President Chirac announced that the headscarf contravened the separation of church and state, or laïcité, and had become a source of social disorder.[39]

In December, Chirac's Stasi Commission (named for its chairman Bernard Stasi, a former minister of State Security) recommended banning the wearing of the headscarf by minors in schools receiving state funds, whether public or private. Then another panel, the Obin Commission (named for the Inspector General of Education, Jean Pierre Obin, who convened it), went to work investigating conditions in French schools.[40] Not one but two state commissions investigated and advised. But, oddly enough, both the recommendation to remove the headscarf from schools and the resulting veil-banning legislation preceded rather than followed the investigations. Verdict first, evidence later. Descartes could not have been happy.

CURIOUS COMMISSIONS

Even as the votes were being cast in the National Assembly in January 2004 to accept overwhelmingly (276 to 29) the Stasi Commission recommendation,[41] the ten members of the Obin Commission were fanning out to some sixty-one schools in twenty-four *départements*.[42] The Obin report would supply hair-raising testimony to support the verdict of the Stasi Commission, and now that of the National Assembly, and suggest that the Islamization of suburban schools had advanced beyond what even the French news was imagining. Jewish students, according to the report, were the targets of "multiple insults, threats and aggressions . . . both in and outside of school . . . made by classmates of Maghrebine [North African] origin." Ever younger girls were donning the veil as a consequence of "rigorous surveillance by men and boys."[43] Here, as elsewhere, the Obin Commission echoed the conclusions of the Stasi Commission, which claimed, despite polling of Muslim women that seemed to indicate that veiling was often voluntary, that "even if the veil was for many a sign of individual affiliation freely chosen, it had become for others—more numerous than official statistics indicated—a choice made under constraint, or a means of pressure on young women who did not want to wear it and who comprised a large majority."[44]

But Obin took Stasi a step further, suggesting that even the month-long daytime Ramadan fast was not a matter of personal choice but one of peer pressure and a "pretext for proselytism."[45] The commission reported that more and more students were being drafted into fasting at ever-younger ages and with a grotesque rigor extending to "the interdiction of swallowing any sort of liquid, including one's own saliva which causes the soiling of the floor with spit."[46] Fasting students often suffered from fatigue and their studies deteriorated. That kept happening even when parents had explicitly requested that the students eat in the school cafeteria and learned to their surprise that their children had not been doing so.[47] Once again, as with Khaled Kelkal and, as we shall see, with Sidique Khan, intemperate second-generation children were flouting the customs of temperate immigrant parents. One teacher told the Obin commissioners that what had once been a celebration of identity had become "'a period of personal mortification' where suffering plays the central role." These excesses explained the manifold student requests for a break during class "or the invasion of libraries or offices used for sleeping or resting during the break."[48] "The boundless obsession with purity" extended to restrooms where in one primary school the students had designated certain sinks and toilets "for the exclusive use of 'Muslims.' The others were for the 'French.'"[49]

Adolescent religious fanaticism progressed from the restroom to the classroom where the secular national curriculum was viewed as a spiritual affront. History teachers complained of constant challenges from students who refused "to look at anything related to . . . Christianity or Judaism." Of course, objections became "more radical and political when the subject at hand [was] the Crusades, the Holocaust, the Algerian war, the Israeli-Palestinian conflicts and the Palestinian question."[50] As an American reader might guess, science, especially biology, was another "object of collective religious challenge, principally in the form of 'creationism.'"[51]

But the Obin Commission found that objections were not confined to subjects elsewhere considered controversial. Math students declined to employ the plus sign, considering it a symbol of the Cross. The teachers of arts and crafts encountered a "refusal to depict a face" and music teachers' pupils would not "play the flute or practice choir songs."[52] Gym teachers reported that Muslims boycotted swimming classes, the girls out of modesty, and the boys because they do not want to enter "girls' water" or "infidel water."[53] Field trips to cultural sites had to be abandoned "because Muslim students refused to visit national architectural works, cathedrals, churches or monasteries because these buildings have or have had a religious function."[54] The same prejudices barred the study of English ("the vehicle of imperialism") and Enlightenment philosophers, "above all Rousseau and Voltaire, and the texts that place religion under the examination of reason."[55] Some teachers tried to resist, courting classroom chaos, but others submitted, adopting a "self-censorship." Still others acquired a Qur'an and, when challenged, had to "resort to justifying their own teaching with that sacred book."[56]

Where did the students' religiosity come from? According to school officials, the "decisive influence" derived not from parents but from those whom teachers, "with a certain amount of hostility," called "'the bearded ones'" and whom the students called, "with a mixture of fear and respect, 'big brothers.'" These militants, the Outsiders, "had often graduated from universities in France, the Maghreb or the Middle East. They were from families established in the neighborhoods or more recent arrivals."[57]

The Obin commission did not hesitate to find a conspiratorial dimension in this student rebellion. Anti-French sentiment was "carrying youth towards resentment and sometimes radicalization." The Obin report pointed to "organizations structured on an international plan," specifying several times that these were "the Muslim Brotherhood and the Tabligh."[58] Moreover, "the overtly segregationist projects of these groups reject integration as a heresy or an oppression." These organizations

> intend to reassemble these populations on a political plane and disassociate them from the French nation, adding them to a vast "Muslim nation." This project seems to us already well diffused and includes . . . middle school and high school students who refuse, sometimes passively, to identify themselves as French and see the partisans of the war against the West as heroes.[59]

We shall have occasion to assess this account of the protagonists, but if the ghetto schoolroom had "become a battleground" in a religious invasion, at stake was more than school discipline.[60] Was France relapsing into the religious combat that had divided the country so many times before? Could teachers, as in the past, stop fanatics from hammering hatred into young minds? Could the school remain a neutral space where national values could be inculcated? The two commissions held that the very principle of laïcité was challenged by le voile. And the attitudes that the Obin commission uncovered, if widespread, posed a challenge not only to France's identity but also to its cohesion and historical mission. In a rare American notice of the Obin report, an essay in the neoconservative *Weekly Standard* concluded that "the schools are only the tip of the iceberg."[61] By piling one appalling story onto the next, the Obin report clearly suggested that its facts and reportage reflected the life of the banlieues. But did they really?

At the outset, the report itself acknowledged that the schools visited were not a cross-section but instances of notorious religiosity, cases that, thanks to public complaints that reached the Education Ministry, constituted "squeaky wheels" that called out for investigation.[62] They were in effect self-selected by the very school personnel whom the commissioners would proceed to interview and then cull from their testimonies the most graphic and arresting stories in the report, each frightful tale amplifying its predecessor and successor in a synergy of wackiness and dreadfulness. And the commissioners did not bother to interview students or their parents. Yet even as the Obin Commission was going about its investigation, a poll appearing in *Le Monde* on February 4 found that 91 percent of French schoolteachers had not so much as run across a headscarf at their current schools.[63] Rather than a cross-section of French schools, or a cross-section of banlieue schools, or even a cross-section of project (or *"cité ghetto"*) schools, the report, designed to justify a conclusion already reached, a law already passed, presented a veritable menagerie, an exhibit of the most monstrous and bizarre anecdotes from the most troubled schools.

Nonetheless, the range of activities and curricula affected, from rest-rooms to classrooms, from history to math, suggested that at least in those schools heard from—threescore, not merely a handful—the infection reached into every limb, into the soul, of school life. If two government commissions, the President of the Republic, its National Assembly, and its Senate had determined that there was a threat of radical Islam, what were neoconservative columnists, already nauseated by radical Islam, supposed to think when they later read of rioting in the same banlieues? Well, they thought that "[t]he poor, disenfranchised Muslim youth who were rioting throughout France this month are the brothers of those who for years have been attacking France's Jewish population. Almost invariably they are members of a largely North African subculture of extremism."[64] The riots had to be the logical extension and the apotheosis of "a low-level intifada against synagogues, kosher butchers, Jewish schools, etc." that "French Arabs have been carrying on . . . for half a decade."[65] This was "Intifada writ large. The coming of Eurabia. Bat Ye'or, Oriana Fallaci, Hirsi Ali, Irshad Manji have warned of this."[66]

ANTICLIMAX

If two expert panels and France's political branches had concluded that radical Islam was running the schools of the banlieues, and if Muslim groups like the UOIF were complicit, as the Obin report suggested more than once, then certainly banning the veil was bound to invite massive Muslim protests, school strikes, the need to expel legions of girls, retaliation against teachers and principals, and even riots.

And so when the riots began, even some foreign correspondents assumed that "laws supposed to promote integration and oppose multiculturalism, such as the ban on Muslim headwear in schools, have often heightened resentment and the feeling of exclusion. This has in turn fed the rise of Muslim radicalism, which has now become the dominant creed of the young in the French ghettos."[67] But following the banning of the veil, none of these dire prophecies came to pass. To be sure, the

UOIF congress at Le Bourget in April 2004 drew more than double the participants from the previous year, 37,000 compared to 16,000.[68] And the UOIF did issue a statement asserting that Muslims in France felt aggrieved by the new legislation. But the statement failed to call for protests; it merely requested that the law be applied "softly."[69] On June 29, 2004, the UOIF published a letter lamenting that the Stasi Commission "too often ignored" the views of Islamic organizations. But the group counseled Muslims to "reflect carefully as to how they want to accommodate to this law."[70] As it became clear that French public opinion supported the government's firmness, the group's declarations became even more conciliatory. Alaoui, its Secretary-General, noted:

> Since the affair of 1989 the UOIF has modified its stance [on the hijab]. We continue to fight for this liberty, but we must take into account the cultural reflexes of our society. The intrusion of religion in the classroom is a shock. We do not seek such an intrusion, but we want to make it understood that the practice of our religion is compatible with the values and foundations of the republic.[71]

This position, on the part of the very group that the Obin report deemed responsible for extremism in the schools, would not have surprised anyone familiar with the UOIF. Months before the law was passed, as John Bowen points out, the Muslim Brotherhood–led group "let it be known that it actually would welcome a law against the *foulard* in schools because it would allow the organization to tell girls that the condition of necessity (the Arabic term *dururat* was used) required that Muslims obey civil laws even when they contradict religious principles."[72]

The UOIF's acquiescence did not go down well with all those attending its Le Bourget congress or with radical sectors of the Muslim community. An Oumma.com article characterized the Islamist UOIF as being a veritable "yes-man" to the government: "Have you noticed that in 'UOIF' there is the word 'oui'? As in *oui* monsieur le minister, *oui* Mr. Prefect, *oui* to those who ripped the veils off of the heads of our mothers and our sisters."[73]

Few Muslim parents and students seemed to share this outrage. More typical of devout girls was the reaction of Nadia, a senior from Seine-Saint-Denis who chose to follow the law and remove her headscarf: "What is essential is not on your head but what is inside, I came to realize that this year." Farah, sixteen years old, also chose to follow the ban, though less cheerfully: "When I approach the school my throat tightens. In class I pass my hand through my hair with the feeling of being nude. But one gets used to it." Farah added that she and her sister would one day like to move to Morocco or Saudi Arabia because in France "one cannot follow Sharia law." However, for now they would stay in France and follow the law because, as she says, "we can do nothing else."[74]

By January 2005, six months into the first school year covered by the law, a grand total of 44 students had been excluded from school for not observing the ban, and 639 students were officially censored for violation of the rule. Of those 639, fully 550 disputes were solved through "dialogue."[75] As schools were drawing to a close in June, a principal at a Seine-Saint-Denis high school summarized the situation: "Last year we were in the middle of a religious revival. During the month of Ramadan the pressure was intense and many students did not dare to eat. This year, all is calm."[76] Muslims had obeyed the ban with hardly a whimper, still less a bang.

That acquiescence alone placed a straw in the wind, but there were other signs that the radical character of French Islam had never been as feral as depicted or else had subsided after public scrutiny and firm government action, not a lesson learned across the Channel as we will see. On August 20, 2004, the terrorist Islamic Army in Iraq seized two French journalists and threatened to kill them, failing a rescission of the "anti-hijab law," which represented "an injustice and aggression against Islam."[77] But the journalists were released unharmed four months later after French Muslims went on the air and took to the streets to condemn what Islamist intellectual Tariq Ramadan called "an odious blackmail."[78] "At this critical moment, when the national allegiance of French Muslims was tested, they passed . . . with flying colors," said one European observer.[79] French Muslims' "refusal to play into the kidnappers' vision of a uniform, transnational *umma*" and their overwhelming compliance with the headscarf law "revealed the depth of integration and nationalization of Islam in France," concluded the scholars Jonathan Laurence and Justin Vaisse after completing their exhaustive study.[80] Anti-Semitic incidents dropped 48 percent in 2005, consistent with the fact that synagogues and other Jewish sites were not targeted in the fall's riots.[81]

Yet even as the controversies over Islam were seeming to ebb, on July 9, 2004, Marie Leblanc, a twenty-three-year-old French mother, claimed that six North African men had attacked her and her sixteen-month-old baby on an RER commuter train that connects Paris both to the banlieues and to well-to-do suburbs.[82] She reported that the men thought she was Jewish because she was traveling to a wealthy district. She told the police that she was beaten and that the six men penned swastikas on her skin with indelible ink and toppled her stroller with the infant inside. The incident agitated the entire country for two days, sparking rallies in support of Madame Leblanc and outraged denunciations from politicians of all stripes, culminating with President Chirac's expression of "horror" on national television.[83] But the police soon proved the story false, a fabrication by the young woman to persuade her parents to support her and her child.[84]

The French media had broadcast the fiction faithfully, failing to observe that neither Arab protestors (*beurs*) nor Islamists were known for drawing swastikas, or that the young mother had a history of psychological problems and had previously concocted stories of her victimization.[85] She was given a suspended sentence of four months in prison and mandatory psychiatric counseling as chagrined journalists flagellated themselves over their willingness to credit uncorroborated Muslim horror stories.[86] Why had a nation celebrated for its Cartesian skepticism been so easily taken in? Undoubtedly, the wave of confirmed anti-Semitic attacks and the testimony favoring the veil ban smoothed the way. But the fire next time, the riots fifteen months later, would find a press corps less credulous toward allegations of Islamist culpability and of a "French intifada." But this rejuvenation of skepticism did not prevail among conservative columnists abroad.

A TEST OF THE PUNDITS

When Walter Lippmann began formulating his views on the press, it was the Russian civil war, during which the United States intervened in support of anticommunist armies, that "aroused the kind of passion which tests most seriously the objectivity of reporting." Examining the reporting of the counter-revolution, Lippmann and his colleague, Charles Merz, sought a standard to assess the reliability of the news, "definite and decisive happenings about which there is no dispute."[87] They decided to measure the news by its accuracy in anticipating the outcome of the major battles of the Russian civil war.

They found the coverage to have been "dominated by the hopes of the men who compose the news organization." The reporting was "a case of seeing not what was, but what men wished to see." The authors were referring to the desire of American journalists "to win the war . . . to ward off Bolshevism."[88] The French riots, like the Russian civil war, the Tet offensive in Vietnam, and the surprise election defeat of Nicaragua's Sandinista government, aroused similar passions and stereotypes and likewise proved a "test of the news"—in the French case, failed not so much by beat reporters, properly chastened by the Marie Leblanc affair, as by editorial pages in and especially out of the country.[89]

The refrain began in France where conservative columns and editorials cried "civil war" and "the beginnings of intifada?"[90] The mantra was promptly echoed by Western neoconservative columnists who stamped the 2005 riots as "a French Intifada: an uprising by French Muslims against the state" or "this civilizational struggle taking place in France" and by radical right-wing blogs.[91] To be sure, such formulations were not confined to neoconservatives or even to the West. The Hungarian leftist newspaper *Le Nepszava* devoted two pages to what it called "the intifada ravaging France." An editorialist in *Romania Libera* saw the uprising as part of "the global Islamist offensive" and another Romanian newspaper worried that the whole continent was on the brink of a "euro-intifada."[92] Nor were the alarms all "Islamophobic." *Al-Jazeera's* editor in chief gave "great importance to this issue because it may spread across Europe and affect the [Arab and Muslim] region."[93] Indeed, the images of Arab-looking youth throwing stones at men in uniforms looked for all the world like Palestine in the fall of 2000. "Parallels can be found with our reality," observed the *Jerusalem Post*.[94] That editorial warned that once "the Arab-Israeli conflict looked predominantly like a territorial one" but "French policy makers would be unwise to overlook the religious ideological dimensions of the battle and the way Islamic radicals preaching from the mosques and spewing out hatred via the Internet are able to prey on this disaffection and import a toxic ideology into France and the heart of Europe."[95] Neoconservative editorialists, who had diligently absorbed the lessons of Israel, assumed the

same wisdom applied to France and then marshaled it against their customary rivals. Two weeks into the riots, the *Washington Times* editorial-
ized that "to ignore the Islamist threat in France, as the U.S. media has
done for 14 days, betrays a politically correct ideology that is willfully
ignorant of the facts."[96]

A FRENCH REVOLT

If it was not an Islamist intifada, what was it? For eighteen days, immigration's offspring had rioted in the *banlieues* of Paris, Lyon, Toulouse, Lille, Nice, and other French cities. 8,700 automobiles and 30,000 trashcans were burned; 140 buses stoned; 255 schools, 233 public buildings, 100 post offices, and more than 20 houses of worship damaged; 200 million euros' worth of property sacked (80 percent public); 4,770 individuals arrested; and 597 imprisoned (including 108 minors.)[1] France had never seen riots lasting so long or covering such large tracts of the country. But in another sense the riots were quite limited, affecting exclusively the banlieues, and more specifically the public housing projects within them, *les cités.*

These were zones with extremely elevated youth unemployment, where half the youngsters were out of work at any one time. The unemployment could be attributed to various factors: employers' prejudices, ill-qualified applicants, and the stagnation of the French economy, among others. But one cause was beyond question: the stratified character of what economists had been calling the "insider-outsider" French labor market. A privileged sector of French workers had lifetime jobs, labor contracts stipulating a thirty-five-hour work week, six-week vacations, and a medical package that the World Health Organization rated the most generous among all its members. These jobs had become so costly that employers simply stopped filling them, preferring to extend short-term contracts without these entitlements. The result was a class system among workers. Not to put too fine a point on it, unionized workers, usually white and native, got steady jobs, even tenure, while immigrants and their offspring, the denizens of the banlieues, got short-term jobs, if any.

The effect for the postmigrants in the banlieues was not outright misery. Their families received welfare payments and housing subsidies. What gnawed was not so much hunger as injustice, the sense of discrimination that fired the American civil rights movement and the riots that James Baldwin described. In a study of the country's urban riots, two French sociologists described it this way:

> This discrimination, between what the republican model of integration promises in terms of equality of opportunity, of meritocracy, of rights and of citizenship, and the real situation of stigmatization, of segregation, stemming from their social hazard and that of their parents and their immigrant origins, constitutes one of the major causes of the frustration and the resentment of French youth.[2]

By the same token, if joblessness is a basic condition of many ghetto youth, and an underlying cause of the riots, there has been no direct correlation in France between unemployment and urban riots.[3] The resentment and anger that erupted in the autumn of 2005 had more to do with cops than with jobs, with identity than with poverty, with breath, so to speak, than with bread.

Interior Minister Nicolas Sarkozy, soon to be president, wrote the prologue to the riots by announcing on June 30, 2005, in the Paris banlieue of La Courneuve, an ambitious plan to reclaim France's "no go zones" (*zones de nondroit*). Sarkozy's announcement came days after a stray bullet from a drug dealer killed an eleven-year-old boy. His plan included vocational training programs to fight unemployment plus dispatching police squads specializing in drug enforcement to the projects.[4]

Along with this heady combination of affirmative action and SWAT teams, carrots and howitzers, Sarkozy demonstrated his flair for the sensational by declaring that he would "wash down" the zones "with Karchers" (a notorious German power fire hose).[5] Then on October 25, the indecorous guest at Le Bourget, whose name had now become an imprecation among street kids, was checking the progress of his program in another suburb, Argenteuil, the heartland of radical Islam in the banlieues, when he was heckled and pelted with stones. He called the attackers *racaille* ("rabble," but alternatively "scum"). So right before the riots, the *banlieuesards* were seething because word had spread that Sarkozy had called them all scum.[6]

Cars were set afire two days later in Clichy-sous-Bois, a grimy suburb in the *departement* of Seine-Saint-Denis ten miles northeast of Paris proper, whose woods, the *bois*, had long since been cleared to make room for leafless, concrete high-rise tenements or cités. The cités housed immigrants and their offspring, who were reportedly 80 percent Muslim.[7] The police were regarded as "an occupying army" when they entered. There is not one police station in the entire town of Clichy-sous-Bois. (Of the 27,000 police in greater Paris, the city of Paris, with two million people and few social problems, had 17,000. The remaining 10,000 were supposed to police the six million people in the banlieues.)[8]

It was rumored that police had chased two boys over a fence surrounding a high-voltage transformer, which promptly electrocuted them. The police denied this adamantly, but an examination of police communications demonstrated that the officers did in fact pursue the boys, that the latter were innocent of any crime beyond playing soccer in a makeshift pitch, and that the officers were aware that the boys were at risk alongside the power station.[9] The boys' companions claimed that what the police called a "routine search" was routine harassment. On "routine searches," young men in Seine-Saint-Denis told me, "the cops address you as *tu* and not *vous*. Then they call you names, make you spread eagle and pad you down and push you around. They might even slug you and beat the shit out of you." These encounters can batter not just the body but the soul, or more precisely, what Homer and Plato called the *thymos*—the organ the ancient Greeks seated in the lungs, in the breath, and which harbored the sense of pride, the routine young male desire for respect, recognition, "*vous* and not *tu*."

Word spread of murder by cops. It was not the first time. Police killings have set off riots in the banlieues for decades, inflaming the smoldering resentment left from innumerable affronts and other "police infractions." As early as 1992, as we saw, such an incident sparked a riot in Khaled Kelkal's Lyon suburb. According to one study, "police infractions against minors" increased six-fold in France between 1988 and 2000.[10]

Sarkozy, the interior minister, was to claim that the riots were organized by drug kingpins, barons protecting their turf against his campaign to abolish no-go areas.[11] Notwithstanding police reports that the riots were organized via text messages, all the car-burners with whom I spoke denied that was the mechanism. Such stories were "stupidity, based on ignorance of the way things are here," one participant told *The Independent*. "Nothing was planned. Nothing was organized. The drug *caids* [lords] did not want these riots; they were bad for business. They gave the kids something else to do. Their business was terrible during the riots."

In my visits both security agents and the rioters themselves insisted that the unrest spread by television, a national, not private, medium that was far more accessible in the banlieue than the cell phone.[12]

The Clichy street kids set cars afire to lure police and firefighters into an ambush of stones and pellets. For years, such traps had become a tried-and-true bait-and-switch (similar tactics were used in the 1965 Los Angeles Watts riots). In the months preceding the autumn 2005 riots, 28,000 cars had been torched around the country.[13] If that old ploy of using burning cars as decoys was the habitual *modus operandi* of the rioters, what was different now was that the car burnings spread from *quartier* to *quartier*.

That night in Clichy, there were TV cameras nearby, hardly a fixture in the banlieues, because they had been coincidentally covering another event there. Images of some thirty burning cars and scores of policemen being stoned made for riveting television, and it was watched eagerly in other banlieues. "Everyone was talking about Clichy-sous-Bois. We said, 'We can top that,'" one young rioter told me. Soon cars were burning in the whole area of Seine-Saint-Denis. "They're burning cars over there in Pierrefitte. Let's get the buses here in Aubervilliers." Soon not just cars and buses, but schools, warehouses, factories, and police stations were ablaze. It became a contest of neighborhoods, led by street gangs, each with a kind of local pride (*le nationalisme de quartier*), virtually the only pride remaining in these desolate zones. Who can set more fires, stone more officers, and attract more cameras? Each neighborhood sought face time in a dismal and dire competition for recognition. And then the rivalry spread to quartiers in other French cities: Rouen, Lille, Lyon, Nice. But the rioting occurred exclusively in the ghettoes; there was no effort to attack the wealthier suburbs or the downtown. Local pride stayed home.

WHO WERE THEY?

If they were not jihadis or Islamists, then who *were* the rioters? Unemployed workers? Unwashed immigrants? Most reporters and Prime Minister de Villepin saw the rioters as jobless workers. Yet the car-burning contests had little in common with the marches of the unemployed during the Western depression of the 1930s. The projects, the cités, offered small likeness to the Hoovervilles built by homeless unemployed families during the American Great Depression. The Depression marches were deterritorialized, but the French car burnings took place only in the neighborhood. The rioters were clothed in underclass hooded sweat-shirts, unlike the marchers of the 1930s, who wore workers' overalls. Street kids, not jobless workers, threw the rocks and set the fires. And the fires of autumn were not, strictly speaking, riots. The burnings were the work not of an angry mob facing the police but typically of small fleeting groups, though occasionally as many as one hundred mutineers banded together.[14] Many of these *enfantes terribles* were schoolchildren on a coin-cidental midterm vacation—they were black West Africans as well as brown North Africans, Caribbeans as well as Africans, Christians as well as Muslims. These kids were more regularly from high school, or junior high, than from the reserve army of the proletariat. More than a third of the rioters were minors, sometimes as young as ten, seeking thrills and revenge more often than jobs and benefits, and all of the above more than Allah's blessings. A study conducted in the Yvelines departement west of Paris found that 23 percent of the rioters were in high school, 13 percent were in junior high, and 6.6 percent were university students. Some 42 percent were students, while only 24 percent came from the ranks of the unemployed. As for ethnicity, 35.5 percent of the rioters questioned by authorities in Yvelines were of North African descent, 28.9 percent were sub-Saharan African, and 33.3 percent were "European" in origin, meaning Eastern Europeans.[15]

They were rarely newly arrived immigrants not usually even from the first generation at all. "One half of them were known to the police," according to a report by the Renseignements Généraux (RG).[16] These were not immigrants who did not speak French, but the children or grandchildren of immigrants who spoke a slangy, perhaps unseemly, French, but rarely Arabic. Born in France, they may choose French citizenship as adults, which is what they almost invariably do.[17] One banli-euesard told me, "When I go back to visit my grandparents, I want to come home after a few weeks. There's no air conditioning. The people there are wild." Several years earlier another second-generation ghetto dweller remembered his unhappiness during family holidays spent in his parents' village in Kabylia, Algeria: "There were kids of my age. They all spoke Kabyle or Arabic, and me, I didn't understand anything. I was excluded. It wasn't fun."[18] The Muslim postmigrant finds recognition neither at home nor back home. That explains why the Islamist *ummah* (the global Muslim community), may look attractive to some. But far stronger is the neighborhood tie to the suffering cité and, by extension, in an estranged, paradoxical way, to France itself. As one neighborhood-hero rapper explained, "We don't take Algeria or Comoros as our point of reference. We compare ourselves to white France."[19] The protesters were not raising the green banner of Islam but demanding to come under the *drapeau tricolore*.

Whether one is of "French stock" (*de souche Française*) matters terribly in the so-called French melting pot, where ethnic or religious identity has officially been banished to the private sphere. The year before the riots, a French think tank, the Institut Montaigne, found that otherwise identical applicants with French surnames secured interviews five times more often than those with Arab names.[20] A year after the riots, young men (who privately acknowledged taking part in them) still could not find even an internship: "On the phone, they say yes. Then you write and as soon as they see your name and where you live, hop, there are no places left. Nothing has changed. Nothing has changed."[21]

Yet even this patent discrimination should not be ascribed *tout court* to "Islamophobia" or racism. Americans watch the rioter's *doppelganger* on *Law & Order,* or they peek at him on subways where he wears a hooded sweatshirt, a baseball cap turned backwards, sneakers and a chip on his shoulder. The rioters exhibited ways that smacked more of the rapper lifestyle than of the immigrant or of Islamism.

POSTMIGRANT ASSIMILATION

These lifestyles represent a certain acculturation and an example of an adversarial assimilation. Gangsta rap and hooded sweatshirts plainly are not Middle Eastern imports. They do not come from the Outside. These are Insider appurtenances, signs of integration into the international underclass. And they tell us something about the content and form of "integration" for the French immigrant postmigrant. The challenge of integration has most often been laid at the feet not of immigrants but of their children. First-generation immigrants rarely assimilate fully. Often they come, as do today's East Europeans to Western Europe, exclusively to work and then return home. They inhabit enclaves where the sender-country language is still spoken. Milton Gordon, in his 1964 classic study of immigrant assimilation, called these enclaves "decompression chambers," where the immigrant who does stay achieves a "reasonable adjustment" to the new society.[22]

The typical first-generation immigrant does not lament his situation, whether in Birmingham, Berlin, or Brussels of the 1960s, in the early twentieth century Lower East Side, or in Los Angeles today.[23] He or she speaks the old tongue and may never master the new one. Much like other first-generation migrants, the Muslim labor migrant maintained a low profile in Europe, kept his head down. He did not demonstrate. He worked long hours and sent much of his earnings back to the village, which he visited periodically, and where he intended to spend his last days. The assimilation process takes place principally in the second generation and in the public school.

Just as much as in the United States, the public school has been the true melting pot throughout French history. There, children from different backgrounds mixed, learned the language, and were introduced to the host culture. Often, that experience created a tension in the immigrant home between the assimilating offspring and parents—over what language is spoken in front of guests, whether to marry outside the community, and so on. Assimilation, as in Richard Rodriguez's haunting autobiographical account, *Hunger of Memory*, even in his most auspicious of cases, throbs with tension, guilt, and confusion.[24]

In the schools of the French banlieue, the assimilation process sometimes warps into a combat for hegemony among ethnic groups, the classroom a "battleground," as the Obin panel put it.[25] As in the surrounding ghettos, three forces compete unevenly: the gangs, the "bearded ones," and the state (embodied by teachers and police officers)—a three-cornered struggle between the underworld, the world above, and this world. In that context, "this world" is weakly represented or, as in the no-go zones, absent. And the street is far more powerful than the mosque.

A Tabligh Jama'at (TJ) missionary in Clichy-sous-Bois, where the car burnings began, acknowledged that his group had stepped up proselytizing since the riots began. "We do rounds every night and talk to these kids. We bring them the good word, we take them to the mosque, and some of them go from being bad to good. That's something the republic doesn't do."[26] Now overcrowded and underfunded, the French ghetto classroom often fails in the integrating mission assigned to the school in the nineteenth century when education became public and gratis. Furthermore, because of family breakdown, these obsolete institutions inherit the task of establishing authority, a role that the family used to perform. The French state and especially its education system never quite recovered the prestige it enjoyed before the student riots of 1968. As David Bell has pointed out, one ramification of that rebellion was the collapse of the magisterial authority hitherto enjoyed by France's teachers, with their surpassing confidence that they could mold students to national specifications.[27] Under these circumstances, "assimilation" may mean entry into gang culture, an adversarial assimilation.

The loss of respect for the French public school corresponds to the deterioration of inner-city schools in most advanced countries. Moreover, Muslim alienation is even greater elsewhere in Europe. Is there any reason why three weeks of riots occurred in Paris and Lyon and not in Barcelona or Berlin, Brussels or Birmingham?

AN INTERNAL EXILE

Britain and Belgium have both hosted ugly Muslim riots, if on a smaller scale. France's slums are more explosive, thanks less perhaps to their marginally higher rate of youth unemployment than to the cité, which is a French invention. French authorities responded to the housing shortage of the 1950s and 1960s with a hasty construction program: inexpensive, uniform "machines for living" inspired by the modernist trendsetter, Le Corbusier. Le Corbusier and the Bauhaus designers saw the new architecture as a radical break from the past, a global style "conceived in the spirit of detachment from place and history and home" as Roger Scruton writes, and as "a gesture against the nation-state and the homeland, an attempt to remake the surface of the earth as a single uniform habitat from which differences and boundaries would finally disappear."[28]

Hundreds of these cités, spectral towers of reinforced concrete, architecturally alien structures, each housing as many as five thousand dwellers, came to surround Paris, Lyon, and other major cities. Marseilles has the highest per capita immigrant and Muslim population of any French city but did not riot. Marseilles, among other features that set it apart, is all but innocent of the Le Corbusier cité. The city has grown horizontally, not vertically. Elsewhere in France, like the labor migrant himself, the cité could be hurriedly and cheaply hurled at a social or economic problem.

Moreover, the same bleak style was exported to Algeria and the Middle East. There, the fashion would later arouse the wrath of an Egyptian city-planning student named Mohammed Atta.

With running water, central heating, and tidy bathrooms, the cité seemed at first to improve tenants' lives at a low rent. But the tenements fell rapidly into disrepair and were soon abandoned by those who could afford to leave when pipes and elevators began giving out. Immigrants replaced blue-collar workers as tenants.[29] When jobs dried up, the cités spawned delinquency and no-go zones.

During the unrest, Jean-Louis Borloo, the Minister for Employment and Housing who was pushing a vast renewal program centered on the demolition of cités, acknowledged that the projects were saturated with immigrants. "We thought, with a kind of republican arrogance, that [integration] would work out naturally," he told a radio station. "Well, we messed up."[30]

Compared to slums and shantytowns I have known in Mexico City, Caracas, Madrid, East London, Beeston, Barcelona, Brussels, and Boston, the banlieues are not particularly ugly or filthy or decrepit. Like most slums, they contain a high proportion of single-parent jobless families living in cramped, unsanitary collective housing. Their members suffer poor nutrition, obesity, decaying teeth, and defective vision and hearing; the children attend overcrowded schools that are ill equipped to cope with their difficulties in mastering French, yielding two generations of unlettered students.

But these conditions can be found in other European immigrant slums. What distinguishes the banlieue is the aroma of exile. "City air makes free" ["*stadtluft macht frei*"] went the adage at the beginning of bourgeois ascendancy. But in the banlieue the reverse is true; the banlieue is a kind of internal Devil's Island, not eleven kilometers off the coast of South America but that distance from downtown Paris or Nice, an hour by public transportation if you can find that, in every sense a *sub*-urb. Geography is what especially stamps most French slums. The layout of the cité, the absence of a movie theater, mall, of a downtown—of anything like a neighborhood—produces in its inhabitants, as one can hardly call the residents, a climate of isolation, and a texture in stark contrast to the rich, distant urban center from which the banlieue is banished, segregated often by unbridgeable chasms of highway, not connecting the city and the cité but separating

them. Bricked off by the impassable ravines, like the Boulevard Péri-
phérique, the six-lane (at times eight-lane) superhighway that sur-
rounds middle- and upper-class Paris like a moat, the banlieue is
bereft of Metro stops and commuter rail stations but is saturated with
cités ghettoes, menacing caldrons dreaded by residents of the chic inner
city or the leafier outer suburbs. These once modernist housing projects, the refuse of the deracinated 1960s, have become, in a supreme
historical irony, a sort of homeland, a source of bitter pride and neighborhood nationalism.

The intelligence chiefs at the RG describe the riots as a "form of
unorganized urban uprising," "a popular revolt of the *cités* with no leader
and no agenda." About half of the insurgents were first offenders, according to the aforementioned confidential RG report. The young people
were animated by "a strong sentiment of identity that does not rest solely
upon their ethnic or geographic origin, but on their social condition of
exclusion from French society."[31] Yes, the pundits notwithstanding, the
protesters wanted not a home elsewhere, in the Middle East or among
the *ummah*, but in the France whose Article I of its Constitution prom-
ises: "an indivisible, secular, democratic and social Republic. It shall
ensure the equality of all citizens before the law, without distinction of
origin, race or religion."

The sociologist Laurent Mucchielli says the banlieuesards

> consider themselves globally unrecognized, stigmatized, and really
> rejected by French society. They are not represented by traditional
> political forces, and find themselves, consequently, powerless to
> construct autonomous collective action that is durable and non-
> violent, as opposed to the emotional outbursts that were the
> riots.[32]

In the banlieue, representatives of the "social Republic" (whether municipal or prefectorial, welfare or community workers, not to mention
schoolteachers and the police) are viewed with attitudes ranging from
distrust to enmity, and the feeling is often mutual. A French sociologist
found "a feeling of dependence and inferiority, combined with expressions of resentment and violence."[33] There are no political institutions
to channel and express these grievances, no political parties, labor unions,
or nongovernmental organizations, all of which are pretty much reserved
for the middle class of the "indivisible Republic."

In autumn 2005, the failure of the French ideal, the isolation and apartheid, produced not Islamism, still less jihad, but rather a curious paradoxical sort of local pride, seen in dress, heard in variations of slang, felt by distinguishing one's own cité or quartier from others and yet by this very act connecting each to the other and to France.

NATIONALISME DE QUARTIER

A decade before the riots, the sociologist David Lepoutre found cité youth processed ostracism in three different ways—with denial, irony, or finally and "rarest," with the "acceptance and assertion of the negative image." The 2005 riots suggested that the "rarest" mode of coping had become primary in, again, a kind of adversarial assimilation. The sociologist noted that notwithstanding that "negative image," the cité still constituted a birthplace, a source of childhood memories, thus evoking a certain affection and "the perception of the neighborhood as their own 'territory.'" Lepoutre noted that this territory was socially constructed, or to borrow Benedict Anderson's phrase for a nation, it was a kind of "imagined community."[34]

The nationalism de quartier is not, of course, a full-fledged nationalism but a stunted, deformed one. In a sense, it is the contraposition of French national pride, the glorification of what is despised and dreaded by those "of French stock" who reflexively turn down job applications with Arabic surnames. These dead-enders somehow manage to inspire "a strong sentiment of identity," to recall the RG analysis, resting not so much on "ethnic origins" as on "their social condition of exclusion from French society." Again, France, not Saudi Arabia or Algeria, is the desideratum.

In the end, France rather easily suppressed the rioting, with the police actually showing surprising restraint once authorities decided, after a lengthy delay, to step in. Forgotten now is the early panic about whether the government could ever gain control and whether the riots would spread throughout Europe. The imposition of a curfew and a few thousand arrests quelled the riots, which actually had begun to wane even before the declaration of emergency. The police who had started the riots with their brutality ended them with their restraint. Troops were not brought in; there was nothing like the National Guard mobilizations

in American inner-city riots. If Napoleon could brag that he scattered
the royalists with a "whiff of grapeshot," the biographer of Napoleon, the
farcical Prime Minister de Villepin, needed no shells at all to disperse
Sarkozy's racaille. Governance by the nation-state and not the intervention of Muslim elders extinguished the crisis.

THE MARCHERS

After the riots, Prime Minister de Villepin devised a plan to loosen the
stratified labor system. "The First Employment Contract" (or CPE) offered a new sort of labor contract and it stipulated a two-year trial period
for recruits under the age of twenty-six. During that period these new
workers could be let go. This introduced an element of flexibility into the
job market and was intended to give unemployed youth a chance at a job.

De Villepin failed to consult with the labor unions before injecting his
reform in the dead of the night as an "amendment" to a larger piece of
legislation. The prime minister was battling Nicolas Sarkozy for the conservative nomination in the next year's presidential election. Sarkozy had
cemented his strongman image during the autumn unrest and was considered to be a candidate who could wrestle votes away from Le Pen. In
disregarding the unions, de Villepin deliberately invited a confrontation
with them. But he had taken insufficient account of his comfortable
countrymen's fears of future unemployment. On learning of the new
law, students at the Sorbonne and then at scores of universities and *lycées*
went on strike, often with the support of school authorities. They called
on the union leaders to join them. Soon hosts of public officials, union
militants, and students were marching all over the country.

In the end the marchers felled the architect of the reform, the prime
minister who had engineered it to provoke the very confrontation with
the unions that would destroy him. The marchers made confetti of the
script in which a triumphant de Villepin was to face down the unions à
la Margaret Thatcher and Ronald Reagan. Instead, the prime minister
and his president, potentates who had withstood U.S. pressure to support
its Iraq intervention, surrendered to French students, labor unions, and
radical sects. De Villepin himself took a backseat to his rival, Sarkozy,
who accordingly a year later would wrest the conservative nomination
from the prime minister and get himself elected president. By obliging

the government to pull back the slender life rope, the modest labor-law reform, it had extended to the banlieues, the marchers actually prolonged economic stagnation and political paralysis and may have kindled a fire for the future.

On Tuesday, March 27, 2006, I stood in the Paris rain and watched the ghosts march. The walking museum exhibited every species of revolutionary familiar to me from a previous life. Followers of Mao Ze Dong and Lyndon Larouche strolled with aging militants of the French Communist party. Trotskyites duly distributed leaflets announcing "world revolution." Lycée students in Che Guevara T-shirts ambled alongside gray-bearded professors chanting slogans from the Spanish Civil War. Blimps hoisted by labor unions dawdled above plump public employees. Class struggle (*la lutte des classes*) got major posterboard. Adorned with hammer and sickle, red flags stood out against black anarchist banners vowing "Death to Capital." Causes that were old a century ago had escaped from their nursing homes in Pyongyang, Havana, and Minsk. The marchers, in the millions around the country, would soon be celebrating victory, but when viewed from the standpoint of economics, this was more like a funeral procession.

The marchers paused and unfurled their umbrellas, chanting solidarity with the *sans papiers*, France's "undocumented workers." But uninvited to the protest party, unmentioned on any of the banners, posters, pins, and leaflets, were the angry young men of the banlieues who had cast terrifying images into French living rooms a mere four months earlier. Not apprised of that conspicuous absence, the latest guru of "the Frankfurt school," Professor Axel Honneth—who had inherited the mantle of Herbert Marcuse and Theodor Adorno—pronounced in *Le Monde*: "The revolt of the *banlieues* has played a decisive role in the current protest movement against the [labor reform] in the sense that it permitted the students to realize that they too could change things."[35] This statement, and the scene at the Paris demonstration that day in March, perfectly represented the musty dream castle of the unreconstructed European Left. In reality, the rioters from the banlieues loathed the marchers, who were protesting a mild labor reform designed in part to assist the slum dwellers, who in turn supported the new law. "It gives us a chance to prove ourselves; that's all we're asking for," I was told in

Asnières, Garges, Stains, Pierrefitte, and Aubervilliers, all quartiers where cars burned and youth unemployment had reached 50 percent.

The marchers saw the February law as a threat to the lifetime jobs that most of them fondly expected to inherit from their parents. But French employers rarely hired, precisely because they could not fire: they could not adjust the size of their work force to the demand for their product. So, sad to say, there was no future for France's lifetime job. What such marchers used to call "the objective forces" were shaping their own economic future in ways undreamt of in their philosophies. The lifetime job was heading to the very "dustbin of history" they envisioned for their adversaries.

Yet a recent survey of French university students had found that a government job was precisely what 70 percent of them aspired to. To secure it, student leaders had reached out to the unions. The unions, the students, the professors, and the sects rallied for privilege. With their signs excoriating the "precariousness" of "savage capitalism," they were marching against economics, history, and the hopes of the banlieuesards.

UNWELCOME GUESTS

Some of the autumn car burners suspected as much, so they crashed the garden party, showing up at the protests like the proverbial skunks. In a packed Paris Metro train, I watched a team in hooded sweatshirts and baggy pants follow a strapping black African teenager who might have had a future as a pulling guard in the National Football League. Exiting at Gare de Lyon, where a similar squad was waiting, the ensemble disappeared in the direction of the procession wending its way towards the Place de la République. The *casseurs*—literally "breakers"—assembled along the route of the march they planned to attack, just as they had at another demonstration a week before, ripping off a cell phone here, breaking a store window there, and sending chills through the bourgeois *arrondissements.* Later, they would attack the march as it reached its final destination. Modern Luddites, burning cars instead of breaking machines, *sans culottes*, storming a twenty-first-century Bastille, the rebels from the slums were not aligned *with* the marchers, as our Frankfurt philosopher imagined, but *against* them.

France is the country where, more than anywhere else, the historical class struggles were each time fought out to a finish, and where,

*consequently, the changing political forms within which they move
and in which their results are summarized have been stamped in
the sharpest outlines.*

So wrote Friedrich Engels, introducing Marx's first historical account of
class war. France still "shows the way to Europe."[36] France, as Honneth
sought to remind *Le Monde*, is still where revolt really happens, as opposed to Germany, where it only gets interpreted. But the class struggle
has taken a form that Marx and Engels did not anticipate. Lenin, who
coined the term "worker aristocracy," came closer; for today's class
struggle sets privileged workers against French citizens from immigrant
backgrounds, the second generation. This class war is being fought on
the terrain of what is called "the insider–outsider labor market." It pits
the insider labor aristocrat and his offspring against the progeny of the
colonies, mostly the children and grandchildren of laborers recruited
from North Africa half a century ago.

Along with the banlieue, Islam was the other notable player unrepre-
sented in the spring demonstrations. Despite neoconservative worries
about a Leftist/Islamist cabal in France and elsewhere,[37] I saw no evidence in the marchers' various posters and flags or in the uniform pallor
of their faces of the fact that Muslims make up 10 percent of France's
population. At the three marches I attended, I saw no sign of the Union
of French Islamic Organizations (UOIF) or any other Islamic group. The
marchers reflected, rather than overcame, their distance from the mosque
and the cité.

I spent the day after the grand march in the banlieues with Rachid
Ech Chetouani, whose father came from Morocco in 1967. At twenty-
seven, Rachid had given up his career as a rapper and now labored
long weeks trying to start a small business importing memory sticks
from China and selling them on eBay. Air Jordans fetched from Chicago and resold in the banlieues and odd jobs in Quebec had gar-
nered Rachid some startup money. After traveling to Shanghai to
establish contacts with suppliers, Rachid went to French banks for
funds. Crédit Lyonnais and Société Générale refused to open an account for him. He finally secured a loan at the Paris branch of Crédit
du Maroc, whose Moroccan manager was an acquaintance of his
Moroccan father.

Unlike the marchers, Chetouani admires the New World:

In America, the boss looks to make a buck, and he expects you to work hard. It's the cash nexus. But that's fine with me. Here we can't get work because everything is based on affinities. The boss hires you only if you have an in. In America no one cares where you came from as long as you can bring in the bucks. But in France you have to know the right people, come from the right neighborhood with the right last name.

THE FIRE NEXT TIME?

The failure of assumptions and premises we have been studying was hardly "a failure of imagination" as in the 9/11 Commission's famous indictment of U.S. antiterrorism. Rather, it was a failure of discrimination. By that I mean that commissions and commentators failed to draw proper distinctions (such as those in the User's Guide that follows) and thus they often took a part for the whole, a supposition, anecdote, or rumor for a finding.

The "Muslim immigrant rioters" proved a veritable United Nations of postmigrant protesters. The "unemployed rioters" were mostly school-age adolescents. "The Islamist intifada" was nonexistent. But how to explain the disparity between two government commissions decrying rampant radical Islam in ghetto schools and the absence of said rampaging radical Islamists in the riots? Did teachers and principals just imagine or even, like Marie Leblanc, fabricate the incidents they described? Their number, detail, and mutual confirmation rule out such suspicions. Did the commissioners simply get carried away in their laïcité and exaggerate the import of what they heard? A bit of that, perhaps. But a more plausible explanation may lie in the cultural gap between commissioners, teachers, and principals (all "French stock") and the Islam of the ghetto, a gap that portended a failure to discern and thus to discriminate.

To the International Crisis Group (ICG), the autumn riots demonstrated not the ascendance of Islamism but its "withering away" in the ghetto and its supersession by Salafism (see glossary and User's Guide for these terms).[38] The commissions and the commentators failed to distinguish between the political Islamism of the UOIF and the apolitical Salafism of the students and between both of those and jihadism (see

User's Guide and glossary for further definition of these terms). But rather than any form of Islamic militancy, if we can speak at all of an ideology of the rioters, it was the "nationalism" of the cité. The young Muslim of the banlieue was more likely to be a "neighborhood nationalist" than an Islamist or even a Salafi.[39]

Islamism's modest leverage in the banlieue was attenuated by its willingness to collaborate with the French Interior Ministry, and specifically with Sarkozy. But the confessional shortfall was offset not by radical Islam but by a feverishly literal Salafism. That sort of Salafism is cultural rather than political. Unlike political Islam, it spurns collaboration with the authorities and rejects the authority of the state in the classroom. Instead, pietist or "sheikhist" Salafism urges its followers, like the sixteen-year-old Farah and her sister, to make a *hijra* (exodus) from the idolatrous Mecca of Paris to the Medina of the Maghreb, or, at the very least, to withdraw from politics. Islamism, as with the Muslim Brotherhood–led UOIF, calls for political participation and collaboration with authorities, hence Sarkozy's presence at the Le Bourget meeting.

Pietist Salafists steer clear of politics, even in its most spontaneous forms such as rioting. The Salafist embraces Muhammad's hijra from Mecca as a prototype for modern life. The Salafist may down pizza and kebabs, but he defies school rules and disparages diplomas. He challenges the curriculum with a Saudi-supplied collection of leaflets, pamphlets, and cassettes. Moreover, when a pietist "takes control of a prayer room in a working-class neighborhood on the outskirts of Paris," according to Gilles Kepel, an authority on the Muslim banlieue, "problems related to veiling often arise in nearby secondary schools in the following weeks and months. The new preacher's injunctions galvanize young male zealots, who reinforce his influence by applying social pressure on the young women in the neighborhood."[40] In the banlieue, Salafism has some purchase in the second generation, TJ among immigrant parents. "Consequently, Salafism . . . implant[s] itself in the strongholds of Tabligh, in particular the unstable *quartiers*."[41]

The heterogeneity of TJ, UOIF, and Salafi appears to have been unknown to the Stasi and Obin commissions, not to mention the pundits. Yet the rise of Salafism and the concomitant decline of Islamism may explain how radical fundamentalism could be so prevalent in ghetto schools and so absent in the riots. Whereas Islamists denounced the riots and cooperated with the police, the apolitical Salafists simply abjured.

EUROPEAN SALIENTS

The same year that second-generation Paris Muslims expressed their anger in neighborhood riots, second-generation British Muslims brought terror to downtown London. The riots expressed neighborhood pride and in a paradoxical way allegiance to France; the London terror was aimed at England itself, at anyone riding the London underground.

To seek out an explanation for this divergence, let's look at some polling numbers. In a 2006 Pew Research Center survey when Muslims were asked whether they considered themselves primarily citizens or Muslims, British and French Muslims formed opposite ends of the European spectrum.[42] In Britain, only 7 percent of Muslims replied that they were British citizens first, while 81 percent said they were Muslims first. In Germany, 66 percent of Muslims claimed to be Muslims first, while 13 percent said they were German citizens first, and 69 percent of Spanish Muslims said they were Muslims first, while only 3 percent said they were Spanish citizens first. Most patriotic were French Muslims, with 42 percent saying they were French citizens first, six times as many as British Muslims, and a comparatively modest 46 percent saying they were Muslims first. Whereas upwards of two-thirds of German and Spanish Muslims and four-fifths of British Muslims identified themselves primarily as Muslims, less than half of French Muslims did the same.[43]

This response was one of a pattern that persists through a series of related questions to the larger public. French citizens were most likely to look askance at an increase of Islamic identity. A high portion, 87 percent, claimed such identification was bad for the country while only 11 percent found it good. By the same token, the British public was least likely to see growing Islamic identity as a bad thing, far less than the other countries polled. Only 59 percent said it was a bad thing, while 27 percent said Islamic identification was good. Spain and Germany were close to France on the issue. In Spain, 82 percent said it was a bad thing and 13 percent said it was a good thing. In Germany, 83 percent said such alignment was bad, with 11 percent saying it was good. Among the four European publics surveyed, the Spanish and German societies felt the most negatively toward Muslims. As one would anticipate from our paradigm, the Pew survey found more tolerance of differences in Britain than elsewhere in Europe.[44] Yet it was the British respondents, Muslims

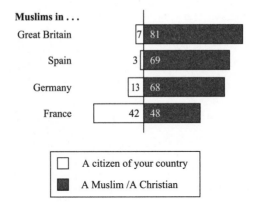

What Do You Consider Yourself First?

Muslims in . . .

Great Britain — 7 | 81

Spain — 3 | 69

Germany — 13 | 68

France — 42 | 48

☐ A citizen of your country

■ A Muslim /A Christian

and non-Muslims alike, in marked contrast to French respondents, who consistently identified Islam as a source of conflict and division in their country. When asked whether they wished to adopt the national customs of the host country or to be distinct from it, 78 percent of French Muslims said fellow Muslims wanted to adopt national customs, with only 21 percent saying they preferred to remain distinct. By contrast, only 41 percent of British Muslims believed their co-religionists wished to espouse national customs, with 35 percent opting to diverge.[45] Muslims were also polled on whether there was a conflict between being a devout Muslim and living in a modern state, and once again, French and British Muslims stood at opposite poles of the spectrum. French Muslims were close to the French general public, but far from British Muslims, with 72 percent of French Muslims saying there was no conflict between Islam and modernity, while only 49 percent of British Muslims found no conflict between the two. (Spanish and German Muslim opinions fell between those of the French and British, with 71 percent of Spanish Muslims and 57 percent of German Muslims saying there was no conflict.)[46] Thus, where Muslims wished to be distinct, as in Britain, the dominant view was that there was more conflict with the host society and with modernity; where they identified with the host country, as in France, the dominant view was that there was less conflict. However, where Muslim identity was most widely tolerated or embraced, in Britain, Muslims felt most alienated! Where Muslim identification was

Is There a Conflict Between Being a Devout Muslim
and Living in a Modern Society?

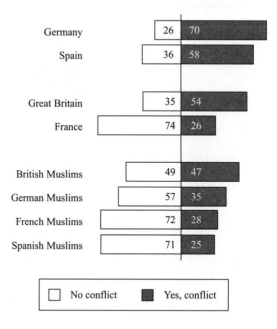

viewed negatively, as in France, there actually was less conflict—a result
that hardly supports the stereotypes about the French riots but does bear
out our analysis of them.

France and Great Britain likewise stood at opposite poles when Pew
consulted their general public on these same questions. In Great Britain,
only 22 percent of the general public thought Muslims wanted to adopt
British customs, and 64 percent said Muslims wanted to be distinct. On
the other hand, non-Muslim French, like their Muslim minority counterparts, reported the highest numbers with the view that Muslims
wished to adopt national customs (46 percent).[47] In results that again
might be considered counterintuitive from a pluralist perspective, the
French public was the most positive about the prospects of Muslim integration. When asked if there was a conflict between being a devout
Muslim and living in a modern society, 74 percent of the French general
public said no. This response was quite different from the responses of
other European countries polled. Only 35 percent of the general public
in Britain, 36 percent of the Spanish general public, and 29 percent of the

German general public saw no conflict.[48] The French were therefore most likely to believe that their Muslim minority wanted to adopt national customs and yet were least likely to see a conflict between being a devout Muslim and living in a modern society.

Surprisingly to some, the country with the greatest tolerance was the one most strongly promoting assimilation. Of the four European countries polled, the French seemed to be most hopeful that Muslims could become a part of their society. It would seem that there is actually less conflict between Muslims and non-Muslims in the European country least tolerant of Muslim identification, than in highly tolerant multiculturalist Britain.

In another variance with the punditry surrounding the riots, French Muslims held far more favorable views of Jews than Muslims in the other European countries polled. While 71 percent of French Muslims had a favorable opinion of Jews, only 32 percent of British Muslims, 38 percent of German Muslims, and 28 percent of Spanish Muslims felt likewise.[49]

One Pew question raised the issue that most interests us, and will absorb much of our attention in coming chapters: Islamist terrorism. Islamist apologetics deny the existence of such a thing, claiming, for example, that the September 11 attacks were confected by the CIA or by Israel's Mossad intelligence agency. Such claims contribute to the jihadi climate of opinion, its narrative, or, to use Walter Lippmann's phrase, its "system of stereotypes."[50] When asked if Arabs carried out the 9/11 attacks, only 17 percent of British Muslims said yes and 27 percent said they did not know, while 56 percent said no. In France, the portion of Muslims affirming Arab involvement was much greater—48 percent believed that Arabs were involved, with 46 percent disagreeing, and only 6 percent pleading ignorance. In Germany, 35 percent affirmed Arab involvement, 44 percent denied it, and 21 percent said they did not know. In Spain, 33 percent agreed, 35 percent disagreed, and 32 percent said they did not know. Thus, 83 percent of British Muslims denied Arab involvement in 9/11, by far the highest among Europeans, while nearly half of French Muslims acknowledged Arab participation in the attacks.[51] The contrasting pattern of responses to the survey questions offers insight into why young British Muslims have proved far more receptive to the jihadi narrative than their French counterparts. The pattern might surprise observers, because Britain offers many indulgences to its

Muslim minorities while France, as we have seen, balks at public conces-
sions to faith. Chapter 7, "Angles of Aggregation," offers an analysis of
the British, French, and German approaches to immigrant integration
that may serve in explaining the responses recorded in the Pew surveys.

The British model, as "Angles of Aggregation" will argue, lost its way
with the loss of empire. The French narrative survived loss of empire but
has been unable to absorb the second generation. That is what the riots
were about, not Islam. The French narrative foundered on the contradic-
tion between its professed equality and the tacit preference for "French
stock" (or de souche Française). One model, professing to assimilate
Muslims into French society, reaped widespread neighborhood riots
that, although alarming and unsettling, were at least bloodless. The
reverse model, with its multiculturalist narrative and grant of considerable Muslim autonomy, hosted withal, somehow, murderous Islamist terrorism. That perplexity we will leave to what follows.

PART TWO

GUIDES FOR
THE PERPLEXED

A USER'S GUIDE

If names be not correct, language is not in accordance with the truth of things.
If language be not in accordance with the truth of things, affairs cannot be carried on to success . . . [and] punishments will not be properly awarded.

—Confucius, *Analects,* XIII, 3

It is now widely recognized that Muslims are usually either Sunni or Shia, the latter an opposition faction that emerged in the seventh century over claims to succession to the Prophet. The Shi'ites are a majority in Iran; the Sunnis a majority in most other Muslim countries. The Shia will rarely play an independent role in our European story. But Sunni Islam, the creed that al Qaeda and most European Muslims share, comes in a variety of shapes. Folk, or Sufi, Islam is permeated by custom. Followers of folk Islam worship at shrines, revere holy men (variously *pirs* or *marabouts*), ornament gravestones, pray in brightly decorated mosques, and sing and dance in festivals. This mystical, often ascetic, sometimes magical Islam is rooted in local culture. Fundamentalist Islam, on the other hand, is austere, literal, orthodox, and scriptural and deplores all folk or popular "innovation" (*bida*). It is often a puritanical import to Europe from Saudi Arabia. As I will show in the case of Mohammed Sidique Khan, the London bomber, the challenge of fundamentalism to folk Islam can generate violent extremism.

Though the distinction between folk and fundamentalist practices is central to other religions—for example, Christianity as sacrament and the Word—in Islam it can be traced back to the Prophet and his dual role as messenger and lawgiver.[1] *Tariqa* (the path or way or method) and *Sharia* (the Law) form the main foundations of Islam: spirituality and learning. Spirituality is the province of sheiks, charismatic vessels of the mystical and Gnostic moment; duty is the domain of the *'ulema* (lawyers and scholars), the guardians of behavioral and legal orthodoxy. Ibn Khaldun in the fourteenth century saw the commerce between these two complementary realms of thought and behavior as essential to the dynamics of the Islamic social order.

But these complementary spheres may come into conflict as when, for example, in the mid-nineteenth-century Indian subcontinent the folk, Barelvi (pronounced BREL-WEE) and fundamentalist, Deobandi (DAY-O-BAHN-DEE) schools began to contend. There, Sufi sheiks had grafted the Muslim faith onto indigenous beliefs producing a popular Islam of festivals, shrines, and saints (something like Roman Catholicism). Fundamentalists (who distantly resemble early Protestants) deemed such practices heretical "innovations" (bida) or even idolatry (*shirk*). Wedded to scripture, fundamentalist reformers through the ages have advanced an alternative divested of accretions. Fundamentalists like the Deobandi, who in this respect resemble Saudi Arabia's Wahhabis (see chapter 5), preached a return to scripture and to the "pure" faith, one based on a direct, unmediated, and individual relation with the Creator. In modern times fundamentalist Islam often has been a faith of the literate city; folk or popular or traditional Islam of the countryside. Fundamentalist Islam, with its fidelity to the Book, migrates more easily than folk Islam with its fixed connection to specific local sites or personages.

Even though most immigrants themselves followed the folk ways, the more portable, fundamentalist mosques and seminaries often set up shop first, in the early days of mass Muslim immigration to Europe. And they would have the more immediate impact on the children of the immigrants. The decision of Mohammed Sidique Khan, to renounce his first-generation immigrant father's folk Islam (which, among other things, would have dictated an arranged marriage to his cousin), to shift mosques and to adopt a fundamentalist version of Islam lit a long fuse that would detonate eventually on July 7, 2005.

But what we have called "fundamentalism" also demands distinctions. Fundamentalist Islam is on offer today in a dizzying variety of brands, shapes, and sizes—from quietist separatists to roving missionaries to political activists, from national revolutionaries to global jihadis. "Fundamentalism" as a catch-all can be promiscuous and crass because conventional fundamentalists, such as the Deobandi, are to be distinguished from Islamists who seek to reform through politics. Olivier Roy, the distinguished scholar of Islamic radicalism, like most of his French compatriots, denominates radical "Salafists" (who invoke Islam's pious patristic ancestors or predecessors, the Salafi). But most Salafists are not violent jihadis and not all Islamists are Salafists. Perhaps for that reason, Roy himself tends to call jihadis "neofundamentalists," and although his term has much to commend it, it remains a neologism.[2] The reader may want guidance through this terminological maze, so what follows is a homespun taxonomy of species of modern fundamentalism including Islamists, who wish to reform; Salafists, who wish to return to the past; and jihadis, who wish to revolt.

Islamists try to change behavior, to reform through politics or preaching, like the Muslim Brotherhood that we will meet presently and the Union of French Islamic Organizations (UOIF) that we encountered in chapters 2 and 3. But the archetypical Salafist renounces society (and much of the subject matter of French schools, as we have seen) to bury himself or herself in ancient precedents. Salafists wish to return to the golden age of the Prophet and his disciples. Islamists accept modern society but want to reform it in a fundamentalist direction. When Islamists dissociate themselves from Salafists, it is typically on the grounds of the latter's preoccupation with individual behavior and often with the minutiae "of correct Islamic dress, rituals of eating, sitting, sleeping, etc."—just now glimpsed in the Obin report.[3] Thus whereas Salafist women don *niqabs* or *burkas* (full-face veils), Islamist women wear only headscarves. The French scholar Gilles Kepel notes a particularly stark difference in the European context: "Unlike the salafists, who preach self-imposed apartheid or advise believers to isolate themselves in a mental ghetto to avoid contamination by European infidels, the associations emerging from the Muslim Brothers have chosen since 1989 to root themselves in civil society."[4] We saw something of this in chapters 2 and 3—the Salafists boycotted school subjects, and the UOIF Islamists hosted Interior Minister Sarkozy at their annual meeting. Though most angry European Muslims are Islamists or Salafists, a few of the angriest of them can become global jihadis, for whom exterminating domestic and international enemies of Islam overrides all other obligations.[5]

These distinctions possess not only heuristic and analytical but also strategic value. To recognize heterogeneity is essential both to understanding the events we describe and to forming a strategy against violent jihad, to single out and isolate the main enemy, to neutralize collateral enemies, to convert neutrals into allies of convenience, and to unite and mobilize allies. If we need to "connect dots," we must draw distinctions.

ISLAMISM

Islamists can be divided into three types: missionary, political, and jihadi. All seek to preserve divine origins while adapting to current conditions, to preserve tradition while borrowing selectively from the West. And despite their diverse interpretations of Islam, they share a "subculture that makes the tenets of Islam permeate every dimension of daily social and cultural life."[6] But these types of Islamists differ in "how they conceive the principal problem facing the Muslim world, and what they believe is necessary, possible and advisable to do about it."[7]

Missionary Islamists (Da'wa)

The most prominent missionary trend in Islamism is Tabligh Jama'at (TJ) (its full name is Jama'at al-Da'wa wal-Tabligh, or the Group for Preaching and Propagation). Since its founding in India in 1926, Tablighi activists have spread throughout the world, including Europe and North America. TJ's special calling is to preserve and fortify minority Muslim communities. That vocation derives from Islam's two-fold subjugation in British India: as a religious minority in an "infidel" Hindu country and as a colonial subject. In the West, where TJ leaders thought they recognized a familiar environment in the minority and quasi-colonial status of Muslims, TJ doctrine changed little from its Indian foundations. Tablighi activists are known for their puritanical orthodoxy, their asceticism, and their strenuous imitation of the Prophet—to the length of copying his supposed style of interrupted sleeping. As the activists travel from mosque to mosque, they make appeals for Muslims to return to a purer form of Islam (much like the Salafis) by forswearing accumulated local practices or accretions (bida). The Tablighi reject politics and instead choose to reform individual behavior and religious practice.

Impatient with TJ's apolitical orientation, many would-be jihadis used TJ's sprawling networks to make contact with jihadis. That was the case not only, as we saw, of Khaled Kelkal but also of members of the 9/11 Hamburg Cell, of Richard Reid the shoe bomber, the London bombers, the 2006 Heathrow airline plotters, the Lackawanna Six, the 2007 Glasgow airport bombers, and the fourteen men arrested in January 2008 with explosives who were intending to bomb Barcelona. Though jihadis come to regard TJ retreats with unremitting scorn, for many, a stop with TJ has been a way station on the pathway to Holy War.

Political Islamists

These Islamists seek the restoration of Islam not through missionary work but through politics. In Muslim countries, Political Islamists typically aim to make restaurants, schools, banks, courts, and ultimately states conform to "Islamic" practices. They seek to replace secular law with some version of Sharia, a set of laws conceived to be divinely inspired. In recent decades this has meant campaigning in elections, most notably in Egypt. That is in sharp contrast to jihadis who hold that man-made laws trespass on Allah's sovereignty. Political Islamists tend to see jihad as a struggle for internal faith or social reform, and they oppose violent jihad against the West and against Muslim regimes. However, Political Islamists have endorsed "resistance" in Soviet Afghanistan and in "occupied" countries such as Iraq, Chechnya, and Kashmir and in Israel's "occupied territories."

The leading exponent of Political Islam is the Society of Muslim Brothers, born in Egypt but with branches or offshoots in some seventy countries, including those of Western Europe. These branches differ considerably from one country to another in their strategy and tactics.[8] In Western countries where Muslims are immigrants, the Muslim Brotherhood, or its front organizations like the UOIF, advocate for the rights of Muslim minorities and do not try to convert the hosts. They engage in electoral politics, and in that respect they resemble European Christian Democrats of the late nineteenth century or Evangelicals in the United States today, though their politics tend to find a home not on the Right but on the Left.

Jihadi Islamists

These are militants who rejected "man-made" electoral politics and embraced violence, abjured the Muslim Brotherhood, and created the first modern jihadi organizations in Egypt in the 1970s. In the following decades, similar jihadi groups spread through the Middle East and into Arab North Africa and South and Central Asia, and eventually to Europe. Those jihadis were of two sorts—revolutionary and putchist. For example, in Egypt the Gamaa Islamiyya sought a utopian Islamic state through popular insurrection, but Ayman al-Zawahiri's al-Jihad, part of which merged into al Qaeda, bent its efforts toward a more pragmatic *coup d'état.*

SALAFISTS

Salafists ("righteous predecessors") draw legitimacy from the *hadith* (the collection of sayings and doings of the Prophet). In *Sahih Bokhari,* the most authoritative collection of hadith, it is recorded that "the Prophet said, 'The best people are those living in my generation, then those coming after them, and then those coming after.'"[9] In the modern context, Salafists are those who look back to the Prophet and his companions for strict instructions on how to live a religious life. We saw some of their extreme followers in action in French ghetto schools—forswearing the plus sign and field trips. However, like Islamism, Salafism is a category difficult to delineate, a task rendered more difficult because the term is debated even among those we seek to label. It is particularly hard to draw the line between Salafists and Tablighis.

As Roy observes,

> Salafism was originally meant to answer the challenge of the West. But "Salafi" no longer refers to a global political project to reform and modernize Muslim societies. The idea is to ignore the West. (Old Salafism meant to compete socially, economically and politically and ideologically with West; new Salafism ignores it—or attacks it militarily.) Salafism is now associated with a conservative program of purifying Islam from cultural influences (from traditional Muslim societies as well as from the West). Contemporary Salafis

have little in common with their predecessors, but much in common with the Wahhabis.[10]

For our purposes, there are two sorts of Salafis: pietists and jihadis.[11]

Pietists are separatists, of the sort we saw in French schools, dedicated to religious study (Roy's "new Salafists" who ignore the West), emphasizing peaceful methods of propagation (*da'wa*), education or "culturing" (*tarbiyya*), and purification (*tahhara*). They view politics as a deviant innovation or bida. Pietists control the state religious establishment in Saudi Arabia, and their quietism suits the regime's domestic and foreign policy. Pietists reject association with "infidels" and pledge loyalty not to their country but to the *ummah* (an imagined worldwide Muslim community) of true believers. Saudi pietist scholars often "advise Muslims in Europe to leave the domain of disbelief to avoid any corrupting influence."[12]

Salafi Jihadis

Salafi jihadis embrace violence, rejecting the political orientation of groups like the Muslim Brotherhood. Would-be Political Islamists usually get exposed to the Muslim Brotherhood analysis during their studies at the university, while jihadis gain their political training on the battlefield, especially in Afghanistan.[13] In Saudi Arabia as elsewhere in the Middle East they tended to remain a marginal current within Political Islam until Saudi government repressed the latter, "leaving a critical void that was eventually filled by the jihadis."[14] These Salafi jihadis adopted the view that warfare against either external or internal enemies of Islam took immediate precedence. Among the most notorious of the Salafi jihadis have been Egyptian president Anwar Sadat's assassin, Khaled Islambouli; Abu Musab al Zarqawi, the vicious leader of al Qaeda in Iraq; Omar Abdel Rahman, the blind sheik who authored the first World Trade Center bombing; two influential strategists, Abu Musab al Suri and Abu Muhammad al Maqdisi; one of our "lords of Londonistan," Abu Qatada al Filistini; and, last but not least, Osama bin Laden. Salafism produces more jihadis than Islamism—if most jihadis are Salafis, most Salafis are not jihadis.

An important distinction among jihadis is between nationalists and globalists. Osama bin Laden pursued global jihad, but several of the groups associated with al Qaeda from time to time began as nationalists, such as Khaled Kelkal's Armed Islamic Group (GIA) and the Libyan Islamic Fighting Group (LIFG). Al-Zawahiri's al Jihad started out as a nationalist group focused on the Egyptian home country, but when its efforts faltered, its leader and some of his followers joined bin Laden's global jihad.

Related but not identical to the distinction between national and global jihadis is the strategic distinction between "near enemy" and "far enemy." The near enemy is the "apostate" regime in Muslim countries (such as the Egyptian secular government and the Jordanian or Saudi royals); the far enemy is the imperialist power that allegedly props it up, today usually the United States. From 1979 to 1998 the "near enemy" strategy took precedence in the jihadi community, with some competition from Fathi Shiqaqi, the founder and leader of the Palestinian Islamic Jihad, who argued for attacking the Israeli far enemy. But most jihadi groups focused, like the GIA in Algeria, on overthrowing their own ("apostate") regimes. In the face of their repeated defeats, Osama bin Laden and Ayman al-Zawahiri argued that proponents of the "near enemy" strategy had failed to identify the true and main enemy, U.S. imperialism, which, according to this analysis, sustained the local Muslim regimes. Hence the sway of the "far enemy" strategy, at least through the U.S. "surge" in Iraq. Then in the Middle East a species of "near enemy" strategy reappeared, targeting the Arab states surrounding Israel.[15] But al Qaeda and its affiliates also retain a "far enemy" orientation, specifically now against the home bases of NATO countries, in the hopes of driving them out of Afghanistan, much as Spanish troops withdrew from Iraq after the Madrid bombings. The clearest example of this Afghanistan-oriented, retaliatory, "far enemy" strategy will present itself in chapter 13.

Jihadis may be Islamist or Salafist, nationalist or globalist, pursue the near enemy or the far, but they also can be differentiated in terms of the constraints they put on their violence against other Muslims; some groups recognize no constraints and are called *Takfiri*. The Kelkal's GIA stretched *takfir* (anathema) to other Muslim groups who were not willing to slaughter the entire anathematized *kuffir* (infidels)—basically saying you are "with us or against us." If against the GIA, you were an apostate; you had renounced Islam. But al Qaeda broke with this group because bin Laden acknowledged the three Salafist qualifications from apostasy.[16] Here, the Salafist jihadis like bin Laden actually part company with the followers of Sayyid Qutb, the Egyptian intellectual who inspired Islamist jihadism, "who denounced entire populations as apostate without meeting these three conditions."[17] As we will see in the chapter titled "Londonistan," these grim and far-fetched distinctions were to cause divisions between the increasingly bloodthirsty GIA and its London supporters.[18]

Again, to summarize, Islamists seek to reform, Salafists to regress, jihadis to raze.

INSIDE MEETS OUTSIDE: WEST MEETS EAST

Our focus is on two classes of European jihadis: aliens and home-grown.[19] Of these the center of our attention is the homegrown: post-migrant jihadis socialized in Europe, only in that sense Insiders. As Insiders they can pose for security officials a unique challenge, thanks to their numbers, invisibility, and skill-set. Postmigrants far outnumber aliens, but they pass through no border checkpoints and prompt no scrutiny. They speak the native language, and they know Western society, hence can obey the injunction of Mao Ze Dong that "The guerrilla . . . move amongst the people as a fish swims in the sea." The Outsiders are the radical preachers who often serve as mentors for Insiders. The convergence of alien prophet and native recruit, of Outside and Inside, of East and West, can make for the most ominous European Holy Warrior: a Westerner with the tongue, information, anonymity, and socialization of a native but with a terrorist skill-set and a dedication to global jihad.

Islamist students and refugees began arriving in Europe in the 1950s, and some began to organize seminars and university Islamic Societies and to publish magazines and journals, efforts that eventually generated Muslim Brotherhood–led organizations in several countries, including Britain, France, and Germany.[20] Without being jihadis, these Islamists, along with the Saudi-funded World Muslim League and Tablighi missionaries, sowed the ideological seeds of Euro-jihad. They sketched the outline of its master or "single" narrative. But jihadism proper first emerged in Europe not in the middle but toward the end of the twentieth century. Though some extremists trickled into Western Europe during the anti-Soviet war in the late 1980s, most extremist refugees settled in Europe at the conclusion of the Afghan jihad, usually after failing to bring jihad to their home countries. Thus they were frequently members of nationalist jihad groups such as the Algerian GIA or the Egyptian Gamaa Islamiyya (GI), an Islamist jihadi group founded in opposition to the Muslim Brotherhood. Some future Outsiders studied in Saudi Arabia but, as emerging Salafi jihadis, they clashed with the rulers of the pietist Kingdom, in a dispute recounted in the next chapter. These groups and individuals began to influence European postmigrant radicals starting in the early 1990s, as we will see in chapter 10. Especially as these groups fell toward the very end of the century under the influence of Bin Laden's global jihad, postmigrants went directly Outside, to Afghanistan, Algeria, or Pakistan to find mentors and trainers in Holy War.

The homegrown postmigrant extremists came from all rungs of the social hierarchy. Products of hardscrabble inner cities or suburbs were Zacarias Moussaoui, the so-called twentieth hijacker; Mohammad Bouyeri, the Dutch slayer of Theo van Gogh; and, of course, Khaled Kelkal. But Jason Burke has found that fewer than 20 percent of British jihadis came from genuinely deprived backgrounds and that more than a third of them possessed university degrees—usually in scientific or technical fields, especially engineering (as is so often the case with Islamist extremists).[21] Ahmed Omar Sayyid Sheik, a wealthy British Pakistani convicted in Pakistan for his role in the murder of the *Wall Street Journal* reporter Daniel Pearl, is a specimen of an exceptionally cruel postmigrant extremist from a privileged background and with a university degree.

It could be said that Europe has managed to replicate the two social types that Kepel found typical of Islamist movements in Muslim countries: the "young urban poor from deprived backgrounds" and "the devout bourgeoisie."[22] But among extremists in Europe, those from the devout bourgeois, such as Sayyid Sheik, are rarer than middle-class professionals, such as engineers, doctors, or university students such as Omar Khyam, who spent a year at university before bringing his middle-class neighbors from Crawley into the 2004 Crevice plot. Khaled Kelkal more closely fits the class of young urban poor, who are increasingly prominent among European jihadis.[23] In between the middle-class and the poor fall men like Mohammad Sidique Khan, the subject of chapter 10, who got a business diploma from a local university before inducing his young working-class comrades to bomb London.

But social origins do not take us far in explaining the appeal of extremism to a small sector of European Muslims from a variety of backgrounds. Nor does immigration by itself explain this phenomenon. But a complex interaction of immigration, European attitudes, and Muslim anger has brought it to pass that our rebels represent the most alarming manifestation of "the crisis of the second generation."

THE REVOLT OF THE SECOND GENERATION

In 2005, the year of terrorist bombings in London and "Islamic" riots in Paris, I studied the public records of the 373 jihadis charged or killed in Europe and North America in the years since the 1993 World Trade Center bombing. The study found fully one-quarter to be European citizens and 65 percent to have resided in Europe. Of the latter, a majority were the offspring of immigrants—postmigrants, typically of the second generation.[24] In December 2006 the Dutch terrorism expert Edwin Bakker cataloged thirty-one terrorist incidents plotted by twenty-eight European networks, and he found postmigrants to be increasing as a proportion of the plotters.[25] Muslim extremism in Europe is typically found not among migrants but among their children.[26]

Spotlighting the second generation limits our view, insofar as certain operations will fall outside that beam—particularly the March 2003 Madrid train bombings conducted by legal residents shunting between Madrid and Morocco. Yet the second-generation focus is also quite broad, because it is common, even typical, for the European Muslim to wed a spouse from home. That means his offspring will be, in good part, once again second generation. Thus the European Muslim second generation is ongoing. For that reason we frequently use the term "postmigrant" as well as "second generation."

In 1979, MIT's Michael Piore identified in America a "sizeable second generation whose upward mobility is blocked," doomed to hold the same "migrant job" as their parents.[27] At that time in Europe, Muslim temporary labor migrants were gaining the right to stay but losing their place in the production process; their residential status was legalized but their jobs downgraded. They now could bring their families, but they could not assure the futures of their children. It was not until the early 1990s that sociologists in the United States began to call attention to "the decline of the second generation."[28] The insecurity of the second generation of immigrants on both sides of the Atlantic shared a derivation: the transition from an industrial to an information economy. Children of immigrants were entering a job market transformed by what the sociologist Daniel Bell called "the rise of post-industrial society."[29]

The central change was from line work that depends on physical labor (i.e., manufacture, mining, and heavy industry) to an information and service economy that relies on mental labor in offices, specifically on the deployment of symbolic forms, the most basic of which was language.[30] Automation cut into assembly-line jobs, often consigning immigrants to low-tech workshops, non-union construction, agriculture, or unskilled work in hospitals, hotels, and restaurants.[31] This would signify that, far from upward mobility, the children of immigrants often found themselves eligible only for jobs inferior to those of their parents. Earlier immigrants moved upward with each generation, proverbially "from peddler, to plumber, to professional," but now postmigrant progress seemed to proceed regularly downward: from "plumber" (or assembly-line worker) in the first generation to "peddler," bagger, car washer, or pizza deliveryman (or drug dealer).[32]

In France in 1975 most foreign workers still worked in industry, but by 1990 three-quarters of them performed low-end service jobs.[33] That was the kind of work left for their children, some of whom were now entering the labor market. In France during the 1970s, "the ebbing of social mobility . . . led to a process of social downgrading, which . . . intensified the social violence in the deprived neighborhoods where ethnic minorities are segregated."[34] In mid-1990s France, Muslims with the same educational levels as their non-Muslim peers were twice as likely to be unemployed.[35] At that time the unemployment rate was hitting 25 percent among young men in the Lyon suburb that produced Khaled Kelkal.[36] By 2003 "numerous qualitative studies [had] shown less favorable integration trajectories for the second generation than for native French youth."[37] Those postmigrants who completed school were channeled "into jobs requiring less skill than their ability."[38]

The emergence of dual labor markets improved job security for adult white males but reduced opportunities for minorities. A 1974 British study found that it had become harder to place unqualified or untrained youths who had previously been able to enter unskilled jobs.[39] The situation was gravest for postmigrants. In 1997, when Mohammed Sidique Khan and his "Mullah Crew" on Beeston Hill were becoming radicalized, 38 percent of Pakistani and 42 percent of Bangladeshi men were unemployed in Britain, and two-thirds of those employed were manual laborers.[40] In Germany's expanding service sector, Turkish migrants were by and large denied jobs that required some kind of qualification.[41] The necessary qualifications could be obtained only via a complicated old-boy system of apprenticeships or through a stratified educational system; both of which handicapped postmigrant youngsters such as the ones we will meet in chapter 13 ("Germany's Young Turks").[42]

Deindustrialization, the insularity of native hosts and arriving guests, residential clustering, dual labor markets and so forth, closed doors against the Muslim postmigrant. Moreover, he was bred among a stern, baffling, and colliding complex of worlds: a home whose expectations had been shaped in a rural village abroad; a secular public school; a traditional mosque with a foreign imam; and Europe's alluring and forbidden mass culture, one that encouraged aspirations to a higher station even as the economy stagnated and labor markets segmented—with secure jobs going to native unionized members and their children, and dead-end jobs to migrants and their children.

For the European Muslim postmigrant, the general turbulence of the postindustrial second generation added to the dilemmas flowing from his attachments to "two linguistic and cultural worlds."[43] How should he respond to his father's demand that he learn Arabic and memorize the Qur'an and marry his rustic illiterate cousin back in Pakistan? What should he do in mixed gender schools with mandatory sexual orientation classes; how could he fend off the drug pusher or cope with such mundane concerns as credit cards based on *haram* (prohibited) interest, or transcendental issues such as grave sites not facing toward Mecca?[44] This is a clash of civilizations on alien and shaky ground. Yet parents placed authority on such delicate and intricate matters at the feet of foreign imams—poorly paid, only semiliterate, whose status even in the home country was roughly equivalent to a barber—now expected to provide guidance to children growing up in the hub of modern Europe and faced with dimming prospects.

American sociologists spotted a two-fold shift in the fate of Latino postmigrants. Along with assimilation into "white" mainstream society, two other tracks had emerged: downward assimilation into the poverty-stricken native underclass, or advancement, but within the ethnic group, involving "deliberate preservation of the immigrant community's values and tight solidarity."[45] All occasions, trends, and circumstances—economic, ethnographic, sociological, familial, and residential—seemed to inform against the Muslim postmigrant and sometimes to spur a dull appetite for revenge. Whether their predicament arose from Europe's cold welcome to newcomers or from the insularity of Muslim communities, a number of these postmigrants felt no attachment to the host country and a fraction embraced jihad and a fierce bond with the ummah.

Of course, as we have seen, it is by no means the case that all European postmigrant jihadis suffer from downward mobility. But those with a university degree and a promising future may be mobilized by solidarity with downtrodden or humiliated "brothers." "Court testimony from recent trials of alleged terrorists in the UK is full of defendants claiming they "'had to act' to protect other [suffering] Muslims" noted Burke's *Observer* survey.[46] Omar Khyam, the leader of the plot to bomb London malls and nightclubs in 2004, grew up in a comfortable middle-class suburb but acted out of fellowship with "oppressed Muslims" at home and abroad. Mohammed Sidique Khan would tell the same story on his martyrdom video released by al Qaeda. If Sidique Khan experienced "second-generation decline" in his own right, his religious zeal and his terrorist vocation were inseparable from his charitable work among his more unfortunate neighbors. For him and others like him, radical Islam provided not only strict discipline and direction but also what Ibn Khaldun, the great Arab sociologist of the fourteenth century, called *asabi-yya*—solidarity, group pride, identity—a motive we have encountered in French neighborhoods and will see again in Britain, and a concept to which we shall return specifically in the concluding chapter.

THE NARRATIVE

The Islam that these angry Muslim postmigrants turn to is decidedly not the Sufi folk Islam of their parents, the immigrant generation, whose faith is carried over from the Punjab or Eastern Anatolia, where religious identity is inseparable from the entire local social, cultural, and physical setting. In traditional society, unlike the Muslim immigrant neighborhood, there is no "search for identity." But postmigrants develop a new and elected Islamic selfhood—a set of maxims and practices and a meta-narrative, a picture of the world learned from itinerant imams and imported tracts, from jihadi videos and Salafist chat rooms, a portable Islam, codified, dogmatic, and, as Olivier Roy has stressed, "deterritorialized." This radical Islam comes from abroad but not from the immigrant sender village. It sustains a revolt not only against the new world that offers only dead-end jobs and discrimination but also against the folk Islam of the old world. For both the convert, so conspicuous among extremists as we will see in chapter 12,[47] and his psychological cousin, the postmigrant radical, Islam is abstract and learned rather than local and lived.

Muslim extremism in Europe involves more than estrangement from new homes and old ways: it is ideological; it recites a story. That master or meta- or "single" narrative is one part political doctrine and one part sacred hagiography; one part an Islamist version of today's events and another part seventh-century prophecy. One part is political, a narrative of real or perceived colonial oppression (in Afghanistan, Algeria, Bosnia, Chechnya, Iraq, Kashmir, Palestine, Somalia, Yemen, and so on). *We Muslims are down because the West is up.* But the other part of the story is cultural and about religious revival. *We Muslims have been cast down because we have gone astray.* If those sentiments are sparked by revulsion at a permissive Western culture, extremists conceive their plight and its remedy, to a marked extent, through the personages, events, and pronouncements of the Salafist "golden age." Thus, for example, we will encounter in chapters 10 and 11 a British extremist group called al Muhajiroun (the Emigrants). The group was composed primarily of second-generation British Pakistanis, second-generation "emigrants." But its name, al Muhajiroun, was contrived not to honor their parents from the old country. The emigration in question is not personal or even contemporary, but designates the *hijra,* or emigration, of the seventy men and their families who accompanied Mohammad and his Companions from Mecca to Yathrib (renamed Medina) in 622 CE.

This exotic and cryptic narrative becomes available to the disaffected Muslim postmigrant, the recovering drug abuser in his neighborhood, the outraged idealist in his classroom, the convict in his cell, the convert in his "encapsulation" (see chapter 13), or the community organizer in his ethnic enclave. He learns to scorn his parents' quiescent, accommodating Islam, reaching outside and back to an offered, self-aggrandizing narrative. In this synthesis of ancient memory and modern legend, the angry European Muslim may find a proud and remorseless identity.

THE OUTSIDE

Violent jihad in Europe derives both from Inside Europe (from inequality, racism, poverty, and generational conflict) and from the Outside (from foreign sources, messengers, and inspirations). Such Outside influences include the propaganda of Islamist states such as Iran and Saudi Arabia; individual "bearded ones" from the Muslim world; jihadis like the Groupe Islamique Armée's (GIA) Khelif B., who indoctrinated Kelkal; clerics like "the lords of Londonistan" we meet in chapter 10; and the stream of jihadis who, having been bested by the "near enemy" in places like Algeria, Egypt, Jordan, and Syria, flowed to Europe as refugees, mingled with the growing numbers of itinerant immigrants, both legal and illegal, and occasionally gained the attention of alienated postmigrants.

These Outsiders channeled and radicalized a potent narrative, one that is shared by violent and peaceful militants alike, which presented Muslims as everywhere oppressed, victimized by regimes propped up by a dissolute imperialist West. The extremists first took aim at "apostate" governments in the Middle East, but presently the entire movement rallied against the Soviet occupation of Afghanistan. Later, the global jihadis among the extremists focused on the "far enemy" in America and Europe. Extremist and mainstream militants alike imbued anti-imperialism with religious revivalism. Sometimes the convergence of politics with culture was explicit, as when Ayatollah Khomeini cobbled together a kind of synthesis between Shiite themes and the Leninist Third World rhetoric of Frantz Fanon's *The Wretched of the Earth,* whereby Fanon's oppressed were Islamicized into *mustadafeen*—"the disinherited."[1]

The movement's dual inspiration corresponded to the twin evils it railed against: colonialism and secularism. If colonialism imposed foreign political rule, direct or indirect, the West simultaneously inflicted an alien culture, one quietly subversive of both Islam and local traditions. As François Burgat argues, "The Trojan horse of secularism was seen as the most pernicious of the West's ideological weapons, which, at the climax of the colonial epic, lent legal respectability to the sacking of the normative Muslim system."[2]

If this narrative relied on a sense of Muslim prostration at Western hands, it sounded a theme often heard in the history of Islam: extend the borders of the faith and purge the heretics. That theme can be understood as the legacy of "a religion of world-conquering warriors" as Max Weber described it. Alison Pargeter, echoing observers such as Bernard Lewis, suggests, "There is a certain cultural mindset that is present in the Islamic world that has proved prone to radicalism."[3]

In any event, three militant trends found their way from the hubs of the Muslim world into the mosques, cultural centers, student societies, bookstores, gymnasia, video players, paintball groups, and jail cells of the European second generation:

- The belligerent, sectarian Wahhabi movement of the eighteenth-century Arabian Peninsula

- The schools and sects that emerged with the disintegration of Moghul rule in the nineteenth-century India subcontinent: Deobandi scripturalism, the missionary Islam of Tabligh Jama'at (TJ; the Group for Preaching and Propagation), and the Political Islam of Abdul al la Maududi's Jama'at-i Islami (JI; the Islamic Bloc)

- The Political Islam of the Muslim Brotherhood, founded after the collapse of Ottoman rule after World War I and by the breakaway followers of Sayyid Qutb

These trends bore a family resemblance; they all wished to see society reorganized in accordance with Islamic law, Sharia. But the strategies for pursuing this goal differed considerably. The Wahhabi movement spread by tribal conquest. The Deobandi generally advocated communalist quietism. Political Islam focused on religious outreach and civic organizing. All sought to return to a purer version of Islam, freed from a perceived unresponsive clerisy (*'ulema*) or from local, mystical, and folk (Sufi) "innovations," such as festivals and the worship of holy men and shrines.

This revivalism evoked a persisting motif in Islamic history: the call to get "back to the basics" of religious practice, to scrape off the rust of accumulated habits clinging to a multitude of local practices, and to restore the Islam of the earliest—the "rightly guided"—caliphs. The constant tension between the universal and the local, the foundation and the evolution, derived in turn from Islam's character as a religion that absorbed vast territories distant in geography, culture, customs, language, and ethnicity.[4]

FROM ARABIA

Lethargy and licentiousness had caused Muslims to fall from Allah's favor, leaving them backward and impotent, scolded the eighteenth-century Arabian preacher Mohammed ibn Abd-al-Wahhab. The reversion to the idolatry that Mohammad had excoriated, the worship of shrines and holy men, had polluted the true, pure Islam of the Prophet and his generation. The way to reestablish Muslim dominance over its competitors was to cauterize the impurities, violently when necessary.

Wahhab's brimstone drew inspiration from Ibn Taymiyya, the thirteenth-century godfather of modern Salafism, who argued that relaxing the practice of Islam had opened the gates to the Mongol Army, which in 1258 sacked Baghdad and toppled the Abbasid Caliphate. Though Ibn Taymiyya, that first Muslim anti-imperialist revivalist, was a respected scholar (*alim*), the Arab clerical authorities ('ulema) deemed Wahhab's teachings to be heretical. But Muhammed Ibn Saud, the ruler of a tiny Nejd city in eastern Arabia, saw in the cruel puissance of the Wahhab's frenzied paramilitary a divine instrument for territorial expansion. Saud sheltered, funded, and armed the Wahhabis to conquer neighboring tribes, entrusting religious governance of the expanding kingdom to the preacher in return for absolute political loyalty. That alliance eventually would make the Saudis kings and Wahhabism the creed of their subjects.[5] This potent partnership would be reinvigorated in the twentieth century and send versions of its doctrine deep into Europe and as far as Kelkal's Lyon and Mohammed Sidique Khan's Beeston.

FROM THE SUBCONTINENT

But in Sidique's Beeston the followers of Islamic sects that arrived from south Asia assembled in far larger numbers. In late nineteenth-century India, Muslims faced a double subjection—to British rule and as minorities in a mainly Hindu space. If politically Islam burst onto the subcontinent through military conquest, culturally it seeped in via missionary conversion as the slow work of Sufi sheiks. Over a period of centuries they grafted Islam onto indigenous Buddhist and Hindu beliefs and practices, bringing forth a religion of holy men, hierarchy, incarnations, shrines, music, dancing, festivals, and cere-monies like 'urs, where the commemoration of saints often lasted sev-eral days and involved rites such as repeating the opening of the Qur'an seven times, reading the entire scripture in a single night, and offering money to Allah.[6]

But as the Islamic imperial rule of the Mogul Dynasty waned in the eighteenth and nineteenth centuries, the political underpinnings of the Sufi synthesis of received faith and local culture eroded. Funda-mentalists began assailing that synergy as a deviation, a shameful "inno-vation" (bida). The literalist and austere reformers of the Deobandi School denounced as shirk (idolatry) the imputed intercession of the Prophet and of pirs, or saints. The Deobandi abjured music at services, tomb and mosque ornamentation, pilgrimages to shrines, and cere-monies like 'urs.

Instead the fundamentalists urged, much like the Salafist Wahhabis who preceded them in Arabia, a return to exclusive reliance on scripture and text. But unlike the Wahhabis, whose Indian sympathizers, the Ahl-i-Hadith, were their rivals, the Deobandi myth of return and their con-ception of the Law included not just the Qur'an, and the hadith, the sayings of the Prophet, but also the fiqh, Islamic jurisprudence. The fun-damentalists' central concern was to instill correct belief and practice according to scripture and classical legal texts.[7]

With their focus on law and scripture, the Deobandis offered a uni-versal Islam as opposed to folk Islam's attachment to family and parochial occasions. Thus, the Deobandis opposed elaborate wedding, birth, and funeral rites.[8] Their attitude toward marriage is worth noting here if only because generational and theological splits on the subject would figure significantly in the radicalization of young men like Sidique Khan and his comrades. In contrast to Sufi institutions, those of the Deobandi stressed doctrine over family.[9] By establishing their seminaries, schools, mosques, and networks, the Deobandis minimized family ties and instead used weddings to reinforce the doctrinal ties between 'ulema, the scholars who led the movement.[10] "Puritanically strict" enforcers of Canon Law, the Deobandis stressed legal scholarship and formal rules over local custom.[11] Barbara Metcalf calls their orientation individualist and "bureaucratic" in the Weberian sense and, in a sense, modern, though the Deobandi, like the Salafi, sanctioned the myth of a return to the "pristine" practices of the seventh century.[12]

The Sufi synthesis was not without its defenders. The Barelvi movement, inspired by Ahmad Riza Khan, from Bareilly [hence, Barelvi, pronounced BREL-WEE] in Uttar Pradesh, India, arose in the late nineteenth century to defend folk Islam. It emerged not from a fundamentalist desire to alter standards of belief and practice but rather out of resistance to the reformist Deobandi and Wahhabi sects.[13] The Barelvi, firmly linked to a time and place, a ceremony or festival, a tomb or shrine, served a constituency that tended to be rural rather than urban. Their organization was hierarchical rather than bureaucratic; its values familial rather than individualistic; its practice customary rather than scriptural; its reach local rather than universal.

The Deobandi were the product of the emergence of an urban print culture in nineteenth-century India. Without print, the influence of the Deobandi, with their stress on correct universal belief, and opposition to localized, customary religious expressions of Islam, would have been diminished.[14] On the other hand, the Barelvi remained tied to the traditional oral and rural culture. If the reader enters a private world, yet, as Walter Ong has stressed, "The spoken word forms people into close-knit groups," probably much more like the original audience for the Prophet's recitations than Deobandi or Wahhabi practice.[15]

Both the Deobandi and Barelvi schools emerged formally in the aftermath of the failed 1857 mutiny against British rule, sobered by that shattering event and persuaded that British power was invincible.[16] But the Deobandi acquiescence was grudging, and the communalist sect would later prove more hospitable to jihad, while the folksy, comparatively tolerant, and apolitical Barelvi "accepted the existence of the colonial authority apparently without question."[17] A continent away, more than a century hence, the conflict between fundamentalist and Sufi, between militant and folk Islam, would divide not only the transported mosques but also the first and second generations of British Muslims (and not least those living on Beeston Hill).

From the Indian subcontinent came two other re-Islamizing movements that also would reach Europe: Tabligh Jama'at (TJ) and Maududi's Jama'at-i Islami (JI). TJ was founded in 1927 as a missionary society shorn of what it claimed was the "pedantry" of the 'ulema. TJ sought to follow the Prophet in every word and act, in sharp contrast to the surrounding majority Hindu society and the mystical Muslim "innovations" it had spawned. The missionary movement would become the planet's most widespread Islamic trend. Like the Deobandi School from which it emerged, TJ put religious reform at the center of its ministry, but TJ is explicitly apolitical. A rigorous missionary movement, it shuns politics because "the world is like a prison cell" and life is but "a fleeting moment." The devout must turn instead to the afterlife, treating the world "like a toilet," as one TJ activist wrote, accessing material goods only when unavoidable.[18] TJ missionaries were to travel the world and spread the faith to the masses, a task neglected by high-born Muslims (the *ashraf*) during Mogul rule. But the apolitical Islamist movement would prove, far more than the Political Islamists, a recurrent antechamber if not an incubator of radical Islam, and nowhere more disastrously than in Beeston.

Rather different was the Islamism of Abdul al la Maududi, the Indian lawyer and journalist who founded the JI party in the early 1940s as the only re-Islamizing movement on the subcontinent with an explicit political orientation. Schooled at a Deobandi seminary or *madrasah*, Maududi, like Wahhab, wanted not to escape history but to alter it. Like Wahhab, Maududi interpreted Islam's decline as evidence of divine wrath, in this case the British conquest of Mogul India. But whereas Wahhab embraced violent jihad as the path to purity, Maududi conceived Islam as a political force. The central Islamic command, the *hisba*, "enjoining good and forbidding evil," needed a political party.[19] Like the TJ, JI wished to reform society to accord with Sharia, but Maududi looked to politics rather than missionary work.[20] The two had in common the myth of return to a pure Islam, but Maududi's prototype was the Prophet's rule in Medina, while TJ modeled itself on his early years in Mecca, devoted entirely to preaching.

OUT OF EGYPT

The third source of the global Islamic revival, the Muslim Brotherhood, emerged from the late nineteenth-century and early twentieth-century reformist circle around Jamal ad Din al Afghani (a Persian—despite his surname—who spent much of his life in Europe as well as Egypt).[21] Afghani, along with his principal disciple, Muhammed Abduh, was to become the forefather of Political Islam. The two argued that slavish deference to traditional authorities, such as the 'ulema, had reduced Islam to a lifeless doctrine unable to adapt to the modern world.[22] Like Wahhab, Afghani believed that Islam's malaise could be cured only by reviving the faith practiced by the Prophet and his companions—they called it Salafism.[23] But unlike Wahhab, Afghani and Abduh were modernizers, seeking to accommodate Islam to contemporary conditions by leveraging the core principles of Islam. Their dream was to liberate the Muslim mind so as to adapt the faith to everyday life.[24] For example, Abduh argued that Muslims in Muslim-minority areas (the South African Transvaal in this case) could adopt the practices of non-Muslims, such as the wearing of a European hat, in such matters as it would be expeditious (such as commerce). Abduh also noted that it was permissible for Muslims to eat meat prepared by non-Muslims (i.e., slaughtered in a non-*halal* manner) in order to ease the position of Muslim minorities. This fatwa produced controversy among those, especially the Wahhabis, who believed Abduh, an overzealous attempt to accommodate Sharia to the requirements of the particular time and place, was making lawful what had been declared unlawful.[25]

In 1928 the Egyptian Hasan al-Banna founded the Muslim Brotherhood, seeking to combine the discipline of certain Sufi orders with Afghani's progressive Salafism into a cohesive political organization.[26] The group would fuse a vanguard party organization with grassroots mobilization while riding the rising trends of revivalism and anti-imperialism. The organization grew steadily and opened branches throughout the Middle East and later in Africa, Asia, and the West, cooperating and clashing with both British occupiers and the British-backed Egyptian monarchy. Driven by antagonism to British rule and the movement for a Jewish state in Palestine, the Brotherhood, like many Arab groups that followed the dictum that "my enemy's enemy is my friend," fell under Nazi influence in the 1930s, forming the paramilitary Green Shirts in imitation of

Nazi Black Shirts, Fascist Brown Shirts, and Communist Red Shirts.[27] Most, if not all, Egyptian political parties during this time had paramilitary wings, whether Blue Shirts or Yellow Shirts or Green Shirts, but the Muslim Brotherhood was a disciplined, cadre party, with round the clock training for its carefully selected members. It participated in elections, running candidates for the feeble parliament of monarchical British-dominated Egypt.[28]

Like the revivalists who came before him, Banna preached that the Islamic heartland had been "subjugated and dominated by the unbelievers."[29] The secularist, westernizing Turkish leader Ataturk's dismantling of the Caliphate in 1924 demonstrated that the West's "sole goal was the weakening of the influence of religion."[30] After Banna's assassination in 1949, the formidable Egyptian intellectual Sayyid Qutb, a latecomer to the Brotherhood, further radicalized the founder's message, much as Lenin did that of Marx, only in this case it was the follower who was the prolix theoretician. His thirty-volume exegesis, *In the Shade of the Quran,* and other assorted works elaborated the concept of Islam as an entire system, guiding every facet of human behavior. His signal contribution to Islamic extremist theory derives from his radicalization of four Islamic notions: *jahiliyya* (ignorance), *tawhid* (monotheism), *kufr* (infidelity), and *jihad.*

Qutb (along with Maududi) converted the Prophet's term for the situation that prevailed in Arabia before his revelation, jahiliyya, into a pejorative to depict contemporary Muslim polities. In these, according to Qutb, the Qur'an's holy light was shrouded by "the dark shadow of colonization" and Muslims, God's chosen people, reduced to idle onlookers while socialism and capitalism contended for global rule.[31] Presiding over jahiliyya were Muslim rulers who violated tawhid by claiming "the right to create values, to legislate rules of collective behavior, and to choose any way of life . . . without regard to what God has prescribed."[32] If Wahhab saw tawhid usurped by devotional practices like saint worship or praying at graves and shrines, Qutb found that desecration not just in prayer but in politics, in all "man-made" regimes— whether monarchy, democracy, or secular republic.[33] Islam, according to Qutb, deems all jahili societies "unIslamic and illegal."[34] Because Islam is the antithesis of jahiliyya, Qutb wrote, "The foremost duty of Islam in this world is to depose *Jahiliyya.*"[35] Whenever such a profanation occurred, it was a Muslim's duty to wage holy war, or jihad, to restore the rule of God.

And jahiliyya was not only political in nature. Qutb directed his righteous wrath equally against the moral turpitude that he saw the West
exporting together with its blasphemous politics. An extended visit to
the United States that featured a sabbatical at a Colorado college in the
1950s offended and radicalized the Egyptian, proving to him that sexual
relations in midcentury America obeyed "the laws of the jungle." "The
word 'bashful' has become a dirty, disparaging word." Qutb was outraged
by a female student who wondered if "from one angle" sex could be
viewed "not a moral matter at all . . . but a question of biology."[36] Qutb
became an intellectual father of contemporary jihadis extremism, in part
by imbuing political violence with moral indignation and a systemic
ideology.[37] But Qutb's signal contribution was to declare existing Muslim regimes infidel, or *kufr,* because they had become apostate (*takfir*)
and thus deserved to be the target of violent jihad.

THE RISE OF THE TAKFIRIS

When Hasan al-Banna was assassinated in 1949, a respected judge, Hasan
al Hudaybi, succeeded him as the Supreme Guide of the Muslim
Brothers. Hudaybi's selection coincided with a military coup that toppled the monarchy. The "Free Officers Movement," led by Colonel
Gamal Abdel Nasser and Anwar Sadat, had worked closely with the
Muslim Brothers, who were attracted by the soldiers' nationalist stance
and Islamic rhetoric. But once in power, the soldiers' promise to Islamize
the new constitution proved illusory. During one of Nasser's notoriously
lengthy speeches, an embittered member of the Brotherhood's clandestine Special Apparatus emptied his pistol at him. Unfazed, Nasser kept
speaking as the bullets flew. Nasser emerged as a stoic hero, the Brotherhood's Special Apparatus the gang that couldn't shoot straight. Much of
the organization, most with no inkling of the hair-brained adventure,
was promptly escorted into Nasser's pitiless prisons.

There, the guards applied the torture that would stain Arab secular
regimes in Iraq and Syria along with Egypt. The jailed Brothers did not
take kindly that those with whom they had stood shoulder to shoulder
against the British and the monarch now set their dogs on them. For those
who asked whether Muslims putting devout Muslims to the rack could
really be Muslims, Qutb had a ready answer, one that would reverberate

as far as Lyon and Beeston. The torturers, and the rulers who sent them, were apostates. Both henchmen and rulers merited expulsion from the Islamic community because they were apostates, men who had confessed themselves, by a process known as takfir, to be infidels, or *kaffir*. As such, they deserved to be overthrown by holy war.

But Hudaybi, the Brotherhood's Supreme Guide, replied that only God could assess faith, not men, not even Muslim Brothers. In *Preachers, Not Judges,* Hudaybi rejected takfir by arguing that "whoever judges that someone is no longer a Muslim . . . deviates from Islam and transgresses God's will."[38] Hudaybi's tolerant response enraged the takfiris, who began renouncing and exiting the Brotherhood. Qutb, who expired on Nasser's gallows in 1966, became the prophet, and the martyr, of takfir and jihad. "Qutb has influenced all those interested in jihad throughout the Islamic world," recounted a founding member of one of the new violent jihadi groups, Gamaa Islamiyya. But the Muslim Brothers, that prominent jihadi sadly continued, "have abandoned the ideas of Sayyid Qutb."[39]

The radicals who left the Brotherhood joined other Qutbists like Ayman al-Zawahiri, whose most prominent work is a ferocious attack on the Muslim Brotherhood,[40] and Omar Abdel Rahman, the blind sheik who inspired the first World Trade Center bombing, in order to form the first modern jihadi groups in the 1970s. Muhammed Abdel-salam Faraj, the leader of Al Jihad, the group to which Zawahiri belonged, proclaimed that "the neglected duty" of devout Muslims was to wage jihad against "apostate" Muslim rulers. Al Jihad assassinated Egyptian president Anwar al Sadat in 1981.[41]

The jihadis' pursuits, in line with Qutb and the whole tradition we are reviewing, were not only political but cultural. Al-Zawahiri demanded to know "who is banning the *hijab* [headscarf] at schools and the *niqab* [face cover] at universities in order to fight the values of Islam and to force our daughters to emulate the West and its immorality?"[42] The charter of Rahman's Gamaa Islamiyya stated that an Islamic state or Caliphate was the answer not only "to the widespread injustice and oppression" of Muslims but also "to the moral bankruptcy into which the Muslims have fallen."[43] While jihadis terrorized governments and tourists in the Arab world, the Brotherhood gained influence through *da'wa,* or preaching. But repressive secular governments in Egypt and Syria suppressed peaceful and violent Islamists alike. Militants fled, sometimes to Europe, but often, in the case of the Muslim Brothers, to Saudi Arabia.

FITNA

But the marriage between the Wahhabis and the Brotherhood soon hit the rocks. The social compact struck by Wahhab and al Saud had kept the 'ulema out of the politics of the Kingdom. But the inventors of Political Islam were not about to halt the political activities that almost defined them merely because of a change of address. Toward the end of the 1970s, seeds of political activism that the Brotherhood had sown began to sprout among the Saudi 'ulema in the form of the *Sahwa* (Awakening) trend.

Even as Islamists were stirring in Saudi Arabia, two events in 1979 propelled Islamism onto the glossy covers of Western news magazines. In January, Ayatollah Ruhollah Khomeini seized power in Iran and proceeded to install a Shiite theocracy and to challenge the Islamist credentials of the Saudis. Then in the following December the Soviet Union invaded Afghanistan. For the beleaguered Saudis, the communist invasion came as an answered prayer. Like other Arab regimes harassed by the Islamist militants, takfiri or not, the Saudis induced critics to go abroad and fight. The leader of the Arab contingent in Afghanistan, and Osama bin Laden's mentor, Abdullah Azzam, featured the blessing of a senior Saudi cleric, Abdel Aziz Bin Baz, in the forward to his rallying cry, *Defense of Muslim Lands.*

The Saudis' regime now found itself engaged on three fronts—against Shiite Iran, against Soviet Afghanistan, and against Saudi dissidents of the Sahwa at home. These campaigns would feature an oxymoron—noisy apolitical quietists. And their noise would reverberate right into Europe.

The Wahhabis centered operations of their World Muslim League in Paris, and Saudi-funded mosques and institutions began appearing across Europe.[44] At Saudi-financed think tanks, publishing houses, seminars, colloquia, and conferences, the "MBs and Wahhabis, mullahs and university professors [would] rub elbows" throughout Europe.[45] Scholarships to the University of Medina became a centerpiece of the Kingdom's efforts to attract European Muslims.[46]

Meanwhile in Peshawar, the Pakistani portal onto the Afghan jihad, the interaction among the various strains of the Islamist revival was less scholarly. Crackdowns forced many Arab Islamists to flee to that haven where they joined a throng of activists, itinerant preachers, refugees, aid workers, and adventurers as well as idealists from other Muslim lands.

Among these was the young Saudi heir, Osama bin Laden, conspicuous and revered for his renunciation of his wealthy upbringing in favor of an austere "Salafi" lifestyle. The struggle between different jihadi contingents to influence bin Laden and his checkbook became a prime example of what Islamists call *fitna,* the discord or civil war that has often characterized the movement since the seventh century.

The fractures of this fitna widened as the Soviets withdrew and questions arose about where to take jihad next and what to do about the Persian Gulf War. When the Kingdom allowed American troops on holy Saudi soil to deter Saddam Hussein's army poised in neighboring Kuwait, prominent *sahwat* rebelled. But as in 1979, the Saudi government procured backing from senior religious leaders.[47] The critics included a not-yet-terrorist bin Laden, who later recalled the Kingdom's decision to welcome U.S. troops as the "biggest shock of [his] entire life."[48]

The Wahhabi state had opposed the sahwat with a pietist Salafism. The pietists rejected political action in favor of an almost obsessive spotlight on individual belief and practice, centered on Qur'anic education, dietary laws, and the *niqab* (face covering), practices followed by Saudi-inspired pietists even in the heart of the West.[49] But if in Saudi Arabia pietist propaganda represented the conservative establishment, in second-generation European Muslim enclaves, as in Mohammed Sidique Khan's Beeston Hill or among German Salafist converts, it would facilitate violent extremism.

On the morrow of the Soviet withdrawal, many jihadis found themselves rebels without a war. Returning home would probably mean jail and torture. To remain in Afghanistan was to choose sides in a fitna, in a civil war pitting not just Muslims against Muslims but *mujahideen* against *mujahideen.* Moreover, the Pakistani government was feeling pressure from Arab governments, especially Egypt, to crack down on jihadis who were using Afghanistan as a base for war back home.

"ISLAM'S BLOODY BORDERS"

Conflicts in Algeria, Bosnia, Chechnya, and Kashmir offered exits from this impasse. The breakup of the Soviet Empire, and the weakening of regimes it had backed, breathed new life into old ethnic and religious clashes along what Samuel Huntington dubbed "Islam's bloody borders."[50]

Whether Muslims were the aggressors or the aggrieved in a given instance is always open to question. But it is indisputable that Muslim Holy Warriors found their way to the "bloody borders" of Europe, while others emigrated to the heart of Europe to take advantage of liberal asylum laws and lax immigration enforcement. If some abandoned violence while remaining Islamists or Salafists, others did not. Now, even in Europe, there would be a fitna (as chapter 10 will illustrate) between those who thought Soviet withdrawal ended the Afghan jihad and others who went on fighting, between Wahhabi pietists and "politicos," and between Political Islamists and jihadis.

The Saudi pietists pursued the remaining sahwat as far as the United Kingdom, where the latter took up residence in exile. The Saudis courted adherents with slickly produced, multilingual books and offers of generous scholarships. If the main recipients of Saudi funding started out as apolitical pietists, some of the beneficiaries became extremists, such as Abdullah el Faisal, one of our "lords of Londonistan" and the mentor of Richard Reid, the shoe bomber, and of Sidique Khan's comrade-in-arms, Germaine Lindsay.[51] Though generally apolitical, the austerity, dogmatism, and separatism of quietist Wahhabism could pave the way to extremism, as it did in el Faisal's case. In this respect, Wahhabi pietism played a role as a way station on the road to radicalization much like TJ has.

In 1993, a Saudi-backed London publishing house saw fit to translate and publish a hitherto obscure master's thesis from the University of Mecca titled *Al-Wala' wa'l-Bara'* (*Loyalty and Repudiation*).[52] *Al-Wala' wa'l-Bara'* fused religious revivalism with anti-imperialism: "The humiliation that the Muslims are today experiencing throughout the world is only a natural consequence of their having abandoned the Shari'ah," having been "[s]educed by the basest of nations." The humiliation of Muslims is the direct outcome of "the rise of European colonialism and the resulting forgetfulness of the Muslims."[53]

In the Saudi homeland the treatise's call to believers to separate themselves from unbelievers raised hardly a ripple in an ocean of Muslim believers. But in multicultural England it seemed to command by fiat the self-segregation of "true Muslims." Whereas the Saudi authorities encouraged doctrinal, textual pietism to counteract Iranian militancy abroad and to ward off political Salafism at home, in Europe, and especially in Britain, its effect would be precisely the opposite. In the hands of radical preachers like Abdullah el Faisal, who studied in Riyadh and preached on Beeston Hill, the pietist concept of *al-wala' wa'l-bara'* was a powerful instrument of radicalization. To differentiate friends from enemies was the primary postmigrant "takeaway" from *Al-Wala' wa'l-Bara.'* In the first instance, all "infidels" or "disbelievers" are enemies. "Do not take the Jews and the Christians for friends. They are friends of one another. And whoever of you takes them for friends is (one) of them." Furthermore it is "forbidden [*haram*] for a Muslim to go to live amongst [the infidels] and acknowledge their authority over him."[54] These messages were transformed in the translation. In Saudi Arabia they worked to shore up national unity and confidence. But in Europe they worked the opposite effect, fomenting or instilling in a minority group an adversarial identity, enmity toward the majority and toward other minorities—the Outside radicalizing Insiders.

THE UNWANTED

T he fathers and grandfathers of today's Muslim postmigrants
came to Europe as temporary workers during the postwar
European economic boom, and eventually settled, bringing
their wives and their religion with them. European and Muslim civilizations had lived side by side for fourteen centuries without mass migration between them. There were wars of conquest, yes, but never
migration, certainly not from the Muslim world to the European, still
less in large numbers. What made Muslims move so massively, what persuaded them then to stay rather than return home, and what persuaded
Europeans to let them stay?

Muslims began to come in numbers to Europe in response to the
same conditions that in the second half of the twentieth century often
gave rise to mass migration from poor to rich countries, from premod-
ern countries of the South and East to advanced capitalist countries of
the North and West. In Western Europe labor migrants were wanted as
a rapid remedy for World War II's decimation of its labor force. As Gary
Freeman points out, those densely populated states were not looking for
immigrants or settlers. "Even when states or employers actively recruited
migrants, it was never for immigration in itself but rather as a necessary
measure to meet labor needs that was pursued at times recklessly and at
times with great trepidation."[1]

Fearful of labor shortages and resulting inflation, not wishing factories
to move to cheaper climes in search of labor (as was often happening in
the United States), and not choosing to meet rising labor costs with
technological innovation (as in Japan), the countries of Northwest

Europe initially recruited their migrant workers from the underdeveloped south of Europe: Italy, Greece, Portugal, and Spain. But soon the labor-hungry advanced countries stalked farther south in their search for cheap labor—to North Africa, Turkey, and the Asian subcontinent, regions with historical ties to Western Europe, but whose populations were commonly Muslim.[2]

Muslims came back to Europe, not as reconquering Moors in Andaluz or Sicily or Turks again at the Gate of Vienna but as lowly labor migrants supplying "an industrial reserve army," to use Karl Marx's phrase.[3] That is to say, Muslim immigrants filled positions that would otherwise have remained vacant or else commanded higher salaries. Thanks to their willingness to work long hours in miserable conditions, to move in and out of available jobs, Muslim laborers afforded employers "a flexibility they would not have otherwise enjoyed," a flexibility benefiting not only the employer who engaged him or her but also employers as a group, insofar as it created a mobile, floating, available sector of surplus workers.[4]

THE MYTH OF RETURN

The Muslim labor migrants had as little intention as their hosts of committing immigration, so to speak. On the contrary, the migrant's "temporary nature [was] tacitly assumed, and apparently guaranteed by the mutual agreement of receiving and sending countries."[5] No one, not the European host governments or the employers or even the workers themselves, entertained the thought of establishing Muslim settlements in Christian Europe (or in a rapidly secularizing post-Christian Europe). Workers were to stay for a time and then be rotated out and replaced by new groups of workers. The migrant workers would be "guests" expected to work a few years and then return home. The workers fully shared that expectation. They intended to stay only as long as necessary to save enough money to buy livestock or open a store, back home, the kind of aspiration that typically animates labor migrants.

These new workers filled what came to be called a "secondary labor market" that subsisted alongside the primary sector in industrial countries and was composed of unskilled workers in fields such as agriculture, low-tech manufacturing, hospitality, health care, and construction.[6]

It became customary to argue that immigrant workers performed a structural role in the European and indeed in the Western industrial economy and that mass migration was inevitable.[7] Hence immigration enabled native workers to escape the social status to which fate had seemed to assign them.[8] In this way the "class struggle" between capital and labor was transformed into an ethnic division between the native workers and immigrants, who were usually Muslims.

Whatever his contractual and formal status, the Muslim labor migrant to Europe almost invariably expected to return home, an expectation that he treasured doggedly. He toiled long hours on the night shift in the worst factory jobs. He hoarded his earnings and sent them back to purchase land or build a flashy new home. He calculated it would take three or five years, the illusion of other "temporary workers" in other times and places. He intended to be a bird of passage.

FAMILY MIGRATION CHANNELS

If there is a single "law" in migration," Myron Weiner wrote, "it is that a migration flow, once begun, induces its own flow. Migrants enable their friends and relatives back home to migrate by providing them with information about how to migrate, resources to facilitate movement, and assistance in finding jobs and housing."[9]

As a result, migration research almost always exhibits a flow from a *particular* point of origin to a *particular* destination as if these two points were somehow metaphysically linked. Two towns just four miles apart in northern Italy sent the bulk of their respective emigrants to opposite sides of the Australian continent. In Buffalo, Chicago, Cleveland, Kansas City, Rochester, and San Francisco (as well as Buenos Aires and Toronto), Italians from specific towns and villages "concentrated in particular neighborhoods or even streets."[10] Polish Jews settled in different Lower East Side New York streets from Russian, Galician and Hungarian, and Romanian Jews, all miles away from the "Uptown [German] Jews."[11] Though mass migration can seem a great sea of people, it invariably flows in channels. In the 1990s, while studying Mexican immigrants in the United States, I found that, in Los Angeles, Mexican immigrants from Cueramaro, Guanajuato, live in Hawaiian Gardens, while those from Leon, Guanajuato, reside in Compton.[12]

In that same decade New York City received some half a million Mexican immigrants, over 50 percent of whom hailed from the state of Puebla.[13] What were families from Puebla doing so far away? How had Poblanos become the fastest growing immigrant cohort in Manhattan and Brooklyn? And why were Mexicans settling in Los Angeles, or Houston, coming not from nearby northern but from central, western, and even southern Mexico? Why does migration not follow a geographic imperative or a demographic logic? The answer to that question also explains why migrants are not, as typically assumed and advertised, the poorest or the most enterprising individuals from the sender country.

Of course, Turks contemplate coming to Germany, Pakistanis to Britain, and Mexicans to the United States because of the wage differential. Wages for laboring jobs in Britain in the early 1960s were more than thirty times those offered for similar jobs in Pakistan. In Mirpur, Pakistan, which is a feeder region not only for Sidique Khan's Beeston but for Birmingham, the average weekly wage was equivalent to approximately 37 pence; in Birmingham, a Pakistani immigrant's average weekly wage was £13.13.[14] In the late twentieth century, wages were thirteen or fourteen times higher in the United States than in Mexico.

But then why didn't every deprived Pakistani get up and move to Britain, every needy Mexican to the United States? How does the selection process work? Two scholars of Mexican migration to the United States, Douglas Massey and Kristin Espinosa, showed that it was the family tie that determined *which* Mexicans came to the United States.[15] These scholars argued that social capital, i.e. family contacts, drove migration rather than the wage differential alone. The differential between the wages of the sender country and the host country may explain *why* there is migration between two areas, but it is the family connection that determines *who* comes from that area.

As migration moves along channels, those conduits deepen to the point that "sender villages" adopt "daughter communities." Daughter communities such as Compton or Beeston send back regular streams of remittances to sender villages in Guanajuato or Mirpur, part of which are reinvested in the travel or dowries of new immigrants. The daughter communities frequently become enclaves where the sender community's language and customs prevail. Thus in the 1950s, more than 60 percent of Algerian immigrants to France were from the Kabylia region of northern

Algeria.[16] The same chain migration channels the Mirpuris of Azad Kashmir to places like Bradford or Birmingham's Ward End or Beeston.

The Kabyles migrated first as a result of a French land grab that displaced peasants in their fertile region.[17] Mirpur first became a migrant sender region, as we will see in the following chapter ("Ghost Towns"), thanks to its rivers and mariners and also to a flood that submerged many of its villages. But the institutionalization and proliferation of immigration channels explain why nearly 93 percent of Algerians who migrate go to France, why most Turkish migrants travel to Germany, and why most Pakistani migrants find themselves in England.

ON THEIR OWN

Far from wives and families, adrift in a foreign country with powerful temptations, many Pakistani migrant males found the enticements of Western culture irresistible. Alison Shaw recounts how, unattached in the West, they sowed their wild oats. To be sure, they worked hard and saved most of what they earned to remit home. To reduce rent, those working on night shifts would share beds with those on day shifts (much as Latino workers in the United States do today). But they apparently fooled around too.[18]

Photos from a studio in the Bradford inner-city neighborhood of Manningham show these Pakistani migrants of the sixties sporting dark glasses to emulate South Asian film stars. To demonstrate their alleged success to the simple folk back home, the migrants brought to the shoot watches, radios, briefcases, and umbrellas. They dress in smart Western suits with rows of pens obtruding ostentatiously from lapels and five-pound notes bulging out of pockets. These self-advertisements indulged in "a special kind of misrepresentation."[19] The pens and briefcases were meant to suggest high-flying office work, but these men were buried in the graveyard shift at mills. And the wives back home, on an extended vacation, could hardly have been comforted to see shots of couples, in which the women were invariably white.

Among the male migrant workers, sleeping in boarding houses, interest in religious matters was nominal.[20] Stephen Barton, in one of the first scholarly studies of a British Muslim community, recounted that early Bangladeshi male migrants in Bradford almost completely suspended their religious activity.[21] To be sure, the men, even without their wives, understood themselves as part and parcel of family and village—that was why they were sent in the first place and why they faithfully mailed photos attesting to their affluence, not to mention regular remittances, back home. It was family honor (*izzat*) that they served by saving every last penny. V. S. Khan observed in 1977 that for these men life in Britain was "an extension of life back home and both must be seen as one system of socio-economic relations."[22] Physically they were in Britain but in almost every other way they were still in Pakistan.

CLIENT POLITICS

The worker's expectation of returning to his home village or region was matched by the desire of host governments, to have him return—though speaking of government expectations accords policy more credit than it deserves.[23] Initially there was little policy worthy of the name, only inertia or what Mark Miller calls "policy adhocracy." Such improvisation was riddled with legal loopholes and scofflaws.[24] Jonas Widgren's observation regarding Sweden applies to most northern Western European countries: "immigration simply took place."[25]

The typical Northwest European immigration regime involved a pure form of what James Q. Wilson classified as "client politics," with direct benefits and indirect costs.[26] The client, the employer, directly benefited from low-wage immigrant labor while his costs (in additional infrastructure: schools, hospitals, transport, etc.) were borne by all taxpayers and residents.[27] Employers, or their associations, basically colluded with government officials in a process, which, as Freeman put it, took place "largely out of public view and with little outside interference."[28] Client immigration politics almost invariably means expansive immigration policies.

Immigration was rarely the subject of parliamentary debate or legislation.[29] In France, for example, politicians rarely tackled the looming racial issue raised by North African migration, and public discussion was just as rare.[30] What dialogue there was in the National Assembly was "highly structured and permitted little give-and-take," even as the main elements of migration policy were arranged in private discussions among the relevant ministers and negotiations with sender countries.[31]

One reason for the absence of public discord about immigration was that, in accordance with the myth of return, it was seen as temporary in a time of perceived "labor shortage."[32] As Yasemin Soysal points out, immigration was one of "the least politicized policy areas" in Europe until the 1980s.[33] European publics were not consulted on the series of ad hoc decisions (as to recruitment programs, residency and work permits, temporary visas, and the like) that began to introduce alien populations with fairly exotic ways into their neighborhoods.

BEATING THE BAN

But in Britain the process was not so straightforward. From 1948 to 1962, Britain ran one of the most generous migration regimes on earth, granting citizenship to hundreds of millions of its colonial subjects across the globe.[34] However, free entry from the Commonwealth was never intended to bring about the metamorphosis of Britain into a multicultural society. On the contrary its purpose was to ensure entry for emigrants from the white "Old Dominions" of Australia, Canada, and New Zealand.[35] The free entry principle originated before mass air travel, when Commonwealth subjects were still unable to migrate to the United Kingdom on a large scale. But with the surge in arrivals of the late fifties, particularly from India and Pakistan, the government devised the Commonwealth Immigrants Act, slated to go into effect in 1962.[36] In 1961 the imminent passage of the act produced a great rush to "beat the ban," with Pakistanis, Mirpuris in particular, in the lead.

The fatal flaw of the 1962 "ban" was that, though it succeeded in stemming primary immigration, it failed to anticipate the capacity for secondary immigration inherent in chain migration and family migration channels. The 1962 act staunched primary immigration by means of mandatory work vouchers, designed to adjust immigration to specific labor needs. But it curtailed primary migration only to institutionalize secondary immigration, or migration via a resident immigrant. South Asians, and Mirpuris in particular, turned the system on its head. They obtained from their supervisors multiple vouchers that enabled them to obtain work visas for kin.[37]

Immigration authorities got wind of this abuse and terminated the voucher system in 1965, limiting immigration to relatives. But Mirpuris, and other Pakistanis, stayed one step ahead of immigration authorities by taking advantage of well-intentioned family reunification policies to gain entry for adolescent children. They exploited their prior seeding of the immigration cohort with relatives and prolonged mass immigration by importing dependents or marrying cousins.[38]

So, while aiming to reduce primary immigration, the 1962 act entirely ignored the potential for massive secondary immigration.[39] As a result there was a massive movement of spouses and dependents, many of them from Mirpur, and the number of arrivals remained as high as in 1960, a number that was only exceeded by the great 1961 rush to beat the 1962 ban.[40] In 1951 Britain hosted roughly 30,000 Indians, 5,000 Pakistanis, 15,000 West Indians, and about 25,000 other nonwhite immigrants in England and Wales. In 1961 the total nonwhite numbers had risen to 336,000. In the sixties the number of nonwhite persons per 1,000 of the total population rose from 1.7 to 7.3.[41]

Muslim migrant workers had entered as subjects of the Crown. The Muslims who moved from the subcontinent to Britain willy-nilly acquired the political rights of citizens. However, "free born Englishmen" were not eager for throngs of dusky "imperial subjects" crowding their workplaces, neighborhoods, and schools.

As the sun set on the British Empire, the old basis of citizenship, the imperial subject, was flooding Britain with unwanted dark-skinned migrants, a policy that British politicians feared would cause racial conflict. It was often acknowledged, if elliptically stated, that "firm immigration controls" were needed for improving "community relations"—in other words, the reason for restricting immigration was public hostility to the immigration of people of color.[42] Henceforth, British immigration policy sought to remove citizenship rights too liberally granted during the colonial period.[43] The logic of that policy was to pare the historical British homeland nation from its vast empire and subject the outlier to immigration restriction.[44] But what could be the formula for excluding nonwhite immigrants while not using overtly racial criteria and yet permit white Commonwealth citizens to enter? The solution in a series of Commonwealth Immigration Acts from 1968 onward was the "patrial." Only individuals with a parent or grandparent born in the United Kingdom ("patrials") could enter freely. Thus by means of *jus sanguinis* (blood ties), Britain sought to get rid of entitlements to citizenship extended to all colonial subjects. But of course the partial ruse, officially deemed "family policy," was, at bottom, racially motivated.[45]

TWENTIETH-CENTURY LOSERS

On April 4, 1968, Martin Luther King Jr. was shot dead in Memphis, Tennessee, occasioning riots, burning, and looting in nearly a hundred American cities. Two weeks later in the Midlands Hotel in Birmingham, Enoch Powell, the rising star in Tory ranks, delivered a jarring address on immigration to a Conservative Party meeting. In the House of Commons, Powell represented Wolverhampton, a city northwest of Birmingham that, according to Powell, was being flooded with Asian immigrants. His constituents were telling the shadow defense minister that their "wives [were] unable to obtain hospital beds in childbirth, *their* children unable to obtain school places, their homes and neighborhoods changed beyond recognition, their plans and prospects for the future defeated." These trueborn Englishmen, Powell claimed, were hearing "more and more voices which told them that they were now the unwanted." They felt themselves to have become "a persecuted minority" even as the press was demanding an "anti-discrimination" act to protect Asian and other dark-skinned minorities.[46] Powell assailed the concept of "integration," a term then rapidly and fashionably supplanting "assimilation" on both sides of the Atlantic:

> There are among the Commonwealth immigrants who have come to live here in the last fifteen years or so, many thousands whose wish and purpose is to be integrated and whose every thought and endeavor is bent in that direction. But to imagine that such a thing enters the heads of a great and growing majority of immigrants and their descendants is a ludicrous misconception, and a dangerous one.[47]

The Tory front bencher and classics scholar in what came to be known as the "Rivers of Blood" speech for its Virgilian augury of disaster[48] flowing from immigration, branded the current policy of permitting the annual inflow of some 50,000 dependents "madness." He calculated that by 1985 the native-born among the immigrants would constitute the majority of immigrants and that by the year 2000 there would be "five to seven million commonwealth immigrants," or approximately one-tenth of the total population. Powell called for a "virtual halt" in immigration and for generous assistance to encourage "re-immigration."[49]

Even more astounding than the speech, defying the political and press taboo on race and immigration, was the public reaction to it. Dock workers and meat porters marched to the House of Commons in solidarity, spontaneous acts of support were recorded in working-class neighborhoods, over 100,000 cards and letters were mailed to Powell, and, most revealing of all, a poll taken after Powell's speech showed that 24 percent named Powell as the favored successor to party leader Edward Heath, an astounding swing in opinion.[50]

Heath forthwith sacked Powell from the Tory shadow cabinet.[51] When Powell refused to drop the subject, Heath took the extraordinary step of announcing that under no circumstances would Powell be a minister in a new Conservative government.[52] Powell's political career was over, and immigration was banished from political discourse for almost the next four decades.

The Times of London titled its editorial "An Evil Speech," finding it "disgraceful," "shameful," "calculated to inflame hatred between the races," and "impractical." Invoking memories of the British prewar fascist Oswald Mosley, the establishment newspaper said the Birmingham event was "the first time that a serious British politician has appealed to racial hatred, in this direct way, in our postwar history." And its worst sin was to have been uttered "within a couple of weeks" of the King assassination, which provoked "burning in many American cities."[53]

In a still smoldering America, the British correspondent for *The New Republic* presented Powell's dire prophecy as a figment of a Coriolanian imagination. Aiming at Waughian wit at a time when the Left was exchanging its class perspective for identity politics, the journalist derided the striking workers and heaped scorn on Powell's followers:"the baying dockers, . . . the buffeted and the put-upon, the stagnant of the middle class and the down trodden of the working class, the twentieth century losers whose plight is directly traceable to that wayward capitalism Powell upholds." *The New Republic's* correspondent questioned Powell's figures and fears. He found Powell's estimate of an annual inflow of some 50,000 dependents to be artificially swollen by a backlog "and not likely to continue above 20,000."

But Powell's figures, for all his wild exaggerations, would prove far closer to the mark. In 2000, for example, the total number of immigrants was roughly 122,000. Of these, some 91,000 were from Africa or Asia.[54] On average, during these years, some 70 percent of resident permits were for immigrants from the Indian subcontinent. In 2009 nearly a quarter of British babies were born to mothers from abroad; in London, more than half of all children were born to foreign-born mothers: the second generation.[55]

THE SECOND GENERATION

What of these children of unwanted foreigners; what of Muslim postmigrants? They were not consulted at all. Much like their neighbors, they were party to no agreement or discussion. They were born to parents who wished to be elsewhere and grew up among neighbors and schoolmates who often wanted no part of them. Their neighbors scorned them, and their parents often raised them in enclaves to be virtual foreigners.

So did they wish to return to the fatherland? Listen to Mohammed, seventeen, and Ahmed, nineteen, hanging out by an East London bus stop, young men who long ago stopped attending Friday prayers with their fathers ("too much hassle, too many old men"). When such young men visit the Mirpuri villages from which their fathers came four decades earlier, they find them "too hot and the food was rubbish and everything was dirty." Ahmed says he had diarrhea all the time he was there.[56] Listen to another East Londoner—this one a Bangladeshi postmigrant—as he answers a query from a Bangladeshi doctoral candidate: "This is a physical space where you call home. But where is your mental and psychological home?"

> Ashraf looked at me with a smile and replied: "I know what you want me to say . . . you want me to say Bangladesh, don't you? But the truth is Bangladesh is not my home. It is just a place where my parents came from. I have been back to Bangladesh twice. . . . On both occasions, I felt weird. I met cousins I never knew I had. I saw it as a holiday and you can never call a holiday place a home. I was born here and this is my home although as a person of colour, I don't think I am welcome here."[57]

Young Muslim men in the slums of Paris or of Amsterdam (or in Mollenbeck in Brussels, in Santa Coloma in Barcelona, in Walthamstow, East London) are outsiders in the land of their birth and strangers in the land of their forebears. In Anatolia or Kabilya or the Rif, they can't hold down the food; in Brussels, Paris, and Rotterdam, these young European Muslims can't get past the bouncer at the nightclub entrance.

ANGLES OF
AGGREGATION

"But there is no such thing as a European Muslim," remonstrated a leading radical Islamist to me in London one evening over dinner. "There are Danish Muslims, German Muslims, Italian Muslims or Spanish Muslims. There are British Muslims: loud and assertive; French Muslims quiet and cowed." But then why, I asked, did his colleague, Tariq Ramadan, the most conspicuous European Islamist, a moderate from the Muslim Brotherhood's most illustrious family, call his best-known book *To Be a European Muslim?*[1]

Muslims in Europe share a complex fate: aliens born domestically, minorities in secular states, Muslims in countries previously largely unfamiliar with either immigrants or Muslims. European Muslims reacted peaceably to the same Danish cartoons that were the object of riots and the torching of consulates in the Middle East.[2] Because they were Europeans, aggrieved Bosnia seized them just as much as occupied Afghanistan had. Yet it is hardly idle to point to variations among European Muslims. The slaughter of Bosnian Muslims fanned more flames in Britain than anywhere in Europe. During the Danish cartoon episode of 2005–2006, British Muslims were louder than Muslims in France and Germany, as they had been far more raucous in the 1989 Rushdie Affair.

Some 20 million Muslims live in the European Union, numbering nearly 5 percent of its population. In France the Muslim population (mainly Algerian and Moroccan) reaches 7 percent.[3] Germany's Muslims (mainly Turkish) number about 4.3 million, or about 5.4 percent of the population. In the United Kingdom, Muslims (mainly South Asian) number about 2.4 million, or nearly 4 percent of the population.

Muslims form the majority of immigrants in most Western European countries, including Belgium, France, Italy, the Netherlands, and Germany. In the United Kingdom, Muslims are the largest single immigrant cohort. Moreover, while America's Muslims are spread out geographically and are fragmented ethnically, European Muslims tend to congregate and remain in enclaves. American Muslims are likely to be integrated and well-educated professionals or business people, more affluent than average Americans (not to mention their European cousins).[4] Most European Muslims are descendants of illiterate labor migrants from rural regions, while American Muslims began to arrive in the country often as college students, and their offspring earn considerably more than the average native-born American and are certainly far more affluent than their coreligionists in Europe.[5]

Unlike Europe, America is a "country of immigration," where immigration is central to the "cultural idiom."[6] Americans proudly invoke our immigrant forebears and laud immigrant enterprise, perseverance, and achievement. In Europe immigration is viewed grudgingly, even resentfully. European immigration is more recent, enters smaller, more crowded countries, and rubs against the ethnicity that tends to characterize its nation-states. As a consequence, immigration became an issue on the other side of the Atlantic well before the anxiety over illegal aliens gained traction in American politics.

Looking at Britain, France, and Germany, the most important European countries—which also happen to be those with the largest Muslim populations—we see that each conceived the integration of Muslims in ways that were broadly reflective of its own particular historical experiences. All three countries admitted large numbers of Muslim laborers beginning in the late 1950s and all eventually allowed them to bring in dependents. However, in each case, prior experience framed the approach to the second generation; each country, facing a massive entry from another culture, fell back on its own past.

Over the centuries France had turned "peasants into Frenchmen," in Eugene Weber's phrase, translating, not without some fierce resistance, the inhabitants of the provinces into members of an indivisible Republic.[7] Centuries of state-building and of the gradual diffusion of a national identity brought into being a French nation-state inside the physical and institutional anatomy of the territorial state. In the words of one French statesman, it has been "a deliberate political construction for whose creation the central power has never ceased to fight."[8] The penetration into the periphery by the institutions, instruments, and networks of the central state (the school, the army, road, rail, and public administration) engineered what Rogers Brubaker calls "the concentric, assimilative expansion of nationhood in France."[9]

By contrast, the German nation was conceived not as the bearer of universal values to which anyone could adhere but as an organic, cultural, linguistic, and racial community. If the French conception of nationhood is "state-centered and assimilationist," Germany's is "*Volk*-centered and differentialist."[10] In France and England, nation-building and state formation went hand in hand from the Middle Ages, but the German people, the *Volk,* had to wait till the late nineteenth-century ascendency of Prussia and its chancellor, Count Otto von Bismarck, before forging a unitary state. From the thirteenth century Germany diverged from England and France, where the trend was increasing centralization. Whereas France became a united Catholic monarchy, and England a united Protestant monarchy, a warring Germany attained only an unsteady religious settlement. Germany became a loose confederacy united solely by language, ancestry, and culture: a nation only in ethnicity. France was the paramount "civic nation"—"a community of citizens" attached to a shared set of political practices and values. Germany was the preeminent "ethnic nation," whose citizenship was defined in terms of ascriptive endowments. In France the state was the engine and the center of national growth; in Germany the source of unity was a shared ethnicity. Britain told a third story: a civic nation mounted on a congeries of ethnic nations.

Nationality in Britain was not, as in France, homogeneous and chemical, the product of the incorporation of peoples and regions, but heterogeneous and arithmetic—the sum of abidingly distinct nationalities. By the end of the seventeenth century England dominated the British Isles, but a sense of separate identity remained important in Ireland and Scotland and even in Wales.[11] These nationalities were separated by history and in some cases by language, with divergent religious organizations, systems of weights and measure, and legal and educational structures, not to mention varying folklore, literature, music, sports, costumes, architecture, agrarian practices, and cuisines.[12] But their cultural distinctiveness did not spawn political separation.[13] In France, by contrast, Brittany, Burgundy, Corsica, Gascony, Normandy, and Picardy among others enjoy slight relative autonomy today. They now retain little sense of cultural identity and their original languages are relics. As opposed to France's submergence of regional identity, Wales, Scotland, and Ireland preserved their cultural and administrative independence under the banner not of England but of the Union Jack. The ruling authorities took care to build up loyalty not to the English people but to British institutions—Church, Crown, and Parliament.[14]

When it came to administering a vast empire, Britain turned to the same model of qualified autonomy. In India colonial authorities pursued policies of cultural tolerance, not assimilation; they preferred oblique rule, not administrative centralism as in the Spanish and French empires.[15] The British Raj preserved the Indian role in governance via a system of "indirect administration" that kept the precolonial power structure intact while rendering it subservient to the Crown. Accordingly, the Raj relied on a few thousand English and Scottish civil servants to govern a quarter of a billion subjects and fanned sectarian discord among Islamic sects so as to reduce the need for Redcoats. As Gilles Kepel points out, this "remarkable economy of means" in faraway India stood in sharp contrast to the dense French colonial presence in nearby and sparsely populated North Africa.[16] "The French policed, at a high cost, every village of Algeria and Senegal, just as the gendarmes did in Provence and Corsica."[17] If the British constructed an empire on loose partnerships with partially self-governing colonies, the French wished to integrate the colonial population so as to form "an indissoluble unity," embracing the citizens of the metropolis and the colonial subjects alike. As opposed to Britain's indirect rule, preserving indigenous cultures and social structures, France's direct rule aspired to forge an equal status for colonial and metropolitan inhabitants alike within *la plus grande France*.[18]

These diverging mechanisms—absorption versus autonomy, direct as opposed to indirect rule—were called on when former colonials became immigrants. In Britain, Muslim immigrants entered a political system with nationalities already present side by side and were inserted, not assimilated, and granted a species of autonomy similar to its colonies, almost as parallel nationalities, allowed to preserve their cultural identity, "leading to a profound adaptation of local public cultures, services and facilities [including schools] to Muslim needs and claims."[19] In France, on the other hand, cultural heritage, viz. religion, was allotted no autonomy, received no place in the public sphere, and to this day there are no Muslims in the National Assembly. In sharp contrast with the United Kingdom, French secondary school students learn next to nothing about Islam.

Postwar Germany had little available colonial practice to draw on when Muslim immigrants arrived. The German Empire's colonial experience was slight and short-lived, beginning in 1884 and ending when Britain and France stripped Germany of its colonies after World War I. Nazi Germany colonized much of Europe, but only briefly, and that chapter of history hardly constituted a model for the democratic Federal Republic. That country wished to start *ab novo,* renouncing the past in a constitutional republic based on the equal rights and obligations of legally vested citizens, a civic nationhood. Yet the Federal Republic could not entirely transcend its past. If there was a historical precedent for Muslims in postwar Germany, it was Polish immigration to Prussia in the late nineteenth century. While Polish enclaves were preserved in eastern Prussia, in the Slavic east, German culture, language, and identity were maintained. Cultures were maintained tenaciously in zones of ethnically and culturally mixed populations. This experience helped to imbue the German elite with what Brubaker calls a "differentialist" model of nationhood.[20]

Ethnicity remained the hallmark of German nationhood, but that criterion was not uncontested. Hence, on the one hand, German courts extended constitutional rights to Muslim labor migrants, but on the other, citizenship was not offered to their German-born children and grandchildren even while it was extended to immigrants of German descent (see chapter 13). At least until 2000 when some reforms were introduced, the availability of citizenship depended on ethnocultural nationality— overseas Germans got it; children of Turks born in Germany did not.[21] German citizenry, understood as a community of descent, restrictive for non-German immigrants and indulgent to ethnic Germans, accents the pronounced ethnic and cultural timbre of the German self-conception. On the other hand, France's routine conversion of second-generation immigrants into citizens mirrors the expansive, state-centered and assimilationist self-conception of the French.[22]

Britain and France each viewed their Muslim immigrants in the light of their considerable colonial experiences, and these experiences themselves reflected divergent nation-building histories. Immigrants arriving in the United Kingdom from the imperial subcontinent were encouraged to look to their communal leaders to resolve their grievances in a polity where Muslims enjoyed autonomy but little chance of entry into British social circles. These leaders in turn exacted political advantage in return for social peace. They became the negotiators of Muslim identity in Britain. In consequence, British Muslims were integrated politically but remained separate socially. Not surprisingly their allegiance was to their community and not to Britain. Muslim domination of local councils and Muslim representation in Parliament were not so much signs of assimilation as of a uniquely British social contract in which Muslims would preserve their identity even in the public sphere.

In France such communal mediation was unknown. As in the French empire, immigrants were to adhere directly to France. In accordance with the official republican ideology that underlies the French model of assimilation, ethnicity has no authorized place in public life. French republicanism doggedly repudiates allegiance to an entity other than the nation itself, whether that be an ethnic group, a territory (such as a French province), or a religion.[23] Referring to the group that until recently has been the touchstone in French discussions of ethnic differences, a speaker in the 1789 National Assembly declared famously: "We must refuse everything to the Jews as a Nation . . . and grant everything to the Jews as individuals." The "melting pot" is far more characteristic of French than of American public life where it is perfectly fine to be Irish-American, Polish-American, Italian-American or Afro-American. French *laïcité* (a secularism that mandates a strict separation of church and state) frowns on expressions of ethnic affinity and religious sentiment, which are unheard in political speech. The British census asks respondents their religion, while the French state stubbornly refuses to compile statistics on the country's racial and ethnic makeup.[24]

As we will see in chapter 13, ambivalent, long-divided Germany, whether Protestant or Catholic, capitalist or socialist, today, vacillates between a nationalist and a multiculturalist approach. On the one hand, only a paltry proportion of Muslims in Germany are citizens, and until 2000, very few had the right to become German nationals. On the other hand, several German states (*länder*) have been quite willing to accommodate the religious claims of their Muslim populations. Education authorities in North Rhine-Westphalia mandate the teaching of Islam in required religion courses in public schools.[25]

Official attitudes toward the Muslim veil in the three countries reflect the broad differences between their models of nation-building, empire, and immigrant aggregation. Under the banner of laïcité the French ban even the modest headscarf in public schools. By contrast, when a legislator in communalist Britain, where the headscarf is permitted everywhere, expressed discomfort with visitors wearing not a mere headscarf but a face-covering veil (niqab) for interviews in his own office, his mild objections raised a storm of outrage.[26] Again, Germany falls somewhere in between, as "something of a hybrid of the British and French responses,"[27] yet with its own idiosyncratic spin on the matter. The nation-building mandate of German public schools is far less extensive than in France, and the right of students to wear the headscarf has never been in doubt. But the wearing of it is denied to German teachers who, as representatives of the state, are expected to observe religious neutrality. However, in some German states these same teachers are allowed to sport crosses because their religion is considered part of the nation's "Christian-occidental" heritage (see chapter 13). As Christian Joppke points out, the "Christian-occidental" label in Germany works as "a substitute for the shattered idiom of ethnic nationhood." "No such crypto-nationalist trope," he adds, "is discernable in France or Britain."[28]

Our examination of policies in the three countries shows the three models in operation—British communalism or multiculturalism, French assimilationism and laïcité, and Germany's ambivalence between a civic and an ethnic nationality. The pattern of responses to the Pew surveys summarized in chapter 3 anticipated the paradigms advanced here for the three countries. In particular, the surveys' antipodes, France and Britain—where unity and national identity predominate in France, division and Muslim identity in Britain—fall closely into line with the tendencies we have described for the two countries: the assimilationist and the pluralist narratives.

The 2005 French riots and London bombings, along with the simmering discontent of German Turks, suggest that none of these models have worked perfectly. France's self-confidence and authority was shaken by wars of liberation in Algeria and Indochina and then by the revolt of its privileged youth in 1968. France's "civilizing mission" no longer animates schoolteachers in immigrant suburbs. Across the Channel, Britain's elites, stripped of colonial possessions, unnerved by charges of ethnocentrism and racism, gave free reign to identity politics. Relative cultural autonomy became absolute. Germany, unable to sort out where an ugly ethnocentric past ends and national pride survives, remains deeply divided over the place of Muslim postmigrants: are the cultures present in the country equal, or is there a *leitkultur,* a leading German culture (see chapter 13)? In all three countries, what has happened to immigrants often is aggregation, not integration. While the French immigration discourse is assimilationist, "the French melting pot" is typically merely formal. British pluralist multiculturalism has often meant, in the words of the Nobel Laureate economist Amartya Sen, "plural monoculturalism."[29] Meanwhile, Germany has been divided in its own way: multicultural in courts, colleges and cant; segregationist in daily life.

Of course, these divergences in orientation are not absolute. France's creation of the Conseil Français du Culte Musulman (CFCM), a body recognized as the official Muslim interlocutor (see chapter 3), has been described as "de facto multiculturalism."[30] German citizenship policies have been evolving toward the European standard of birthplace as opposed to blood. The judiciary in Britain dismissed suits against schools that restricted the wearing of the niqab, forming a "counterpoint to the situation in France and Germany, where headscarf restrictions originated from the political branches of the state against rights-protecting courts."[31]

To compute the impact of these variations in host-country reception, we must figure in differences in Muslim immigrant provenance. The Muslims who migrated to Britain from the subcontinent after World War II had been minorities in a Hindu land as well as British subjects, developing in response a communal religiosity. The North Africans entering France at the same time came from Muslim-majority countries and felt no need to develop their religious idiosyncrasies. Moreover, the French, as Gilles Kepel notes, were oblivious of the kind of "self-imposed apartheid" that got transplanted to and implemented on British soil.[32] Turks who started coming to Germany in this period had lived under an aggressively secular regime for most of the century. In Britain the Pakistanis and in Germany the Turks do not speak the host country's language as French North Africans often do. Turkish jihadis have been extremely rare until very recently; militants for a decade and a half have waged holy war against an Algerian government that has aided the French in counterterrorism; and the Pakistani government has fostered jihad for geopolitical ends, an opportunity not lost on British would-be terrorists.

One can find similar variations in every European country that hosts Muslims. For example, while Muslims began arriving en masse in northern Europe (Belgium, Britain, France, Germany, the Netherlands, and Scandinavia) in the mid-1950s, they only began coming to southern Europe (Greece, Italy, and Spain) in the 1980s. Thus, Muslim postmigrancy, so to speak, is embryonic in southern Europe; meanwhile, Muslims have been in the Balkans for centuries, though hardly at all elsewhere in Eastern Europe.

THE BRITISH DIFFERENTIA

But the most arresting European variant is that Britain's jihadis outnumber by an order of magnitude those of any of its continental neighbors, and their sum widely exceeds the total for the rest of the region. In November 2007 Jonathan Evans, the director of Britain's internal security service, the MI5, in a dramatic and rare public appearance, revealed that there were two thousand individuals known to be "involved in terrorist-related activity in the UK," and that there were "as many again that we don't yet know of." The service was aware of two hundred terrorist networks and thirty active plots.[33] A year later authorities viewed the threat as growing "increasingly complex" and the numbers "even higher."[34] In May 2010 Evans told me that while his service had identified more "subjects of interest" and thwarted many plots, the threat remained severe.[35] In a September 2010 speech the internal security director stated that the United Kingdom "continues to face a real threat from Al Qaida–related terrorism. That threat is diverse in both geography and levels of skill involved but it is persistent and dangerous and trying to control it involves a continual invisible struggle." Evans saw "no reason to believe that the position will significantly improve in the immediate future."[36]

Nowhere else in Europe have intelligence officials seen the need to reveal a jihad count, but in confidential briefings Belgian, Danish, Dutch, French, German, Italian, and Spanish security officials have never offered me estimates exceeding a fraction of the British.[37] Jean-François Clair, of the Direction de la Surveillance du Territoire (DST), France's internal security agency, briefed me several times on the record.[38] In 2008 he explained that while, he gathered, it had been for the British "important to show the size of the problem to the public," in France conditions had not made it "useful to make open declarations." In any case the number in France of those "under investigation is far less than thousands." Only "about a dozen" groups of different sizes "had been neutralized, the majority of them planning or preparing terrorist actions in France, some others concerned by the conflict in Iraq after March 2003."[39]

On the public record, Michael Taarnby, a security analyst who has worked for the Danish government, estimated in 2006 that of 180,000 Muslims residing in Denmark, which, thanks to the cartoon episode, became a stated target of al Qaeda, "only a few dozen, if that, have actually crossed the line and chosen to engage in illegal or violent activities."[40] The Dutch security service that tracked the Hofstad group that murdered Theo van Gogh, had by 2006 identified only "some ten to twenty loose-knit structures in the Netherlands that can be qualified as jihadist networks" within a "relatively small" "hard core of radical Islam encompassing several hundreds of people only."[41] In Spain the comparable number is "around 300 radicals," a feeble figure compared with Britain's more than four thousand complicit individuals who form only a small portion of its "radicals."

These numbers are merely illustrative and should not be construed as a metric. But the outsize British numbers are rooted, as we shall see, in a radical social movement without its like elsewhere in Europe. To recur to numerical estimates once more: Hizb ut-Tahrir, the Party of Liberation, a virulently anti-Semitic group that wishes to install Islamic regimes by *coup d'état* and thereafter to conduct jihads, had some ten thousand British members in 2009. In that same year, in Germany there were 350 members of Hizb ut-Tahrir; in Denmark, there were fewer than 200.[42]

Intelligence sources in that year viewed British-born Pakistani extremists entering the United States under the visa waiver program as a likely source of another attack on American soil. That is why in 2006, prompted by a failed attack on transatlantic airliners leaving London's Heathrow Airport, the CIA launched a major intelligence operation in the United Kingdom, according to a report in the London-based *Telegraph*. Bruce Reidel, a respected former CIA analyst, told the paper,

"The British Pakistani community is recognized as probably al-Qaeda's best mechanism for launching an attack against North America."[43]

According to one line of analysis, "Islamist terrorism has become a pan-European phenomenon. . . . The activities of Islamist extremists in 'Londonistan' have been matched by those in 'Milanistan,' 'Hamburgistan' or "Madridistan. . . . [T]he network has spread across the entire continent;"[44] and "every other European country finds itself in the same predicament" as Britain.[45] But is there really a "pan-European" terrorist network, or are "Londonistan" and British jihadism sui generis?

PART THREE

IN BRITAIN

GHOST TOWNS

B eeston is a twenty-minute bus ride south from downtown
Leeds; Leeds is a three-hour train ride north from London into
West Yorkshire. The four attackers of London's transport system
in 2005 are known in Britain as "the Beeston bombers." Three of the
four hailed from or next to Beeston, including Mohammed Sidique
Khan (who was thirty in 2005) and his chief accomplice, his boyhood
friend Shehzad Tanweer (then twenty-two). [1]

Beeston is one of the five wards of South Leeds. The latter contains
65,000 souls living in 29,000 households, at least half of which are leased. [2]
To the north of Beeston passes a six-lane highway, severing it from the
rest of Leeds not unlike the artery that quarantines the Parisian *banlieues*
and their ghostly *cités*. On the eastern slope of Beeston sits shabby, care-
worn Beeston Hill, population 16,000, housing the South Asian community, predominantly Pakistani, along with other South Asians,
Caribbeans, and, most recently, Poles.

Beeston Hill's Pakistanis hail from Mirpur, a district of Azad Kashmir, the Pakistani-administered portion of the territory that is dis-
puted with India. [3] Seventy percent of British Pakistani families, and an
even higher portion of those on Beeston Hill, are from Mirpur. [4] The
Mirpur district, whose capital city is also called Mirpur (population
400,000), sits astride a riverbed in the foothills of the Himalayas about
seventy-five miles northeast of Islamabad, at the extreme south of
Azad Kashmir.

HOMES

The Manchester anthropologist Roger Ballard, exploring Mirpur's stagnant sender villages, could not help but notice enormous houses "as
many as five or six stories high," bazaars with "two-story off-street shopping malls selling all manner of consumer goods," and streets filled with
cars and the "teeming shoals of motor cycles." But on further inspection
those apparent signs of prosperity proved wholly misleading. Most of the
grand houses turned out to be bereft of furnishings, with the exception
of the inevitable vast sitting room for entertaining guests. Yet no one was
at home. The owners of these facades had simply bolted the doors and
repaired to England where they actually lived.[5]

They left behind an indigenous economy, based on small, unimproved
farms. Alison Shaw, an Oxford anthropologist, noticed on a similar trip
that the traditional houses of nonmigrating villagers were built of mud
bricks: "*Pakka* (literally 'cooked') houses usually belong to wealthier
people (such as those with relatives abroad) and are built of kiln-baked
bricks and mortar, usually covered in a layer of concrete and often
brightly painted."[6]

Moreover, such buildings are often found in clusters where each suc-
cessive structure is slightly taller than its predecessor. The architectural
style of these monuments to emigrant family pride confirms the status-
seeking logic of this competition in construction. Whereas the residences
of Pakistan's old elite are invariably concealed behind tall walls to hide
their private spaces, the gaudy new multistoried edifices tower *above* the
destitute landscape, flaunting their sprawling balconies, ornate porticoes,
stuccoed gables, and other glossy embellishments, each garish crown
overtopping its predecessor.[7]

This performance architecture was certainly not meant to impress
Professor Ballard or the world outside the village, but the builders'
humble relatives and tribesmen remaining in Mirpur, or their not-so-
humble fellow emigrants, the splendor of whose edifices just down the
road has been topped by the new. An elaborate and exotic "game of
status competition is being played here—and very little else."[8]

This invidious, conspicuous consumption proceeds in splendid isolation from the torpid indigence of the local economy and contributes
little to alleviating the latter. What is not spent on mansions is deposited

Mirpuri ghost houses. © Raja Qaiser; used by permission.

in local bank accounts; there is thus scant investment in production or infrastructure. Mirpur, like similar villages in western or central Mexico, is condemned to "the migrant syndrome" of dependency and economic stagnation.[9] A wry comment from one of Ballard's informants summarized Mirpur concisely: "We don't cultivate wheat here anymore, we cultivate visas."[10]

In contrast to the pallid serial "machines for living" of the Paris slums or Beeston Hill's dingy row houses, each emigrant edifice in Mirpur is a differentiated and public boast of the owner's personal attainments overseas and his wish that these be recognized at home. The rioters in Paris and Lyon, Lyon's and Beeston's bombers, all sought a very different sort of recognition, from the great world, on rapt television screens. In Mirpur, recognition is narrow, familial, directed at the clan, the *biradari*. But tribal recognition is not what the Beeston bombers sought in London on July 7, 2005. They were playing to the wider world, to which they addressed their martyrdom videos. The recognition that the parents desire is local, embedded, and territorialized. What the parents seek in the tiny village back home is *izzat,* which is the Urdu term for honor, reputation, status or image, the *sine qua non* of traditional society. Disputes with fathers over izzat will figure frequently in the radicalization of the sons of Beeston.

Mirpur is not only a "remittance economy," to echo the phrase V. S. Naipaul used three decades earlier to describe a younger, less inveterate Pakistan, but it is also a remittance *society*.[11] Remittances build houses and reputations; they carve out a new social hierarchy where England's hard-working drudge becomes king for a day—or a week or a month—in Mirpur, because the empty mansions are designed not for every day but for holidays and special occasions such as weddings, birthdays, vacations, or funerals.

I found Andrew and three other lonely Englishmen downing beers under Muslim eyes outside a row house off Tempest Road, Beeston Hill's main drag. At least one of the carousers, judging by his maladroit attempts at humor and his distracted demeanor, had ingested something a lot stronger. Andrew offered to point out the Hardy Street mosque, where Sidique Khan worshipped before he renounced his father's Sufi saints and shrines, and the Fish N' Chips that Tanweer's father owned before it discreetly changed hands after July 2005.

As Andrew and I set forth he confides that he has spent half his life in Beeston, half in jail, where he had done time for burglary before he got off speed and smack. He tells me about a neighborhood "Asian gang" that fought crime and drugs and bullied whites. A few weeks earlier, "two Asian chaps" hustled him into a car where he was questioned for several hours about the break-in of a store down on the bedraggled section of Dewsbury Road that leads haltingly to metropolitan Leeds.

Andrew's abduction was my first concrete corroboration of Shiv Malik's deduction that Sidique Kahn's "Mullah Boys" gang, whom we will meet in chapter 11, still stalked Beeston Hill, notwithstanding the police and press spotlight after the London bombings. Tanweer and Sidique had been charter members. Malik was a BBC journalist who had lived in Leeds previously for several years, and he had returned for a six-month attempt to loosen Beeston tongues. His BBC feature was to be aired on the first anniversary of the bombings. But nobody wanted to talk with Shiv or his colleagues. "At first it seemed that the community was just fed up with journalists asking dumb questions," Shiv recalls.

Beeston Hill back-to-backs. © James W. Bell; used by permission.

"But eventually, we realized that it wasn't just irritation keeping people silent; it was intimidation."[12]

The streets that Andrew and I walk are furrows between rows of two-story "back-to-back terraces" as they have been generously denominated since they were first installed for Irish immigrants in late Victorian days.[13] George Orwell got to know these dwellings well during the Depression; he described them as "two houses built in one, each side of the house being somebody's front door, so that if you walk down a row of what is apparently twelve houses you are in reality seeing not twelve houses but twenty-four. The front houses give on the street and the back ones on the yard, and there is only one way out of each house."[14] Hardly designed for neighborliness or comfort, in Orwell's day, if you lived on the side facing the street, you had to walk around to the end of the block to reach the outhouse in the yard, a distance as long as two hundred yards. And if you lived at the back you looked out on a row of outhouses. Even today few of the back-to-backs have indoor bathrooms, but most now have indoor toilets, though outhouses remain in use.[15]

A century ago, in 1909, the Housing and Town Planning Act forbade any further building of back-to-backs, declaring such accommodations unfit for human habitation. But the Leeds City Council exploited a loophole in the act that permitted houses approved prior to the legislation to be built and their construction continued until 1937.[16]

Orwell visited them seventy years ago, when they were merely four decades old, and he found interiors so dark that indoor lights had to be kept burning all day. Rain came through the roof; sewers ran under the houses and reeked in the summer, if you could smell them above the stink of "chamber-pots standing about in your living-room." Upstairs rooms were thinly partitioned so that quite often the budding novelist found "eight or ten people sleeping in two small rooms, probably in at most four beds."[17] Family size hardly shrunk when fecund Pakistani Muslims replaced prolific Irish Catholics. Orwell was certain that such circumstances did "not encourage self-respect." But they could, when grafted onto an *al-wala' wa'l-bara* doctrine holding Muslims to be a superior breed, in straitened, undeserved circumstances, generate a touchy, thymotic and retaliatory sense of identity and injustice.

Some homes were "so appalling," the immortal chronicler of social conditions confessed, that he had "no hope of describing them adequately. To begin with, the smell, the dominant and essential thing, is indescribable." And what was "the use of a brief phrase like 'roof leaks' or 'four beds for eight people'? It is the kind of thing your eye slides over, registering nothing," the British master observed. "And yet what a wealth of misery it can cover!"[18]

And I haven't mentioned the bugs. "Once bugs get into a house they are in it till the crack of doom; there is no sure way of exterminating them. Then there are the windows that will not open. I need not point out what this must mean, in summer, in a tiny stuffy living-room where the fire, on which all the cooking is done, has to be kept burning more or less constantly."[19] At the opposite extreme, winter in harsh northern England afforded little relief, with fireplaces that gave out little warmth and "the misery of leaking roofs and oozing walls, which in winter makes some rooms almost uninhabitable."

The back-to-backs that Andrew and I pass are now more than seventy hard years older. A recent Leeds City Council survey found that 73 percent of back-to-backs in Leeds failed the decent homes standard or the Housing Health and Safety System thanks to the presence of "category 1 hazards" and their general lack of maintenance, heating, safe stairwells, and fire-safety precautions.[20]

The families of Beeston coal miners or of workers at mills and foundries in nearby Hunslet first occupied these houses, and, with the installation of an electrified tram in 1900, their lettered children could finally commute to offices downtown. But their grandchildren and great-grandchildren began departing for the new suburbs as South Asians started arriving in the sixties. Among these South Asians were Sidique's father, Tika, destined for a Hunslet foundry. Pakistani immigrants lengthened the shelf life of Beeston's tenements as steam gave way to diesel, steel to plastic.

ALL GOOD WORKERS

The legendary machines pulled in the Pakistanis as it had Irishmen before them and Englishmen before that. Leeds stood at the forefront when little Britain bore the torch of modernization—and remained there from the sixteenth century, with the enclosure of common land to raise sheep for woolen manufacture, well past the nineteenth-century industrial revolution, based on the factory, the railway, and the coal mine, not forgetting the steam engine.

The city owed its original prominence to the booming woolen trade as England became the clothier of Europe, producing the first commodity of large-scale manufacture. Leeds sits on the Aire, which empties into the Ouse, which flows into the Humber and thence to Hull, the North Sea, and Europe; an ideal spot for export and a convenient source of waterpower to operate fulling mills. The city owed its emergence during the sixteenth century to those natural advantages and the incredible growth of the woolen cloth industry in West Riding.[21] By 1698 Leeds was "esteemed the wealthyest town of its bigness in the Countrye."[22]

A century hence, the natural blessing of the West Riding of Yorkshire was coal, as the steam engine supplanted the water wheel. Railway engines were to become Leeds's leading merchandise, but in 1758 its railway first saw the light as a horse-drawn carriage mounted on rails of wood to carry coal from pits in Middletown, next door to Beeston, over to factories around Leeds. In 1807 the wooden tracks began to be replaced with iron edge rails. In 1812 the Middleton Steam Railway became the first commercial railway to employ steam locomotives. In

1816 the Leeds–Liverpool Canal was completed, making Leeds the center of a cross-country waterway.

Two years later Emily Brontë was born in Thornton, now part of Bradford, the country's preeminent Muslim settlement and a short ride from Leeds. Emily grew up believing that spirits lurked in the surrounding moors, barren rolling wastes of bogs and grasses and sedges, which form the setting of *Wuthering Heights,* her masterpiece of religion, revenge, and terror. In the year of her birth Leeds boasted more than a hundred woolen mills employing ten thousand workers.[23] As factories proliferated, so did dreadful working conditions, of the kind recounted not by Brontë but by Charles Dickens and Friedrich Engels. Such conditions, along with unsafe housing and acute air pollution, led to a very high death rate.[24] Leeds's cemeteries became the targets of a highly coordinated gang of body-snatchers known locally as "the resurrectionists."[25] Body-snatching became such a menace in Leeds that the townsfolk organized "Grave Clubs" to bury corpses twelve feet down and to guard newly interred remains for as long as five weeks, just the sort of thing that haunted the imagination of Miss Brontë.

In the later days of Queen Victoria, South Leeds, dotted with coal pits, was producing everything from ale to iron, steam engines to hydraulic pumps, glass to ready-made clothes as well as textile machines, printing presses, and armament for war in the Crimea and colonial repression in south Asia. The Irish came to fill job openings and occupy the new-fangled "back-to-backs" on Beeston Hill.[26] These were the days when the sun did not set on the British Empire, consolidating its rule in India, without a hint that the descendants of these colonial subjects would someday haunt its engines of glory.

By 1960 immigrants from Mirpur had started taking the jobs that neither the English nor even the Irish wanted, working double shifts, taking three-per-day turns on mattresses in Leeds flophouses, much like Mexican migrants in their American enclaves today. Barry, who had been a line boss in the sixties in the foundries of Hunslet, told me that the Pakistanis were "all good workers" who took the night shift and worked "sixty or seventy hours a week" without complaint. By the late sixties Muslim wives were coming over from Mirpur to join their husbands in decaying back-to-backs and to hustle them and the kids to mosques installed in converted flats. The Irish were departing, not as pleased to have South Asians as neighbors as Barry was to have them as hands. The displeasure was mutual. The Asian immigrant nursed his "myth of return," and nowhere was this treasured more strongly than among those moving into the back-to-backs on Beeston Hill. But by the recession of the mid-1970s it had become clear that what was temporary was not the worker but the workplace. The migrant worker would stay; his factory went off to East Asia.

The mass introduction of South Asian labor foreshadowed the relocation of entire trades to the sources of plentiful cheap labor, a sure sign of the beginning of the end for industrial Leeds and for British heavy industry.[27] Leeds's hallmark trade unfurled the early warning signs of the coming collapse of British industrial competiveness. Until the 1960s, Leeds produced about half of all suits bought by British men. Famed clothing factories located in Holbeck and Hunslet populated the back-to-backs in bedroom suburbs like Beeston.[28] But in that same decade the European Common Market started making inroads into the British cloth market without British manufacturers achieving reciprocal gains in mainland markets.[29] To compete, British textiles had to be cheaper. That could be achieved by modernizing, by substituting machines for men, as England had done since the sixteenth century. Or it could be done by finding cheaper men. Mills in West Yorkshire sent recruitment officers to Mirpur and Punjab for workers.[30] The new low-wage arrivals seemed to obviate the need for plant modernization.[31] But immigration turned out to be only a temporary lifeline, and before long those same employers would simply ship overseas their capital and their machines, but not their workers, leaving behind the spectral remains of better days in places like Beeston.[32]

The sixties brought changes in clothing fashions as well as intellectual ones. Multiculturalism brought to the metropolis the identity politics long employed in Britain's famous "indirect" colonial rule.[33] Suits, vests, and blazers fell out of favor as styles became more casual.[34] One preeminent Leeds clothier tried "adapting suit style to the requirements of Teddy boys,"[35] but such marginal changes could not save the old firms. Wholesale "bespoke tailoring" in large shops became unprofitable.[36] It could not withstand competition from high-tech European exporters and low-tech low-wage workforces in East Asia.[37]

By 1987 the proud clothing trade of Leeds had reverted to small workshops or even private homes, and South Asian immigrants performed

95 percent of the work.[38] The decline was general in West Riding.[39] Those fated to shoulder the heaviest burdens of this radical de-industrialization were the laid-off Pakistani millhands, many of whom had just bought homes on Beeston Hill. Their sons would inherit the presumption of advancement usually found in the second generation but faced instead the harsh reality of downward mobility. West Riding towns would produce ongoing street battles between white and Asian gangs, which in the summer of 1995 and again on July 7, 2001—precisely four years before the Beeston bombings—burst into riots that attracted national attention and concern.

LASCARS

Why do most of Beeston's Pakistanis, and most of British Pakistanis, come from rural and remote Mirpur? Why from lonely Mirpur and not from the teeming slums of Lahore, Karachi, or even nearby Rawalpindi?

Mirpur lies between the foothills of the Himalayas to the north and the more fertile plains of the Punjab province of Pakistan to the south. Mirpur is basically Punjabi in culture, and the language is a dialect of the Punjabi tongue, though for centuries the region formed part of the neighboring princely domain of Kashmir, which, with the partition of India in 1947, was split into three parts (Pakistani, Indian, and Chinese).[40] But, unlike Hindu Punjab, Mirpur is an area of subsistence agriculture, or it certainly was in the late fifties and early sixties when farmers began leaving for England. The terrain is generally rough and irrigation is rare. Rainfall is plentiful, often overly plentiful, leading to flooding. Infrastructure has always been minimal in Kashmir (where princely rule meant high taxes and scant investment in roads, bridges, wells, electricity, and schools), a situation not rectified when Pakistan began to govern its portion of Kashmir. Adding to these burdens has been the fragmentary character of the holdings, owing to the practice, general among Muslims in the entire Punjab region, of dividing the deceased's property in fixed shares among male siblings.[41] As a consequence of all these conditions, most farms have been too tiny for the harvesting of cash crops.[42]

Mirpuris are not untypical representatives of the 95 percent of British Pakistanis of rural origin.[43] If small plots and subsistence farming alone

accounted for migration, though, most of Pakistan would be in West
Yorkshire or Birmingham today. Besides, after Mirpur the next major
source of Pakistani migration to Britain has been the relatively prosperous districts to the south around Faisalabad, lying in the Punjab plains, a
region of irrigation canals where the villages generally have electricity
and are accessible by paved roads, and the farmers have access to tube
wells and tractors and harvest cash crops.[44] One factor that helps to
explain the Punjabi presence in Britain is the mass migration into the
region after Partition. Practically the whole of the Muslim, Hindu, and
Sikh populations of East and West Punjab traded places during that dire
and bloody event.[45]

But in Mirpur, flood and not war, natural and not man-made events,
pushed families from their homes. Mirpur, like Leeds, is a river district.
Though, of course, it would be idle to imagine that Mirpuris went to
Leeds as "river people" drawn to the water, water in various forms does
flow and hiss through the entire Mirpur/Beeston migration story. Mirpur lies at the point where the Jhelum River pours down from the
heavily forested foothills of the northern mountains into treeless Punjab,
the very spot to build boats to carry lumber and other resources down
the five rivers of the Punjab to the Indus and onto the seaports of the
delta and the Indian Ocean. For more than three thousand years, boatmen
have embarked from Mirpur to sail into the Indian Ocean. However,
when the British arrived and built railroads deep into the Punjab from
Bombay and Karachi, the skippers of Mirpur were outflanked. But another kind of water job presently surfaced, for the Leeds steam engines
that pulled trains could also propel boats, and the railway age soon also
became the age of the steam ship.

Europeans were not keen to work below, feeding coal into boilers in
the blistering stokeholds, and certainly not in the tropical conditions of
the Indian Ocean. The Brits took the deck jobs, thank you very much.
So a century before the Irish left to the Mirpuris the nightshifts of
Hunslet foundries and the back-to-backs of Beeston Hill, there had
been another opening that fit the needs, backgrounds, and capacities of
unemployed Mirpuri seamen. These seamen, known as *lascars,* became
engine-room stokers on steamships sailing out of Karachi and Bombay,
monopolizing a position they were to hold until oil replaced coal after
World War II.[46] Heathcliff, the obsessed and vengeful protagonist of
obscure origins in Brontë's *Wuthering Heights,* is described as a "lascar."

He was a fictional pacesetter among that first contingent of dusky pioneers to West Yorkshire.

British steamship companies recruited many of their lascar seamen from the Mirpur district, men who were happy to work on the water and leave their forlorn smallholdings. Then when the steam engine gave way to the diesel, often also built in Leeds foundries and engineering plants, and boiler-room jobs began disappearing, Mirpuris joined the Queen's Navy and some, as subjects of the Crown, settled in Britain.[47]

As a result, a number of Mirpuri lascars had established themselves in Britain before World War II. Their numbers swelled as sailors who saw their ships torpedoed from beneath them by German U-boats and Japanese submarines were drafted to work in Britain's labor-short munitions factories, foundries, and textile mills in places like West Yorkshire.[48] These men established the first Mirpuri migratory communities in Britain.[49] Emigration from the Punjab stemmed from a similar series of conjunctures that formed "a tradition of internal colonization" that originally attracted migrants to the prosperous canal colonies of Punjab.[50]

In the second or mass stage of Mirpuri immigration, water was to play an even greater role—with the building in the 1960s of the vast Mangla Dam, the world's sixth largest, across the river Jhelum. Funded by the World Bank, the project was designed primarily to offset the irregular seasonal flow of the Indus and its tributaries and to provide a steady source of irrigation as well as electricity. But the construction of the dam flooded most of Mirpur's most fertile land, drowning some three hundred villages in the district, sinking the town of Mirpur itself (now the ghostly Old Mirpur) and displacing more than one hundred thousand of the region's residents. To compensate those affected, the Pakistani government promoted the migration of five thousand individuals in 1961.[51] But those who availed themselves of these paltry awards needed the further assistance of settled migrants, "prior contacts"—such as relatives or friends—who encouraged them to emigrate, offering temporary housing and job connections. "No villager would go without some established contact."[52] Had the Mirpur flood occurred where there was no previous pattern of migration, probably very few refugees would have ended up in West Yorkshire. Ballard, who for four decades has studied South Asian migration to England, reinforces the point: those affected would have had to settle for the Pakistani government's "grossly inadequate offers of compensation and resettlement" were it not for their "established transnational connections."[53]

Those "prior contacts," usually families of seamen who had settled in England, advised their relatives not only of jobs in the labor-hungry mills and foundries of West Yorkshire but also of the imminent introduction of immigration controls. Hence, Mirpuris hastened to join the Pakistani rush to "beat the ban" and catalyzed the principal period of mass migration from Pakistan to Britain.[54] Mass immigration from Pakistan would increasingly take on a family character, thanks both to the household nature of migration and to British policies that, as became the rule elsewhere in the West, promoted immigrant family reunification, in this case with heavy consequences.

LINKS

In immigration parlance, Mirpur's floods "pushed" Asian migrants out, and Leeds machines "pulled" them in. But "prior contacts" are what explain why so many migrants pushed from Mirpur got pulled into little Beeston Hill and why Beeston Hill has such a disproportionate population of Mirpuris among its immigrants. The logic of immigration lies not only in the push and pull of localities but also in the channels between them. As we saw in chapter 6, the link between pull and push is usually family, and here it is the extended family or clan, the biradari, the building blocks of the tribe. Pakistanis' accounts of their arrival in Britain display a pattern: brothers join brothers, sons follow fathers, nephews follow uncles, cousins join cousins, and neighbors join neighbors. In her study of Pakistanis settled in Oxford, Alison Shaw found that "in most cases" the migrants had "prior contacts" in Britain.[55] Her findings match the results of my own queries among Pakistani and Bangladeshi migrants in Leeds, East London (Walthamstow and Tower Hamlets), Crawley, and Birmingham.

Family networks are integral to migration. A painstaking study of the migration of Mexicans to the United States discovered it to be anything but a random movement of poor individuals simply seeking higher wages. Instead, it found customary decisions made deliberately by family members acting through preestablished and extensive social networks. Immigration constituted an institutionalized element in the income portfolio of these households and a ready escape ladder in a crisis.[56]

Pakistanis from Mirpur who settled in tiny Beeston Hill were behaving as migrants have always done, as links in a chain. What turns temporary labor migration into mass migration and settlement is chain migration. The historical and social construction of migratory networks explains why Pakistani migrants came from the Punjab or Mirpur rather than from other parts of the country, such as the far more indigent Baluchistan and Pashtun provinces.

If Mexican mass migration is a network-driven family enterprise, Mirpuri migration is that in spades. As Shaw discovered in a field trip to Mirpur, "The migration itself was generally regarded as a means of improving the status of close kin 'at home' rather than as a route to individual social advancement."[57] The Mirpuri villager, visiting home every year, is well aware that his circumstances dictate that he can rise socially only in his native surrounding, not in England.[58] The migrant's bountiful gift-giving, his eager purchase of land, his erecting an ostentatious villa: all express his fealty to the home village and the kinship group.[59] Mexicans who migrate are expected to remember their families, but they are free to build their lives in the United States. On vacations they will return home, where big spenders are local heroes.[60] Yet once migrants marry and have children—once they have settled—remittances shrink and life begins to revolve around their new home abroad.

But this is not the case in Mirpuri migration. Rather, as Shaw discovered in her interviews with Pakistanis in Oxford, most of whom came from Mirpur, their families in Britain are satellites whose orbit around the home village have been temporarily diverted, but not fundamentally altered, by migration.[61] Unlike the Mexican migrant, the Mirpuri migrant never loses his focus on home, not in life or in death. The Mirpuri father does all he can to see that his children retain that focus.

Migration begins with an investment. Someone has to put up the funds for passage and for food and lodging until the first paycheck. Almost invariably that someone is a family member, and typically the cash is not a gift but an advance. In the Pakistani context, the initial investment represents the first in a customary and standardized exchange of gifts (in Urdu, *lena dena*). That advance, that gift with strings attached, will often constitute a first step that will lead eventually to an arranged marriage back home with, for example, the daughter or niece of the patron. But postmigrants, socialized in modern European countries, sometimes resent and reject the marriage endgame.

Pakistani immigration to Britain is not so much a leaving of home as an aggrandizing of it, one that preserves rather than severs the elaborate, socially constructed linkage between birth, marriage, family, death, and creed. To cut any thread in that social fabric, as when a postmigrant refuses the family obligation to wed a cousin back home, rends an integral chain of obligations, throws into question an entire social system, a gift economy, and a code of honor. In the case of Sidique Khan and the Mullah Boys, as we will see in chapter 11, that momentous refusal constituted both a thunderous declaration of radical dissent and a big step on the road to jihad.

GRAVES

In 1990 Ballard found Mirpur families to have devoted colossal efforts and scarce savings to flying corpses back home.[62] A decade later, Shaw encountered the same arresting evidence of "continuing links with relatives in Pakistan."[63] The graveyard embodies the territoriality and embeddedness of the kinship group. In Mirpuri villages, every biraderi, or clan, possesses its own carefully tended graveyard where each member "gradually reassembles after death."[64]

If the writ of Sidique Khan and Shezhad Tanweer and the Mullah Crew still runs on Beeston Hill, and their spirits still haunt London law courts, Tanweer's body rests in apparent peace in the village of Chak-477 in Samoondran, in Punjab province, which owes its strange bureaucratic name to the irrigation canals devised by the British in colonial times. Tanweer's remains, like those of many departed British Pakistanis, had been sent home. The whereabouts of those of his partner Sidique are unknown but were not likely to be similarly honored by his estranged family.[65] But at the ancestral graveyard in Chak-477, Tanweer's headstone towers above all the others and bears that famous inscription about there being "no God but Allah, and Mohammad is his messenger." A week before my visit to Beeston Hill, while Britain mourned the third anniversary of the July 7 bombing, the relatives of the Beeston bomber in Pakistan gaily celebrated their "shadid," their martyr.[66] Though jihad has long been a national cause in Pakistan, the police had told them to be discreet and to avoid observing the death publicly. But in Chak-477, as on Beeston Hill, cooperation with the police is scant. One officer explained to *The Daily Mail* that "people in the area have accepted his grave as a shrine of a big saint."[67]

Nobody remains to extol the departed at the lonely graveyard on the peak of Beeston Hill, where "the rude forefathers of the hamlet sleep."[68] The cemetery sits in disrepair, weeds having overgrown every plot without exception. Gravestones lie like fallen soldiers. The local primary school's head teacher, keen to defend Beeston Hill against all comers, claims that government officials toppled the headstones because the plots were untended. I was unable to verify the existence of a government program for overturning gravestones. Though a slim majority of headstones remain standing, all the plots are untended. No, these defeats are the arbitrary work of vandals loose among the spirits, men toking or shooting-up, unrepentant wards of the Mullah Boys perhaps, exacting an enduring revenge against the departed town fathers.

The stones bear crosses and Irish names like Mulveany, Butler, Morgan, and Atkinson. In their hundreds not a single one marks a death after 1974. This graveyard is itself dead. The untended plots and the overturned headstones mark a demise and an exodus, signs that a community once inhabiting Beeston moved out as another, of a different faith, moved in. Thomas and Miriam Commersol left behind among the weeds an imposing and intact gravestone, proclaiming "In the midst of life we are in Death," and "We plan but God decides," the somber certainty of a Christian Beeston, sentiments oddly concordant with today's Friday prayers in Beeston Hill's three mosques.

DESH PARDESH

If Beeston Hill's Mirpuris erect ghostly vacation homes and fill graves in Kashmir, they create in English neighborhoods a "home away from home"—in Urdu they call it *desh pardesh*. If Mirpur's mansions and tombs are conspicuous symbols of absence, in Britain desh pardesh is a present and intact way of life . . . and death.

Muslim rules of *purdah* (literally, a veil or screen) are enforced especially sternly in Mirpur where women are banned from all public places including the bazaar. That means the men do the shopping in Mirpur. When traveling outside the village, to visit kin or a shrine, women wear a *burka* from whose hood two strips of cloth can be lowered to cover the face. But V. S. Khan found in Bradford in the 1970s that "Mirpuri women are subject to a stricter form of *purdah* . . . than in the home village," a phenomenon that ran "contrary to the frequent assumption that traditional forms of behavior are bound to modify and become more westernized in Britain."[69] Two decades later Alison Shaw noted how "despite the very different physical layout" strict Muslim rules for the seclusion of women "continue to be very important in almost all east Oxford Pakistani homes." When male visitors arrive and a male is home, the visitor is detained at the door while the women of the household, "modestly adjusting their *dupattas* [scarves] over their heads, leave the front room and retreat to the backroom or kitchen with requests for food and tea for the guests."[70] That is precisely my reception when visiting Pakistani and Bangladeshi homes in East London and Birmingham. And that is how the home of Gultasab, Mohammed Sidique Khan's brother, received the British journalist Shiv Malik on Beeston Hill.[71]

Shaw delineates how the physical layout of a British Pakistani home is made to resemble, insofar as possible, the layout of a home in a Punjab or Mirpur village.[72] Thus, Pakistanis and Bangladeshis, on moving into a Beeston Hill back-to-back, will turn the downstairs of a "one-on-one" into a sitting room for guests while sleeping the entire family in the one room upstairs, just as Shaw found in east Oxford.[73] The architectural revolution is not only physical but also spiritual. As Pnina Werbner points out, in building "close-knit social networks," the families "reconstitute[d] a moral community and transform[ed] the space, the house, the neighborhood, and the city in which they live, into a moral space" where the customs of the village would be perpetuated and deepened.[74]

The central event in the life of the British Pakistani community, the wedding, is likewise stamped with the character of the village and the clan. Marriage is an alliance between families rather than individuals, and the wedding is the premium event that immigrants stage locally.[75] Female guests don their costliest silks and their golden jewels. "The bride herself literally glitters with gold and embroidered sequins from head to foot."[76]

The exchange of nuptials is only the climax of a train of "customary transactional activity" occurring throughout the wedding cycle, an extensive period of gift exchange that serves to repay accumulated debts and to initiate new ones. That is because the wedding ceremony is the very "nexus of the Punjabi Muslim gift economy," the commencement and culmination of all reciprocity. The exchange of gifts expands the network of people tied to each other by mutual liabilities.[77] Gifts are the prime index of social status and these reciprocal marriage-related transactions often the wonder of the attendant congregation.[78] The prodigality of the imported nuptial celebration, seemingly so contrary to the frugality that marks the ordinary course of British Muslim life, reflects the crucial role of marriage in articulating social and political standing. These rituals may strike native Britons, whose ancient tribes have been whittled down over centuries to nuclear families, as all the more bizarre when they learn that the second-generation bride and groom are customarily cousins.

Migration, cousin marriage, seclusion of women, the return of remains . . . these practices occur not in isolation but as part of a way of life, a culture. They are the threads of a fabric that binds the British Pakistani in general, and the Mirpuri in particular, to his family place of origin. In marriage and death, and everywhere in between, the homeland and family, kith and kin, imprint themselves in exceptionally powerful ways. To turn against any one of them, as the Mullah Boys did when they conducted, as we will see in chapter 11, wedding ceremonies unauthorized by their elders, was to revolt against an entire social system imported from Pakistan.

In the Bradford Mirpuri community studied by V. S. Khan in the 1970s, the norms and institutions of village life remained "the guiding principles of daily life."[79] This holds true by and large today. Shaw observed a generation later that most Oxford Pakistanis had a number of close relatives living nearby.[80] She also observed that the kin- and village-based social structure established during early settlement had allowed the migrants' families back in Pakistan to control men's activities by arranging their marriages or by having his wife and children join the migrant.[81] That arrangement, she asserted, should be viewed not as merely a rejoinder to immigration regulations but as a fundamental part of the machinery for maintaining clan integrity and guaranteeing that a man continued to recognize his obligations to his kin.[82] The institutions of the Mirpuri village went along on the migrant journey in order to regulate behavior against the temptations of Western culture. That regulation was the immediate corollary of the arrival of women and children.[83] At the same time a British immigration policy that centered on family reunion cemented the control by the dead hand back home of its colony in Britain.

Izzat, honor and status back home, governs even those activities that appear to represent acclimatization to England and to the Protestant ethic. Shaw found that such seeming adaptations as moving to the suburbs or women undertaking paid work were "rooted in *biradari* values" and were actually enterprises for acquiring goods and status within the traditional framework.[84] What Werbner found regarding caste distinctions in Manchester is just as true for Beeston Hill: they are not simply "residual categories imported from Pakistan." But rather their viability and continued relevance for migrants are certified in marriage strategy and religious performance. Pakistanis' obedience to the imported hierarchy, she found, remains just as enveloping as it was back home and is registered in the riches sent home.[85]

Parsimony in Beeston Hill makes for extravagance in Mirpur. But the conspicuous consumption is not that of Thorsten Veblen's leisure class, nor is the thrift that of Max Weber's Puritans. To be sure, in both cases asceticism turns "with all its force against one thing: the spontaneous enjoyment of life and all it had to offer."[86] But labor and frugality on Beeston Hill serve not as Calvinist proof of "the state of grace" but for the high life in Mirpur. Neither the Puritans nor the Muslims wished "to impose mortification on the man of wealth," but one mandated "the use of his means for necessary and practical things" and the other for a prodigal affluence back home.[87]

Thrifty in their "home away from home," lavish in Mirpur, the British Muslims are not building the spiritual foundations of thrift or asceticism but rather family prestige to be paraded back home.[88] The devotion to biradari or clan status, to the tribal way, is what distinguishes izzat from the Protestant ethic. The impressive savings rate of Pakistani immigrants in England does not engender capitalist accumulation, as did the Protestant ethic; it builds the mansions that haunt Mirpur. It signals not grace in an afterworld but status (izzat) in these ghost towns.

CONVERSATION STOPPERS

From the top of Beeston Hill, you can make out the cranes on the office towers against the skyline. Today, among the Pakistanis, many of whom survive on welfare inside these rundown houses built by Victorian industry, live Poles. They have come to build the postindustrial skyscrapers of

downtown Leeds. They too send earnings home but, unlike their Mirpuri neighbors, their return home will not be mythical. Except for
Andrew, his mates, and the schoolteachers, only the Poles readily speak to
me. But they can usually only manage a few English phrases, only enough
to tell me that they have been here for just a few months and know
nothing of the late suicide bombers that continue to haunt Beeston Hill.

In odd contrast to the bedraggled antiquity of the Hill, a good many
of its back-to-backs sport satellite dishes. But these are less signs of modernization than of an intense connection to the past. Inside, the old-timers
from Mirpur are watching broadcasts in Urdu. Outside, beneath the post-
industrial antennas run preindustrial laundry lines. The juxtaposition offers a peek inside where old men, weary from a life of hard labor, tune in,
while their wives wash their clothes and their children chafe. The imple-
ments outside allow a glimpse of patriarchal priorities: satellite TV but no
washing machine. Outdoors, these women are covered in black cloth.
Their teenage sons hang on the corner, smoking and frowning at me.

Beeston Hill is not chatty. No one I approached, however circumspectly, would answer even the most rudimentary questions about its
most famous native sons. The head teacher at the Greenmount Primary
School claimed this was because reporters had depicted "the entire community as a nest of terrorists" after July 7.

But neither the locked silence nor the dismal isolation is entirely of
recent making. Tahir Abbas, a professor at Birmingham University, who
has written and edited several books about British Muslims, told me that
the resentment of the Asian communities in northern England "has a
long history dating back to the first assaults by racists a generation ago."
Beeston Hill, now three years free of packs of reporters, reminds me of
the shared, stony, and studied resentment I encountered as a community
organizer in strife-torn Boston a generation ago. In its white inner city I
advanced the romantic and detested mission of desegregation. In Beeston
I was finding my investigations even more quixotic and abominated.

At the Hamara Centre for Healthy Living where Sidique worked
with Beeston Hill's deprived youth, the colloquy ceases when I come
near to asking about their former colleague. I am ushered out the door
unceremoniously by a bald, bearded man with fierce eyebrows. Not
much friendlier was my reception at the Fish N' Chips that used to
belong to Tanweer's father. At noon the establishment is doing a steady
business. As I wait in line exchanging pleasantries with the server, in

walk two elderly bearded gentlemen in identical beige robes. They exchange greetings with my interlocutor in Urdu. He ceremoniously fetches from behind the counter a large plastic container bearing the name of the Huraira mosque that the robed men empty into a hefty sack displaying the same letters. The mosque on Hardy Street is a stone's throw away. There, the Mullah Boys had first established its "al Qaeda gym" before Sidique and his colleagues decamped in a now obscure dispute that we shall learn more about. The robed gentlemen tell me they are from Mirpur. Our chat is perfectly cordial until I ask if the establishment has "changed hands recently." Glances are exchanged all around the establishment and down again drops the drape of silence.

If my awkward transition was a conversation stopper, Scotland Yard ran into the same stony silence. Deputy Assistant Commissioner Peter Clarke, head of the Metropolitan Police's counterterrorist command, the dour officer heading the London bombing investigation, complained loudly and often about the lack of cooperation from Beeston: "I do understand that some of you will have real concerns about the consequences of telling us what you know. I also know that some of you have been actively dissuaded from speaking to us. Surely this must stop."[89]

Car burners in the Parisian banlieues were far more willing to talk to me about their exploits than Mirpuris on Beeston Hill were disposed even to acknowledge the day that now haunts them. The last time I met with such reticence was in Sandinista Nicaragua during the Contra war of the 1980s. But there, when prompted, people declaimed loudly in favor of *la Revolución,* if only through a protective veil of authorized clichés. To pierce it I learned to avoid the patois of the despised foreign revolutionary tourists, the "Sandalistas," and to refrain from questions about "la Revolución" and not to address my interlocutors as "*compañero.*" Living under an oppressive but politically correct dictatorship, Nicaraguans would divulge their private horror stories only after you had earned their "*confianza.*"[90]

On Beeston Hill such revelations were not to come even had I not been an American. Nazreen Suleaman, a Muslim woman from neighboring Sheffield who tried gamely to report on Sidique Khan for the BBC, told me that the Muslim community despised "the mainstream media." Shiv Malik rented a neighboring flat for three months but also found the silence impenetrable. Scotland Yard and the Yorkshire police could not assemble enough evidence to convince a London jury to convict Khan's surviving accomplices in 2008. In 2010 Shiv Malik of the

BBC remarked, "Even today, I don't know a single reporter who hadn't come away from that place maddened and broken by the silence."[91] Malik and his BBC team could not secure even background interviews thanks to "intimidation."[92] And the source of the fear was clear to Malik. It was the Mullah Boys, whom we will meet again in chapter 11, the same "Asian gang" that had coercively "de-briefed" Andrew, that took up the fight against drugs when the community elders threw up their hands, that warred with Anglo and Caribbean gangs and organized paintball expeditions to practice jihad, that married Muslims outside the family.

Halfway down the Hill, the steeple of a Victorian neo-Gothic church peers down from a corner of Tempest Road on the serried back-to-backs below. No one seems to know the name of this pious towering landmark. There's a police CCTV surveillance camera in operation, one of only twenty in the entire South Leeds area.[93] I search for some identifying plaque or tablet. I find only a large black garbage pail reading "Trinity Church." The building must be a Catholic relic from the days when the Irish were the immigrant folk on Beeston Hill, when coal was still mined here and the forges and engineering plants were still busy in Hunslet. Then I come upon the buzzers and nameplates: "42 Trenthnam St. flats 1–10." This cathedral, with its imposing steeple, has been converted into flats, the reason for its inscrutability. Another ghost. Did departed white Christian Beeston Hill also vacate it back in the 1970s?

As I look up from returning my dictaphone to my pocket I notice four young men in their late teens glaring at me, and one is beginning to make small menacing circles around me on a bicycle. "Excuse me, do you happen to know how long it has been since this church was in operation?" The bicycle approached: "How should I know? Anyway, you shouldn't be recording without people's permission."

"But I was only recording myself, not other people."

"I don't trust Americans," was the ominous reply.

"Oh, is that right? And where are you from?"

"I'm from Allah," he sneered, pointing to the darkening sky with a look of menace. It was as close as I was able to get to Sidique Khan's Mullah Boys.

COUSINS

We have seen how Muslims came to Beeston Hill and yet stayed home. They performed that feat in Walthamstow and Tower Hamlets in East London, in Ward End and Sparkbrook in Birmingham, in Manchester and Luton, in Bradford and Dewsbury and the other mill towns of West Yorkshire that surround Beeston. Across Islamic Britannia, remittances and cadavers were translated to Punjab and Kashmir, the *izzat* and authority of the clan were honored, women covered themselves, and eligible bachelors were told to marry their cousins back home. However, a portion of the latter refused to comply, and among them were the Mullah Boys of Beeston Hill. These outliers, Romeos flouting fathers and clans, will be not heroes but villains in our drama.

But before we turn to the unfolding of this catastrophe, we will look at the incidence and impact of the "feat" I just alluded to and that I described in the previous chapter. How did British Muslims, so powerfully linked to home, fare in the years before the London bombings? How well did they register on social-economic indices regarding income, employment, education, and housing? The results will tell us much not only about the condition and standing of British Muslims but also about the "feat."

UNEMPLOYMENT, INCOME, AND ECONOMIC ACTIVITY

In 2002 13 percent of Muslims were unemployed compared to 5 percent of the general population.[1] Moreover, a British government–sponsored survey by four highly respected and independent scholars found the unemployment rates of British Muslims to be the highest of any faith community based on figures from the 2001 census.[2] Thus, it is hardly surprising that when looking at the proportion of those economically active in the same age group, Muslims performed more poorly than any other faith community. Only 50 percent of Muslims were economically active versus 67 percent of all residents and 71 percent of Hindus and 70 percent of Sikhs.[3] Much of the disparity was due to the low Muslim female participation in the workforce, comprising only half that of other faith communities and of natives.[4]

Muslims also showed the lowest proportion of men in white-collar professions and the highest percentage of men working in semiskilled and unskilled occupations at 33.7 percent versus 17.7 percent of Hindus.[5] According to data from the Office for National Statistics, in 2002 one in ten Muslim men worked as a taxi driver, cab driver, or chauffeur. That percentage was much higher than for any other faith group.[6] Ethnic groups have received more scrutiny than faith communities. A study performed by two scholars at the University of Leeds in conjunction with the Office of the Deputy Prime Minister found income for Pakistani and Bangladeshi households to lag behind Indians and blacks as well as whites.[7]

EDUCATION

Muslims also trailed in educational achievement. The 2001 census showed that 41 percent of Muslims over the age of fifteen were without a high school diploma. For Sikhs the figure was 32 percent, for Hindus 26 percent, and for all other faith communities it was 30 percent.[8] Young Muslims in inner-city London fared even worse. Thirty-seven percent of Muslims between the ages of sixteen and twenty-four failed in this zone to complete high school versus 25 percent of their neighbors.[9] In London, at 33 percent, Pakistanis and Bangladeshis were the ethnic groups least likely to have education beyond high school (such as vocational or other courses).[10] In December 1991 schools in Bradford, the "Islamabad of Britain," a twenty-minute ride from Leeds, scored last overall when seven-year-olds were tested for English, science, and math.[11]

HOUSING

The Leeds University study found that Pakistanis and Bangladeshis, at 35 percent, were most likely to reside in poor housing and living conditions compared to 18.6 percent of Indians, 13.7 percent of whites, and 22.9 percent of blacks.[12] Forty percent of Muslims lived in overcrowded homes, compared to 20 percent of Sikhs and 30 percent of Hindus and the national average of 10 percent.[13] The government study found that, in general, Hindus tend to live in affluent areas, Sikhs in middle-class areas, and Muslims in poor areas; Muslims recorded the highest percentage of the population living in public housing.[14]

Residential clustering, or the concentration of minorities in enclaves, is an illustrative indicator of a low level of assimilation. Jane Lakey found that 51 percent of Pakistanis and 42 percent of Bangladeshis would prefer to live in an area where people from their own ethnic groups were in the majority.[15] When the 2006 study looked at ten urban areas with at least one thousand members of the named religious groups, Muslims topped the "Index of Segregation" at 54 (with 0 meaning there was no segregation and 100 at total segregation); Sikhs were at 48, and Hindus at 38.[16]

The government study illustrated both the clustering of Muslims in enclaves and the official mind-set that helped put them there. In the words of the study,

> the South Asian populations map sufficiently well onto the religious groups to allow us to suggest that the South Asian Muslims, Hindus, and Sikhs were following a pluralist rather than an assimilationist pattern. This is to say that their residential patterns will allow them to create the critical mass necessary to maintain their institutional completeness, religious, social and cultural values rather than being absorbed into the wider society through dispersal.[17]

In general, according to the government review,

> Hindus, Sikhs, and Muslims are found in large numbers in only a limited number of the English regions and . . . within them, they are concentrated into a small number of large cities. The regional distribution of the larger ethnic groups . . . showed substantial

stability in their settlement patterns between the 1960s and the 2000s with growth concentrated in and at the edges of existing areas.[18]

These results are hardly surprising given the patterns of discrimination in the indigenous population and the insular tendencies of South Asian immigrants. But host policies and mind-sets cannot escape blame; especially those that, with all good will and high-mindedness, allowed Britain, as the civil rights activist Trevor Phillips memorably phrased it, to "sleepwalk into segregation."[19] Even in the context of the formidable disparity in outcomes between Britain's native majority and its South Asian minority, the Muslim performance within the South Asian minority demands attention.

The surveys showing that Pakistani (and Bangladeshi) Muslims fared poorest of all ethnic groups in Britain (in terms of income, employment, education, housing, and integration) confirmed earlier investigations.[20] But why do Pakistanis (and Bangladeshis) register so singularly low on social indicators? Though both racism and Islamophobia figure in the equation, neither offers a satisfactory explanation. Racial prejudice should affect Hindus and Sikhs, not just Pakistanis and Bangladeshis. On the other hand, there is nothing to suggest that indigenous racists differentiated between South Asians who were Muslims and those who were Sikhs or Hindus—all were commonly called "Pakis." To attribute these differences to "Islamophobia," an animus directed against Pakistanis and Bangladeshis but not Sikhs and Hindus, is to suppose a measure of nuanced differentiation hard to square with the purblind bigotry of Islamophobes.

BALLARD'S ANTHROPOLOGY

The Manchester University anthropologist Roger Ballard is anything but an Islamophobe. Yet his findings on the cultural patterns of Punjabi Hindus, Muslims, and Sikhs must be classified as politically incorrect. In one investigation he compared Sikhs and Muslims from the Punjab with Sikhs from Jullundur in India and Muslims from Mirpur. The entire greater Punjab, where up to three-fourths of British South Asian families originate, bears "strong social, cultural and linguistic commonalities."[21]

The region is home to substantial communities of Muslims, Hindus, and Sikhs. Muslims live almost exclusively in the Pakistani half of the greater Punjab (including Pakistan-administered Kashmir, of which Mirpur forms a part) while Sikhs and Hindus live largely in the Indian Punjab, with Sikhs in the majority. As we have seen, Mirpuris are hardly an unrepresentative sample of British Pakistanis. The same goes for Jullunduris when it comes to Sikhs. For as Ballard states, "The great majority of British Punjabis can . . . trace their roots . . . either to the Jullundur Doab or to the Mirpur district in Azad Kashmir," and "indeed as many as three quarters of British Punjabis [themselves three-quarters of British South Asians] may well be either Jullunduris or Mirpuris" in origin.[22]

If these two groups as Punjabis share occupational, cultural, and linguistic markers, their fates in England, as we just saw, diverge sharply. That led Ballard to look more closely at their different Punjabi starting points. Both communities were drawn from small peasant farmers, but India's Punjab has thrived and Jullundur has become exceptionally affluent. Meanwhile, Mirpur, as we have seen, has stagnated. Consequently, "Jullunduris were much more likely to possess marketable craft and business skills, and also to be literate, at least in Punjabi, and sometimes in English too."[23] In Britain their superior skill-sets and educational levels helped Sikhs attain preferable jobs, start their own businesses, move into the suburbs, whose better schools enabled their children to perform competitively with other middle-class Britons. On the other hand, British Mirpuris stayed largely in unskilled jobs in engineering plants, textile mills, take-out counters, and taxi ranks and in slums like Beeston Hill where they often reared children with a limited grasp of English and knowledge of the world and a low level of academic achievement, like those we met at the Stratford Street Mosque in the prologue. Their poor performances in the job market and schools, their residential clustering, and their lack of English earned Mirpuris, Ballard says, "a reputation for 'backwardness' amongst their fellow South Asian settlers."[24]

However, Ballard found that the material disparity of starting points did not "provide a *sufficient* basis for understanding all the dimensions of difference"—in particular why Mirpuri migrants "in common with most other Muslims . . . tend to sustain much tighter and more inward-looking social networks." He forthrightly asks whether "cultural—and or specifically religious—variables [could] be a partial determinant of such differences."[25]

Ballard entered this heretical path of inquiry mindful of committing "Orientalism," a charge that has shadowed scholarly investigation of Islam and the Greater Middle East since Edward Said's 1978 work by that name. Since then, as Jerrold Green has observed, "the mere recognition that cultural factors matter" has led "their more dogmatic colleagues" to brand "specialists as anti-scientific heretics."[26] To adduce culture as an explanatory factor was to reduce Muslims, in Stanley Kurtz's formulation, to "exotic and implicitly irrational 'Others,' over whom we, supposedly-more-rational Westerners, have an unspoken right to rule."[27]

So Ballard was careful to steer clear of what he calls "unhelpful and unilluminating," "essentialist" stereotypes of Islam as "more 'authoritarian,' and less 'open-minded,' than either Hinduism or Sikhism." He limited himself to the question of "just how difference has been precipitated."[28] In keeping to this minimalist agenda, Ballard largely skirts a question that Kurtz broaches: to what extent were the initial economic discrepancies between Mirpur and Jullundur "themselves . . . rooted in cultural differences?[29] Ballard focuses not on how Mirpur and Jullundur got that way, but on three conventions that differentiate Mirpuris from Jullunduris: mortuary rites, gender rules, and marriage arrangements.

Muslims bury their dead; Sikhs and Hindus cremate the bodies. Alone among these groups, Muslims enforce the seclusion of women. Sikh and Hindu women move circumspectly around the village to shop or to work in the fields. Punjabi Sikhs and Hindus are barred from marrying their close kin, while Mirpuri Muslims are not only permitted but also encouraged to do so. As arcane as these differences may appear, Ballard argues that, taken together, they "have had . . . a very substantial differential impact on both the character of kinship structures in Punjab and on processes of overseas migration."[30] Of these, most resonant in our story is the one on which Ballard focuses: cousin marriage.[31]

Ballard starts by noting that many basic kinship conventions in the Punjab are uniform. Arranged marriages are standard and their guiding principles are "patrilineal descent and patri-virilocal residence"—that is, descent is through the male line with a wedded couple taking up residence with the groom's father's family, or *ghar*. The Punjabi household typically holds a father, his sons, and his sons' sons, together with their wives and unmarried daughters, and this extended family "is a strongly corporate group" in which members live communally under the same roof and jointly exploit their common property.[32]

But one practice sharply sets off Punjab's Muslims. Punjabi Sikhs and Hindus marry outside the family, the Muslims inside; Ballard's Jullunduris are exogamous; his Mirpuris endogamous. Punjabi Hindus and Sikhs do not marry within the extended family.[33] A Sikh or Hindu bride moves out of the village to join her husband's family. On the other hand, in Muslim law marriage is restricted only by the incest taboo proclaimed in Leviticus (18:7–18) and echoed in the Qur'an (3:23), excluding as spouses only parents, siblings and parents' siblings (parents, brothers, sisters, uncles, and aunts). Ballard believes that "conversion to Islam . . . had a dramatic impact" on Muslims in the Punjab. They "not only abandoned clan exogamy but adopted an active *preference* for cousin-marriage."[34]

In this they took up a practice rare in the West, and banned in thirty-nine U.S. states, but very widespread in the Muslim world, especially in the Middle East and Pakistan. Consanguinity rates in most Middle Eastern countries are the highest in the world, ranging from 30 to over 50 percent as in parts of Saudi Arabia and Yemen. Pakistani rates are similar to those in Saudi Arabia.[35] In the Asian subcontinent, consanguinity ranges three times higher in Muslim compared to Hindu and Sikh areas. The most authoritative study found 46.8 percent of consanguinity in marriages in eight Punjabi cities.[36] Another study found that "the highest rates of consanguineous marriage have been associated with low socioeconomic status, illiteracy, and rural residence."[37]

Yet there is reason to suppose that cousin marriage emerges from tribal practice more than religious edict. Though Muhammad took his cousin Zaybnab as one of his brides and married his daughter Fatima to her cousin, the Qur'an nowhere prescribes cousin marriage.[38] Kinship is the basic structural principle of organizing tribal society based on plant and animal domestication—the stage of human social development that follows hunter-gathering bands and precedes the formation of rudimentary and then modern states.[39]

Whatever motives lay at the historical root of Muslim consanguineous marriage, a recent study found that in twentieth-century Pakistan the incentive for clan endogamy was pride; the practice implied the family was desirable and therefore of high social standing.[40] Shaw explains that to be considered a worthy man one must have a reputation for honoring obligations to this kin. Consanguineous marriage is a clear and important fulfillment of this obligation.[41]

The Urdu word for such pride, for the concern with family status is, of course, *izzat*—better rendered as honor or respect, or "face," as in "not to lose face." Izzat, and specifically a concern with family honor or status, lies at the heart of other mysteries associated with the "feat" of simultaneously leaving and staying—ranging from lavish uninhabited Mirpuri houses to honor killings in Birmingham. As for cousin marriage, as Ballard points out, brothers and sisters *expect* their children to be given that option, so much so that rejection "causes great offense."[42]

European aristocratic and royal families made use of cross-cousin marriages to cement political alliances, but Muslim cousin marriage generally eschews such alliances and, as Ballard suggests, aims instead to preserve an impermeable and exclusive arrangement of marrying kin. To be sure, marriage cannot invariably join close kin—a consanguineous spouse of suitable age and gender may not be available. But Ballard estimates that at least 60 percent of all Mirpuri marriages are contracted between first cousins,[43] and a very substantial proportion of the remainder is contracted between slightly more distant kin.[44]

On marrying her cousin, a Mirpuri bride, rather than relocating to another village and moving in with a different family, simply moves into the home of a beloved aunt, who becomes her mother-in-law. That means that kinship networks in Mirpur are less extensive than those in Jullundur, and relationships among the former are thus more encompassing.[45] This helps to explain why the "starting points" in Mirpur and Jullundur, of Punjabi Muslims and Sikhs, are so different. Moreover, as we are about to see, the impact of cousin marriage is every bit as dramatic when it comes to the "ending points" in Britain. And the mother-in-law continues to rule the roost in Britain. Shaw was told by many Pakistani women in Oxford "that the personality of the mother-in-law is more important in marriage than what the husband is like, for she will influence her son's attitude to his wife."[46]

The aunt/mother-in-law nexus unravels another mystery. Why did Sikh and Hindu wives and children follow migrant heads of household to England promptly, as early as the late 1950s, while Muslim women and children were delayed more than a decade? Though marrying outside of her family and thus outside of her village, a Hindu or Sikh bride does not establish a new autonomous household, as she would in Western marriage. Instead the Hindu or Sikh bride removes to her husband's family home where she may bridle under the rule of her mother-in-law.

As a result the initial years of married life for a Hindu or Sikh bride are notoriously stressful.[47] But when marrying her cousin, the Mirpuri bride leaves neither the village nor her relatives. Her mother-in-law has been her cherished aunt since infancy, and failing that, other kinswomen invariably reside nearby.[48] Contented at home, Muslim women were loath to leave the surroundings they had known all their lives to follow their migrant husbands to tramontane England. As late as the 1971 census, a full decade after the rush to "beat the ban," less than a quarter of British Pakistanis were women.[49] In 1979 Anwar related that "many Mirpuris" told him that "they would not bring over their wives and young children if they were given the surety that they [the kin] would never lose the right of entry to this country."[50] On the other hand, Sikh and Hindu women often were eager to get out from under the tutelage of an alien mother-in-law. That gave Jullunduri women a huge head start in adjusting to English life and language.

But for Mirpuris the opposite was the case. Phillip Lewis showed that in 1990, a good generation after the first influx of Asians, in Bradford, a Midlands community with a high proportion of Mirpuris, Muslim residential zones were the rule. There, Muslim communities lived in a relatively self-contained world of businesses and institutions, religious and cultural, which they created to service their communal needs. The concentration of Muslim voters had already been translated by British communal politics into "a sizable number of local councilors."[51] In Britain, as a consequence of the tradition of decentralization and "indirect rule," it is local government that dispenses the benefits of the welfare state: housing, education, welfare, and a host of other public benefits. The hence highly coveted local council seats became the main site of identity politics, or what the British call "race politics." Minorities became entrenched in school boards, housing associations, and local government, both among elected officials and as staff.[52] Whole neighborhoods in Northern, Midlands, and West Yorkshire cities such as Birmingham, Manchester, and Leeds became conspicuous examples. Towns like Bradford or Dewsbury, as Barbara Metcalf observed, the latter looked "more like Pakistan than does Pakistan itself."[53] In 1981 the Bradford City Council referred to "settlement by tiptoe," signifying that, as Lewis glossed the term, "a dual society had emerged whose members looked outward to mainstream British society for jobs, schools and services, but who still looked inward in their desire to preserve their traditional culture, religion and language."[54] Urdu weeklies and monthlies and radio stations proliferated. Many children found work in Asian businesses: halal butcheries, producers of audio and videocassettes in Urdu, goldsmith and jewelry specialists, and clothing retailers.[55] And if British Muslims were occasionally obliged to look outward for jobs, schools, and services, they still looked inward to preserve their traditions, religion, and language. The two perspectives would prove, in some cases, hard to reconcile.

Like *purdah* (the veiling and seclusion of women) and the sending of remains home to be buried, cousin marriage has lingered among British Pakistanis and has even grown. A study of British Pakistani mothers in the postnatal wards of two West Yorkshire hospitals in the 1980s suggested an accelerating rate of consanguineous marriage that contrasted with the decreasing rates observed in other countries like Japan.[56] In 1990, Pnina Werbner found recorded in Manchester genealogies a very high rate of first- and second-cousin marriage.[57] Among Pakistanis in Oxford a decade later Shaw's analysis of the marriages of the sons and daughters of twenty-four first-generation couples showed 76 percent of the marriages were with kin: 59 percent with cousins and 17 percent with other relatives.[58] She concluded that "if you are born into an east Oxford Pakistani family, then it is very likely that the person you will marry and the people with whom you will have life-long kinship obligations will be relatives from the extended family, *biradari,* or caste."[59]

Ballard concludes that Muslim singularity in purdah, mortuary rites, and marriage rules "all reinforce the same tendency." Thanks to their aggregate impact, Muslim kinship networks not only inhibit the physical and social mobility of Muslim women but tend to be "tighter and focused more locally than those of Sikhs and Hindus."[60] Moreover, none of these practices represent isolated or exceptional occasions but are part and parcel of a familial and lifelong structure that ties the British Pakistani in general, and the Mirpuri in particular, to the family's place of origin and hinders adjustment to Britain. In marriage, death, and everything in between, the homeland and family, kith and kin, imprint themselves on British Mirpuris in a singularly profound way.

This influence begins in migration. As we have seen, the migrant sets off with the blessing, the funding, and the mission of his extended family. He will travel four thousand miles from home, but he settles and works among kinsmen and townsmen. Moreover, his objective is not to secure personal advantage but to fulfill his fundamental obligation as a member of his family—to make the utmost contribution to the shared resources of the group. He becomes not so much a member of British society as a colonial of his clan and village.

As the surveys previously reviewed showed, these are not happy circumstances for advancement in new surroundings. Indeed, these circumstances take us far toward explaining the poor economic, social, and educational performances of Pakistanis when compared with Hindus and Sikhs. The observance of purdah in itself partly explains Pakistanis' low rate of economic activity. Furthermore, cousin marriage generally means the importation of spouses unfamiliar with England or English whereas young Hindus and Sikhs are far freer to marry spouses who will introduce them to British social and economic networks. In contrast, as Ballard notes, Mirpuri relatives living in England will not fail to remind their kinsmen there of the family obligation of cousin marriage. And this expectation will be redoubled by the immigrant's relative prosperity, deepening the obligation to relatives back home.[61]

These pressures are hard to resist. Aside from their loyalty to and affection for their relatives in the homeland, the migrants are aware that the rejection of marriage offers from their relatives will certainly be felt as dishonorable, demeaning, and disgraceful. It means rupturing the chain of mutual obligation and reciprocity, the *lena dena* of the gift exchange society. As a consequence, "slighted kinsfolk may well take every opportunity to blacken their name"—a major sanction in a society where izzat is so crucial.

If, upon arrival in England, the ties of the Sikhs to Jullunduri begin to attenuate and those to Britain to thicken, for Muslims insular, familial, and homeland social networks and moral codes work to set their community apart from the surrounding British culture. Sikhs left manual jobs to start businesses and move to the suburbs, while Mirpuris continue to work the night shift, to live in the inner city, and to return home for long vacations and lavish weddings. Mirpuri wives, as we have seen, arrive in England later than their Sikh and Hindu counterparts, thus delaying or even waylaying the process of learning English and adjusting to British culture. As a consequence, whereas the Sikh children learn English from their neighbors, many Mirpuri children grow up with parents who speak little or no English, and many attend schools dominated by Punjabi speakers like themselves, with far less opportunity to learn fluent English from direct contact with native English speakers. On top of that, their time after school may be spent, as with the children we met outside of Beeston's Stratford Street mosque, memorizing Arabic sounds instead of capering on English playgrounds. "No wonder then, that the many Mirpuri (and Bangladeshi) children who grow up in such circumstances, and who receive little or no relevant educational assistance to enhance their linguistic competence, tend to fare much less well in examinations than do their Sikh counterparts."[62]

Schools and children will prove strong motifs in the story of Sidique Khan's radicalization. The data suggest that prevailing cousin marriage serves, in Stanley Kurtz's words, to "seal off" British Muslims from the larger society. Kurtz's commentaries on Roger Ballard's analysis of Mirpuri cousin marriage were titled "Marriage and the Terror War."[63] But is *terrorism* characteristic of those who marry their cousins? What would Kurtz make of a Sidique Khan, a terrorist who in a mixed school had more white friends than Pakistanis and who defied family authority in refusing to wed his cousin, and instead exchanged vows with his Indian Deobandi sweetheart even as he was embracing jihad? But before we recount the story of Sidique's forbidden passions, we must pass through "Londonistan," just as he did on his fateful pilgrimage toward his feat of fanaticism.

THE LORDS OF
LONDONISTAN

The anxious prince had heard the cannon long,
And from that length of time dire omens drew
Of English overmatch'd. . . .
He sees the dire contagion spread so fast . . .
And therefore must unwillingly lay waste
That country. . . .

—John Dryden, "Annus Mirabilis"

During the early 1990s, London hosted and subsidized extremist preachers holding forth in mosques, cultural centers, bookstores, assemblies, and colloquia as well as in journals, magazines, and newspapers. Under what the extremists called "a covenant of security," security officials allowed them to incite freely and to preach homophobia, anti-Semitism, and subversion if they refrained from terrorist acts inside Britain. After they learned that Rachid Ramda of the Algerian Groupe Islamique Armé (GIA) had, from London, funded Khaled Kelkal's terror attacks in France, French security officials devised the sobriquet "Londonistan."[1] This chapter will trace the evolution of Londonistan from a traditional haven for dissenters into a terror powder keg.

We will focus on four extremist preachers, the "lords of Londonistan," who begot this metamorphosis:

- Abu Qatada, who inspired the 9/11 pilots and who was, according to the United Nations Security Council, "al-Qaeda's spiritual ambassador to Europe"[2]

- One of Qatada's many disciples, Abu Hamza, the one-eyed demagogue who presided over London's most prominent radical mosque at Finsbury Park

- Abdullah el Faisal, the Jamaican convert who tutored Richard Reid, the shoe bomber; Zacarias Moussaoui, "the twentieth hijacker"; Umar Farouk Abdulmutallab, the underwear bomber; and one of the Beeston bombers

- Omar Bakri, whose party established an underground railroad to Pakistan for second-generation British Muslim suicide bombers

Yet these men were important less for hands-on assistance than for creating an ideological atmosphere, a theological justification and a political narrative, for extreme action that easily reached Beeston. All four were immigrants, all became recipients of generous welfare benefits, and all were well known to, when not actually informing for, British security services.

ANNUS MIRABILIS

In 1989, when repudiation of totalitarianism shook the Soviet empire, tore down the Berlin Wall, and filled Beijing's Tiananmen Square, Britain had an uprising of its own. Salman Rushdie's abstruse, semiautobiographical, postmodern fable of British Muslim life, *The Satanic Verses,* became the target of furious demands to ban it, as if secular England were obliged to respect some ancient vestige of Sharia law. The public book burnings, the bookstore fire bombings, and the assassination bounties were the first indications to many native Britons that the importation of Muslim families, the self-segregation of their communities, and the indulgence of their prejudices might entail shocking and pernicious consequences.

The Rushdie Affair temporarily united Shia with Sunni and the folk Islam of the Barelvi (shocked by Rushdie's "insult to the Prophet") with the fundamentalist Deobandi. Few of these constituents were inclined to or perhaps even capable of distinguishing art from propaganda, fiction from documentary, and religion from politics.

The reaction to the Rushdie Affair was not homogeneous among native Britons. There was an unprecedented questioning of multiculturalism by one of its champions, Roy Jenkins, who, as Labor Home Secretary in 1966, had cast aside assimilation in favor of "cultural diversity."[3] Now in 1989 he would dare to suggest that "we might have been more cautious about allowing the creation in the 1950s of substantial Muslim communities here."[4] On the other hand, sections of the Labor Party, especially those dependent on the Muslim vote, sided with the Rushdie protestors. Jack Straw, as its education spokesman, used the controversy to commit the party to Muslim demands for single-sex education and state-financed Muslim schools.[5]

Britain was confused. How was its hallowed allegiance to free speech to partner with its equally proud and long-standing devotion to communalism? And where did the two attachments stand with respect to another fundamental value—the rule of law? How were these ideals to be translated into immigration policy? Were dissenters welcome even if they fomented terror in their countries of origin? Was there no distinction between free speech and hate speech?

It was also "a confusing time to be a young Muslim in Britain," in the words of a Muslim journalist covering an April 1990 conference of Barelvi youth convened in Bradford to weigh the future of the second generation.

> Responding to the Rushdie Affair, Muslim cries for unity and renewal of an Islamic identity, has exposed disunity and the fractured intellectual tradition of a religion transported from several different countries. Several of the younger delegates said the Muslim leadership in Britain was bankrupt of ideas. But it is the difficulty of living a religious life in a secular society which should be addressed . . . [instead] elders insist on fighting the battle of Pakistan in Bradford. There is a communication gap between the elders and the young. . . . The Koran says we are caretakers of the world. We should be involved in Green politics. We are not taking part in our host country enough.[6]

A lot was being asked of Islam: preservation of its fundamentals, guidance in adapting to a secular society, progressive politics. This was a tall order for the typical *imam* imported from Pakistan who often could not even speak the tongue of his young congregants.

Young Muslims saw this importation as an affront to the needs of the British-born members of the community. The latter's needs were pedagogical and ministerial as well as linguistic. Qur'an schools held in mosques like the one on Stratford Street on Beeston Hill were unappealing to children used to the variety of teaching methods in state schools. Postmigrants viewed only a handful of mosques as "providing programs specifically for them."[7]

At state-sponsored Muslim supplementary schools, teachers were brutally authoritarian. Sometimes the religion was literally beaten into the students. The Bradford Council for Mosque (Britain's premier first-generation Muslim organization), for example, encouraged pedagogues to strike their students with canes, despite the state ban on corporal punishment.[8] As a consequence of such conditions and practices, first-generation elders were discovering that their traditional Islam often did not resonate with their children.[9] Where would young Muslims turn instead?

To the music scene? By the early 1990s Bradford featured several Asian bands whose live performances were more like political rallies than concerts. Muslim youth, who in other times would be called avant-garde, were striking out on their own, forging an adversarial synthesis between their religion and their new home. An Urdu daily newspaper produced in London featured a Muslim band with lyrics praising Qur'anic scriptures and Asian culture while condemning the West's oppression of Muslims.[10] A shadow of dire things to come, but at this point all apparently innocent and joyful, if highly politicized. This was a fusion that would become potent: an anti-Western yet modern message, breaking ranks with the older generation but remaining within a fundamentalist framework. The name of the group? Fun-da-Mental.

These signs of second-generation alienation had Muslim authorities worried. Islamic thinkers were faced with the difficult task of translating "a residual Muslim identity into a self-conscious Islamic identity."[11] How much of traditional South Asian religiosity was accessible, relevant, and conveyable to youngsters in Bradford or Beeston? And who was even trusted and respected enough by young Muslims to preside over such a transmission?

According to Elizabeth Scantlebury, a significant number of young Muslims were then "rejecting a religio-ethnic identity in favor of a search for 'True Islam.'"[12] The door was wide open for an authority from the Muslim world, an Outsider, preferably an Arab, but one who could speak persuasively in English, to a second generation already rejecting the institutions that their parents struggled to implant in Britain. Young Muslims were looking for something different, and the lords of Londonistan would create a baleful alternative, with an inadvertent assist from British policymakers. These Outsiders could speak English and could negotiate contemporary life, even while preaching a fundamentalism more austere than the Deobandis. They could offer modern solutions for postmigrant Muslim predicaments and yet could present themselves as bearers of ancient Islamic authority.

A comprehensive history of the British second generation's radical Islamic movement has to begin in the early eighties with the amorphous study circles that formed among college students in the wake of the Iranian revolution and the Afghan jihad.[13] Omar Bakri, one of our four lords of Londonistan, took a lead here as an Islamist party-builder. The first sign in the mainstream press of these things came also in 1989, as communism toppled in Moscow and infidel books burned in London. An August *Guardian* account of a meeting conducted by Bakri's Hizb ut-Tahrir (the Party of Liberation) in Walthamstow, East London, reported that "whereas 'older generations of Muslims . . . continue to be mainly concerned with worship, the young have become more interested in Islam as an ideology and a way of life.'"[14] The *Guardian* did not appear worried, but Bakri was creating in the second generation a British branch of a party based on radical Islamist ideology and on Leninist organizational principles.

Omar Bakri Mohammed, who would become known in the British media as "the Tottenham Ayatollah," was born in 1958 in Aleppo where he joined the Syrian Muslim Brotherhood at fifteen. In 1977, after a failed Islamist revolt against the secular government of Hafaz Assad, he fled to Beirut where he became a member of Hizb ut-Tahrir (HT). Bakri studied at Sharia University in Damascus and at the prestigious al-Azhar University in Egypt, where he clashed with his professors over his activism. He then moved to Mecca where, with the aid of a Saudi royal, he established an HT cell.[15] He settled in Britain in 1986 and formed the British HT subsidiary from a handful of seasoned activists who had found refuge in London, having been banished from various parts of the Arab world as a result of their activities.[16]

Hizb ut–Tahrir had been launched in Jordan in 1952 by Taqiuddin al-Nabhani, a Palestinian judge dissatisfied with the Muslim Brotherhood.[17] Nabhani was inspired by the Syrian Baath Party's dream of a unified nation based on Arab socialism, but in this case the unification would transcend ethnic and regional boundaries and unite the entire Muslim world, the *ummah,* in a modern Islamic Caliphate or dominion.[18] Like the Baath, Nabhani's new Islamist party replicated Marxist Leninism in its theory of party development, organizational structure, cadre selection, discipline, work methods, outreach, and its use of front organizations.[19] HT was a "democratic centralist" organization. Clandestine members in separate cells had no knowledge of one another but were connected hierarchically. The disciplined cadre inhabited a triple-decked structure whose "Amir" based in Jordan set the general lines of policy.[20] But though the leadership was based in the Middle East, London would become, under Omar Bakri, HT's global communications center, maintaining contact with and providing educational materials, funding, and support for other national branches.[21]

HT's stage theory of party development recommended an initial focus on aliens, usually students or professionals.[22] The British HT first was to "culture" a core group of dedicated cadre, a vanguard.[23] But for that mission to be completed in three years, Bakri's innovation was to shift attention from fellow expatriates to homegrown Muslims.[24] By the late 1980s HT's study groups were composed largely of young second-generation college students.[25] "Culturing" (*tarbiyya*) can best be understood as a kind of internal conversion process because most HT activists were born-again Muslims.[26] Some of the militants, in a trendy phrase, were "reverts," though many had never been observant before. One of them, Ed Husain, stressed that whereas Bakri's previous audience—Arab asylum seekers like Bakri himself—had heard Islamist rhetoric in their home countries and paid little attention to Hizb ut–Tahrir, "it was mostly second-generation British Muslims and converts who were seduced by the 'Tottenham Ayatollah.' His mastery of the Arabic language, his ready and seemingly relevant quotes from the Koran and other sources, silenced us impressionable Muslims of Britain."[27]

By 1990 there were four hundred HT members in England.[28] The cornerstone of HT's detailed theory of radicalization was what Bakri and his followers called the "cognitive opening." Receptivity to radical ideology, to the Islamist narrative, could result from a crisis. That could be economic (a dead-end job), personal (loss of a loved one or drug addiction), cultural (humiliation or a racial insult), or directly political (discrimination or repression).[29] When established religious or political authorities proved incapable of addressing such a crisis, as was typically the case, HT would pounce on this "cognitive opening." Neither parents nor their imported imams offered guidance in such crises. Communist and socialist parties no longer offered a viable political alternative. Maajid Nawas, a national leader of the HT in the 1990s, told me that his own crisis resulted from attacks on Muslims by black and white gangs in his Essex neighborhood in the early 1990s. "Had it been a decade or two earlier I might have become a Marxist. But there were no active Communists by that time. HT on the other hand was everywhere. They told me Marxism was dead, and the jihadis had defeated it."[30]

ANNUS MIRABILIS II

In the dark lecture theatre there were sobs at what people were seeing; gasps of shock at what was going on two hours away from Heathrow airport: the serving of Muslim men's testicles on trays, Serbs slaughtering pregnant Muslim women, reports of group rape within the borders of Europe.[31]

The year was 1993, the place a packed lecture hall at Tower Hamlets College in East London. The president of the school's Islamic Society, Ed Husain, had advised that the thirty-minute video called *The Killing Fields of Bosnia* would be "unlike any you have ever seen." When it ended, Husain, the activist from the Young Muslim Organization (YMO), soon to become a secret member of Hizb ut-Tahrir, delivered his homily: "While our sisters are raped in Bosnia, our brothers slaughtered, the enemies of Islam organize disco parties for us here at college. . . . Next week there will be a talk on how to stop the horrors of Bosnia. Pass the word."[32]

Asked to choose a year or an event from which to date the emergence of "Londonistan" and British Muslim radicalism, the miracle year of

1989 would not be my choice. To be sure, the collapse of Marxism left the stage empty for Islamic radicalism, and the protest over the "apostate" Rushdie's novel established, for better or worse, a public British Muslim identity. But for most aggrieved Muslims, the narrative described in chapter 5 had already routed Marxist ideology. The Rushdie protest of that year was run by first-generation elders, not their second-generation offspring.

The event that sparked second-generation radicalism was the April 1993 massacre in Srebrenica. Serbians killed eight thousand Bosnian Muslim men and boys in an enclave that was under the United Nations' protection. It was then that radicals like Omar Bakri and HT burst on the public Muslim scene with videos, newspapers, magazines, lectures, and demonstrations all advancing the following syllogism: *Europeans are slaughtering Bosnian Muslims in the thousands, though they are fair, blonde, and blue-eyed, and have coexisted in the Balkans for six centuries. What chance of survival then do we, dark-skinned, recent arrivals, have in Britain, whose armies have colonized Muslims in India and Egypt? Naturally this sworn enemy of Islam cannot tolerate an awakening Muslim community at home.* For certain second-generation British Muslims, many now in their formative college years, this was a mighty argument.[33]

Hizb ut-Tahrir did not, of course, create the radical second generation alone. At this time, several elements were conjoining in what would prove to be a "dire contagion" of demographic trends, cultural legacies, and historical contingencies, of push and pull. These included the entry en masse of second-generation Muslims to community colleges and metropolitan universities; their exposure to Saudi Salafism; their easy, familiar access to Pakistan and hence to the anti-Soviet jihad in Afghanistan; the arrival of numbers of jihadi refugees attracted by traditional British hospitality to dissidents; and finally the proximity of war in Bosnia.

University students went to study in Saudi Arabia and returned to introduce contemporary Salafi ideas to the embryonic British movement. These young men brought back with them a literal interpretation of scripture. In Britain, many joined the edgy Saudi-backed Salafist group Jamiat Ihyaa Minhaaj Al Sunnah (JIMAS; The Association to Revive the Way of the Messenger). Followers of JIMAS had an impressive bluntness, a ragged appearance, and a constant need to quote scripture. Their women companions wore gloves, covered their faces,

and displayed a holier-than-thou attitude toward unveiled women.[34]
These practices, so remote from the customs of the host country, but
also from those of the immigrant fathers, became symbolic weapons to
wield against the backward-facing caps, jeans, and hooded sweatshirts
of gangster hip hop, and against the designer outfits of the assimilated.
Not a few of these freshly turned-out Salafists then made the pilgrimage to Afghanistan.[35]

Scores of Britons had peregrinated to Afghanistan to fight the Soviets
in the 1980s, but most returned to their previous noncombatant lives.
They had not been motivated by politics, but by a spiritual call to assist
oppressed coreligionists.[36] When the Soviets left Afghanistan, they
returned home, not tempted by the ensuing internecine jihadi warfare
there. But some had been politicized and would return to cultivate comrades in Britain among the budding Salafists.

Altogether, Iran, Afghanistan, Saudi Salafism, Omar Bakri's "culturing," and the arrival of numbers of jihadi refugees gave birth to Islamic
radicalism in Britain. They "pulled" in postmigrants like Beeston Hill's
Mullah Crew, young men "pushed" toward radicalism by dead-end jobs,
drug abuse, forced marriage, or racial discrimination. They formed, in
the words of Jonathan Birt, a "grievance theology"—blending religion
and politics into a "theo-political discourse."[37] It is important to take
account of both these dimensions. Often, cultural, not political, issues
figured most in Londonistan sermons.[38] Preachers excoriated homosexuality, lewdness, fornication, alcohol, and drugs. Militants had given up
promiscuity, drugs, and alcohol. This dual critique, this fusion of grievances on two separate fronts—cultural/religious and political—attracted
followers whether one was first radicalized by a burst of personal religious zeal or by a perceived affront to the religion itself.[39] Londonistan
deserves the credit, if that is the word, for the public articulation of this
theology-cum-political ideology.

It was at this point, around 1993, that a segment of the pietist Salafist
British subculture began to get politically active, much as their godfa-
thers did in Saudi Arabia with the rise of the Awakening Sheiks (see
chapter 5). But two forces that influenced young British Muslims had
little impact in Saudi Arabia: the Bosnian tragedy (occurring only a
thirty-hour drive from London) and the old moles of Hizb ut-Tahrir,
still under Bakr's leadership. The Syrian charmer and his comrades
pounced on the Bosnian evidence to prove to postmigrants that Muslims

were under attack everywhere: in Chechnya, Kashmir, Palestine, and in Britain. With this worldview, young Muslims were now primed for radical activism.

The scholar who would become the most respected and influential individual in British jihadi circles also arrived in London in the seminal year of 1993. He was Abu Qatada, "the most significant extremist preacher in the UK," in the words of David Blunkett, Tony Blair's Home Secretary in the years leading up to the London bombings.[40] Brynjar Lia, the prominent Norwegian authority on Islamism, designated him "the foremost jihadi cleric in London."[41] Abu Qatada al-Filistini, born Omar Uthman in Bethlehem in 1960, studied for a time with a renowned pietist imam in a small circle of teenage students that included at least two eventual luminaries of the nonviolent Salafi community. But the Palestinian broke with the pietists over the issue of violence. He pursued his studies in Jordan and the West Bank until 1989 when he fled, alleging political persecution. The radical scholar reached the United Kingdom from Pakistan in September 1993 on a forged United Arab Emirates passport. The United Kingdom granted him refugee status in 1994.[42]

Abu Qatada began preaching in Arabic on Fridays at the Four Feathers Youth Centre in Marylebone, central London, with the Algerian jihad as his principal cause.[43] Arab exiles, mainly North African, gathered for these public services, along with a smattering of South Asians and a handful of blacks.[44] They were largely flotsam and jetsam of the Afghan jihad and its aftershocks.

The city offered a safe haven where the mujahideen could regroup and, with the assistance of Western appurtenances, dedicate themselves to producing and distributing propaganda in support of their holy wars against the "near enemy" back home. The GIA, especially after its suppression in Paris in 1995, centered its extensive propaganda operations in London. The Libyan Islamic Fighting Group (LIFG) burrowed into the growing Libyan community in Manchester as well as in London. London also housed Egyptian jihadi groups such as the blind sheik Abdel Rahman's Gamaa Islamiyya and Ayman al-Zawahiri's Islamic Jihad, soon to join up with al Qaeda. A Saudi opposition group linked to the *sahwa* current in the Kingdom (discussed in chapter 5), the Coalition for the Defense of Legitimate Rights (CDLR), was headquartered in London.

Another London-based Saudi organization, the Advice and Reform Committee, served as bin Laden's representation in Europe, from which he barraged the Saudi Kingdom with faxes and "letters of advice."[45] A number of foreign jihadi groups issued their propaganda and ran their media centers from London, with its burgeoning Muslim community, friendly universities, lax asylum laws, generous welfare benefits, permissive legal system, convivial multiculturalism, and its agglomeration of press outlets.

The jihadi strategist Abu Musab al-Suri, who also advised al Qaeda and lived in London at this time, catalogued the city's resources for "Islamic activity." He found seventy-five daily newspapers, weekly and monthly magazines published in Arabic; huge libraries; diverse literary schools; and political opposition movements of every stripe. "Everyone from Shaykh Muhammad Surur [a prominent fundamentalist scholar] to the jihadis," met in London he noted, and "lately it has become a refuge for everyone."[46]

The city's allure went beyond propinquity, propaganda, prose, and poetry; typically the jihadis, in addition to largesse from the Gulf, commanded British welfare benefits.[47] That support led jihadi beneficiaries such as Suri to conclude that "London must have acted according to a well-studied and well-known international plan and opened its doors to the Islamists and the jihadis."[48] Such inferences also led the extremists to conceive that Britain had entered with them into a "covenant of security" (see below).

At the Four Feathers Youth Centre near Regent's Park, Abu Qatada would hold forth to as many as two hundred followers stretched out on prayer rugs on a basketball court. It became a place where bulletins were distributed, donations were collected, and jihadis gathered. It also became a place where the British security service observed the jihadis.[49]

In February 1994, a London reporter captured the black carnival aspect of the scene outside Friday prayers at Four Feathers and at mosques around London.

The departing congregation . . . has to run the gauntlet of dozens of young men raising money for holy wars against foreign governments. "Fight the Algerian junta!" A bearded man in his 20s stands beside a grisly montage of photographs portraying, he says, victims of torture by the Algerian government. One youth says he comes from Nubia and is raising money for the overthrow of the Mubarak government. "Help the jihad in Egypt," he cries, trying to out-shout another youth who says he is collecting for Palestine.[50]

According to the jihadi strategist Suri, Abu Qatada soon became "the religious reference point" for Algerians and Arab-Afghans in London as well as for "many others in European capitals." This occurred even though Abu Qatada was not a jihadi militant himself. What made Qatada into a sheik—what earned him a devoted following of violent extremists— were his Salafi philosophies, which he proselytized vigorously, and his oratory brio.[51]

Suri attributed Abu Qatada's rhetorical talents and his down-to-earth manner to his participation in the Islamist missionary group Tabligh Jama'at (TJ) before he became a Salafist.[52] The Palestinian's subsequent affiliations were more striking. Police discovered tapes of his sermons in a Hamburg flat used by the pilots of the 9/11 attacks.[53] The would-be shoe bomber Richard Reid, and Zacarias Moussaoui, the man found guilty of preparing for a "second wave" of al Qaeda attacks on America, repaired to Four Feathers for "spiritual counseling."[54]

Abu Qatada's advice easily transcended the merely spiritual realm. Jordanian authorities indicted him on charges of conspiring to attack U.S. and Jordanian targets before millennium celebrations in January 2000. His co-conspirator was none other than Abu Musab al-Zarqawi, the Jordanian who later led al Qaeda forces in Iraq. A German police informant described the Palestinian as a leader of Tawhid, an anti-Semitic jihadi group founded by Zarqawi.[55] Imad Eddin Barakat Yarkas, alias Abu Dahdah, the chief of the Madrid cell that helped organize 9/11, met often with the sheik in London.[56] The crusading Spanish judge Baltasar Garzon, who led the investigation into the Spanish links to the 9/11 attacks, labeled Abu Qatada, rather extravagantly, "Osama bin Laden's right-hand man."[57] Though the Palestinian claimed that he had never met bin Laden, Omar Nasiri states that he himself passed messages from jihadi organizers in Afghanistan to Abu Qatada in London, and it has been reported that the Palestinian met Osama bin Laden in Peshawar in 1989.[58] The British immigration court reviewing his case in 2007 determined that Abu Qatada was "heavily involved, indeed was at the centre in the United Kingdom of terrorist activities associated with al-Qaeda."[59] The court found "the reach and the depth of his influence . . . formidable, even incalculable."[60]

Wanted on terrorism charges in Algeria, Belgium, France, Germany, Italy, the United States, and his native Jordan, Abu Qatada was allowed to roam free in London until December 2001. He was imprisoned in 2002 but released on bail in 2004, when he was re-arrested and tried for violating his asylum status. The British high court, the Law Lords, overturned his conviction the next year and he was freed. In 2007, he was put under house arrest and then placed in Long Lartin prison in Worcestershire in 2008, where he fought a deportation order and smuggled religious decrees (*fatwas*) out to followers.[61]

Among the many who gathered at the knees of Abu Qatada at Four Feathers was Abu Hamza al-Masri, a charismatic speaker himself and a shameless adventurer who became the Palestinian's best pupil and later his most formidable rival. His eyepatch and hook-hand earned the telegenic Egyptian the moniker in the British media of "Doctor Hook." He came to preside over North London's ample Finsbury Park Mosque, to which he attracted an all-star team of jihadis and radical preachers and throngs of postmigrants from as far away as Beeston Hill. Among the second generation, the English-speaking one-eyed man was king, because in that realm Abu Qatada, for all of his oratorical skills, was powerless. He did not speak English.

The pupil also differed from his teacher, and from our other Londonistan preachers, in his extremist provenance. The other lords of Londonistan became radical Islamists in the Middle East. But if Abu Hamza, born in 1958 in Alexandria as Mostafa Kamel Mostafa, also must be classified an Outsider, his radicalization occurred after he had reached British shores. A civil engineering student, the Egyptian entered Britain in July 1979 on an ordinary tourist visa that he proceeded to overstay. He was arrested as an illegal immigrant in December 1980, but he was granted leave to remain thanks to his marriage with an unsuspecting pregnant Briton, a Catholic convert to Islam, who, it would later turn out, was herself already married—a case of mutual fraud that would eventually ensnare the future imam.[62]

Mostafa took a job as a bouncer and pimp in a seedy Soho nightclub. Soon his unloved British wife caught him cheating. His immigration status in jeopardy, Mostafa promised to reform and to get religion.[63] Until that moment, he displayed little interest in Islam. The Egypt he had known was Islamic mainly in the turgid humbug of the sort the novelist Naguib Mahfouz captured vividly. In 1982, Mostafa gained permission to reside permanently in Britain as a political refugee, but like many who learned to abuse European asylum systems, originally set up for refugees escaping from totalitarianism, Mostafa had no politics, still less a "well-founded fear of persecution." He stayed by gaming the system, as he would continue to do brilliantly for two decades. Scotland Yard finally arrested him in 2004 per a request from the United States, after a federal indictment charged him with attempting to set up a jihad training camp in Oregon.[64]

Returning to his engineering studies at Brighton Polytechnic, Mostafa was exposed to Islamic radicalism. But his path to Londonistan stardom began with his apprenticeship under the father of the Afghan Arab jihad, the Palestinian Abdullah Azzam. When he returned from Afghanistan, the imam at the Brighton Islamic Centre and Mosque found him "a changed man."[65] So while this conversion to radicalism was "brewed" in Britain, there were some imported spirits in the concoction.

A second tour of Afghan training camps left the Egyptian maimed with a sealed left eye and stumps for arms—to one of which was attached a leather-and-steel hook-handed prosthetic. Mostafa would fashion himself a jihadi fighter, but his injury reportedly resulted from an amateurishly mixed explosive.[66] If Mostafa could no longer aspire to be an engineer, his eyepatch and hook-hand, together with his soft voice and eloquent tongue, would make him an entrancing figure from the pulpit. As the imam of the prominent Finsbury Park Mosque, Abu Hamza became a stellar attraction for estranged postmigrants, including Sidique Khan and Shezhad Tanweer, who heeded the imam's exhortations, as well as those of the Egyptian's guest preachers, such as Omar Bakri and Abdullah el Faisal.

El Faisal was born Trevor William Forrest in 1964 to a Jamaican family of devout Christians soldiering in the ranks of the Salvation Army. At sixteen, el Faisal converted to Islam and began studying at an Islamic institute in Guyana before migrating to the United Kingdom some years later.[67] He left England to study in Saudi Arabia and returned to England on a ticket bought by the Islamic Rajhi Company, a Saudi organization that sponsors Muslim clerics.[68]

In late 1991, el Faisal landed a job as a lay imam and instructor at the Masjid Ibn Taymiyyah, also known as the Brixton Mosque and Islamic Cultural Centre, a Salafist mosque in south London, which was attended also, as we have seen, by Abu Hamza. Brixton is an inner-city neighborhood known for endemic drug and gang problems, periodic riots, and as the unofficial capital of the United Kingdom's African-Caribbean community. El Faisal's degree in Islamic Studies from Imam Muhammad bin Saud Islamic University in Riyadh gave him Salafist legitimacy, and the Jamaican convert's English secured direct access to Brixton's profuse Muslim second generation.

Abdullah's fiery attacks on pietists and his attempt to gain control of the Brixton mosque got him dismissed in 1993.[69] Embittered, he found employment at other mosques and Islamic Centers in London, and he formed a road show on which the convert redoubled his fire against "the false Salafists" and "the *Taghout* [idolatrous] Saudi regime." Tapes of the former Saudi Arabian student's lectures, in which he also thundered at the Barelvis, became best-sellers at Islamic bookshops like the Mullah Boys' Iqra, which we will inspect in the chapter that follows.[70] The Jamaican reportedly traveled to Beeston with Abu Hamza on at least three occasions and witnesses recall Sidique Khan peppering el Faisal with questions at their meetings. Sidique became an "avid collector" of el Faisal's taped sermons.[71]

El Faisal was convicted in February 2003 of soliciting the murder of Jews, Americans, Christians, and Hindus, and of using threatening words to stir up racial hatred.[72] He was deported to Jamaica in May 2007.[73] Before that in London, Umar Farouk Abdulmutallab, the underwear bomber, had come under his influence.[74] And when el Faisal preached at the al-Madina mosque in Beeston, Sidique Khan was joined by another Beeston bomber, Germaine Lindsay, who was a disciple of his fellow Jamaican convert.[75]

Another foreign-born English-speaking preacher who became famous in Londonistan and who animated terrorist cells in Britain was Anwar al-Awlaki. The Yemeni-American would later inspire the Fort Hood massacre and conspire with Abdulmutallab, the underwear bomber. Awlaki preached in various prominent London mosques and universities from 2002 to 2004. His CDs earned him notoriety throughout Islamic

Britannia, and he toured the island denouncing the "kuffar" until he left for Yemen in early 2004. He continued to be seen and heard on London-based websites and via video links at conferences hosted by university Islamic Societies such as the one Abdulmutallab led at University College London.[76] Awlaki's exhortations, albeit in a prerecorded posthumous form, hardly ceased after the preacher cum commander perished in a U.S. drone strike in Yemen on September 30, 2011.

However, the Londonistan preacher most central to the terrorist careers of the London bombers was Omar Bakri. Bakri, who had been living and organizing in London since 1986, was granted political asylum in 1990. But the grant was revoked when the Syrian declared that Islamic jurisprudence authorized the assassination of Prime Minister John Major should he travel to Saudi Arabia in support of the Persian Gulf War. Thereupon, the HT sheik left for Pakistan, where he expected a military coup would install a radical Islamic state. However, he could not obtain a visa in Pakistan, so he returned to Britain where his asylum status was reinstated a year later.[77] The granting of asylum to a man who had issued a death threat against the country's elected leader may strike some observers as a peculiar way of honoring international refugee law, but it was only one of a long train of dispensations to such individuals.

Having eagerly sought asylum in the United Kingdom, Bakri would soon find harsh words for anyone "willing to sacrifice the *Shahada* [the profession of faith] for the purpose to [*sic*] gain a British passport."[78] Omar Bakri forthwith advised his followers to renounce their British nationality, to disobey the law, to reject integration, and to boycott elections. According to Ed Husain, his former follower, the Syrian "was the first Muslim cleric to drive a wedge between Muslims and the law." Within a decade, his policy of "non-cooperation with *kafir* [infidel] legislation" would set many radical Islamists and Muslim youth against the British police force.[79] Following reports that the government was planning to try him under treason laws following the July 2005 bombings, Bakri left for Lebanon. He was barred from returning by the Home Secretary on the grounds that his presence in Britain would not be "conducive to the public good."[80]

What set Bakri apart in Londonistan was not his stridency or his knavery but his organization. That is, unlike the other lords of Londonistan, Bakri had HT at his disposal, and later, its more radical, properly jihadi, spinoff, al-Muhajiroun: both organizations were centralist, disciplined enterprises that could systematically recruit, indoctrinate, and train.[81] After that party-building "stage" was completed, the organization was supposed to choose the "revolutionary moment" to take power by means of a coup. As far-fetched as Bakri's ideas were, they would attract an earnest and devoted following in Britain.

The *Guardian's* 1989 report on Bakri's HT had betrayed no sense of danger or threat, portraying the group merely as dedicated "to raise [Muslims'] awareness of Islam."[82] But five years later, the liberal daily's picture of HT events had darkened perceptibly, its multicultural suppositions perhaps somewhat rattled. Now the quondam Islam consciousness raisers were, a *Guardian* headline proclaimed, a "Radical Time-Bomb Under British Islam." The piece covered Farid Qassim, a leader of "the most influential of Britain's new radical Islamic groups, the Hizb ut-Tahrir or Liberation Party" delivering a "rambling three-hour outpouring of hatred of the West, Arab governments, Israel, democracy and any form of *kafr* or heathen authority" as well as a "commitment to the jihad or holy war for which Qassim has called." The "new radical parties, of which Hizb ut-Tahrir is the fastest growing," had launched

> a two-pronged offensive. They are challenging the managements of Britain's mosques by making humiliating public criticisms of the local imams' sermons. And Hizb ut-Tahrir has taken over nearly all the Muslim student societies at London University colleges and campuses in other areas where Muslims form a large part of the community.[83]

The *Guardian* article quoted Ehsan Massoud of *Q News,* the progressive and constructive Muslim monthly, who explained that "this pre-packaged Islam" is "very attractive . . . particularly for those young Muslims who want to break out of the '*biraderi*' [clan] politics which dominate the society of their parents."[84] HT mounted its challenge to the Muslim and British establishments just when many young British Muslims were pondering their future in a Europe that, in their view, had stood idly by during the massacre of Bosnian Muslims, the suppression of Algerian democracy, and the occupation of Muslim land in Palestine.[85]

The 1994 *Guardian* report also quoted one recent recruit to a radical group:

> No matter how much I want to be British, I never will be because of my brown skin. I used to see everything as blacks versus whites,

but now I see the struggle as Muslims against non–Muslims. . . . Our children should be clear that they are not allowed from Islam to participate in elections that work within a democratic framework, as it would mean that they would be accepting the foundation, ideals and a governmental structure that clearly contradicts Islam.[86]

Integration was a "euphemism" for secularization and "contrary to Islam."[87] Even the multicultural option of attending Islamic "supplementary schools" would not be proof against secularization, and hence apostasy, because, it was believed, the teachers at such institutions were generally either ignorant of Sharia or were so enmeshed in Western life that they abjectly adopted British customs and laws.[88]

In 1996, Pnina Werbner observed that for the young generation of Muslims coming of age in Britain, Islam was being defined more and more by clashing political ideologies and less and less by the Qur'an. "[Their] texts increasingly fuse a multicultural rhetoric of antiracism and equal opportunity with the ethical edicts of the Qur'an and *Hadith*."[89] It is a safe bet that the anthropologist had Hizb ut-Tahrir in mind.

HT, and Bakri's 1996 HT offshoot, al-Muhajiroun, reached out to young men in places like Beeston, Luton, Tipton, Crawley, East London, and Birmingham's Ward End. Prospects were encouraged to view Muslims as oppressed wherever there was no caliphate, no imperial Muslim state, including Muslims in Britain.[90] They enlisted family and friends, and infiltrated charities, cultural and professional associations (typically university Islamic Societies), mosques, and political parties. They organized quiet study circles and noisy demonstrations; everything to take advantage of the many "cognitive openings" and cultural interstices on offer in *fin-de-siècle* Islamic Britannia.[91]

Bakri's display of Arabic scholarship wowed recruits, in the same way that impressionable wannabes of another era were swept away by recondite quotations from Marx or Lenin. But there were now also homegrown alumni of HT's "culturing" programs available to assist with recruitment. Husain remembers Maajid Nawas from back then. The national HT leader "oozed street cred. He wore the latest baggy jeans, expensive trainers, and had good hair. He had once worn an earring and the empty piercing spoke volumes to East London rude boys. Maajid was equally at ease among aspiring black rappers and budding Asian bhangra singers."[92]

In 1995, after a spate of bad publicity and calls by the National Union of Students to ban the group, the Middle East leadership of HT ordered the organization to lower its profile and told Bakri to restrict his activities. The party center considered Bakri's high-profile activities, such as "public conversions," inappropriate, not to mention Bakri's endorsement of "direct political struggle" for a caliphate in Britain. Such activities belonged to "more advanced stages of the party's strategy," really apt only in Muslim countries Outside.[93] Its Middle Eastern leadership wanted HT to concentrate on "removing the rulers of the Muslim world" and urged "the duty of Muslims in the West to help advance the cause of our brothers in Muslim countries."[94] The leadership wanted its London branch to remain its portal to the global media, its propaganda hub, and a fertile recruiting ground for the establishment of a caliphate in a *Muslim* country, in the Middle East, not to pursue the quixotic mission of turning Britain into an Islamic state.

HT reduced its visibility, and Bakri forthwith quit HT. With disciples from Hizb ut-Tahrir, the Syrian asylum claimant promptly formed a similarly structured cadre organization, al-Muhajiroun, in 1996, and set up headquarters in Tottenham, North London. The new organization's name, Arabic for "emigrants," as we have seen, referred to the Prophet's migration, or *hjira,* to Medina in 622. Quintan Wiktorowicz's definitive 2002 study estimated the group had 160 members, 700 study-circle participants, and 7,000 contacts or potential participants.[95] The lives of the activists centered on the movement, with an array of required weekly activities that were fast-paced, demanding, and relentless. Members regularly engaged in outreach (*da'wa*) outside local tube stops, libraries, municipal buildings, and other public locales from noon to 5 PM on Saturdays. On Friday afternoons, the Muslim Sabbath, they organized demonstrations. In addition, activists engaged worshippers in mosques, opening dialogue and encouraging correct beliefs. On campus, they recruited inside Islamic Societies.

Notwithstanding al-Muhajiroun's political character, the foundation of its activism was religious training, including a mandatory two-hour study circle every week (*halaqah*). These sessions were not book-club chats but rigorous seminars requiring hours of preparation. Members were known to tape-record the discussions and study them. New members underwent "encapsulation," as often happens to converts (see chapter 12).[96] That is to say, all their information came from extremist sources,

such as websites, brimming with conspiracy theories. With this ammu-
nition, Bakri launched ideological battles against more moderate Muslims. Time was devoted to understanding the ideology of rivals within
the fundamentalist community.[97] Al-Muhajiroun cadre were instructed
to raid rival groups for recruits.

In their zeal, activists went far beyond these strenuous minimum requirements. They organized public "propagation tables," demonstrations
and public religious seminars to supplement their leaflets, press releases,
magazines, and books. Intramurally, cadre poured over private texts and
courses as well as training manuals and internal bylaws. Members who
slipped were disciplined, leading to suspension or exclusion.[98] This rigorous routine has been likened to the dawn-to-dusk memorization exercises of Islamic religious schools, or *madrasahs,* but it reminds me of my
time overseeing cadre training in Marxist-Leninist organizations.

Like Hizb ut-Tahrir and communist organizations of yore, al-Muhajiroun fathered a bewildering variety of front groups that managed to
gain access to community centers, libraries, local Muslim cultural centers, and mosques.[99] Typically administrators of these venues were
unaware of the group's radical agenda. Bakri's organization insinuated
itself into several more moderate Islamic groups, including campus
Islamic Societies, the Society of Muslim Lawyers, the Shariah Court of
the United Kingdom, the Society of Converts to Islam, the International
Islamic Front, and the Muslim Youth League.[100] Identity politics frequently opened the doors to well-meaning non-Muslim organizations
as well. A meeting scheduled for the pacifist Quaker Friends House was
canceled only when al-Muhajiroun's positions were brought to the attention of administrators.[101]

Though Omar Bakri's group deployed traditional conspiratorial tactics, it also prided itself on being contemporary to the cutting edge. The
"emigrants" wished to return to the time of "the rightly guided caliphs,"
by capitalizing on the popularity and utility of the postmodern Internet.
Within hours of news events, activists updated the al-Muhajiroun website, offering English commentary for the second generation and links to
Arabic sources.[102] Bakri eventually would dispatch second-generation
recruits to Pakistan for jihad training. They were allegedly creating conditions for the establishment of an Islamic state, but most of these militants went directly to jihad, many first Outside, in Pakistan or Afghanistan,
but some later in Britain, the Inside.

INSIDE OR OUTSIDE?

Olivier Roy argues that radical Islamist preachers in Europe have been Insiders not Outsiders, renouncing their families to leave their country of origin to fight or study abroad. The militants are pariahs, cultural outcasts in both their adopted and home countries, who live among clusters of likeminded individuals, clusters often centered around a particular radical mosque. These men are "all westernized," Roy writes. "The mosques of Hamburg (Al Quds), London (Finsbury Park), Marseilles and even Montreal played a far greater role in their religious radicalization than any Saudi madrasa."[103]

Indeed, Roy wants to see the entire Islamic radical movement as the latest in a line of Western protest movements. "Al Qaeda is heir to the ultra-leftist and Third Worldist movements of the 1970s."[104] By the 1990s, radical leftism had all but disappeared. Today, Roy says,

> the only networks of radical protest are Islamic, but they recruit from among the same social categories (outcasts from the educated middle class and dropouts from the working class), carry the same hatred for "bourgeois" values and attitudes, have the same targets (imperialists) and often the same pet guerrillas (Palestine), claim to be internationalist (*ummah* instead of the international working class), and are built on the same generation gap.[105]

On occasion, however, Roy exaggerates his important perception of the Inside, the Western component of radical Islam, as when he asserts that "Osama Bin Laden is far more within the legacy of a tradition of Western radicalism than merely an expression of traditional political violence in Islam."[106]

Roy's Westernization thesis does not account very well for the lords of Londonistan. It comes closest to describing Abu Hamza's trajectory, but even his radicalization cannot be understood apart from his sojourn in Afghanistan with Abdullah Azzam. Omar Bakri was a card-carrying member of Hizb ut-Tahrir before stepping on English shores. Far from being "westernized," Abu Qatada did not have sufficient command of English to conduct a conversation. Abdullah el Faisal, born in the West, was trained in Saudi Arabia.

Alison Pargeter notes that the purism and dogmatism of Europe's angry Muslims "is exactly the approach used by revivalist Islamist movements all over the Islamic world who sought to strip Islam of its local traditions and to bolt politics onto the faith, enabling Muslims to express their frustrations with the state through the lens of Islam."[107] Fundamentalists in Muslim lands produced Wahhabism, the Deobandi movement, TJ, Jema'at-i Islami, the Muslim Brotherhood, and all their jihadi offshoots. Pargeter, echoing Bernard Lewis and Samuel Huntington, contravenes Roy's Insider thesis with an Outsider thesis: she contends, as we have seen, that "a certain cultural mindset" current in the Muslim world is disposed to extremism.[108] Yet Roy is certainly correct to dissociate radical Islam from traditional practice.[109] We do not have to choose between these formulae, or between Inside and Outside. They are both dimensions of European jihad. The lords of Londonistan fastened their Outside narrative to the Inside alienation of numerous British Pakistanis. When the Eastern message of the Outside found Western alienation in the Inside, the mixture proved explosive.

IF YOU BUILD IT, WE WILL COME

Like the 1995–1996 rupture of Hizb ut-Tahrir, the conflict generated by the GIA within the fissiparous world of Londonistan would demonstrate the influence of the Outside. Soon after he secured asylum in Britain, Abu Qatada took charge of the Algerian jihadis' official organ in Europe, the GIA's *al-Ansar.* The weekly had moved its headquarters from Paris to London because, according to Abu Hamza himself, Britain "allowed more freedom of speech."[110] Abu Qatada bestowed legitimacy on the Algerian jihadis even as they turned more murderous.[111] Finally, in mid-1996, after a spree of executions in Algeria of school teachers, journalists, artists, musicians, political leaders, French monks, and Muslim clerics deemed heretics, Abu Qatada, along with the Gamaa Islamiyya, the Libyan Armed Group, and even Osama bin Laden himself, denounced the bloodthirsty Algerians for "Takfiri deviations" and "innovation."[112]

However, many in Londonistan believed the GIA's account that the Algerian army actually had carried out the massacres, and Abu Qatada's popularity dipped.[113] Abu Hamza saw an opportunity to outflank his Palestinian tutor. At a public debate, the one-eyed Egyptian and his temporary ally, Omar Bakri, defended the GIA. They attacked critics like Abu Qatada as slanderers.[114] But a few weeks later, after a direct, public

THE LORDS OF LONDONISTAN

admission of guilt by a GIA commander, Abu Qatada's former disciple reversed course. To informant-cum-jihadi Omar Nasiri, this proved Abu Hamza was unreliable; "his objectives shifted with the wind." The Egyptian supported the GIA, regardless of their conduct, to win followers from Abu Qatada and to attract donors.[115]

———

Cash was on Abu Hamza's mind again in 1996, when he lowballed his far more learned and prominent Palestinian mentor to land the coveted slot of *khateeb,* official Friday preacher, at Finsbury Park Mosque (FPM). The North London Central Mosque in Finsbury Park (one of the first of the great leafy London parks laid out in the Victorian era) had been built with funds from Saudi King Fahd, in response to a request from the Prince of Wales. The royal collaboration, a modern red brick building with a towering minaret and dome and five floors of prayer halls, one underground, had opened its doors in 1994.[116] One of the original trustees recounted that what the royals had envisioned as a genteel, cosmopolitan center of study ended up with a radical management committee backed by a threatening gang of militants. Enter the slick, soft-spoken, reassuringly bilingual Abu Hamza to offer himself as mediator. The young militants wanted someone who spoke English, but the trustees had chosen English-less Abu Qatada, without checking into his background with the Saudis or with reputable Muslim scholars. Abu Qatada was demanding 50 percent of collections, but the Palestinian's fluent former student, now his low-wage competition, asked only for lunch money. Short of funds, the trustees leapt at the bargain.[117]

But Abu Hamza, equally unvetted by the trustees, only appeared to come cheaper. Later the trustees learned that their mosque was a mark on his hit list. The one-eyed Egyptian had previously targeted several mosques, including the prestigious Central London Mosque in Regent's Park, and his henchmen, the Supporters of Shariah (SOS), had infiltrated a number of mosques including, it emerged, Finsbury Park.[118] When he couldn't hoodwink bargain-hunting employers, the former bouncer employed other tactics. As he explained in a sermon entered as evidence in his eventual trial:

> Get some brothers, you don't need to be a majority, you need to
> be firm. . . . I used to go to Regent's Park mosque. Three thousand

Finsbury Park Mosque. © Ben Kelly; used by permission.

people pray in Regent's Park Mosque. And only ten people holy, ten people, and [the mosque authorities, elders tell us] we'll [Abu Hamza's men] never stand up and deliver the *Khutbah* [official sermon]. . . . But if the people know you are firm, they will back down. They all back down. All what you need is somebody who's making himself [indecipherable] you give him a couple of slaps. You give him a flat tire outside, then the police take you and make you, give you a record. You go outside, somebody else next day, finish, finish. They will all surrender: give me the keys for the mosque.[119]

The man with the hook made it clear that the correct way to take over a mosque was not by election ("you don't need a majority, you need to be firm") but by conquest. To conquer, he advised, "give a couple of punches for the cause of Allah. That's it. Don't ask anybody for your right. The *Masjid* [mosque] is a house of Allah. Anybody hindering the cause of Allah inside the Masjid, he should be thrown out."[120] The one-eyed preacher was employing fear tactics in Britain that surpassed in brazenness even Hizb ut-Tahrir in its clandestine usurpations of university Islamic Societies and its "dropping" prayers at rival mosques, as well as JIMAS's bullying of girls to veil themselves. Abu Hamza's next target was Finsbury Park.

THE *JAHILIYYA* OF "THE GREYBEARDS"

The Egyptian's tenure at Finsbury Park Mosque began smoothly enough. Abu Hamza's public message was reassuring. Britain was an adopted home, a haven, for hard-pressed Muslims around the world who should reciprocate by learning English and speaking it as often as they could.[121] But in the private prayer room upstairs, there was a different message to the band of followers, the Supporters of Shariah who accompanied "Doctor Hook" from Luton: the trustees were stealing from the collection jar, siphoning off mosque funds for personal use. The corruption of existing Muslim authorities has been a central theme of radical Islamist discourse ever since Sayyid Qutb made *jahiliyya* the cornerstone of his radical critique (see chapter 5). We will soon see the emotional force of the charge of corruption and hypocrisy on Sidique Khan's Beeston Hill. On this occasion, Abu Hamza's accusation sent a frisson through the private prayer room, recalled Achiou, a postmigrant Londoner in attendance.[122]

The former bouncer soon began publicly to rail against the "greybeards" who ran the mosque. Their project to renovate flats near the mosque had been a cover for a house of prostitution for which they now served as pimps. Young Muslims flocked to the sleaze-buster. "It felt exciting to be stopping corruption," remembered Achiou, who himself had amassed a tidy sum as a computer analyst in the latter years of the Margaret Thatcher boom economy. Within weeks, attendance quadrupled, overflowing the prayer hall. Loudspeakers blared on the street outside the mosque. At Friday prayers, the disfigured preacher brandished slips of paper theatrically between the two prongs of his terrible hook, claiming they were the mosque's accounts and that they showed hundreds of thousands of pounds missing. Once he flung a supposed receipt into the crowd that claimed to show a charge of £70,000 for hanging doors. The trustees, he charged, were colluding with local tradesmen in a kickback scheme. Accordingly, the new imam sent brawny followers to menace businessmen who had performed work for the mosque. When terrified builders and shopkeepers went to the police, they received the same answer that frightened Muslims got in Brixton and Luton—the government could not get involved in religious disputes.[123]

Abu Hamza's rabble-rousing campaign against "corruption," his fiery, colloquial English, and earthy familiarity with the British street gained him respect and rapport with estranged young Muslim men. The traditional mosque "was boring," recalled Achiou: "The sermons didn't strike a chord with my generation, who were restless. We wanted something but weren't sure what it was. Then along comes this preacher who is speaking our language, and we wanted to follow him."[124] Should a young follower desire to marry against his parents' wishes, the Egyptian would intercede with the parents. If they balked, Doctor Hook would conduct the wedding himself right in the mosque—exactly what the Mullah Boys were doing on Beeston Hill, as we shall see in the next chapter.[125] The Egyptian would explain that the parents and the imams they imported were saddled with superstitions from the old country, and that they both were prey to Western deviations.

Young Muslims in Europe, Abu Hamza believed, were finding the usual Islamic verdicts from local mosques unsuitable for their complicated lives.[126] The charlatanry of the mosques was a key theme in the Londonistan discourse; it was becoming one for Sidique Khan in Beeston. Abu Hamza devoted five sermons, captured on audiotape, to an attack on "so-called Muslim leaders" titled "The Hypocrites." There, following in the path of Sayyid Qutb, he scavenged Muslim history to unearth supposed correspondences with modern-day deviations, especially instances of those who "jump between Islam and *kufr* (infidelity)" by preaching the Word but forgoing true jihad; such people were "part-time believers and part-time hypocrites."[127] In his own videotape series, Abdullah el Faisal directed the brunt of his fire at Muslim "hypocrites," preeminently traditionalist Barelvi Sufis and the Salafist pietists.[128] Abu Qatada declared that violent jihad distinguished the Muslim from the hypocrite.[129] Omar Bakri regularly denounced "the so-called Salafis" (Wahhabis) as refusing to "struggle against *kufr* (infidelity), *shirk* (poly-theism) or the *Tawaagheet* (idolatry)."[130] The Saudi Salafis, el Faisal thundered, are your enemies: "In fact they are your greatest enemies because they disguise themselves. They hide themselves in clothing of righteous-ness and piety with a beard and a white *thawb* [robe]. Some of them speak Arabic, yet they use their knowledge of Arabic to cement the throne of the apostate leaders."[131]

The Saudi Salafists' first apostasy was treachery, allowing the American "crusaders" into the Holy Land to fight Saddam Hussein, but such trea-son flowed naturally from its source in "hypocrisy." The pietist hypocrisy

> spread negativity in the ranks of the believers for them to give up
> the jihad. So if you are going on the battlefield, you're marching
> forward with your Kalashnikov on your shoulder to fight, then listen
> to the hypocrite in your rank "O the sun is too hot, my shoes
> squeezing is me, the journey is too far we're gonna faint and die
> before we reach there."[132]

For el Faisal, the false prophet was one and the same with the infidel: "Every *kaafir* [infidel] is a hypocrite and every hypocrite is a *kaafir!*" These hypocrites were "the Jews of the Ummah."

The Jamaican's prescription for the Jews? "You have no choice but to hate them. How do you fight the Jews? You kill the Jews." Lest the con-vert's bigotry be considered narrowly focused, he also advised: "If you go to India and you see a Hindu walking down the road, you are allowed to kill him and take his money."[133]

But as we have seen before in Londonistan, and will see in Beeston, the main burden of radical rage is against other Muslim currents like the Sufi. For el Faisal, "the greatest enemies" of those who preach the truth "are not the *kaffirs*. We are not being slandered by *kaffirs*. The deviant groups, are our greatest enemies."[134]

Unsurprisingly, double-dealing was common among those so devoted to exposing hypocrisy and corruption. All four of our lords of

Londonistan were recipients of generous welfare benefits, and most, if not all, were informants for the British domestic security service. A British immigration court reported that in a string of conversations with an MI5 officer during the mid-1990s Abu Qatada offered to cooperate with British authorities, claiming to wield powerful religious influence over the Algerian community in London, which he would use to prevent terrorism in the United Kingdom.[135] He promised he "would 'not bite the hand that fed him.'"[136] And feed him the British welfare system did, at the clip of over £400 a week in government benefits, including £322 for housing and £70 because he was judged too sick to work.[137]

But the glib English-speaking Abu Hamza far outdid his mentor in gaming the British system. The disabled imam also reported to the MI5, but he collected disability payments and had his home renovated at public expense. One of his wives collected nearly £1,000 a week from the very British taxpayers whom her husband execrated and cursed regularly from the pulpit.[138] Omar Bakri, when he was not too busy publicly celebrating 9/11 or calling for attacks on elected British officials, was collecting a total of nearly half a million pounds in state benefits.[139] We will soon look at the British side of this "covenant," but one wonders if idealistic apostles like Sidique Khan, attracted by his icons' denunciations of the corruption of traditional imams, would have been appalled by their hypocrisy or gratified by their contempt for non-Salafis? El Faisal offers an answer: "You're allowed to take all these benefits that these *kaffirs* offer you, because everything that the *kaffir* owns is yours. . . . [A]nd you're even allowed to have four wives and put them on benefit. So hope that they give you a mansion in Hampstead Heath!"[140]

After all, as Abu Hamza declared, by "giving" Palestine to "the dirty Jews," the British "have given what they do not own to those who do not deserve, and we are working like monkeys."[141]

LONDONISTAN JIHADIS

Not all of Londonistan was jihadi, nor did all of the jihadis turn their fire on the West. Hizb ut-Tahrir and Omar Bakri held until September 11 that jihad had to await the establishment of a caliphate that could install Sharia and dispatch armies. In addition, the jihadis who pursued the "near enemy" strategy endorsed Holy War in Muslim lands but not in

Britain. In the late nineties, al Qaeda's turn to global jihad began to influence some of the latter, including the lords of Londonistan. All these
extremists claimed to operate under "a covenant of security" with the
United Kingdom, under which they agreed not to strike their UK safe
haven in return for freedom to agitate and organize in the country. But
the lords of Londonistan would work not merely to inculcate a "grievance theology" but to turn it into operative violence.

If Bakri needed a caliphate for jihad, and establishing a caliphate
required a prior revolution, the Syrian was also the lord of Londonistan
who would most directly facilitate attacks, both successful and not, on
London. In November 1999, Bakri dispatched several high-level cadre
members to Lahore, Pakistan, to establish the Pakistan branch of al-
Muhajiroun. Their mission was to organize a revolution to topple the
Pakistani regime and establish an Islamic state there. But Bakri's Pakistani deployment led by turns to active jihad—terror plots and suicide
bombings—in Britain.

Far from concealing its Pakistani deployment from British and Pakistani intelligence services, the al-Muhajiroun organizers in Lahore held
a press conference in the teeming Punjab city to announce it.[142] Six
months later, Bakri told *The Guardian* that al-Muhajiroun comprised
both a "*Da'wa* (propagation) Network" and a "Jihad Network." While
the Da'wa phalanx spread "the word of Islam," the Jihad Network
recruited for armed struggle. The Da'wa Network recruited followers
who later would be deployed by the Jihad Network in warfare "for the
sake of Islam."[143] Bakri called training for jihad "National Service" and
declared that it was "part of a young Muslim's religious obligations to go
for three months' military training" in Pakistan.[144] It was a call not un-
heeded in Beeston.

In December 2000, Bakri sent Mohammed Bilal to Pakistan, a follower who would become Europe's first postmigrant suicide bomber. In
Lahore, the al-Muhajiroun cell hooked up the young Birmingham
recruit with Jaish e Mohammed (The Army of Mohammad), a group
fostered by the Pakistani intelligence agency ISI (Inter-Service Intelligence) to wage jihad in Indian Kashmir. Jaish would later be implicated
in the 2002 murder of the *Wall Street Journal* reporter Daniel Pearl and in
the 2006 Heathrow airliner liquid bomb plot. On Christmas Day 2000,
after receiving explosives training, Bilal blew himself up outside an
Indian army barracks in Srinagar, Kashmir, killing six soldiers and three

local students.[145] In Pakistan Jaish proclaimed the British postmigrant a martyr; in Britain, Bakri also proudly laid claim. Because the United Kingdom's new Terrorism Act did not come into force until February 2001, Bakri remained within the law in urging Muslims to receive terror training abroad.[146] Bilal's exploit became a kind of aspirational template for scores of British Muslims who, like Mohammed Sidique Khan, would travel to Lahore for jihad.

The Terrorism Act failed to trim Bakri's terror sails. His Lahore operation expanded, and in 2002 it quietly gained control of the state-owned Pakistan Software Export Board (PSEB). The state company provided Bakri's operation access to government guesthouses throughout the country. The group appropriated PSEB servers to operate its jihadi websites. Junaid Babar, who defected from al-Muhajiroun, testified at the trial of Omar Khyam and his "Crevice" plotters (see below), that, while working for the Pakistani company, he was able to forge official passes that enabled him and his al-Muhajiroun comrades safe passage to al Qaeda camps in the Federally Administrated Tribal Areas and the Northwest Frontier Province.[147] British volunteers, including Sidique Khan as well as the Crevice plotters, slept in al-Muhajiroun's rented rooms in Lahore. On one occasion, the raucous behavior of the neophyte conspirators brought in the police. When Pakistan intelligence agencies learned that the men had gone to the border for training, they informed Britain's MI5, but al-Muhajiroun recruitment and conveyance went on apace.[148]

On April 30, 2003, two British Muslims attempted to blow up Mike's Place, a Tel Aviv beachside café bar, killing three civilians and wounding fifty more. Both had passed through al-Muhajiroun study circles and had attended the Finsbury Park Mosque for good measure. In October 2002, after the two had visited Taliban camps, one of them returned to Lahore and stayed with al-Muhajiroun cadre.[149]

Omar Khyam was another al-Muhajiroun recruit, this time from Crawley. He became the ringleader of the Crevice Plot, the first Islamist terror plot against Britain itself and the first conducted by second-generation Muslims in Europe since Khaled Kelkal. In early 2004, Khyam's conspiracy became the target of the largest sting operation in British history to that date. Operation Crevice involved 700 police officers (every officer in the south of England) and a grand total of 7,600 individuals, including police, witnesses, and security services. Investigators collected 3,500 hours of audio material, 3,600 witness statements, and

24,000 hours of video evidence as well as 33,800 man-hours of surveil-lance.[150] The April 2004 arrests thwarted a plot to construct massive fer-tilizer bombs intended for London's biggest nightclub, the Ministry of Sound, and for the Bluewater shopping mall, as well as gas and electric utilities. More than half a ton of ammonium nitrate was seized and eigh-teen Pakistani British citizens were arrested, of whom seven were tried and five convicted.[151] The probe was prompted by surveillance of a sus-pected al Qaeda leader living in Britain known as Mohammed Quayyum Khan. MI5 noticed that Quayyum, whom they believed to be an aide to the al Qaeda leader Abd al-Hadi al-Iraqi, met repeatedly with Khyam.[152]

Omar Khyam told his jury at the Old Bailey, "At the time that I started to practice Islam, there was one group that was quite active in our area which is called al-Muhajiroun. . . . I started to attend the circles that they were doing in the mosques and in community centres."[153] Khyam's connection with al-Muhajiroun began with Bakri's visit to the Langley Green Muslim Centre, a tatty, one-story mosque located several blocks from Khyam's home in a solidly middle-class section of Crawley, an hour's drive south from London. Khyam recruited neighbors and cousins for the enterprise.[154] According to Khyam's uncle, Bakri's group "preyed on boys at the mosque and even in the shopping centers," indoctrinating them when they were young and impressionable by showing them videos of Muslims suffering and then channeling their anger into hatred. "Omar was a normal kid until al-Muhajiroun started preaching their hatred round here," he says.[155]

In Luton, a town on the other side of London, Salahuddin Amin, one of Khyam's second-generation co-conspirators, had also answered al-Muhajiroun's call. In his videotaped confession to the police, he described first meeting the Crevice ringleader at a Luton prayer center where Bakri held forth. Amin added that Abu Hamza's sermons at Finsbury Park helped to persuade him to join the Taliban's fight against the NATO-sponsored government.[156]

———————

Salahuddin Amin was not the only impressionable young man whom the lords of Londonistan implicated in violent jihad. One widely repro-duced video, shot in Finsbury Park on October 13, 2000, two weeks into the Second Intifada, showed the mosque's three floors of prayer halls crowded with more than one thousand men. In the basement were a handful of women. Abu Hamza stood on the top floor facing Mecca, his words resounding through loudspeakers. The Intifida was just one battle of many facing the ummah. Muslims were being oppressed by the kaffir in Kashmir and Chechnya, and by apostate rulers in Egypt, Yemen, and Saudi Arabia. "These are your people." There could be only "one solution: jihad." "My dear brothers, if you can go, then go. If you can't go, sponsor. If you can't sponsor, speak, If you can't do all of this, do all of that. If you can send your children, send them, you must help, you must have a stand. . . . If it is killing, do it. If it is paying, pay, if it is ambushing, ambush, if it is poisoning, poison."[157]

Likewise, Abdullah el Faisal could be heard calling for the death of nonbelievers and urging schoolboys to train to shoot Kalashnikovs in seminars held around the country and available on tape in Islamic bookstores.[158] One of those who heeded his exhortations was Umar Farouk Abdulmutallab, the "underwear bomber."[159]

During his seven-year reign at Finsbury Park, Abu Hamza assembled a star-studded cast of terrorists. The names most familiar today are Richard Reid, the hapless "shoe bomber"; Zacarias Moussaoui, 9/11's reputed "twentieth hijacker"; Ahmed Ressam, the would-be Los Angeles airport Millennium Bomber; Ahmed Omar Saeed Sheikh, the alleged murderer of Daniel Pearl; and Earnest James Ujaama, a young Afro-American civil rights activist who, like Reid, had converted to Islam. Abu Hamza sent Ujaama off to inspect a site for a camp in Klamath County, Oregon. The area, Ujaama reported, was suitable because it was "a pro-militia and firearms state."[160] Ujaama has said the plan was to build a community of American Muslims to be trained in jihad.[161]

Less familiar, but more lethal, guests of Abu Hamza included Rashid Ramda, then facing extradition to France from London for his central role in the French transit bombings, and the spur for the French coinage of "Londonistan." Another lodger was Nizar Trabelsi, a Tunisian and former German football star, who was arrested while preparing to drive a truck bomb into a NATO base in Belgium. Also boarding at Finsbury Park at one time or another were David and Jerome Courtailler, brother converts to Islam who assisted in the bombing of the U.S. Embassy in Kenya; Abu Dahdah, convicted in Spain for masterminding the Madrid bombing; and Dhiren Barot, convicted in a British court for plotting to bomb various U.S. East Coast banks in 2004.

The keeper of this menagerie was Djamel Beghal, an Algerian computer expert, who had arrived from France in 1997 "frustrated by the tough anti-Islamist climate in Paris."[162] The former GIA militant eventually was arrested in Dubai in July 2001, while en route from Afghanistan to France for alleged involvement in a plot to blow up the American embassy in Paris.[163] Beghal circulated among the postmigrant aficionados attracted to Abu Hamza's sermons, inviting some to linger after Friday prayers and join "prayer groups." Talent spotters, who were men trained in Afghanistan or other war zones, were then sprinkled among the study circles in order to weed out the poseurs and exhibitionists. Beghal's Algerian lieutenants spotted those ripe for special instruction.[164] A typical second-generation recruit was Haroon Rashid Aswat, born in Dewsbury, a half-hour from Beeston, in a Gujarati Indian community. He left home after reprimanding his parents for failing to live like "good Muslims." He found a new home in Finsbury Park, where he memorized the Qur'an, led daily prayers, and became Abu Hamza's trusted lieutenant.[165]

As many as two hundred worshippers bedded down on sleeping bags and flimsy mattresses in the mosque basement on any given evening. There were body builders and drifters, but mainly students and young adults who shared quarters with contingents of asylum seekers, many of them Algerian.[166] The guests were entertained and instructed by "an endless supply" of videos featuring Muslim victims and *mujahideen* retribution.[167] One terrified young worshipper reported later that he was taught, along with six others in the mosque basement, to strip down, load, and fire a Kalashnikov rifle.[168]

Those advancing in this recruitment process received plane tickets for Afghanistan, along with spending money and a letter of introduction from the crippled imam. Abu Hamza's recommendation guaranteed entry into the generic jihadi training camp at Khalden, run by Abu Zubaydah, who was later reportedly tortured at Guantánamo.[169] Of these recruits, the brightest were sent to Darunta to learn to manage poisons and explosives.[170] The CIA would discover in safe houses in Afghanistan the dossiers of many admitted for field training. Finsbury Park Mosque was listed as the reference in proportions that shocked the agents.[171]

It is impossible to determine how many young men left Britain for camps overseas in the 1990s and the 2000s in part because so many groups were poaching each other's recruits and squabbling over funding. Sir John Stevens, a former Scotland Yard Commissioner, claimed that, days after the London bombings, more than three thousand recruits had been sent for training, but months before, he had cited only two hundred returnees from the camps.[172] In 1999, *The Sunday Times* reported that "about 2,000 young Muslims travel abroad each year for training."[173] The article quoted Omar Bakri, hardly a disinterested source, who claimed that 1,800 young British Muslims went abroad annually to fight in places like Kashmir, Palestine, and Chechnya.[174] The authors of the definitive study of Finsbury Park Mosque's "suicide factory" write that "what is clear, if astonishing, is that not a single jihadist attending these camps was detained upon return to UK."[175] More recruits embarked on jihadi training missions from Britain than from all the other countries of Europe combined.[176]

The Italian terrorism prosecutor Stefano Dambruso was astounded at how often Abu Hamza cropped up in his investigations of Milan's extremist circles. He told me that his repeated attempts to interview Abu Hamza were politely but firmly turned down by Scotland Yard officers, who explained they could not force the imam of Finsbury Park to talk to anybody, even to them.[177]

THE COVENANT OF SECURITY

When asked to throw light upon their forbearance in earshot of hate speech, incitement to murder, and recruitment for terror, British officials cite the information gathered from informants such as Abu Hamza or Abu Qatada, or the identities disclosed by photographing their public meetings. But a full explanation of their lenience would extend to British traditions, history, culture, law, and courts; the due honor to the country's tradition of refuge; prosecutorial constraints in Britain's adversarial court system; and to widespread skepticism of authority; to the decline in patriotism among elites; and to the end of empire, with its resulting self-absorption and loss of confidence. But the Outsider jihadis had their own explanation; their immunity was one side of a bargain. In return for a safe haven, they would refrain from attacking Britain. Indeed, there was "a covenant of security" between the extremists and their hosts.

Thus, according to Omar Bakri,

When a Muslim enters a non-Muslim country with a covenant of
security, he/she has agreed not to violate the sanctity of the other
party (i.e. the government or ruler), and that they will not violate
yours. The government however represents all of the other people
and so the covenant is applicable to all the people, and so you
cannot kill or steal from anybody in that country, while you are
under covenant.[178]

The expression was pretentious—even under Sharia, governments, not
private individuals, make treaties or "covenants."[179] But Crispin Black, a
former intelligence analyst for the Ministry of Defense, in a post-7/7
critique, acknowledged his government's inveterate policy of providing
tacit refuge to Islamist extremists on the condition that they won't attack
the Queen's shores.[180] According to Michael Clarke, a don at King's College, the "covenant of security" was an accepted agreement between
leaders of the British and Muslim communities. Toleration was granted
for self-regulation.[181]

Of course, Bakri and his confederates exhibited little respect for "the
sanctity of the other party." And Abu Hamza, once ensconced at Finsbury Park, discovered that his "adopted home" of Britain was less to his
liking. He and his listeners were only *visiting* "the land of *kufr* [infidels]
and *haram* [shame]." "And don't hope that you can stay here for long
doing anything and treat yourself in this country. [A] person who comes
to the toilet, he should be very keen to go out of it quickly because it
smells, and changes the human's nature and you can't really worship
very good in a toilet as you all know."[182] The country that harbored the
Egyptian and his colleagues, sustaining them with handsome welfare
allowances, was "a *Kaffir* country,"[183] and "a country of *kaffir* is a country of war."[184] "Some scholars, they can say you have to respect the law
of this country. You have to look like the people of this country, shave
your beard, wear like they wear, speak like they speak, talk like they talk.
This is Fatwa [judgment] from (scholars), or so-called (scholars) in your
local mosque."[185]

It was a discourse of double enmity: against the "toilet" of Britain
but also against the postmigrant's elders—the imam and the *alim,* the
preacher, the scholar, and the head of family. Abu Hamza had found a
way of addressing the second generation's twofold alienation. He was

mobilizing them to disobedience, to jihad, under the noses of a police immobilized by public skepticism toward the security forces, a legacy of their highly publicized abuses in the war against the Irish Republican Army.

The police could not arrest if British laws were not broken or without a case that could obtain a conviction. A conviction could only be secured with a tractable jury. Juries reflect public opinion. Public opinion is shaped by the media. The media often transmit the wisdom of the academic world. So how did the journalists and the scholars present Londonistan?

If *The Guardian,* as we saw, was starting to take Omar Bakri and his group seriously in 1994, public service television found the extremist to be little more than an amusing diversion. The journalist Jon Ronson followed Bakri for a year in 1996. His award-winning documentary for Channel 4 posed the question, "Is Omar Bakri really a danger to this country or has the government gone after a very silly man because it is easy to do so?" Ronson presents his subject as a harmless, even loveable, bumbling clown engaged in a series of misadventures. The film shows the al-Muhajiroun leader purchasing outsized plastic Coca Cola bottles to use to collect donations for Hamas; stopping by a newsstand to gather specimens of British porn to embellish reproving Islamist propaganda; shrinking, to the ridicule of other Islamists, from handling a fish he has caught trawling with them; and jovially handing out homophobic leaflets at a subway station. His "jihad training camp" in Crawley (where he would later recruit Omar Khyam) features a middle-aged man flailing at a punching bag. Hecklers from Queer Nation accost his Hyde Park rally.

Ronson made it appear comically preposterous that this jolly, overweight, bespectacled wisecracker could be a danger, and it's hard not to laugh along with him. But the self-mocking "ayatollah" got the last laugh, as Ronson ruefully admitted in an epilogue after the London bombings of 2005. Even then, Ronson assured us that there "is no evidence that Omar Bakri or al-Muhajiroun were involved in any way with the London bombing."[186]

Ronson's condescension was matched by Professor Clarke's insouciance. In the face of widespread outrage after the London bombings, Clarke, who teaches "Defense Studies" at King's College, insisted that the "covenant," whether formal or informal, was sound policy because it recognized the multiplicity and diversity of norms among British Muslim communities.

Self-policing and improved relationships with the police, and working the "grain of different national and religious minorities," he argued, are fundamental to preventing England's "gentleman-amateur suicide bombers from becoming figureheads for a national revolt among Muslim youth."[187]

If the professor had a point about the amateurism, we will see in the next chapter how distant the police were from "the grain" of Beeston's "religious and national minority." In actuality, the insularity of the university and the flippancy of the media were matched by the complacency of the authorities. In the doublespeak apologetics of the first official report on the London bombings, "Understanding of the potential threat from British citizens, including those born and brought up in the UK, appears to have developed over the period 2001–2005."[188] Peter Clarke, Scotland Yard's chief investigating counterterrorism officer, was more forthcoming at a conference in May 2005 when he acknowledged that the security services had "the perception that the terrorist threat was something that came from abroad."[189] Put even more bluntly, the British government was unaware that "Insiders," British citizens all, could convert Londonistan's invective and networking into bombs and detonate them right in London. In the university, as in the media, the "covenant" represented a corollary of multiculturalist condescension, while in the security realm, it purchased a complacent, cynical, and self-centered insurance policy on the assumption that the lords of Londonistan were dangerous only to foreign countries. But UK security services, as we have seen, had not counted on the radicalization of the children of Muslim immigrants. They had failed to imagine that *British* young men would learn the lessons of Londonistan and deliver those lessons to London itself. Londonistan and our "ghost towns," separate in the minds of the British guardian class, would intersect. Mohammed Sidique Khan was a child of that dire convergence.

THE LIFE AND LOVES
OF A SUICIDE BOMBER

Verona brags of him
To be a virtuous and well-govern'd youth.

—William Shakespeare, *Romeo and Juliet*

The concurrent blasts by the four Beeston bombers at four sites in the morning rush hour of July 7, 2005, killed fifty-two commuters on trains and buses, injured another seven hundred, disabled the city's transport system and the country's mobile telecommunications infrastructure, triggered special measures on the London Stock Exchange to restrict panic selling, precipitated the longest uninterrupted stretch of broadcasting in the history of British television, and raised terror alerts throughout Europe and in North America. Two weeks after the attacks, four new jihadis attempted to duplicate the attacks, presenting Scotland Yard with its "greatest operational challenge since the Second World War," according to its commissioner.[1] For weeks the events unnerved the city that had braved the Nazi blitz.

If Mohammed Sidique Khan, the ringleader of the Beeston bombers, was an updated, deadlier Khaled Kelkal, the Englishman was not, like his French forerunner, the agent of an external network but instead the product of a homegrown movement. But Khan left no record of his radicalization and falls into no ready sociological category—he was neither downwardly nor upwardly mobile, not a petty criminal nor a dropout yet not a success story either. On Beeston Hill the London bomber was known for his kindness and gentleness and for his extensive community service.

What turned this tolerant, compassionate, and integrated young Muslim into a mass murderer? Was Sidique "born again" like so many jihadis? Did his teenage time in the white "in-crowd" presage an identity crisis? Did his mother's demise during his adolescence precipitate melancholia and then radicalization? Or did his break with his father after he had refused to marry his cousin lead him to a new family of jihadis? The House of Commons admits that it knows neither how nor when Sidique Khan developed his extreme views. Its best guess is the unsupported and implausible conjecture that after a life-altering "incident in a nightclub" Sidique found religion.[2] His half-brother Gultasab dismisses that claim as "bullshit."[3]

But neither Gultasab nor his father, Tika, nor any other family members nor their neighbors on Beeston Hill will shed any further light on any of these matters as packs of British reporters learned, and as I found after numerous conversation-stoppers. As I mentioned in "Ghost Towns," Shiv Malik, the most persistent of the reporters, ascribes the deadly, uneasy hush to the unabridged reign of Sidique's Mullah Boys and the institutions and individuals associated with them. I found no cause to doubt him.

If the reporters were confined to the same slight available light, resulting in scores of nearly identical shallow stories, could the security agencies fill in the blanks? During several long sessions with the Joint Terrorism Analysis Center (an organization that pulls together all three British intelligence agencies as well as Scotland Yard and five cabinet departments), my probes almost invariably were met with one of the following replies: "We cannot comment on an ongoing investigation" or "Our *sub judice* laws prevent us from commenting on a case that may go to trial."

Did intelligence agencies know any more than the media did? Peter Clarke, Scotland Yard's counterterrorism chief (who was later to head its investigation into phone hacking by news organizations headed by Rupert Murdoch) attempted to collect evidence on Beeston Hill for the trial of three of Khan's suspected accomplices. He expressed his frustration publicly: "I firmly believe that there are other people who have knowledge of what lay behind the attacks in July 2005—knowledge they have not shared with us. In fact, I don't only believe it, I know it for a fact." But in vain he pleaded with Beeston Hill residents to "share information and ignore those who would try to use intimidation to silence them."[4] The three suspected accomplices, the only individuals brought to trial in connection with the London bombings, were acquitted for lack of evidence. Senior security officials conceded that "no one is now likely to be brought to justice" for Britain's worst peacetime atrocity.[5] Transcripts from the trial might have disclosed something about the relationships on Beeston Hill. But U.K. court records carry exorbitant charges for access, beyond the budget even of daily newspapers, not to mention individual scholars. In short Beeston was silent, the press trivial and redundant, the intelligence services mute, the police thwarted, the prosecutors frustrated and court records unavailable.

When did Sidique radicalize and under whose influence and at what tempo? Those who know will not tell, and those who would tell do not know. A chasm, as profound as the M61 highway that divides Beeston from Leeds, segregates British journalists, scholars, intelligence services, and lawmen from Muslim life. A nation that prides itself on the transparency of its institutions and its pluralism dwells in darkness when it comes to its Muslim minorities. Britain's notorious libel laws are so restrictive that journalists who suspect that a prominent resident had orchestrated the Beeston blackout cannot share what they've learned with the very public that has been assaulted and terrorized by this conspiracy. Those who do probe Beeston Hill's ghostly silence seldom meet with candor or even courtesy, as I found out not for the last time among schoolchildren and their elders on Stratford Street.

Every weekday morning at eight, Mohammed Sidique Khan arrived at the home of Deborah Quick to collect her two daughters, Harley and Robyn, to drive them to breakfast at Hillside Primary School where Sidique worked as a "learning mentor." The two girls, ages six and four, belonged to what the young man called his "breakfast club" of children on welfare. As word spread of his kindness, other parents on Beeston Hill asked Sidique to pick up their children, too. When they could not squeeze into his small, navy blue Vauxhall Corsa, Sidique started walking them all to school.[6]

This nice man, was a kind of community hero. One day a troubled eleven-year-old burst out of class and started running away. While the teachers dithered, Sidique leapt into his Vauxhall and in due course brought Jason Giles (hardly a Muslim name) back to school.[7]

When he applied for his position as a teaching assistant at Hillside Primary, Khan noted his "extensive experience in managing difficult children" as a youth worker. The affable man was generous with his time, devoted to the community and skilled at mediating crises. It was not unusual for troubled youngsters—often kids suspended from school—to seek his support when dealing with distressed parents and the police.[8]

The future terrorist bomber also aided expelled children wishing to return to school, arbitrated disputes between rival gangs, and arranged interventions for young drug abusers. "I feel patience and understanding comes through experience and maturity," he wrote on the job application. "I constantly analyze society and speak to people regarding current issues. I consider my ability to empathize with others and listen to their problems as well as offer viable solutions to be one of my strong assets."[9]

Yet all the while, the community organizer, the empathetic aide who cheered problem students and who dedicated after-hours to troubled youngsters, was training for Holy War and learning how to make bombs in visits to Pakistan. He began mentoring his fellow bombers—Shezhad Tanweer (twenty-two at the time of the bombing), Hasib Hussain (eighteen), and Germaine Lindsay (nineteen). Each of them was nearly a decade younger than Sidique.[10] The young conspirators routinely visited Sidique at the Hamara Centre for Healthy Living, where he worked part time, and where, like the school children he took to breakfast, the teenage plotters looked up to him as "a father figure."[11]

SID'S DREAMS

Tika Khan sent his son Sidique to Hugh Gaitskill Middle School, which not only was outside the local school zone but also enrolled fewer Asians than the Cross Flatts School on his doorstep.[12] Right away, Sidique's mischievousness and sense of humor endeared him to his schoolmates who baptized him "Sid" because he was "the most English of Pakistanis."[13] Even at Matthew Murray High School, where Pakistanis attended in greater numbers, the future jihadi "seemed to have more white friends than he did Asian friends."[14] His integration stood out in a school where "the slightest thing could spark a race war" in which sometimes "the uncles of the Asian pupils . . . would turn up at school to join in." According to his schoolmates, the Holy Warrior-to-be somehow managed to avoid taking sides. "Sid . . . was friends with the in-crowd. He had white mates as well as Asian, and he would quite often be round the back of the gym at break-time smoking a fag with the rest of us. He didn't have any girlfriends that I know of, but he'd talk to girls."[15]

He was "remembered as a quiet, studious boy who was never in trouble but was sometimes bullied."[16] For the BBC's Nazreen Suleaman, a Muslim woman of Sidique's generation, "it was a real surprise to discover how Anglicised Khan was at school."[17] She was also struck by Sidique's temporality. Growing up in nearby Sheffield, Nazreen and her contemporaries were sent to study the Qur'an in Arabic, much like the pupils on Stratford Street.[18] But Sid was an enigma among his friends. One of them could not remember him discussing religion even once. Most Pakistani boys went to the mosque because their families made them—"you're going," they would say, and that was that. But Sid didn't go. He didn't even seem interested in Islam. "With Sidique," another friend recalled, "you'd never really know what religion he was from."[19]

Suleaman was even more startled to learn that the lead Beeston bomber had once nursed the hope of becoming an American and had spent several months in the United States.[20] He returned with cowboy boots and a leather jacket, telling his peers he wanted a life in the States.[21] To be sure, between that time and his "martyrdom" video damning the Yankee imperialists, Khan underwent what one school friend called "a total reversal in his outlook." [22] But the evidence suggests his *volte-face* was not sudden; it evolved over a period of years. Sidique's one constant was his penchant for going against the grain and his slow but inexorable alienation from his father, his father's clan, and his *izzat* and faith.

We have only hints of what befell Sid Khan in the years immediately following his 1992 high school graduation. One of them surfaced only in May 2009 when the Intelligence and Security Committee of the House of Commons issued a second official report on the London bombings. According to the report, on December 26, 1992, a man named Sidique Khan was arrested and cautioned for a Section 47 assault (medium level)— after which police took Khan's photograph and created his police record.[23]

That we had to wait four years to learn that the London bomber had been arrested previously illustrates how little was revealed in that interval by news accounts, court proceedings, police reports, relatives, or neighbors. The arrest report tells us that Sidique continued to live at the family home on Stratford Street after his graduation from high school. It also suggests that something was amiss with the complicated young man who had been so gentle in his school years. These appear to have been wild times for Sidique—punctuated by hard drinking and drugs, quite a change for the reportedly quiet friendly boy who was sometimes bullied in school.[24]

According to the official Home Office account of the London bombings, after leaving school, MSK (as MI5 denominated him) worked locally as an administrative assistant for the government's Benefits Agency and for the Department of Trade and Industry.[25] He then found employment with the Inland Revenue Office not, as he told a schoolmate who bumped into him then, "auditing company books" but filing papers as a lowly clerk. After only five weeks, he left the job.[26] The struggling young man apparently was learning that the wide world would rarely offer the second-generation opportunities beyond, or even equivalent to, the foundry work of his father. Instead, perhaps he would have only a place in the taxi ranks next to Gultasab.

Maybe that is why Sidique hinted then to his schoolmate that he had earned a college degree, even though he would not enter Park Lane College until 1996, a time when his aspirations found temporary abode back on Beeston Hill. We know little about this period—Park Lane College, as its registrar told me, destroys student records after seven years—but it is clear that around this time "Sid" began the reformation that would flame out in the Edgeware Road Underground on July 7, 2005. American dreams yielded to jihadi prophecy.

SID'S DRUGS

Like many eventual jihadis, it seems that Sidique did a turn as a prodigal son, later telling associates that he had turned to religion "after a far from blameless youth that had seen him involved in fights, as well as bouts of drinking and drug-taking."[27] Sidique's "bouts" were symptomatic of an epidemic among males then coming of age on Beeston Hill. Legion are the tales of young Muslims finding Allah at the bottom of a bottle. In the late 1980s crack cocaine dealers set up shop in Beeston.[28] By the mid-1990s, as one of Sidique's Beeston Hill contemporaries told Shiv Malik,

there were a lot of drug addicts in the area, which dragged everything down. . . . I wouldn't say that we're stuck-up people, but you
move to an area and spend money on your property. You want to
live there, and if somebody's gonna come up and throw syringes in
your garden and put a brick through your window, you want to
fight the battle. At the end of the day it's your pride more than
anything. [29]

Beeston's elders were helpless against the crack scourge. The parents
were often illiterate and spoke little English, and the Urdu-speaking
imams they imported from Mirpur or the Punjab to guide their offspring knew nothing of their new surroundings. The gritty problems of
the Beeston street were left to the second generation to cope with.

The gang of south Asian youth that formed on Beeston Hill in the
mid-1990s was a fluid group of fifteen to twenty members. The Pakistanis and Bangladeshis took on not only the rival Caribbean and Anglo
gangs but also their drug-addicted mates. When persuasion and inspiration failed, the group used coercion. The crusaders abducted crack addicts and, with the consent of the abusers' families, removed them to a
flat above a launderette belonging to one Farouk Butt who also owned
the Stratford Street mosque. There the gang forcibly detoxified the addicts, cold turkey, over five days, and then sent them to pray. This was, in
Christopher Caldwell's words, "a sort of street gang organized for social
work."[30] Rescuing addicts from crack was a spiritual duty and recovery
was a religious event. At some point Beeston's drug warriors began
calling themselves the Mullah Crew or the Mullah Boys.[31]

Sidique became a leading member of the Mullah Boys, probably the
eldest as well as the wisest. He appears to have embraced a Muslim identity with the zeal of a convert and a latecomer. Of Sidique's spiritual
transformation we have no real record. A fellow community worker
remembers him as not particularly observant when they first met around
1997, when Sidique was twenty-three. "He sometimes got what we call
'the Friday feeling' and would go to mosque for services, but he otherwise didn't pray much."[32] But in these years Sidique was changing again;
he was exploring the religious identity he once ignored. In molting the
Anglicized self that had landed him only a dead-end job, he did not
revert to the folk Islam of his parents. Instead he was becoming, if not yet
a jihadi, a fundamentalist.

Gultasab dates that conversion from when Sidique started to pray "like a Wahhabi."[33] But that ascription begs examination. Gultasab followed his father Tika's Barelvi faith, brought from the old country, the Sufi denomination that resisted the reformist incursions of the fundamentalist school that arose in nineteenth-century India. Back then, Barelvis learned to brand their austere urban fundamentalist rivals, the Deobandi, with the name of the violent sect allied with the Saud tribe in eastern Arabia. However, the Wahhabis' actual affiliates on the subcontinent were not the Deobandi but the smaller and more extreme Ahl-e-Hadith sect. The Deobandis, the Wahhabis, and the Ahl-e-Hadith all raise their hands to their chests in prayer, unlike the Barelvi, who lift praying hands only to the waist; hence, this explains what appears to be a misunderstanding on Gultasab's part.

There are three mosques on Beeston Hill, each catering to a different clientele. Sidique frequented all three. The Kashmir Muslims' Community Centre and Mosque, a.k.a. Jamia Masjid Abu Huraira, on Hardy Street is Barelvi, run by Mirpuri, and was attended by the Khan family. In its basement Sidique and the Mullah Boys would set up a weight room that earned the derisive epithet "the al Qaeda gym."[34] The al Madina mosque on Tunstall Road is Bangladeshi. There, Sidique met the firebrand Jamaican preacher Abdullah el Faisal, one of several Londonistan agitators to visit the area.

The Masjid-e-Umar, the mosque on Stratford Street, is overseen by Deobandis. After souring on the Barelvi Hardy Street mosque of their parents, the Mullah Crew reportedly moved to the Deoband mosque whose literal interpretation of the Qu'ran was far better suited to their newfound beliefs.[35] The now devout Sidique prayed there three to four times a day.[36] A reporter who tried to investigate the mosque judged it to be "dominated" by Tabligh Jama'at (TJ), the Deoband missionary movement that also played a role in Khaled Kelkal's radicalization process.[37] Senior Stratford congregants traveled regularly to TJ's European headquarters ten miles away in Dewsbury, where Sidique later lived in the home of his Deobandi wife. Yet Sidique continued to attend services at all three Beeston mosques, and it would be wrong to characterize either the Deobandi or TJ sects as radical. In any event Sidique and his colleagues grew impatient with both the Stratford Street mosque and the apolitical TJ. The Mullah Boys had their own agenda.[38]

For postmigrant youth in West Yorkshire, Phillip Lewis observes, "The Barelvi or Deobandi are likely to be less accessible and the traditional religious practices of their parents problematic. For such people religious belonging has to be more self-conscious."[39] Moreover, Sidique and his Mullah Crew would not just profess and exhort; they would be the change they preached. The pietist imams liked to invoke Mohammad, but the Prophet had created a social movement, governed a city, and assembled an army that conquered an empire. Those who merely inveighed against license, degeneration, and disgrace were worse than merely outdated, impotent and irrelevant; they were charlatans, frauds, and "hypocrites," to use the term Sidique was learning not on Stratford Street but from and in Londonistan.

In 2002 Sidique first visited the Finsbury Park Mosque with its flamboyant preacher, Abu Hamza. He and Tanweer returned a number of times, even sleeping over in the mosque basement next to veteran jihadis. Prior to that, with the Jamaican-born Germaine Lindsay, the future Beeston bomber, MSK had become a follower of Abdullah el Faisal.[40] And prior to that, Sidique and the Mullah Boys had been exposed to the agitation of Omar Bakri's followers.

Those on Beeston Hill who were drawn to Londonistan were not first-generation migrants clinging to an insular culture oriented to the old country but rebels against that way of life. To embrace jihad was to spurn family, clan, and tribe, ascriptive ties to a concrete place and community, and to choose an affiliation, like a modern political party or Londonistan's networks.

The Mullah Boys, while reaching out to Londonistan, established on Beeston Hill the customary haunts of Islamic radicals: a prayer room, a gym, and an Islamic bookstore. This was done with the assistance of Stratford Street's Farouk Butt and Hanif Malik. The BBC's Shiv Malik recounts asking two of Sidique's fellow youth workers for interviews: "Both said they would talk only if I got permission from Hanif Malik."[41]

With his radiant bald head, arched eyebrows and beard, Hanif Malik looks a bit like Ming the Merciless from Flash Gordon. Following 7/7, Malik said in various press interviews that he was shocked and outraged by the bombings. No one has ever suspected Malik of being involved in violence, but we [Shiv Malik and his BBC collaborators] discovered deleted web pages that revealed that he had helped to spread radical Islamist ideas.[42]

Shiv Malik's description of Hanif Malik fits the man who met my in-
quiries by hustling me out of the Hamara Centre.

SIDIQUE'S FUNDING

Hanif Malik was certainly responsible for one striking aspect of Sidique's
diverse activities on indigent Beeston Hill: their funding. Malik, with
Farouk Butt's help, presided over a veritable welfare conglomerate that
embraced the Hamara Centre, its youth annex, and a community school
as well as Sidique's pet projects, the gym and the bookstore.

Together these enterprises received nearly a million pounds from the
European Union as well as from the Yorkshire Forward, a regional development agency, and from the Leeds City Council and local churches and
charities. The Leeds Community School obtained a grant of over £106,000
for staffing and construction costs. The Hamara Centre, raided by police
after the London bombing, received two £200,000 grants for building
costs and an £189,000 European Union building grant.[43] The Hamara
Centre, where MSK's inner circle gathered, with its multifunctional hall,
IT suite, training room, meeting rooms, and kitchen, was inaugurated by
Hilary and Tony Benn. The latter, then the leading radical Labor Member
of Parliament, championed multiculturalism. His son, who represented
Leeds as a Labor MP, has said he is "a Benn but not a Bennite."[44]

All this time Sidique was counseling and rescuing Beeston's youth
24/7—in his work with the Mullah Boys, at the Hillside Primary School,
in his job with the Leeds City Council afternoons at the Hamara Youth
Centre for Healthy Living, and in his evening hours counseling. He did
all this while he juggled a job at a gas station in nearby Ilkley and completed his degree at Leeds Metropolitan University.[45] Part of Sidique's
mystery was that even as he radicalized he remained "a switched-on
modernizer," in the words of his Leeds City Council supervisor.[46] Samuel Huntington contended that Islamic radicalization is "both a product
of and an effort to come to grips with modernization." He found its
"underlying causes" to be "urbanization, social mobilization, high levels
of literacy and education, intensified communication and media consumption which undermine traditional village and clan ties and create
alienation and an identity crisis."[47] Sidique, the "switched-on modernizer," was a product of all these "underlying causes"; he was a "marginal

man" torn between old and new, between kinship and autonomy as the basic structuring principal of society.

In February 2000 Sidique procured an EU-backed grant from the Leeds City Council for the Kashmir Muslims Welfare Association to outfit a gym in the basement of the Hardy Street Mosque. Along with Islamic devotion, bodybuilding typically is part of both radical Islamist drug treatment and grounding for jihad. (The 9/11 bomber Mohammed Atta's Al Quds Mosque in Hamburg was snugly nestled above a small "fitness center.") Tanweer's uncle says the gym beneath the Hardy Street Mosque was open only to MSK and his disciples and it was where Sidique "brainwashed" his nephew.[48]

But within a year Sidique and the Barelvi mosque leadership parted ways bitterly. After the London bombings the mosque authorities claimed that they were worried about the radical message that Sidique was promoting in the gym, outfitted with punching bags and martial arts equipment.[49] However, Gultalab Khan told Shiv Malik another story, which Shiv related to me: Sidique grew angry that the mosque elders were spending the resources he had raised on shoddy, second-hand equipment, and he accused them of siphoning off funds meant for the gym. This was just the kind of corruption, the *jahilyya,* of which Londonistan preachers accused the "greybeards."[50] Sidique in his second and last "martyrdom video" would inveigh against such authorities who were

> content with their Toyotas and semi-detached houses to think that their responsibilities lie in pleasing the *kuffar* [infidels] instead of Allah. So they tell us ludicrous things like you must obey the law of the land! . . . How did we ever conquer lands in the past if we were to obey this law? . . . [T]hey need to sit at home with the useless and leave the job to the real men, the true inheritors of the prophets.[51]

REAL MEN

With another government grant, in April 2000, near the gym, the Mullah Boys had opened a bookstore called Iqra ("recite" in Arabic, the first word of the Qur'an, also translated as "knowledge"). Resembling left-wing bookshops that I used to scour in the 1970s or Islamic ones I've explored more recently, it shared space with Hanif Malik's community school in a small, squat building owned, like the Stratford Street Mosque, by Farouk Butt. As might be expected, this was no ordinary Muslim bookshop. Iqra provided not just Islamic literature but also media services, youth activities, orphan sponsorship, seminars, and presentations. Sidique, one of the six trustees listed on "The Iqra Trust" declaration form sent to the UK Charity Commission in 2002, saw it as a "*da'wa* centre," a vehicle for a self-described "dedicated core of brothers and sisters who have taken it upon themselves to propagate the message of Islam."[52] Their "Salafi jihadist creed" resounded from every corner of the bookstore's three diminutive, cramped floors—from its prayer room, its Internet café, and its digital video-editing suite.[53]

Upon entering the store, you would encounter a small room of shelves and tables heaped with skull caps, dresses, prayer beads, and wooden Qur'an boxes. Besides piles of books and CDs and videotapes, you would also encounter one of the Mullah Boys, dressed in long robes and a cap, sitting austerely by the door, helping customers navigate the labyrinth of wares and scouting for potential adherents. On the walls, in whatever bare space was left, were posters of Mecca and Medina. Only posters with Arabic quotes were sold.

You could also visit the Iqra website, where you could browse a list of what "Iqra has to offer": weekly Islamic seminars for men and women; a meeting room that could be booked for "Islamic purposes"; a clothing collection facility (in which the clothes were donated to charity); *Jum'uah* (Friday prayer stalls); a "Discovering Islam" exhibition for the local community; a da'wa stall for the general public; and a reference library of Islamic works.

On the face of it, Iqra might appear to be a typical radical bookstore, offering a paradoxical combo of "outreach" and solipsism. But Iqra specialized in hate. An IT consultant who worked at the bookstore for two years, helping its team of extremists operate sophisticated and secure computer systems, told the press he became sickened by the fanatical atmosphere and the "racist rhetoric about filthy *kafirs* [unbelievers], Jews and America and Britain."[54] Presumably Sidique used different expressions when shepherding kafir children to school.

The Salafist Ur-text among radicalizing British Muslim youth at this time, certainly prominent in the bookshop on Bude Road, was not Sayyid Qutb's notorious *Milestones*, which had inspired radical youth throughout the Greater Middle East, but the Saudi *Al-Wala' wa'l Bara'* (*Loyalty and Repudiation*) treatise discussed at the end of chapter 5. Turning the pages of *Al-Wala' wa'l Bara'* (*AWWB*), it is not hard to imagine its impact on readers such as Sidique and Tanweer and their Mullah Crew. At the outset the tome instructed them that Muslims possess "a unique character" because they belong to "a great civilization" and that the way to recover that civilization is through faith and jihad. Faith provides "honor and self esteem"; "as a believer you feel a sense of your own worth and dignity."[55] *AWWB* became a manifesto of separate and supreme group identity, reminiscent of the "black pride" advanced in the 1960s by the extremist Black Panthers.

If the protagonist of *AWWB* was Islamic identity, its enterprise was hate. "Love," we are told, "is the source of *wala'* [loyalty], and hate is the source of *bara'* [dissociation]."[56] But *AWWB* has far less to say about love, about valuing and praising *us*, than about hate, about abjuring and despising *them*. If the express subject of the tract is "Whom shall we choose as friends? Who are our enemies? Whom shall we love? Whom shall we hate?" then its thrust is hate and repudiation.[57] For *AWWB*, Allah, like Jehovah, is an angry god. To adopt the faith is to share his anger and even more important to have your own anger sanctified. "Opposition for the sake of Allah is to feel anger at the enemies of Allah and to struggle against them." That struggle is holy; it is a jihad.

"Do not take the Jews and the Christians for friends. . . . And whoever of you takes them for friends is (one) of them." Thus all "infidels" or "disbelievers" are enemies—so much so that it is "forbidden [*haram*] for a Muslim to go to live amongst [the infidels] and acknowledge their authority over him." In Saudi Arabia, bereft of "infidels," such bigotry was inconspicuous. But among the patrons of Iqra, the anathemas resonated. For a young man to live among the infidels is to "make him feel weak and isolated and, then he would become docile and apologetic before them."[58] Did our complex Sid actually feel "docile and apologetic" during his integrated school years or perhaps later as a lowly administrative clerk or teacher's assistant, a "dog's body" as Tahir Abbas, a Muslim specialist on extremism, described his school job to me?

The advice of *AWWB* to those forced to live among infidels was to "proclaim their religion." Doing so "exonerates a person from the obligation to emigrate." Moreover, you must not merely declare your own religion but "assert" it. "Asserting your own religion does not mean that you

simply leave people to worship whatever they please without comment,
like the Christians and the Jews do. It means that you must clearly and
plainly disapprove of what they worship, and show enmity toward the disbelievers.[59] This was not the ad hoc self-segregation of first-generation
tribal immigrant enclaves in *desh pardesh,* a "home away from home," or
the unintended "separate development" often resulting from multicultural
policies. Rather, *Al-Wala' wa'l-Bara'* put a doctrinal gloss on a Muslim
second-generation alienation, some of whose members were already angry.

There were two more crucial radical messages for Sidique in *AWWB.*
"The habits and customs of the *jahiliyya,* inherited from parents and
grandparents, [had] no place" in the group. At the very least, Sidique's
father, Tika, would be "one of those who," according to *AWWB,* "like to
call themselves Muslims," who follow "the tradition of their people, traditions which have nothing to do with the Revelation of Allah."[60] I have
stressed in the User's Guide and elsewhere the antagonism of fundamentalist Islam to traditional Islam.

In line with that antagonism, but even more shattering, more divisive,
more of a repudiation of the father, was *AWWB*'s proposition that "the
abandonment of heterodox sects and innovators [i.e., traditional Islam] is
the essence of the doctrine of alliance and dissociation [*al-wala' wa'l
bara'*]." "Adopting some unfounded and false belief," which certainly
would include the Sufi shrines and saints of Sidique's father, "is *Bidah* or
religious innovation."[61] Such practices are worse than sins, worse than
denying the faith, worse than disobedience. "Satan loves *Bidah* . . . more
than disobedience, since there is no repentance from *Bidah* while disobedience may be repented for."[62] The fathers of the Mullah Boys, use-
less with the drug lords, sedulously saving for their gaudy homes in
Mirpur, insisting their sons marry their cousins in accord with clan and
tribe tradition, are more cursed than idolaters. "Alliance and dissociation
[*al-wala' wa'l bara'*] require that we not only denounce their positions but
also that we have nothing to do with them on any level."[63]

SIDIQUE'S LOVE

At first Beeston's fathers welcomed the Mullah Boys' newfound godli-
ness, of which they had only a vague and mild notion. The youngsters
were confronting the drug problem that the elders couldn't. But then

the Mullah Boys started conducting weddings in the Iqra bookstore. Two of them married white girls, and a Bangladeshi girl married an Afro-Caribbean guy. The very fact that the marriages were not paternally arranged offended the elders.

During his year at Leeds Metropolitan University, where he would convert his Higher National Diploma from Park Lane College in business and marketing to a bachelor's degree in business management, Sidique fell in love with Hasina Patel.[64] Dazzling Hasina, far from being a cousin, was Indian, not Pakistani, and Deobandi, not Barelvi. Sidique's "bright angel" was a Montague, not a Capulet.

By 1999 it was apparently clear to Tika that his youngest son, unlike his older brothers, Hanif and Gultasab, had no intention of marrying his cousin and returning to the Sufi Barelvi way. To bring him back to the flock, to save his son, his family, and his izzat, Tika sent his son to meet with the family's Sufi *pir* (spiritual guide), Sultan Fiaz ul-Hassan—"who with his fancy cars, sizeable entourage and heavy spiritualism comes across as part Pope, part witchdoctor and part Vito Corleone." Fiaz ul-Hassan recounted to Shiv Malik that when Sidique was sent to him, "he was no longer the boy who used to look up to him." He told the holy man that he had changed his views on Islam and that he wanted to go for jihad training in Afghanistan.[65]

Two years later Tika made a last desperate attempt to rein in his son and save the family honor. With his eldest son, his daughter, and his second wife, Tika Khan moved sixty miles southeast to Nottingham, away from the "al Qaeda gym," the Iqra bookstore, and the Mullah Crew, in the hope that his twenty-six-year-old son would follow and leave behind his "Wahhabi" comrades and his Deobandi sweetheart.[66] Instead, Sidique went right ahead and married his "Juliet." Marriage outside the extended family, marriage based on "doctrinal ties," as we saw in chapter 5, was standard practice for Deobandis like the Patels. But Tika Khan, a Barelvi, would never speak to his son again. He also never would lay eyes on his granddaughter, who was one year old at the time of his son's suicide.

Many unhappy British Muslim families were unhappy in the same way. Sons did not want to marry girls who came to Europe straight from Pakistan, girls who could not speak English and knew nothing of Western life; and parents were unwilling to leave their *lena dena* unfulfilled, to reject their families back home for newfangled values their children had adopted in Britain. Sons believed that their parents "regard[ed] women as property," as Hasan of East Oxford put it, and that they were more concerned about "face" than following the commands of Islam. Parents believed their children were misguided, that arranged marriage was tradition, an obligation as much as a chance to strengthen kinship ties.[67]

The second-generation British Muslim, lodged between traditional and modern, tribal and urban, was an acute case of a "marginal man," to use the term of Robert Park, a founder of the Chicago school of sociology and a pioneer in the study of immigrant assimilation. Park wrote that one consequence of immigration has been to create "the marginal man," one whom fate has condemned to live in two societies and in two different but antagonistic cultures. The result can be "an unstable character" in whose mind "conflicting cultures meet and fuse."[68] In Muslim Europe, fusion does not take place without fail. Defiant sons avail themselves of justifications they learn from radical recruiters. In Sidique's England they maintained against their fathers, against the tribal tradition, that cousin marriage was un-Islamic and a heretical import from Hindu India.[69] "Our Muslim *nikah* [marriage ceremony] is a contract between a man and a woman who have to consent to the marriage in front of witnesses, that's all," they said. "You don't have to marry your cousin."[70]

The Mullah Crew had their infidel brides convert, a victory for Islam against "tribal superstition." Sidique and his comrades refused to follow their old-fashioned parents. They would have the liberty of fellow Westerners to wed whom they chose. They would leave behind immigrant imports and parochial conventions, and they would confront the community's social problems. But the ideology that framed their altogether standard second-generation impulse was not Western reformism and certainly not British national pride (whatever that now meant). As for socialism, class struggle had yielded to identity politics in the United Kingdom well before the Berlin Wall collapsed.

The multiculturalism of identity politics actually led away from Britain and back to Islam, or rather to a scriptural, revivalist, and dogmatic version of Islam. That Islam, prescriptive and portable, offered a seeming solution to the second-generation conundrum. Traditional Islam and tribal, clan, and family honor demanded marriage with a cousin back in rural Mirpur, a doubtful partner in urban England. Hormones and the surrounding society led to dates, drink, and dope. Dishonor lay that way. Salafism solved the conundrum. You could be good as well as free, pious but autonomous.

The wedding of Mohammed Sidique Khan and Hasina Patel.
© Daily Mail Online; used by permission.

Is terrorism characteristic of those who marry their cousins as Stanley
Kurtz suggests in "Marriage and the Terror War"?[71] Roger Ballard's data
indicate that the prevailing cousin marriage helped, in Kurtz's words, to
"seal off" British Muslims from the larger society. But did it lead to terrorism? Not according to Olivier Roy, who, in surveying al Qaeda militants, found that

> most of these militants eschewed a traditional Muslim marriage,
> which favors a union from within a kinship group (and preferen-
> tially between first cousins), or at least an arranged marriage, which
> was normal among Al Qaeda's first generation. Its second generation
> chose their own partners without family interference.[72]

Indeed, Roy learned that "many activists cut their family ties when
joining groups associated with Al Qaeda and that quite a few actually
"married a 'Western' girl or at least a Muslim woman from another
country."[73] Such behavior, Roy found, was "congruent with the generation gap that is the hallmark of neo-fundamentalism," his term for radical Islam.[74] Mohammed Sidique Khan and his ilk were "switched-on
modernizers," not cousin-marrying provincials.

Sidique and Hasina married six weeks after 9/11. The link between
father and son was severed, but Sidique had a new family. "When
you're cut off from your family," Hassan Butt told Malik, "the jihadi
network then becomes your family. It becomes your backbone and
support."[75]

SIDIQUE'S JIHAD

Al-Wala' wa'l-Bara' (*AWWB*), the Saudi treatise treasured in Islamist bookstores such as Beeston Hill's Iqra, explicates jihad as follows: "Jihad, in Arabic means 'hardship' or 'struggle.' In religious terminology this means to struggle against disbelievers."[76] But "Jihad is also a profitable exchange to be made with Allah," in which you will be saved "from a painful punishment" and "He will forgive you your sins and bring you into gardens beneath which rivers flow."[77] "When you are called for Jihad, you should immediately respond to the call."[78] Whatever that may have meant in Saudi Arabia, for Sidique and Tanweer it meant Pakistan.

The earliest indication that MSK had passed from fundamentalism to extremism is that in 1999 he and the Mullah Crew were playing paintball, an ostensibly innocent, even childish, diversion involving camouflage dress and guns that shoot paint, a game popular among Western boys.[79] It was part of the Mullah Boys' exercise program, supplementing lifting in the Hardy Street gym, climbing the moors of Yorkshire, and canoeing in Wales. Before "playing" paintball, Sidique and his comrades would prep by viewing videos that featured graphic scenes of Muslims being tortured in Chechnya or Bosnia balanced with beheadings of "infidels"—jihadi videos.[80] Such video-cum-paintball groups are common among budding jihadis. It was in this paintball group that Sidique met Germaine Lindsay, the Caribbean convert who became one of the London bombers.[81]

To find violence, however, Sidique did not have to train for foreign war. The Mullah Crew appears to have been a kind of Muslim Defense League, shielding Beeston Hill's South Asians against black and white gangs. Illustrative is an episode one year before the London bombings, which attracted the attention of local news. After one of the racial gang fights on Beeston Hill, the windows of Tanweer's father's Fish N' Chips shop were smashed. The Mullah Boys sought revenge on the other side of the hill.[82] The gang cornered Tyrone Clarke, a black Caribbean, and before stabbing him to death, struck him with baseball bats, poles, and thick pieces of wood.[83] Four men received life sentences, but one fled to Punjab.[84]

By this time Sidique and Tanweer were visiting Pakistan regularly for jihad training. As with the other Britons who would follow them, such as Omar Khyam, or as with American wannabes a decade later—such as

the five Northern Virginia men arrested in Pakistan in December 2009—
it was the Insiders who sought out the Outsiders, the Pakistanis. The
lifeline between Beeston Hill and Pakistan was now serving in a far different way from the steadfast family connection.

When the *London Times Educational Supplement* did a story about
Beeston's Hillside Primary in 2002, it chose to feature the "learning
mentor Sidique Khan." The reader learned that the school had the worst
pupil turnover level in Leeds in one of the most transient school zones
in the country. More than half the students came or went in a single
school year. For the *Supplement*, a clue to the school's predicament was
found in the neighborhood. "Closely packed, slightly dilapidated, back-
to-back houses carry adverts in their windows for bedsits to rent. There
is a hostel for the homeless round the corner." The new students were
typically children of immigrants or asylum claimants. It was Sidique's job
to obtain and assess their records, show them the grounds, and gain their
confidence. He told the reporter "it will still be years before government
regeneration cash transforms the area."[85] Had Sidique, like many revolutionaries before him, grown impatient with the slow slog of reform?
Months earlier he had traveled to a jihadi training camp in Azad Kashmir.
Welfare worker or terrorist? Babysitter or mass murderer? These would
seem totally incongruous vocations, puzzling, even bedeviling, contradictions. But they also appear to have constituted way stations on a trajectory of reformation—the way up from prodigal son to recovering
profligate to religious reformer to religious militant to suicide bomber.
In the process kindness and solicitude turned earnestly and inexorably to
hatred and terrorism.

   We have no testimony respecting this progression, no accounts from
relatives, friends, neighbors, or coworkers. Sidique kept no journal or
diary that we know of. But on the Iqra website were two hints of his
evolution. The first was posted by a former Ecstasy (or "E") user. We
don't know if Sidique himself was the author, but the author clearly
speaks from experience and had "thought long and hard about what
compels people to take this drug." There were three inducements: physical pleasure, peer pressure, and exaltation (a "high"). For all three, the
remedy was to be found not in government programs but in Allah. Governments had previously taken "a moral stance and wanted to avoid a

hedonistic, or pleasure-seeking, society." But "with the breakdown in moral consensus and the increasing demand to live one's life without any constraints," that approach has become "unfeasible." Warnings about medical consequences are also ineffective because "the probability of suffering an adverse reaction to taking E is very low especially if one takes the necessary safety measures (e.g. drink lots of water, cool off etc.)." However, the real danger from "taking E is not simply the physical harm which it can do, but the mental and spiritual damage as well." The pleasure of the drug is fleeting, and moreover it "distracts us from meaningful pursuits in our lives, primarily the worship of Allah." The "high" of Ecstasy is an ersatz surrogate for religion. "You see, taking an E makes you feel happy and content with yourself as a person and, moreover, your mind reaches a higher plane of existence. Both of these occurrences are similar to religious experiences. It seems to me that some people are taking E as a kind of substitute for religious commitments in their lives."

Also relevant to our story is Iqra's account of the social solidarity when "you are on an E, and everybody else at the rave, party etc. is also on one. . . . Everybody is your best friend; they offer to share their drinks with you, or give you a sniff of their 'poppers' or Vicks inhalers (which brings on the 'rush')." But once the drug has worn off, the "artificial community" dissolves and "you no longer feel that 'love buzz' and you go back to work or studies on the Monday morning facing the same cold world." But through Islam "the sense of community is phenomenal and not at all transitory."

These accounts may sketch the mental journey from Sidique's down period, the degradation of dissembling about his dead-end job, his "bout of drinking and drug-taking" to his recovery and profession of faith. But what process of thought took him from there to activism—to community service, and then to jihad?

The Iqra website hastened to make clear that reading was not the point: "Today, Islam is only in the books and very few places see Islam in reality. . . . Great things are waiting to be done. . . . [T]his is a battle. . . . Those who . . . slide into apathy will be the losers."

Sidique never wanted to be a loser. In school he sought "the in-crowd" even if it meant turning away from his Pakistani identity. Later he fibbed about his lowly job. And then he recovered from his "slide into apathy" through Islam. Through Islam he would do "great things" and enter the ultimate "in-crowd."

Iqra had the algorithm: "The first step here is to get up and commit our lives to His Cause. Allah Himself will offer us the opportunity of doing some special deeds and earning vast amounts of reward."

Would we like to spend the rest of eternity with people like our-selves: mediocre people? Or would we prefer the company of those who are the closest to Allah: Muhammad, Ibrahim, Isa, Musa [aka Abraham, Issac, Moses]. . . . Imagine spending the rest of eternity with the best that ever lived at the highest stage in Paradise. . . . Allah will then out of His Mercy reveal His Face. . . . To be in the com-pany of the most beautiful, dignified, noble, gentle, kind and hon-ourable servants of Allah.

"Noble, gentle, kind, honourable": the very adjectives his neighbors and colleagues had reserved for Sidique. But which are the "special deeds" that will earn "vast rewards?" According to the website, "The world is asking for some people to step forward and bring Islam before our eyes. . . . Great people are needed. These people will be great in this world and in the hereafter. So Allah will send us tests to see who will get up and do something and who will remain as passive spectators."

In his second "martyrdom video," Mohammed Sidique Khan would say this to the world:

I myself I ask Allah to raise me amongst those I love like the Prophets, the messengers and the martyrs and today's heroes like our beloved Shiekh Osama bin Laden, Dr Ayman al Zawahiri and Zarkawi and all the other brothers and sisters who are fighting in Allah's cause. With this I leave you to make up your own mind and I ask you to make da'wa to Allah almighty to accept the word from me and my brothers and enter us into the gardens of paradise.[86]

SID'S "NEW FAMILY"

What did Hasina know about her husband's beliefs and companions, the institutions he built, the preachers he followed, his preparations, and his plans? Rupert Murdoch's richly endowed Sky News secured the only media interview with MSK's Deobandi love bride, whom Sidique had romanced even as he was training for jihad. The syrupy Sky correspondent pitched softballs to her deceived, wronged, victimized sister. In veteran British crime reporter Sean O'Neill's summary of the Sky charade, Hasina contended that "in the eight years she spent with him he transformed from a moderate young man to one who was interested in religious fundamentalism and then active jihad. But she insisted that she had no idea he was involved with extremists."[87] Hasina, the patient Griselda, professed total ignorance, on cue wrapping herself in the stereotype of the Muslim woman: "We were trying to be good Muslims and, in our religion, we are told that men and women have to be segregated. I never sat in the same room with his friends, he never sat in the same room as my friends, so it is a completely different life."[88] Sky's reporter failed to bring up the pair's visit to Israel in February 2003 on what some believe was MSK's "reconnaissance mission" for the two British Tel Aviv bombers.[89]

Hasina Khan's account is even harder to square with her performance on her husband's family farewell videotape, which was first exhibited in court in April 2008, eight months after the Sky News interview. With his infant daughter, Maryam, in his lap, perched on a bed at Hasina's family home, MSK tells his child in his West Yorkshire accent and British jargon: "Look, I absolutely love you to bits and you have been the happiest thing in my life. You and your Mom, absolutely brilliant."[90] Then he adds: "Fighting is good. . . . Take care of mummy— you can both do things together like fighting and stuff."[91] It was Hasina herself who filmed that video, two days before her husband traveled on a one-way ticket to Pakistan in November 2004 with the intention of joining the Taliban to battle British and American forces in Afghanistan.[92] If not conclusive evidence of collusion, this hardly suggests of "separate lives." Later in the recording Mrs. Khan is heard telling her husband that the tape has almost come to the end, warning: "There are two minutes left so say your piece."[93] The court was also shown footage taken a month earlier of MSK introducing little Maryam, in Hasina's presence, to her "uncles"—his "brothers," fellow London bombers Shehzad Tanweer and Hasib Hussain and their alleged co-conspirator Waheed Ali. Sidique's "new family" excluded his father but evidently not his Deobandi wife.

MSK'S CONSEQUENCES

A month after the July 2005 bombings Omar Bakri left the United Kingdom following stories that the UK government was planning to investigate certain Muslim clerics under little-used treason laws. A week later, the Home Office deemed his presence "not conducive to the public good" and banned his return.[94] In February 2006 Abu Hamza was found guilty of soliciting murder and was sentenced to seven years' imprisonment. In May 2007 Abdullah el Faisal was deported to Jamaica and permanently banned from the United Kingdom. Meanwhile, Abu Qatada remained in jail pending deportation. Under the eyes of Scotland Yard, in the winter of 2005 Finsbury Park Mosque was cleansed of Abu Hamza's Supporters of Sharia and was reclaimed by mainstream Muslims, including representatives of the Muslim Brotherhood–led Muslim Association of Britain, which installed a new board of trustees and imam. The mosque began offering courses open to the general public that promoted Islam as a religion of tolerance.[95]

The grand lords of Londonistan were gone, but other jihadi preachers continued to hold forth around the United Kingdom, and second-generation jihadis continued to fashion plots. On August 9, 2006, Scotland Yard and MI5, the country's domestic spy agency, detained twenty-four Pakistani postmigrants who were planning to explode some ten transatlantic airliners bound for American cities. International air traffic was thrown into chaos. Flights from London were canceled for several days. US law enforcement officials were put on emergency alert, and liquids were banned from carry-on bags. The suspects had been planning to detonate a volatile peroxide-based explosive, similar to that used in the London bombings, by an electrical charge from a cell phone.[96] In the next several days, officers would recover seven martyrdom videos, four hundred computers, two hundred mobile telephones, and eight thousand CDs, DVDs, and memory sticks on raids at sixty-nine sites around the country.[97] The *Observer* called the plot "an atrocity that had the potential to dwarf 11 September."[98]

In the years following the London bombings, the directors of MI5 began speaking out publicly on the magnitude of the terrorist danger. In November 2006, Dame Eliza Manningham-Buller announced that she and her officers were working to neutralize two hundred networks, consisting of more than 1,600 identified individuals, actively planning or advancing terrorist attacks in Britain and abroad. The extremists were motivated, she stated,

> by a sense of grievance and injustice driven by their interpretation of the history between the West and the Muslim world. This view is shared, in some degree, by a far wider constituency. If the opinion polls conducted in the UK since July 2005 are only broadly accurate, over 100,000 of our citizens consider that the July 2005 attacks in London were justified.[99]

The next year, her successor, Jonathan Evans, raised the estimate of those thought to be involved in terrorist-related activity in the United Kingdom to four thousand. In November 2008, a report compiled by the intelligence branch of the Ministry of Defence, MI5, and Scotland Yard's Special Branch, found that although most extremists, typically between eighteen and thirty years old, are British nationals of Pakistani origin, there are extremists who are aliens from northern Africa, Iraq, and the Middle East.[100]

According to *The Daily Telegraph*, that latest security assessment indicated that the number of individuals now posing a threat to the United Kingdom was "even higher" than the previous year's estimate by Evans. Though the document named London, Birmingham, and southeast England as areas of extremist activity, "the MI5 indicated that the threat posed by Islamist extremists came from across the UK."[101]

In 2009 Evans stated that British citizens influenced or directed by "al-Qaeda's high command in Pakistan" remained intent on carrying out attacks on British soil, forcing his agency to maintain "constant surveillance" on thousands of suspects.[102] In May 2010 Evans told me that the threat remained just as severe.[103]

SID'S MYSTERY

We do not know what led "Sid" to adopt a Muslim in place of a British identity and to abandon American for jihadi dreams, but a comparable transformation was occurring among second-generation immigrants and minority communities throughout the country during the 1980s and early 1990s. In joint actions "blacks"—a term then commonly used to group Africans, Caribbeans, Hindus, Sikhs, Pakistanis, and Bangladeshis—squared off against attacks by white gangs and anti-immigrant groups like the National Front as well as against the "sus law" (a stop-and-search law that permitted a police officer to act on suspicion, or "sus," alone) that appeared to target young "blacks." Minority unity reached its apex in the 1981 Brixton riots in opposition to "Operation Swamp 81." That campaign against street crime consisted of constant police stops and searches of ethnic minority youth in the slum community in south London. It took more than 2,500 police to quell the hurling of Molotov cocktails and the burning of vehicles in protest of alleged police brutality. During the disturbances, nearly three hundred police were injured and 120 vehicles were burned (half of them belonging to the police). "There had been no such event in England in living memory," according to Scotland Yard.[104]

But Brixton was only one in a string of violent engagements between "black" youth and the police or anti-immigrant gangs dating back to Nottingham and Notting Hill in 1958. The long line of confrontations registered the country's difficulty digesting the masses of immigrants and their children deposited on its shores. But it was the disturbances that followed that made the Brixton riots a symbol of the collapse of British race relations. The eruptions spread into and beyond London into the Midlands, the North, and into Sidique's West Yorkshire, to the usually quiet south, and even to Wales. Kenan Malik cites one commentator's claim that "not since the insurrections of the 1830's—the Chartist movement, has English society experienced such extensive revolt."[105]

The chain of violence alarmed Prime Minister Margaret Thatcher's government into abandoning the police stop-and-search operations and embracing Labor's policy of "community engagement." Sir George Young, whom the Tories after Brixton promptly made Britain's first minister for race relations, defined the new policy as support for "the leaders of ethnic groups."[106] It was an approach in line with the country's communalist traditions. It soon evolved into a program of promoting local councils, of the sort already dominated in Muslim communities by clan chiefs and mosque committees and by the Labor Party.[107] The Greater London Council took the lead, not only in reallocating resources to ethnic groups, but also in redefining the very meaning of racism. In the future, it argued, "black people" should not be forced to assimilate to a British identity or to embrace British values. Instead, they "should express their own identities, explore their own histories, formulate their own values, pursue their own lifestyles." This transvaluation of values would "transform," in Kenan Malik's analysis, "the very meaning of equality," from universal to group rights, "from possessing the same rights as everyone else, to possessing different rights appropriate to different communities."[108]

The mid-1980s sundering of a united "black" movement focused on civil rights into ethnic and religious factions devoted to group rights occurred on both sides of the English Channel. In France, Islamism supplanted the French *beur* and antiracist movements.[109] In Britain where Brixton had featured a broad "black" movement, the 1985 Handsworth riots featured ugly confrontations between young West Indians and Asian shopkeepers, badly bruising the notion of an identity of interests within a single "black" movement.

The 1989 Rushdie Affair completed the breakup of the antiracist coalition of Left and Islamic associations, as the former refused to support the demand by the latter that the government ban the novel of an author who was well known for his progressive, antiracist views.

The anti-establishment Left would make its own contribution to the establishment's promotion of communalism. The withering of Soviet communism and the decline of the workers' movement fostered the same ascendancy of identity politics and multiculturalism, displacing social class and civil rights in the Left agenda. If black power and feminism seemed at first to be the pacesetters of the group rights trend, among Muslims, it was Salafism that reaped the harvest. Thus as Sidique Khan came of age politically, the ideological environment he encountered was not the broad "black" movement of the early 1980s centered on civil rights but militant Islam in a world of group rights. Had the fledgling community organizer on Beeston Hill consulted (attracted by its glowing preface from the head of the government-funded Commission for Racial Equality) the Leicester Foundation's *Muslim Guide* to "teachers, employers, community workers and social administrators in Britain," Sidique would have been directed, as "recommended reading," not to the Sufi and Barelvi tradition favored by his father, but to the works of Mawdudi and Qutb.[110]

If there is a key to the contradictions of Sidique Khan's life, it is buried in the ghostly silences of Beeston Hill. Yet it is hard not to imagine that seeking to save first himself, then others around him, Sidique learned at every turn—from media, from university as well as from mosque—that it was essential to liberate himself from the British values, the British identity, of Sid's world; that he and his wards and companions "should express their own identities, explore their own histories, formulate their own values, pursue their own lifestyles."

If we cannot ascertain a moment of radicalization, an epiphany (if there was one), we can trace the arc of Sid's radicalization, its wave-form or probability function. Sidique Khan, a "marginal man," was born into a country foreign to his family, to parents who wanted their son to be a literate, integrated Englishman but also to remain Mirpuri in faith and fealty. The elders observed a rural, a tribal, tradition in an urban secular country, but his father sent Sidique to a magnet school where he spread the wings of the dove amid embattled natives and outlanders.

Sid dreamed to be an American, or at least a "Sid" with a respectable job to be displayed for old schoolfriends, much like Mirpuri factory workers sent home beguiling photos of themselves adorned with the trophies of Western success. But Sid's schooling and his integration conduced only to dead-end jobs; a "second-generation decline" and around him British Pakistani scores and emoluments trailed even those of other postmigrant minorities. Down jobs, hypocritical imams, homely, unlettered cousins awaiting his hand in marriage, crack and Ecstasy on the street offering a transient, illusory escape. No secular adversarial tradition was active and available for protest, salvation, and solidarity. What was left of that, the Labor Party, catered to the clan chiefs in the local councils. The media, the wider culture, and even government officials regularly placed value not in Britain, the land of Shakespeare and Locke, but in one's "roots."

Sidique may have been unwanted Inside, but he could always turn Outside. First to the outlaw Mullah Boys, foiling the crack lords who baffled their elders, preaching a new God and a new credo—*al-wala' wa'l-bara'*—with true friends and clear enemies. It was a religion that said identity came not from any country—not from grudging, dissolute, infidel Britain, nor from backward, idolatrous, tribal Mirpur—but from the Islam of Wahhab and Qutb. This new and powerful Islam made short work of fusty foreign imams and offered the coherence of a narrative, the solidarity of a movement, and the romance of Holy War, if for the moment mimed in paintball groups, soon to be performed in Pakistan in the company of "great men." Outside also was the beautiful Hasina, a full-time student, not a night-school-type like himself; a Deobandi from an upscale family, not an ugly illiterate cousin practicing an idolatrous folk religion. Here was an ample new family to supplant the narrow old one.

"Are British Muslim terrorists motivated by poverty?" I was asked recently by a U.S. State Department official administering the Counter-terrorism Office. "Not really," I answered, "not in any direct way." Sidique had a degree; Omar Khayam came from a solid middle-class section of Crawley; Omar Saeed Sheikh, Daniel Pearl's British Pakistani murderer, was wealthy. The lords of Londonistan railed not against Muslim poverty but against kaffir hypocrisy and against homosexuals and Hebrews. If the poverty of Muslims could be an occasion and an inspiration, that was far down the list of grievances, below the "oppression" and "occupation" of Muslim lands, well below any perceived slight to the Prophet.

"If not poverty, what then?" Deposited from another world, brought from tribe to city, "a marginal man" thrust from the first-generation immigrant "decompression chamber" into a difficult, debauched terrain, rejecting the summons back to the village but then offered a sublime, a glorious, life Outside, Sidique and those like him lived, just as Omar Bakri and his acolytes had formulated it, a "crisis" of identity.

PART FOUR

IN GERMANY

GERMANY'S HOT
SUMMER

In the summer of 2007, homegrown terrorists set Germany's teeth on edge. Forty young German jihadis, predominantly postmigrant ethnic Turks but also native German converts to Islam, were implicated in plots to attack their home country.[1] These extremists made up what became known as the Sauerland Cell and all of them were radicalized in Germany. Several members of the cell traveled to Pakistan for military training, where they completed courses in camps in Pakistan run by the Islamic Jihad Union (IJU), a global jihadi group allied with al Qaeda. Other Sauerland members received IJU training online in Germany. The realization that Germany was now a target for terrorists, for German-born terrorists, mobilized both the Right and Left opposition and sowed division within the ruling coalition government.

The specter of Germans training in foreign jihadi camps and of a colossal plot against Germany itself ratcheted up tensions that had been building since the previous summer's disclosure of a shocking plot engineered by two Lebanese men studying in Germany (these "Suitcase Bombers" will be discussed below). The spring of 2007 had seen deadly attacks on German troops in Afghanistan and the kidnapping there of two German aid workers (one was killed). That same spring a Moroccan-German, Redouane el Habhab, accused of supporting al Qaeda, went on trial and the media carried stories that al Qaeda was targeting the June G8 summit in Heiligendamm.[2] Along with the subsequent arrest of German jihadis in Pakistan, all this augured that, notwithstanding its studied opposition to the Iraq War, Germany had become a terror target, not merely a venue as on September 11, and that this time the terrorists were Germans themselves.

AUSLÄNDER JIHADIS IN GERMANY

The Hamburg Cell that planned and piloted the September 11 attacks is thought to have comprised as many as several dozen men, all aliens and visitors.[3] Turkish intelligence and the CIA supplied leads that led to the surveillance of cell members, but German police felt obliged to close the investigation for fear of infringing on "the rights of a religious minority." The 9/11 hijackers themselves lived in plain and rather noisy sight, frequenting extremist mosques, social events, and study groups. But they were not the secular nationalist radicals (such as the PLO militants of the Olympic killings of 1972) whom Germans were familiar with. As Rainer Münz, a German immigration scholar, facetiously remarked, "To us they seemed ideal guests. They were not studying French structuralism but structural engineering. They were Silicon Valley boys."[4]

The Hamburg Cell radicalized and organized under post-Nazi constitutional protections thanks to its connection to a prayer group. But after September 11 this immunity was removed. In April 2003, German authorities raided some eighty offices and dwellings belonging to the German branch of Hizb ut-Tahrir (HT), as "a clear warning to everyone," and seized computers. The Social Democrat interior minister, Otto Schily, then affirmed "that [Germany] will act against violent propaganda and anti-Semitic agitation." This was the second crackdown against HT, which was then banned in January 2004.[5] At its height, the group had perhaps three hundred members in Germany, versus ten thousand in Britain.[6] No ethnic Turks were reported among them. Most HT members in Germany were probably foreigners, mainly Arab students, much like the composition of HT in its early days in Britain.

After September 11, Germany passed two counterterrorist legislative packages, which, among other provisions, provided for the introduction of air marshals on airplanes and increased oversight of money transfers to potential terrorist organizations. The new laws also authorized intelligence services to monitor extremist religious organizations and foreign terrorist groups. But despite these changes, small *foreign* cells continued to operate within Germany. The most notorious, composed mainly of

Palestinians, was directed by Abu Musab al Zarqawi, the notorious Palestinian-Jordanian global terrorist who designed suicide attacks against Shia worshippers and others after the 2003 American invasion of Iraq. Zarqawi's group in Germany was known as the Tawhid (Monotheism) Group. The group later shifted operations to Iraq and eventually became al Qaeda in Mesopotamia. In Germany, the group focused first on logistics: forging travel documents, collecting funds, and facilitating jihadi travel. Its German structure was dismantled in April 2002, shortly after Zarqawi had personally ordered attacks against a discotheque in Düsseldorf and a Jewish institution in Berlin. Another small group that met the same fate in Germany at this time was Ansar al-Islam. Founded in the Kurdish autonomous zone in Iraq after the first Gulf War, this outfit came closer to tapping into actual German support, specifically within the Iraqi-Kurdish diaspora. But the German police arrested most of its leaders in 2003.[7]

In March 2003 German authorities arrested six men with ties to the al-Nur mosque in Berlin, and again it was a group that consisted of foreigners, not Germans. At that time a senior Interior Ministry official told me that the six belonged to an organization working to recruit Arab students to conduct a terrorist operation timed to coincide with the outbreak of war in Iraq.[8] The recruiter was a thirty-two-year-old Tunisian named Ihsan Garnoaui who had entered the country on a false Portuguese passport similar to one used by other jihadis. The passport was one of a batch of five hundred that had been stolen from the Portuguese consulate in Luxembourg.[9] The press reported that Garnoaui had been in personal contact with Osama bin Laden and had spent five years conducting the training of Islamic militants in camps in Afghanistan.[10] At al-Nur, authorities found bomb-making materials, a toxicology manual, a video showing Germany from the air, a loaded Glock pistol, and various passports.[11]

On March 20, 2003, German police spied Garnoaui in a car with familiar diplomatic license plates. Within minutes Garnoaui was arrested. The driver was Mohamed J. Fakihi, the director of the Islamic Affairs Department of the Saudi Embassy in Berlin. The diplomat already had attracted the attention of the Office for the Protection of the Constitution (Bundesamt für Verfassungsschutz) after his business card was found in the possession of the Hamburg Cell's Mounir el-Motassadeq, a Moroccan student who was a close friend of Mohammed Atta (the chief

9/11 hijacker).[12] Motassadeq was convicted for conspiracy to aid the 9/11 conspirators, and he received Germany's maximum sentence of fifteen years.[13]

German investigators told me that Fakihi channeled more than $1 million to the al-Nur mosque. The mosque was moved from a shabby courtyard inside a rundown apartment building to a four-story complex on a gentle side street; the edifice had shops, kitchens, classrooms, and an Internet server. Most of al-Nur's worshipers were from Arab countries. In addition, documents containing the mosque's address were seized from men alleged to have received military training in 2001 at al Qaeda camps in Afghanistan. German prosecutors submitted copies of the documents to a court in Hamburg during Motassadeq's trial.[14]

As part of the Fakihi probe, German investigators sought to determine why the Saudi Embassy in Berlin housed its Islamic Affairs Department far from its elegant residence in West Berlin. Fakihi operated from a former East Berlin–era high rise on Torstrasse in Kruezberg/Neue Koln, a district known for its mixture of immigrants and counterculture. It was an improbable location for a legation whose mission was, according to what the Saudi Embassy told German investigators, "the dissemination of the glories of Islamic culture." A senior German intelligence official claimed its real mission was to propagate Wahhabism.[15]

Fakihi did not speak German, and though he functioned as a cultural attaché, he refused to attend concerts, plays, or movies because as a pietist Salafi he shunned music.[16] But he did meet regularly with known Islamic extremists, according to German officials. U.S. officials alleged that Fakihi was "more than just a sympathizer of bin Laden. He was organizationally involved" with al Qaeda.[17] According to a letter obtained by the *Wall Street Journal*, Fakihi "told his superiors in Saudi Arabia that his ultimate goal was to turn Berlin into an Islamic proselytizing center for Eastern Europe." The Saudi diplomat envisioned moving his office to the al-Nur Mosque, which he proposed should carry the Islamic message to Poland, the Czech Republic, and Hungary, the last of which "once belonged to the Islamic Caliphate under Ottoman Empire rule."[18] Though the diplomat's purpose was almost certainly bluster, not bombs, two days after the arrests, the German Foreign Ministry, following a recommendation from the country's domestic intelligence service, ordered Fakihi to leave the country. The next day Fakihi was on a flight to Riyadh. Protected by diplomatic immunity, he was not subject to charges.[19] Once again, it was an alien, not a German, who sought to take advantage of the country's legal loopholes, its safe haven. The Saudi diplomat's connection with extremists, though not evidence of a terrorist conspiracy, illustrated the role that Wahhabi doctrine can play in radicalization. We shall see below how Wahhabi doctrine influenced an entirely German terrorist, the convert Eric Breininger, a leading member of the Sauerland Cell.

THE SUITCASE BOMBERS

In 2006 a different set of foreign jihadis fixed their sights on Germany. The group was small but its ambitions were large. During the July World Cup football matches in Cologne, two operatives placed suitcases filled with bombs on trains heading for the stadium. They failed to detonate, but if they had, the explosions would have killed hundreds according to an official investigation. The group also planned to bomb the football stadium itself and Cologne's main bridge.[20]

The principal plotters were a pair of Lebanese nationals who were studying in the Baltic Sea port of Kiel, located in the north of Germany. One of the plotters, the appropriately named Jihad Hamad, turned himself in to Lebanese authorities in August 2006. Following a trial in Beirut, he was sentenced to twelve years in jail. After he was identified from security camera footage, the second plotter, Yousef Mohammed el-Hajdib, was arrested by police in Kiel, where he studied engineering. In December 2008 he received a life sentence from a jury in Dusseldorf. Editorials in the major German dailies considered the verdict confirmation that the country was in danger of attacks on the scale of Madrid in 2003 and London in 2005.[21]

Hajdib's indictment stated that the bombs were intended as revenge for the cartoons mocking the Prophet Muhammad that were originally published in the Danish newspaper *Jyllands Posten* in September 2005, and which eventually led to violent demonstrations in the Middle East.[22] The suitcase operation was first described as a prime example of "leaderless jihad."[23] But by the start of the Beirut trial, eight months into the investigation, German authorities, who had interrogated the suspects and examined their email and mobile phone data, computer hard drives, and DNA traces, reached a grimmer conclusion: the attacks were commissioned by an operative linked to al Qaeda. The plot was designed to assess the plotters' capacity for assaulting U.S. troops in Iraq. An email message from Hajdib to Hamad urged patience "until we have passed the initiation test. Then we'll travel to Iraq together." [24]

Neither the suitcase bombers nor any of the other previously cited jihadi cells in Germany involved homegrown terrorists or postmigrants. But the suitcase bombers did shatter the confidence that Germany, thanks to its government's strong opposition to the war in Iraq, had earned immunity to terrorist attack.

A SUMMER'S HEAT

On the summer solstice of 2007, right after the arrests in the border region between Pakistan and Afghanistan, Deputy Interior Minister August Hanning, previously the head of the *Bundesnachrichtendienst*, the German equivalent of the CIA, hosted an unusual press briefing. His subject was terrorist threats to Germany, and he stated that the sort of "noise" heard in the summer of 2001—which became intelligible only after the 9/11 attacks—was being heard again.[25] A month later, Hanning added, "The danger that there could be terrorist attacks here [in Germany] is very real. . . . There is a new quality in the threat to Germany."[26] The official added: "Germany is being threatened by suicide bombers. We now find ourselves right in the crosshairs of Islamist terrorism."[27]

Two weeks earlier Hanning's boss, Interior Minister Wolfgang Schäuble, confined to a wheelchair after suffering an assassination attempt as interior minister in 1990, had called for a bolstering of the antiterrorist tools available to German authorities. He told the German weekly *Der Spiegel* that "the old categories no longer apply. . . . We have to clarify whether our constitutional state is sufficient for confronting the new threats." The minister called for the preventive detentions of suspects, the option of deploying *Bundeswehr* (national armed force) troops within the country, the clandestine seizure of private computer data, and the contemplation of preventive extrajudicial assassinations of individuals planning terrorist attacks.[28] Schäuble's recommendations supplemented his previous requests for more effective surveillance methods and a reformed version of protective custody called *Schutzhaft* (a term, opposition politicians hastened to point out, that had been used by Adolf Hitler to jail his entire opposition).[29] A group promoting data privacy began selling T-shirts on the Internet with Schäuble's image above the slogan "Stasi 2.0"—suggesting that he was reviving the reviled State Security Ministry of Communist East Germany.[30] The leader of the Social Democrats, Kurt Beck, raised temperatures another notch, accusing the Christian Democrat interior minister of seeking to "protect freedom to death."[31]

If the Left opposition (and Social Democratic members of the coalition government) deemed Schäuble's proposals undemocratic, the conservative Bavarian Christian Socialist Union (CSU) considered them feeble. The CSU spokesperson on terrorism claimed that the minister was "just talking" instead of redrafting a law that would make participation in a terrorist training camp illegal. The conservative politician was referring to changes made in 2002 to paragraph 129 of the Penal Code, which criminalized membership of and support for a terrorist group. The original law was passed in 1976 at the tail end of the Red Army Faction's terror wave. In 2002 Gerhard Schröder's Social Democratic government added paragraph 129b, including groups like al Qaeda but only if they had three or more members. That meant that a mere terrorist pair, such as the Suitcase Bombers, heading for an anonymous training camp would have to be detained by other legal means if at all.

The usually apolitical and mainly ceremonial German president, Horst Köhler, expressed concern about the Interior Ministry proposals.[32] However, Chancellor Angela Merkel staunchly backed Schäuble's effort to change the terms of debate, even as she emphasized that she would not endorse preventive detentions or targeted killings. "We have threats that we didn't even know ten years ago," the chancellor said on German television. "I want an interior minister who will grapple with these new threats." Guido Steinberg, who had been the terrorism advisor to the former Social Democrat Chancellor Schröder, allowed that if some of Schäuble's proposals went too far, Germany nonetheless did need to close legal loopholes such as one that distinguished between material support to a terrorist group, which is a crime, and solely promoting its message, which is not.[33]

As June turned to July, jihadi car bombs in London and Glasgow led the chancellor and the interior minister to issue strongly worded statements. Merkel, who had been content to let Schäuble handle terror issues, now called for deploying German troops to combat domestic terrorism: "The old separation between internal and external security is yesterday's thinking. We need to think in completely new ways." Schäuble added, "Something like this can also happen in Germany."[34]

As the summer's heat escalated, in the second week of July, *Bild Zeitung,* the newspaper with the largest circulation in Germany, a tabloid marginally more respectable than its British counterparts, published excerpts from a sensational new book. One of its chapters recounted the life of Said Bahaji, the missing Hamburg Cell member who was born and raised in Germany with a German mother. Another included an interview with a jihadi, "Abu Osama," who claimed to have traveled from Germany regularly to fight Americans in Iraq. *Bild* led each article with factoids, including the Interior Ministry's estimate that some 32,000 "extremist" Muslims resided in Germany. Sandwiched among the *Bild* stories was a lengthy description of the conversion of Thomas Keller. Keller was part of what would come to be known as "the Ulm scene" (see chapter 13).[35]

Then on July 25, the trial of Redouane el Habhab began in Schleswig in northern Germany. The thirty-seven-year-old Moroccan German was accused of supporting al Qaeda and starting his own terrorist network in Sudan. He had moved to Germany, having learned German to read Karl Heidegger in his native language.[36] By all accounts the student of the philosopher notorious for his Nazi affiliations had integrated into his Kiel environment where he ran an Internet café and sold cell phones—much like the 2003 Madrid bombers. That is, until the sudden death of his brother, after which he turned to Islam. He was alleged to have ties with both Mohammed Atta's Hamburg Cell and the Suitcase Bombers. Atta, Redouane el Habhab, and Yousef el-Hajdib all lived in Kiel at the same time. The bulk of evidence produced by the police was from online chat rooms, and much of it was apparently gathered from computers in the Internet café that el Habhab himself ran.[37] On January 24, 2008, the Heidegger acolyte was convicted on six counts of aiding a foreign terrorist organization and one count of founding such an organization. He was sentenced to five years and nine months in prison.[38] In early March, a trial for one of his accomplices, Abdelali Miftah, began: another, Thaer Alhalah, was convicted in February 2008.[39]

In the meantime, the German forces in the UN-NATO mission to Afghanistan had become jihadi targets. In August three German police officers seconded to Afghanistan were murdered. The three officers, who were not part of the NATO mission but were assigned to protect the

German ambassador, were commemorated in a ceremony at the *Berliner Dom* (the gigantic Prussian-era cathedral in the heart of Berlin) that was presided over by Chancellor Merkel and attended by half of her cabinet. With major television crews present, it was the most public display of mourning in Germany's then six-year Afghan engagement.[40] Notwithstanding American criticism that German forces had been reluctant to deploy in more dangerous parts of the country, the Afghan mission was highly controversial in Germany. Speculation started that jihadis would make reprisal, as they had to powerful and consequential effect in 2003 in Madrid.[41]

The newspapers, from the stately *Frankfurter Allgemeine Zeitung* through *Bild Zeitung*, covered each story at "*Sommarloch*" length (the slow news cycle during the sunny months, or, "the silly season"). If these reports seemed to generate more press heat than antiterrorist light, as *Sommarloch* dragged on, German and U.S. intelligence teams were working a deadly serious lead.

THE PLOT

On New Year's Eve 2006, Fritz Gelowicz and Attila Selek, a convert and an ethnic Turk, both from the southeastern city of Ulm, were stopped after driving slowly by the U.S. military barracks in the western city of Hanau, near Frankfurt. They told the police that they were curious to see how Americans celebrated the New Year. Ulm was known as an Islamist center, and the two men had spent time together in Saudi Arabia.[42] The incident mobilized an American surveillance operation that enabled U.S. officials in the spring of 2007 to advise their German counterparts about the suspicious travels of a group of Germans to Mir Ali in North Waziristan.

Mir Ali, the hub for foreign militants in Pakistan, houses, along with al Qaeda, the aforementioned Islamic Jihad Union (IJU). The IJU is an Uzbek jihadi group allied with al Qaeda but with no previously known presence in Europe. In 2002 the IJU split off from the Islamic Movement of Uzbekistan (IMU). The IMU had focused on "the near enemy," the oppressive regime of that Central Asian country.[43] But IJU, apparently won over to bin Laden's "far enemy" orientation, claimed responsibility for the suicide attacks on the Israeli and American embassies in Tashkent in 2004.[44] There is a German base in Termes, Uzbekistan, but the IJU was targeting Germany for more ambitious global reasons.[45] The group was designated as a terrorist organization by the State Department, and German prosecutors said it was characterized by a "profound hatred of U.S. citizens."[46] The IJU cooperates closely with both al Qaeda and Taliban warriors and runs its own training camp in North Waziristan. Though the IJU retains Uzbekistan as a target, the West is now central to its ideology. The alliance with the IJU suited the organizational priorities of al Qaeda, which wished to expand beyond its Arab core.[47]

For the IJU, the "far enemy" is the NATO force occupying Afghanistan. Of those forces the IJU considers the Germans the weakest link, the most likely to retreat under pressure at home. Therefore, the IJU targets Germany in the hopes of exploiting the German public's growing dissatisfaction with the country's involvement in the Afghan counterinsurgency campaign. In that hot summer of 2007, weeks before a parliamentary (*Bundestag*) debate scheduled for the fall, the IJU and its German terror collaborators were seeking to cause a panic that would lead to a German withdrawal from Afghanistan, much as the Madrid bombings had procured the Spanish withdrawal from Iraq three years earlier and much as al Qaeda and the IJU would attempt to do once more in Germany in the fall of 2009 (see the next chapter).

German authorities told the Americans that Gelowicz and Selek had rented a house in Hanau near the U.S. Army base.[48] That prompted the U.S. embassy in Berlin to announce on April 20 that it was enhancing security at American facilities and to warn against a blossoming terrorist threat in Germany, particularly against Americans.[49] From that time on, information was exchanged regularly between U.S. and German intelligence officials. The United States mostly provided electronic intercepts, while the Germans handled operations in the field.[50]

In June 2007, three Germans were arrested in the border region between Afghanistan and Pakistan. Authorities said that during the same time period another dozen German nationals had traveled for training there, usually through Iran or Turkey.[51] Part of the terrorist tradecraft imparted in these camps encompassed the making of peroxide-based explosives, readily assembled from materials available at drugstores and difficult for police to detect. Sure enough, the cell was observed gradually acquiring and then storing 1,600 pounds of liquid hydrogen peroxide in twelve barrels around Germany. This was the same chemical, but in far larger quantities, that the Beeston bombers had detonated in London three years earlier. Prosecutors said that the assembled material could yield bombs more powerful than those that produced 191 deaths in Madrid. In July German security agents managed stealthily to swap out the chemicals.[52]

The next month Gelowicz rented another house, a white two-story cottage in Oberschledorn, a hilly village northwest of Frankfurt in the Sauerland region. Gelowicz; another German convert, Daniel Martin Schneider; and another ethnic Turk named Adem Yilmez— leaders of the Sauerland Cell, as it came to be known—began transporting the now harmless chemicals to the chalet where they had also collected detonators and electronic components. That prompted police to close in and detain the three men on September 4 after raids in some thirty locations across the country.[53] Those detentions came hours after Danish authorities in Copenhagen arrested eight jihadis with links to senior al Qaeda operatives.[54] The German action failed to apprehend some ten other suspects who had provided support for the three operatives.[55]

The IJU claimed responsibility for the foiled bomb plot. Reportedly targeted were the Frankfurt International Airport, the U.S. and Uzbek consulates, and the military base at Ramstein, which supports operations in both Afghanistan and Iraq and houses the largest American military hospital outside of the United States.[56]

THE CONVERTS

To many Germans the most frightening feature of the fraught summer was participation in the plot by several native-born ethnic German converts to Islam—such as cell leader Fritz Gelowicz and his colleagues Daniel Martin Schneider and Eric Breininger. Interior Minister Schäuble stressed the role of converts in what he took to be the recruitment strategy of the jihadis: "They are expressly targeting converts. These are not members of the underclass, but rather social climbers. In the Hamburg cell, there were academics; recently in the UK, doctors; and now here the children of the middle class."[57] Though it seems odd to characterize converts to radical Islam in Germany as "social climbers," the minister

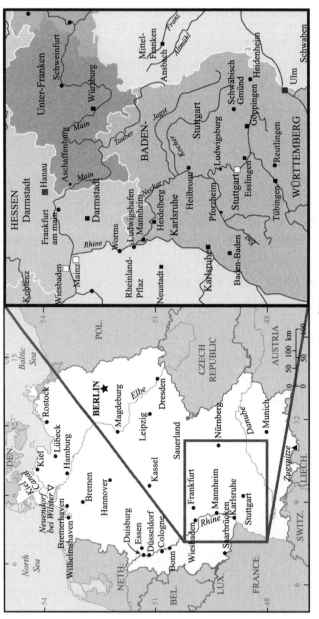

Map of Germany.

reiterated that the threat of "homegrown terror" (in German, the English expression is used) was mounting and that terrorists might soon get their hands on a nuclear device. Schäuble went on to say the threat could be increasing because terrorists were learning from the public debate.[58]

Of the 3.3 million Muslims in Germany, about 18,000 are converts, according to the Islam Archive, a government-funded research group.[59] Most convert simply in order to wed Muslims and pose little threat of radicalization. But Daniel Schneider had attracted the attention of German authorities for three years.[60] He had been arrested on the Afghan-Pakistan border in 2006 and was only allowed to return to Germany in early 2007 upon the intercession of the German Embassy.[61] The domestic intelligence agency, the *Verfassungsschutz* (the Office for the Protection of the Constitution), interrogated Schneider upon his return from Pakistan. Though the agency had learned that the convert belonged to a group of Islamists, some of whom were prone to violence, it decided against trying to make him an informer.[62] Schneider's group came to be known as the Sauerland Cell.

The Sauerland converts alarmed their countrymen in a special way. Like millions of young Germans—in 2007, Breininger was twenty-two; Schneider, twenty-two; and Gelowicz, twenty-eight—they grew up in middle-class Christian homes and went to high schools in sleepy suburban neighborhoods. Schneider even served in the German military. To be sure, our Mohammed Sidique Kahn spoke with a Yorkshire accent and was highly assimilated, but the leader of the London bombers was born Muslim, had an Asian name and his dusky skin allowed whites to maintain psychological distance. In Germany that summer the distance shrank. Germans now had to ask themselves how such ostensibly conventional upbringings could nourish such intense hatreds.[63]

Like Adem Yilmaz, a third member of the German IJU cell, Schneider was living off welfare benefits. And like Gelowicz, who converted to Islam following his parents' divorce when he was in his early teens (his brother, not implicated in the plot, was also a convert), Schneider became a Muslim against the backdrop of an unhappy family life.[64] Schneider's parents divorced in 1996 and, following a major custody battle, the boy moved in with his father in 2001. A good, if inconspicuous, student who excelled at sports, Schneider abruptly left high school two years before graduating to enroll in a technical college, according to the *Süddeutsche Zeitung*, because he wanted to go to a school "where only men teach."[65]

Schneider's protégé, fellow convert Eric Breininger, before his death in Afghanistan, recorded a memoir, which reads like propaganda as much as autobiography. Breininger relates that he originally attended business school and lived the life "of a typical Western teenager"—"Satan's ways," as he would later denominate them—with lots of partying and promiscuity. The turning point, he says, came when a Muslim coworker took him to a Saarland mosque. He was thereupon introduced to Mohammed ibn Abd-al-Wahhab, the fanatical eighteenth-century cofounder of Saudi Arabia's Wahhabi dynasty. According to his account, Breininger immediately saw "the importance of *Al-Wala' wa'l Bara'* to Islam," and grasped "the obligation of jihad."[66] Under the spell of his conversion, Breininger quit school, left his bride, and moved in with Schneider to devote himself to the Qur'an, Wahhabi literature, and jihadi audiotapes, under the supervision of his new "brothers."

> We followed the events in the region where Jihad was taking
> place and watched videos on how the Mujahideen fought against
> the Crusaders. What really shocked us the most was the news
> about the prisons, and how the Crusaders treated our brothers;
> how they tortured and oppressed them. And also the fact that
> these infidels are putting innocent women in prison, raping them
> day after day and then afterwards some of them would have to
> carry the babies in their bellies. That these honorable women
> were being treated like crap just fanned the flames of hatred
> within me towards the infidels.[67]

Breininger's conversion, radicalization, and jihadization converged in rapid and dire succession: "I quickly realized that I had to do something against these Crusaders, who are humiliating our brothers and sisters." A mere four months after his conversion, he set out for the Middle East to learn Arabic. He studied Arabic in Egypt for three months and then traveled to Pakistan's Federally Administered Tribal Areas where he linked up with the IJU. But Breininger languished among peers with whom he could not communicate. Learning that several German Muslims had recently completed their training to enter the Taliban, Breininger secured permission to join them. The Taliban had no objections to the founding of a subgroup, the "German Taliban Mujahidin" (GTM).

Breininger ends his tale with a fundraising appeal to German Muslims: "If the brothers would buy one doner kebab less a week we could buy almost 20 sniper bullets to fight the *kuffar* [the infidels]." But better yet, he urged, you could come and join us; start a family, and raise children "free from the kufr of western society." This new generation of *mujahideen* would arise "multilingual: commanding Arabic, Turkish, English, Pashtu, Urdu and their parents' tongue."[68]

Like fellow converts-cum-jihadis Gelowicz and Schneider, Breininger came from a family shattered by divorce, and it is tempting to see his conversion as a stab at recovery and replacement. In William James's classic *Varieties of Religious Experience*, conversions serve to "integrate" the "divided self" and heal the "sick soul." Those suffering from "morbid-mindedness" were likely candidates for "re-birth" and to find salvation in "self-surrender."[69] Sidique Khan's radicalization appears to have moved in measured steps, the kind of "conversion" that, in James's account, shows "a gradual growth of holiness without a cataclysm."[70] But James also finds "sudden conversion" frequent, where "a complete division is established in the twinkling of an eye between the old life and the new."[71] The convert then often attains "an entirely new level of spiritual vitality, a relatively heroic level, in which impossible things have become possible, and new energies and endurances are shown."[72] In this course "the sweetest delights" ("Satan's ways") are repudiated "with a ferocious pleasure" the moment they present themselves as hazards to a cause that calls forth "our higher indignations." For such a convert it is nothing to spurn friends, to relinquish privileges and possessions, and to sever social ties. "[A] stern joy" is taken "in astringency and desolation."[73]

William James insisted that "converted men as a class are no different from natural men."[74] But converts and radicals share certitude—whether by virtue of Holy Writ or ideological manifesto. In any case, converts constitute a remarkably high proportion of jihadis. A 2005 database that I created with a colleague recorded a striking proportion of converts among jihadis—more than 9 percent of the total jihadis in the West from 1993 to 2005, and more than a third of those born in Europe or the United States.[75]

James found Christian conversion, being "born again," to happen typically in late adolescence, over a short period of time, as the culmination of an emotional, or even pathological, episode. Breininger and Schneider were barely adults when they converted. The median and average age of conversion in our jihadi database was twenty-one.

Scholars such as Larry Poston and Ali Kose have contrasted Muslim conversion to the classic Christian conversion studied by James along with Edwin Starbuck and J. H. Leuba.[76] In contrast to that model, Poston and Kose found conversion to Islam in the modern West to be a protracted process, culminating in maturity. In their view, Muslim conversion is the product of a prolonged search for a simplified and rational religion, dispensing with paradoxes such as the Trinity. Those scholars located Muslim conversion on average at approximately thirty years old.

The vogue of Salafist conversions accounts for the discrepancy between our findings and those of these earlier scholars. Latter-day conversions are often fostered, as in the case of Breininger, by Wahhabi propaganda and the adversarial Islamist narrative we described earlier. Breininger's appears to have been a typical "protest conversion," as Olivier Roy has christened these twenty-first-century Islamic versions of a radicalization process that has been familiar among Western youth since the 1960s.[77] These politicized conversions, in which Islam has become the favored mode of repudiating what used to be called "bourgeois society," in an earlier day might have befallen as a radicalization facilitated not by the Qur'an or jihadi videos but by *The Communist Manifesto* or *The Little Red Book*. According to the police, Breininger's fellow convert and mentor Daniel Schneider could just as well have become "a Scientologist or Neo-Nazi—it was just a matter of who got to him first."[78]

Conversion in Lewis Rambo's words involves "a profound revolution"; the experience has a "foundational quality."[79] James's divided self is made whole. The convert and the radical become individuals driven by their convictions. As I have hinted, radicalization itself can be regarded as a conversion process: it involves a wholesale transformation of outlook and praxis. Indeed, the psychology and sociology of radicalization bear a striking resemblance to the experiences studied by students of the conversion process.[80] The radical, like the convert, typically experiences a moral crisis and becomes a seeker of answers. The subject arrives at a watershed through contact with a mentor or, increasingly today, via Internet chat rooms. He is welcomed into the fold of true believers.

Eric Breininger's sister recounts how her brother suddenly not only gave up pork but "stopped styling his hair," shaving, and watching TV, and that he "began waking up in the morning to pray." "He no longer went out; he broke off contact with friends. His only interest was the mosque where he went to pray, to read the Qur'an and to learn Arabic. . . . He was no longer interested in conversation with outsiders."[81] Breininger's mother awoke one morning four months after his conversion to see her son's packed luggage in the apartment they shared. Breininger informed his mother that he was leaving for another country to learn more about Islam. He said goodbye to her as she got ready for work and that was the last time she saw him.[82]

Eric Breininger's story matches that of Mohammad Bouyeri, the ritual slayer of the Dutch filmmaker Theo van Gogh, and of "Sid" Kahn, who spurned relatives and eventually colleagues. All of these stories feature kind and likable men who become disdainful and distant. To families, colleagues, and friends, such behavior is baffling, yet it is characteristic of the conversion process. The radical, like Rambo's convert, becomes "encapsulated" by the institution he joins, one that bars information from external sources.[83] Abd Samad Moussaoui, the brother of Zacharias, the would-be twentieth 9/11 hijacker, describes the latter's return home from Londonistan: "when he landed . . . in Montpelier, I saw right away that my younger brother had changed. . . . He had renounced all his old attachments; he had always been quiet, but now he became secretive."[84] "The preferred strategy of Wahhabi and Qutbist gurus," the bereaved brother laments, "is to try to cut people off from their families."[85]

Radicalization and conversion share more than a family resemblance. The radical and the convert each undergo a "transvaluation of all values" (*Umwertung aller Werte*) in Nietzsche's phrase.[86] They share a comprehensive transformation—not just in appearance (a beard, a veil), but in company and surroundings; not only in philosophy (ethics, epistemology, susceptibility to revelation or dogma), but in psychology (bearing, confidence, and abnegation); not just in beliefs, but also in behavior; not just in values, but also in actions; a change not only in lifestyle, but also in one's attitude toward life; not just in opinions and views, but also in sources of information.

The more conspicuous converts in jihadi ranks have included the ringleader of the African embassy bombings, Wadih el Hage; "Assam the American" (*ne* Adam Gadahn), Osama bin Laden's American spokesman; Jose Padilla, who reportedly planned a "dirty bomb" attack in the United States; the failed "shoe bomber" Richard Reid; a Polish-born German, Christian

Ganczarski, who served as Khalid Sheikh Mohammed's European coordinator; the Belgian female convert, Muriel Degauque, who suicide-bombed
a squad of U.S. troops in Iraq; and two pairs of convert jihadist brothers: the
American-Dutch Jason and Jermaine Walters, of the Hofstadt Group, who
were arrested in a raid after they threw a grenade at Dutch police; and the
Frenchmen David and Jerome Courtailler, ringleaders of the Beghal group
(the Algerian organizers at the Finsbury Park Mosque). The Beghal group
was implicated in numerous terrorist plots, including a planned attack on
the U.S. Embassy in Paris. Three of the twenty-three Britons arrested in
the Heathrow airliner plot in August 2007 were converts.

The 35 percent incidence of converts among European-born jihadis
in our database contrasts strikingly with the scant portion of converts in
general Muslim populations. In France, converts make up only 0.009 of
the overall Muslim population.[87] In Britain, they make up 0.004 of the
entire Muslim population; in Germany, slightly above 0.005, about half
of a percent.[88] Thus if a German Muslim is a convert, he is eighty times
more likely to become a jihadi than is a born Muslim.

Conversion to Islam requires little more than thrice uttering the *Shahada*, swearing "no God but Allah." But that may signify that the convert
has little religious training and no cultural bearings. As with postmigrant
"reversion," a convert's Islam can be abstract and absolute, an appropriated and prehensile devotion, divorced from the moderating influence of
daily life in a traditional community in a specific place and time. Second-generation "reverts" and converts can pass through their radicalization without the speed bumps provided in Muslim cultures. They are
deracinated, looking afar for a set of principles that become a codified,
deterritorialized religiosity.

Consequently, the convert, like the second-generation revert, may be
more disposed to extreme action so as to demonstrate his bona fides.
Jean-François Clair of France's Direction de la Surveillance du Territoire
observed that converts are often "willing to go further to prove themselves" and told me "they are our most critical problem."[89] The zealous
Breininger moved from the threshold of a Saarland mosque in a matter
of months to violent jihad and death in Afghanistan. The surfeit of ardor,
matching an absence of experience, connection, learning, and stature,
may steer the fresh convert to extremes. But Germany has an even more
critical jihadi problem—its angry young Turks.

GERMANY'S YOUNG TURKS

O n March 3, 2008, exactly six months after the arrest of the leaders of the Sauerland Cell, twenty-eight-year-old Cüneyt Ciftci steered a pickup truck loaded with five tons of explosives into a guard post in Khost province in southeastern Afghanistan. The second-generation German Turk remained inside the blue Toyota to detonate its payload.[1] Two American soldiers and two Afghans were slain and another seven individuals, including four U.S. soldiers, were wounded. The Islamic Jihad Union (IJU), the al Qaeda–affiliated group that took responsibility for the attack, claimed sixty dead in both the explosion itself and a follow-on Taliban attack.[2]

The IJU website carried a video of Ciftci's last moments. "When I press this button, eternal life in paradise will fill me with God's reward."[3] The bearded young Bavarian, who had taken the name Hafiz, sits behind a steering wheel wearing a backpack and an ear-to-ear grin. His hands are raised: one holds a gun, the other lifts forefinger to Allah. He looks straight into the camera, beams, and announces his eagerness for death and destruction.

If the German media were obsessed with the converts in the 2007 Sauerland plot, the cell's Turkish coloration presented more worrying implications. The majority of the forty or so implicated in the Sauerland plot were ethnic Turks, which make up an incomparably larger component of the German Muslim population than converts. There is reason to suppose that radicalization is occurring within this isolated and often alienated population. A global jihadi group, allied with al Qaeda, is focused on abetting and exploiting this alienation.

German authorities were slow to acknowledge that an ethnic Turk, the father of two, who had worked at McDonald's and for Bosch, had volunteered for a suicide mission at the behest of global jihadis. The videotape notwithstanding, the Federal Criminal Office (BKA)—Germany's equivalent of the FBI—refused to confirm the identity of the remains for nearly two months. Finally in May the BKA president Jörg Ziercke announced that DNA analysis corroborated that Ciftci was indeed the bomber—the first German suicide bomber, even if, of course, not the first to radicalize in Germany.

Though the title of the book you are reading may bring to mind Mohammed Atta and the 9/11 Hamburg Cell, of course those angry Muslims were not Europeans. They were not even settlers in Europe. They were visitors—not immigrants (still less second-generation immigrants), and not Insiders. The cognoscenti could note a paradox—that the country whose Hamburg bombers had focused counterterrorist attention on Europe did not, unlike Britain, Belgium, Denmark, France, Italy, the Netherlands, and Spain, appear to harbor indigenous terrorists and was not itself a target of terror. They could note that though Germany hosted the second largest Muslim population in Europe, her Muslim extremists were fewer in numbers than those in any of the enumerated countries; that her homegrown terrorists were too few to mention, and none had forged a link with global jihadis outside the country.[4] As late as the spring of 2007 it seemed correct to assert:

> The experience of Germany, with the largest Muslim population in Western Europe after France, shows that a significant Muslim population at the heart of Europe need not produce either violent Islamist groups or destabilizing social unrest. . . . Neither political nor jihadi currents of Islamism have had much appeal for those of Turkish origin, three quarters of the Muslim population, and the handful of terrorist suspects that have been found have been either German converts or dual nationals of Arab origin.[5]

That a jihadi movement could find recruits in this particular demographic was considered Islamophobic hysterics. But beginning in Germany's hot summer of 2007, homegrown terrorism situated in the Turkish second generation, tied to al Qaeda, and targeting Germany began to confound those knowing assumptions.

THE COMING

Turkish immigration to Germany began with the labor recruitment for the economic recovery and expansion after World War II. Then, after labor migration stopped abruptly with the downturn following the 1973 Arab oil embargo, the bulk of Turkish immigrants entered Germany via family reunification programs.[6]

Muslims first came en masse to Germany as Turkish guest workers (*Gastarbeiter*). Guest workers were laborers recruited mainly by employers, a process facilitated by government treaties. Germany's guest worker program began in 1955 thanks to a labor shortage caused by its *Wirtschaftswunder* ("economic miracle"). The erection of the Berlin Wall in August 1961 created a new shortage, ending the inflow of East German workers virtually overnight. Germany previously had negotiated guest worker treaties with southern European countries suffering high unemployment. Now West Germany began to reach out to Turkey and then to Morocco. Even before making pacts with Portugal (1964) and Yugoslavia (1968), in 1961 Germany signed its first agreement with Turkey, with whom it had enjoyed close relations during the Ottoman Empire. Turkish citizens (largely from rural eastern Anatolia) quickly became its largest group of guest workers. By 1970 there were three million foreigners (two million of them employed) residing in Germany making up nearly 5 percent of the German population. Turkish workers ballooned from 13,000 in 1962 to 800,000 in 1974.

Employers and workers, the German and the Turkish governments, all embrace the myth of return. All assumed that the stay of the "guests" would be temporary. The migrant's temporary nature was presumed, and apparently assured, by the mutual agreement of receiving and sending countries. Working under the principle of "rotation," the migrants, mostly male, were to work in Germany for two years before returning to the home country in order to make room for other migrants.

THE STAYING

In Germany, as everywhere in host Europe, politicians who had quietly authorized entry policies favorable to business interests feared that agitators opposing immigration might seize on the issue and foment a nativist backlash. Keeping immigration, or race, out of politics was an imperative, not just in Germany—and as we have seen, in Britain—but also in France and in the smaller European countries also facing a mass influx.[7] Germans, like other host European publics, were not consulted on the series of decisions pertaining to immigrant recruitment: work permits, residency, and visas—so the accommodations of client politics had injected foreign populations into their midst.

Germany, like France and other Western European host governments, devised a complex system of residency and work permits.[8] Residency rights were usually tied to employment, and thus unemployment carried legal ramifications. If one belonged to the worker's immediate family, he or she could stay without working. But neither the worker nor his family was supposed to stay when his job terminated. Residence permits became, in the words of one German scholar, "acts of grace," which were granted usually by local officials.[9]

If residency rules were intended to control immigration, they failed. Relatives of guest workers came in clandestinely or overstayed their visas when there was no other way to join their families. Where individual state rules were highly restrictive, they were gradually relaxed so that labor recruits often became *de facto*, and soon *de jure,* immigrants.[10] Moreover, the restrictions only convinced migrants to stay put—if they were to leave, they could forfeit the option of return. And then the system of work and residence permits, which usually had to be acquired through cumbersome procedures before arrival, led to a rise in illegal immigrants.

The guest worker program was terminated in 1973, when the worldwide oil crisis slowed the German economy. Unemployment soared, and labor migration became redundant. Would guest workers be invited to leave? Would "temporary" workers return to their homeland as originally envisioned and contracted? To the contrary: not only did the workers stay but their families joined them. Family reunification would grow many times greater than the initial guest worker migration, to become in Germany, as in other European host countries, the largest component of immigration.[11]

It spurred the growth of Islam as well. Before family reunification, mosques were few and far between and Islam did not play a salient role in the lives of guest workers. But the arrival of women and children fostered a concern for customary culture and traditions. Consequently, Islamic communities began to require mosques. Indeed, by the mid-nineties, according to Germany's Central Islam Institute Archive, the number of mosque associations has soared in two decades from single figures to more than 2,200.[12]

We have seen in Britain following family reunification the same religious, cultural, and behavioral consequences—heightened observance, marriage endogeny, and mosque building. In 1965 there were thirteen mosques registered in England. By 1980 there were 203.[13] In 1970 France counted approximately 20 mosques; by 1980, the figure had risen to 250.[14] As for the Low Countries and Belgium, while in the early 1970s there were merely a handful of mosques in the two countries combined, by the mid-1980s, there were two hundred in the Netherlands and more than one hundred in Belgium.[15]

Guest workers imported families, rediscovered their religion, and procured juridical status even as their economic function turned superfluous. Under "the right to reside" (*aufenthaltsberechtigung*), the children of guest workers were granted the right to stay in Germany but not citizenship (see below).

The guest worker's obligation to return was abrogated and immigrant families were united, as elsewhere in host Europe, not as a result of popular consultation or through the legislative process but by the courts. The latter filled with alacrity a vacuum created by passive legislatures, reluctant to approach the heated immigration issue. Germany's Constitutional Court, its highest court, ruled that the German Basic Law, its constitution, covered not just citizens but all those living in the country.[16] A series of decisions from the Constitutional Court secured the residency rights of de facto immigrants, effectively prohibiting the government from deporting, terminating residency permits, or even extending the waiting period for a noncitizen resident to bring in a spouse on the basis of family reunification.[17]

In the Indian Case (1978), the Court told the executive that workers who had stayed a long time had thereby acquired a constitutionally protected "reliance interest" that overrode the official state policy of zero immigration. That is to say, the national interest was considered inferior to the interests of foreigners. Germany's supreme court ruled that de facto immigration, to quote Christian Joppke, "could not remain limited to the directly recruited guest-worker population, but had become a recurrent, self-reproducing process for constitutional reasons alone."[18] The Court restricted government policy relating to aliens.

Deportations and forced repatriation were also ruled out for allegedly constitutional reasons.[19]

The Court thereby spirited away from the executive branch the option of repatriating most classes of foreigners. The foreigner was awarded progressively heightened rights, corresponding to a process of self-limitation on the part of the state.[20] The guest worker, without lifting a finger, acquired what James Hollifield denominated "embedded rights."[21] The constitutional rights of settled foreigners got so securely fortified that only parliamentary legislation could abridge them (something highly unlikely as we shall see), thus limiting executive discretion and tilting courts in the foreigner's direction. A restrictive executive policy was henceforth unconstitutional.

Another straw in the wind was the "Arab Case." Two Palestinian students with ties to terrorists were deported as "security risks" after the 1972 Munich Olympics when Palestinian terrorists kidnapped and then murdered eleven Israeli athletes as well as a German police officer. The court ruled that expelling the Palestinians violated their constitutional rights. It was the first time that the Constitutional Court ruled that foreigners had rights that outweighed state interests, in this case security interests. "Public interest had to be weighed against . . . the private interest" of foreigners and the latter prevailed.[22] In so ruling, the Court came down on one side of an argument that we shall see would continue to roil the German Federal Republic: is Germany a civic or an ethnic nation? Is modern Germany an ethnocultural or a postnational state?

In 1981, with majorities of up to two-thirds of German voters favoring return migration, the Christian Democrats launched a campaign against family reunification.[23] They charged that the procedure circumvented the guest worker recruitment stoppage, and they demanded repatriation.[24] In an indication of the prevailing elite *zeitgeist,* the Christian Democratic Union felt constrained to stipulate that return migration was "not immoral."[25] By then it had already become second nature to prefer putative moral imperatives to the state or national interest.

In 1988 the CDU proposed a generous Foreigner Integration Law (offering benefits and entitlements for the historic guest worker population) together with a restrictive Foreigner Residence Law.[26] But the proposal had to be withdrawn in the face of broad opposition from a coalition of charities, unions, political parties, nongovernment organizations, and churches including the Organization of Catholic Bishops, which criticized the "narrow pursuit of national interest."[27] The new CDU Interior Minister Wolfgang Schäuble, whom we shall meet presently, retreated, extending an olive branch to the pro-foreigner lobby, and secured the 1990 Foreigner Law "just in time to keep the issue out of the federal election campaign of 1990."[28]

————————————

On the question of immigrant rights, or more precisely the right to remain in the country after the expiration of the labor contract, to move from sojourner to settler, the guest workers and their allies achieved only a partial and paradoxical victory. Immigrants won the right to remain in the country but not access to citizenship. In contrast to most other European countries, citizenship for Muslims in Germany, though no longer simply unavailable, remains problematic. Although Germany's citizenship law was liberalized in 2000, postmigrant German Turks, who were born and raised in Germany, were denied citizenship. Only in 2000 did Germany shift the basis of citizenship from *jus sanguinis* (blood) to *jus soli* (territory) as in other European countries. But obtaining citizenship for a nonethnic German still required a probationary residency of at least fifteen years in Germany. More pertinently, the new dispensation affected directly only those born after December 31, 1999—leaving unredeemed the embittered and susceptible young men we shall meet presently.[29]

A TURKISH HOME

Today there are between 3.8 and 4.3 million Muslims living in Germany, roughly 5 percent of the total population.[30] Nearly two-thirds are of Turkish origins, about 2.5 million; of these about four out of five are Sunni Muslims.[31] Less than a third of these, about 700,000 Turkish Germans, have German citizenship.[32] The vast majority of Germans of Turkish origin are found in the former West Germany, especially in industrial states such as Baden-Wurttemberg and Bavaria in the southeast and North Rhine-Westphalia in the northwest and in sections of the working-class neighborhoods of cities like Berlin, Cologne, Duisburg, Dusseldorf, Frankfurt, Mannheim, Mainz, Munich, and Stuttgart.[33] Some parts of these neighborhoods are overwhelmingly Turkish, with

Turkish doctors, lawyers, and newspapers as well as shops and eateries
alongside salons and apartments sporting satellite dishes to pick up Turkish TV signals. German Muslim undertakers estimate that three quarters
of their coreligionists choose to have their remains sent home rather
than undergo interment in cold German ground.[34]

The original Turkish guest workers were skilled and arrived from
urban areas in Turkey, but by the early 1970s the bulk of new entrants
were unskilled and often hailed from rural eastern Anatolia, arriving
via chain migration, which sometimes transplanted entire village networks into the German diaspora.[35] German ethnocentrism helped
keep these rural Turks compartmentalized. If German separatism found
an echo in these Turks, it was not Turkish nationalism but folk tradition
that resonated. Chain-migrating Turks arriving in Berlin tended to
keep company only with families from the same village—reproducing
as far as possible the sender village with its patriarchal family structure
and customs of reciprocity.[36]

Accordingly, as among British Pakistanis, the nuptials of German Turks
were less often Western-style love matches than unions arranged by parents. One journalist reported that about half the Turkish men in Berlin
bring their wives from the old country.[37] The Federal Ministry of Family
found that a quarter of Turkish women in Germany in 2003 did not
know their partners before they married. Another study estimated that
over 90 percent of Turks choose Turkish marriage partners and that less
than 10 percent of the marriages among Turks are exogenous.[38] A third
study concluded that "over half of the second-generation continue to
choose their partners from among the residents of Turkey."[39] Second-
generation men, says Ali Ucar, a professor of pedagogy at Berlin's Technical University, often choose spouses from among their relatives back
home rather than partners raised in Germany "because they consider [the
latter] too progressive." Since the new immigrants have no command of
German, conversations among family members—including the children—are inevitably held in the mother tongue.[40] Hence, only a minority
of Turkish postmigrants are fluent in German. Just 40 percent of second-
generation Turks as opposed to 80 percent of second-generation migrants
from the former Yugoslavia claim to speak German very well.[41]

A comparative treatment found that marriages of Turks in Germany
were far more endogenous than those of Algerians in France—by a
factor of two or three for males and five times that for women.[42] The

rural Anatolian practice of wedding relatives, usually first cousins, is common. According to the Center for Turkey Studies at the University of Duisburg-Essen, the latter accounts for between a sixth and a quarter of endogenous pairings, not as common as among British Mirpuri but still an arresting number.[43] Yet like postmigrant British Mirpuri, Dutch Moroccans, and French Algerians, young German Turks inhabit a netherland. They do not find *Gemuchlichkeit* in the fatherland. Instead, during family summer vacation visits to their parents' homeland, they find themselves labeled *Almanicilar* ("Germaners").[44] They belong nowhere.

That estrangement notwithstanding, arranged marriages with spouses from home can mean the perpetual reduplication of parents who speak Turkish and not German. Such families may speak Turkish at home and raise offspring accustomed to speaking Turkish rather than German and are slow to integrate. Though nominally of the third generation, these postmigrant Muslims, much like the British Pakistanis we have studied, remain effectively in the second generation, with one parent always an immigrant. Most Turkish first-graders reportedly do not master the German language because they are raised in settings where Turkish is spoken almost exclusively. A study in Kreuzberg, a Berlin neighborhood with a high Turkish ethnic concentration, found 63 percent of all children born to foreign parents speak no German when they enter the first year of school.[45] Also, four out of five Turkish first-graders have no knowledge of German, which severely hampers their ability to learn. Eighty percent of their parents cannot participate in parent-teacher conferences because their command of German is limited.[46] Their children, thanks to poor language skills, are likely to land in *Sonderschule*, special schools for pupils with learning disabilities. Thus it comes as no surprise that the school drop-out rate for Turkish German postmigrants is nearly three times as high as among native Germans.[47] The extent to which "the children of Turkish immigrants in Germany are failing at school" led one reporter to conclude they were "in danger of solidifying into a permanent underclass."[48]

While nearly a quarter of all Turkish students go to *Hauptschule* (the lowest track of secondary education), only 13 percent of all German students do. In the highest school track, *Gymnasium,* the only college track, the situation is reversed: while nearly a quarter[49] of native German students attend Gymnasium, only 6 percent of Turkish students do so.[50] Several years ago the Turkish embassy, worried by reports that the grandchildren of the first guest workers still could not master German, sent out circulars urging parents to persuade their children to learn German.[51] But, beyond such exhortations, German Turks often find little reason to speak German outside of the classroom or the office. Nearly three-quarters of them live in Turkish enclaves with thick concentrations of mosques, shops, restaurants, and professional services. They can tune Turkish TV on more than a dozen channels via cable or satellite. Hanim Han, a teenager in the "Little Istanbul" enclave of Duisburg, told a *Time* correspondent: "You just don't need to know any German to get along."[52] But you do need German to avoid being slotted into an inferior school track and an inferior job.

Compared with Turkish postmigrants in France, Turkish-German postmigrants start school three years late, have fewer face-to-face contact hours with teachers, and are slotted into a vocational track earlier and receive less supplementary support and assistance.[53] As a result, the Turkish-German student is afforded little time and assistance to pull himself out of his disadvantaged starting position. Similarly, the Turkish girl, though outperforming her male counterpart in school, is likely to drop out to wed or work.[54] On the other hand, a highly developed vocational training system has improved the chances of the second generation to find jobs, especially in those humble occupations, such as mechanic, painter, or hairdresser, where German Turks benefit from their social networks. Yet German Turks are less likely than both native Germans and other migrants to land skilled jobs and more likely to find themselves in dead-end unskilled jobs.[55] Moreover, at 40 percent, ethnic Turks in their twenties are five times more likely to be without vocational qualifications than their German opposite numbers and suffer twice the rate of employment. About 18 percent of German Turks are unemployed, at twice the level of native unemployment and higher than for other minorities.[56]

In the face of structural discrimination outside the family and poor incentives within it, it is hardly surprising that criminal suspects of Turkish origin outnumber Poles, Italians, Serbs, and Romanians by margins upwards of five to one and by even larger margins with respect to suspects from other diaspora communities in Germany.[57] Second- or third-generation immigrants displayed "considerably higher offender rates than did the first generations of immigrant workers."[58] In the 2010 integration rankings of the Berlin Institute for Population and Development, based on annual population statistics, postmigrant Turks trail their counterparts in other immigrant groups, as well as native Germans, by large margins not only in education but also in earnings and employment. And their performance improves little even after decades of residence.[59] All told, with respect to their minority counterparts, "children of Turkish migrants are the most disadvantaged group among the second generation."[60] And if certainly not all Turkish German offspring are downwardly mobile—women, for example, score better in school and on the job market—even optimistic observers have acknowledged that a "significant portion" of these postmigrants have "inherited the status of their immigrant parents."[61]

If there is little to sustain the idea that the German Turkish postmigrant sees himself or herself as Turkish as opposed to German, there is persuasive evidence that his standing in society and in the law is inferior, that he has fewer contacts with Germans, and speaks German less well than both autochthonous Germans and other German minorities.[62] He is unlikely to enjoy a clear, consistent, and reliable identity. It is a situation that can lead to frustration, anger, and religiosity among these youngsters, especially men, and "makes many of them susceptible to political and religious extremism."[63] In the twenty-first century these susceptibilities appear to have deepened: a study from the Centre for Turkish Studies found that among Muslims of Turkish descent aged eighteen to thirty, those who characterized themselves as devout, rose from 63 percent in 2000 to almost 80 percent in 2005.[64]

WHEN IN ROME?

According to surveys conducted by the German Marshall Fund, 76 percent of Germans in 2005 said that immigration was "an important" or an "extremely important threat," and in 2007 74 percent of Germans felt "personally affected" by immigration.[65] In 2009 the Allensbach Institute found that a majority of Germans thought the country had too many immigrants.[66] In the Pew surveys that were reviewed in chapter 3, Germans harbored a more negative view of Muslims than any other European public. Fifty-nine percent said immigration from Muslim countries was a "bad thing," compared with 41 percent of French and 32 percent of Britons.[67]

Immigration's advocates and opponents spent the 1990s locked in a bitter debate that produced a reform of Germany's citizenship laws that satisfied few. Though major restrictions were removed, liberals continued to complain that a child of foreign descent born and raised in Germany was still not routinely entitled to a German passport. Yet conservatives were unhappy with easing access to citizenship for a German Turk community notable for its poor German and for its insularity. On these grounds the CDU and its Bavarian partner the CSU (Christian Social Union) openly questioned whether the ruling Social Democratic Party (SPD) was fit to run the country, accusing it of jeopardizing "German cultural identity" by liberalizing immigration.[68]

That set the stage for the *Leitkulturdebatte*—a heated dispute about whether Germany should have a "leading culture." Conservatives declared that the country needed such a "guiding culture"—first, in order to structure immigrant, read Muslim, integration, but also, in the words of then CDU chairperson Angela Merkel, "to go into the united Europe as a joint and self-confident nation . . . a country that is sure of itself." The Leitkulturdebatte was thus, in Merkel's words, about "what holds our country together."[69] Her colleagues aimed the concept at the Social Democrat and Green party multiculturalists who, in the view of the leitkulturists, were promoting a Turkish "parallel society."[70] "There should be no doubt," as Christian Democrat General Secretary Laurenz Meyer put it, "about who has the rights of a house owner and who is the guest."[71]

The recurring debate goes beyond immigration policy and reflects the profound doubts and divisions that have haunted postwar Germany about what it means to be German. Periodic disputes on the rights of immigrants to residency, asylum, citizenship, and suffrage et al. are chapters in a foundational argument over the country's identity. Each side regularly invokes principles enshrined in the constitution, the Basic Law: national unity or universal rights. The Left upholds the constitution's championing of "the open state," a civic nation defined by democracy and human rights, while the Right hews to an ethnocultural exclusivity enshrined in the same document's embrace of the *Volk*.

The leitkultur proposal bore on three dimensions of the German self: language, law, and history. Even multiculturalists agreed that language was a valid part of German identity. But were ethnic Turks slow to learn German as a result of their own or of Germany's insularity?

On the constitution, again there could be apparent agreement. Jürgen Habermas, a leading liberal philosopher, had formulated the concept of "constitutional patriotism" (*Verfassungspatriotismus*). But the conservative leitkultur camp happily invoked it also. The leitkulturists cited national elements of the German constitution; their opponents, the universal principles inscribed in it. For the Left, the Basic Law's postulate of the inviolability of human dignity and its prohibition of discrimination of any sort were shaping values that formed the embryo of a postnational collective identity, one designed to supplant a German identity forever fouled by Nazism. In place of a genetic national self, the Left invoked the Verfassungspatriotismus based on the universal and abstract values of the Enlightenment. For them, the Basic Law guaranteed "a republic open to anybody who is willing to accept the rules of this particular nation." The Right countered that citizenship was the birthright of the German Volk exclusively, transferred only by blood, that the Basic Law was designed to preserve the German people, and that the concept of the multicultural society was unconstitutional.[72]

When leitkultur proponents established citizenship tests in several Christian Democrat majority states, such as Baden-Wurtenburg, Islamists cried foul, complaining of constitutional hypocrisy. The tests, they complained, skirted questions about the rule of law, party pluralism, elections, or democratic rights, values that Islamists could argue they subscribed to with no reservation. Instead of these things, they claimed, the tests focused on cultural issues such as polygamy, female equality, spousal rights, and homosexuality, ones the leitkulturists rightly presumed problematic for many Muslims.[73]

It was not uncommon for the Left to insist that the country owned an historical responsibility for foreigners and refugees due to the Holocaust.[74] For the ethnoculturalist Right, modern Germany had a title to reclaim all that remained worthy in the German identity. Many proponents of multiculturalism tended to hold Germany morally responsible for immigrants who were, in their view, compelled to migrate as a consequence of "colonial oppression" and "global inequality." Immigrants had saved the postwar German economy when it needed cheap labor and then were rewarded with segregation. By that logic, multiculturalism constitutes the only moral solution.[75] The leitkulturists ridicule such reasoning as the product of the counterculture, the "sixty-eighters," whose views were adopted by "media school masters" who have "hammered into German minds that it was the people's destiny to be ashamed until the end of time to belong to a *Volk* that had committed the most appalling genocide in history."[76] Clearly in Germany's civil war there can be no Lincolnesque appeal to "the mystic chords of memory."

Germany's Turkish Muslim minorities compose the subtext of this debate. So the events of the summer of 2007 and Cüneyt Ciftci's deadly smile could not help but elevate axial temperatures, with respect not only to Islam but also to the large Turkish German community, hitherto unsullied by implication in terrorist plots.

YOUNG TURKS

Turkish immigrants had been regarded, far from would-be terrorists, "as a comically conservative population—good people, calm people, hard-working law-and-order-people who were grateful to be in Germany."[77] What was now making the isolation of German Turks a national security issue was not just the general availability of the radical Islamic narrative, in Saudi mosques, in videos and audiocassettes, in prisons and universities but the fact that a global jihadi group had trained its sights on them.[78]

The Islamic Jihad Union (IJU) September declaration of responsibility for the Sauerland plot at first surprised German security analysts not only because it is unusual to claim responsibility for a failed plot, but also because it appeared in Turkish, not Uzbek.[79] The IJU, the group that six months later would broadcast Ciftci's grinning suicide video, appears to cooperate with both al Qaeda and the Haqqani faction of the Taliban and runs its own training camp in North Waziristan.[80] The alliance with the IJU suits bin Laden's organizational priority of expansion beyond his Arab core. Guido Steinberg, the German terrorism expert, observes that the integration of Turks would strengthen a trend that has been apparent since 2003: the expansion of al Qaeda to Pakistanis, Kurds, "and an increasing number of European Muslims."[81] Al Qaeda had failed to recruit Turks in large numbers, but partnering with the IJU was "an opportunity to rectify this deficit."[82]

As we have seen, the IJU, with al Qaeda, turned its attention to Germany as "the weakest link" in the NATO presence in Afghanistan. But the interest in German Turks embraced another salient. The Uzbeks are a Turkic people (Uzbek belongs to the Qarluq family of Turkic languages) and speak a language similar to Turkish. Moreover, as we have seen, many second- and even third-generation German Turks speak Turkish better than German. That makes Germany's postmigrant young Turk a target of opportunity for the IJU, one that it seeks to address with a Turkish website called "Time for Martyrdom" (www.sehadetvakti. com), online since November 2006. Steinberg notes that many of the postings on the website "are written in faulty Turkish, suggesting that the authors might be Uzbeks or perhaps Turks who have spent most of their lives in Germany."[83]

Wolfgang Schäuble, Angela Merkel's Interior Minister, was asked if the German security services had been wrong to assume that "Turks living in Germany" were not prone to terrorism. His response was that "most Muslims in Germany are Turks, and while most Turks are not likely to be involved in terrorism, some will be."[84] Schäuble's counterterrorism proposals, discussed in the previous chapter, came at a time of rising acrimony in Germany's mostly Turkish, Muslim population and as four major Turkish groups boycotted Chancellor Merkel's annual meeting on integration to protest citizenship tests aimed at Muslims.[85]

Following the Ciftci "martyrdom" video, the IJU website carried videos showing the converts Eric Breininger and Daniel Martin Schneider training in an IJU camp and calling for Muslims living in Germany to join the jihad against the West. Both Breininger and his masked "interviewer" speak in German in the video. As we have seen, like Ciftci, Breininger and Schneider were linked to the Sauerland Cell.[86] Adem Yilmaz of the Sauerland Cell reportedly organized the trips of numerous German recruits to IJU camps in Pakistan.[87] Before making an appeal for new recruits, Breininger can be heard singling out Ciftci for praise for killing Americans. Its website, the Turkic connection, and the plight of young German Turks cast the IJU in a position to recruit to global jihad among Germany's Turkish diaspora.[88] With this in mind, let's take a closer look at Cüneyt Ciftci, Germany's most unforgettable young Turk and our last angry European Muslim.

HAFIZ

Cüneyt Ciftci, the son of Turkish immigrants, was born on Bastille Day, July 14, 1979. He grew up in Ansbach, a prosperous town twenty-five miles southwest of Nuremburg. "Surrounded by gentle hills, fields,

meadows, forests and picturesque Bavarian villages," Ansbach bears no
obvious resemblance to Beeston. Boasting "attractive new apartment
buildings with curtained windows and solid middle-class cars parked out
front," the area where Ciftci lived, according to Deutsche Presse Agentur,
appeared "anything but a nest of violent Islamist extremists."[89] Ansbach
does host a number of Turkish families who migrated there in the 1960s
to work as unskilled laborers in nearby factories. Because of Germany's
restrictive citizenship laws, many of them remained Turkish citizens.

Ethnic Turks make up most of the worshippers at the town's two small
mosques. The Hilal Mosque gets support from the Turkish government's
religious affairs office known as Diyanet, which until recently had a Sufi
orientation. The city's other mosque is affiliated with the Milli Görüs
(National View), an Islamist group based in the Turkish immigrant community that has been controversial in Germany. The *Verfassungschutz*
classifies Milli Görüs as extremist, and monitors the mosque, but the
group resembles in many respects the French UOIF, the Muslim Brotherhood–led group discussed in chapter 2.[90] The militant Milli Görüs
movement tends to fundamentalism, in contrast to the moderate popular
Islam of the Diyanet-linked mosques.[91] But Milli Görüs does encourage
followers to apply for German citizenship and to pursue minority rights
as Germans.[92]

Cüneyt Ciftci's father was a founding member of that Ansbach Milli
Görüs mosque, making him "no stranger to the authorities at the
Bavarian-based Office for the Protection of the Constitution [Verfas-
sungschutz]."[93] He sent Cüneyt at the age of twelve for three years to
study in a state-run religious school in Turkey, where he learned to
recite the Qur'an from memory and came back with the name Hafiz.
But then Ciftci turned away from his father's fundamentalism and tried
to pursue a secular life.

Integration did not go smoothly. Hafiz abandoned school, then a ma-
sonry apprenticeship, landing in a series of odd jobs, including one at
McDonald's. Stefan Meining and Ahmet Senyurt suggest that the young
man felt torn between Germany and Islam, between a yearning to integrate and a fundamentalist father. Yet Hafiz seemed to have landed on his
feet when he found a warehouse job with Bosch that provided steady
income, a health plan, generous vacations, and other fringe benefits.[94]
Acquaintances told Meining and Senyurt that Ciftci was not at all a religious extremist or even "especially religious." He ate at restaurants,

grooved on fast cars, and joined a soccer team. His former coach and teammates later described him as very quiet and reserved.[95]

German authorities consistently rejected Ciftci's repeated applications for citizenship after several rounds of "security conversations," a procedure mandatory for all "foreigners" whose loyalty to the constitution is in question. Meining and Senyurt believe Ciftci was turned down because of his father's Milli Görüs affiliation. Was the integration of Ciftci, torn between his desire for German normalcy and his strict father, thwarted in the end by the German government—a government that deemed a great number of native-born to be "foreigners," that judged that those who frequent a Milli Görüs mosque were "extremists"? In December 2007 the Interior Ministry had released a 509-page document that arrived at an estimate of 32,000 "extremists" by conflating fundamentalists of different stripes—Islamists (including the Muslim Brotherhood and Turkish Milli Görüs [see below], Tabligh Jama'at [TJ], and assorted Salafists).[96] Hafiz would soon convert this questionable judgment into a kind of perverse prophecy.

First, the son, in a pattern with which we have become familiar, offended his orthodox father by marrying a secular Turkish woman he met in a *döner kebab* bistro. She did not wear a headscarf. But unlike the Beeston Khans, the Ciftci father and son seemed to patch their rift. Hafiz and his wife moved in with his parents, and the daughter-in-law presently began wearing a headscarf. She became estranged from her mother whom Ciftci now judged too "Western." At the same time Hafiz grew a beard and donned the long tunic and flowing trousers of a *salwar kameez*. Just before moving in with his parents, Ciftci had returned to the father's mosque and even began preaching there, capitalizing on his Qur'anic study and a "beautiful, clear voice." But in the supposedly "extremist" Milli Görüs mosque his Friday sermons met resistance, especially when he cited the holy book to claim that Muslims had a duty to kill Americans in Iraq. Following that sermon, the mosque board prohibited Ciftci from preaching.[97]

What radicalized Hafiz? Information is thin here, even thinner than for Khaled Kelkal or for Sidique Khan, but German security authorities believe that Ciftci's radicalization may have begun around 2001 or 2002 with his involvement with TJ, the international Islamist missionary movement. TJ, as we have seen repeatedly, has often been a way station for radicalization, as it was for "the American Taliban" John Walker Lindh; for

members of the 9/11 Hamburg Cell; Richard Reid, the shoe bomber; the
Lackawanna Six; Khaled Kelkal; Sidique Khan; and the 2006 Heathrow
airliner plotters. Jihadis, like those who trained with Omar Nasiri, the
Moroccan double agent, revile TJ retreats as holidays for obese hypocrites.
But far more frequently than the Muslim Brotherhood, a group regularly
impeached for this sort of thing, TJ has served as a launching pad for
would-be jihadis. Nasiri, for example, made his contacts with the training
camps in TJ mosques.[98] Observers described TJ as a "sieve" in which
jihadis covertly sift out likely candidates for "martyrdom."[99] The contrast
in Ciftci's radicalization process between the roles of TJ and the political
Islamists of his father's Milli Görüs seems more than incidental.

There are approximately a thousand Tablighi in Germany.[100] The
Bavarian Verfassungschutz has followed twelve TJ circles, including the
one Hafiz frequented in Pappenheim, a village forty miles south of Ansbach.[101] Since the 1960s Pappenheim has been home to Turkish immigrants laboring in nearby quarries and auto factories. In 2006, two TJ
hate-preachers from Bosnia-Herzegovina, who had been active in Pappenheim as well as in the neighboring city of Treuchtlingen, were
expelled from Germany.[102]

Up until 2002, TJ missionary groups visited the Milli Görüs mosque
in nearby Ansbach. After 2002, the Milli Görüs mosque apparently
became more wary of the TJ missionaries, and it seemed to have prevented them from proselytizing in the area. But meanwhile, in 2001 and
2002, authorities believe that Cüneyt Ciftci first came into contact with
TJ through family relations. Although the details remain obscure, German security authorities assume that TJ helped to put Ciftci on the path
toward extremist Islam.[103]

On April 2, 2007, after giving proper notice to his employer and to the
government, but without supplying a new address, Ciftci left Germany
with his wife and two children and headed for Pakistan where, after settling his family, Hafiz proceeded to a training camp run by the IJU.[104]

GERMANY'S TWIN CITIES OF ISLAMISM

In the IJU camp, Hafiz joined Eric Breininger and other members of the
Sauerland Cell who arrived via a different route—not from TJ but from
Germany's version of "Londonistan," the twin cities of Ulm and Neu

Ulm, nestled in Baden-Württemberg and next-door Bavaria, respectively. It is worth noting that these two southern states, with their very low unemployment and superior educational opportunities, are often cited in Germany as models of immigrant integration.[105] But the Islamic Information Center in Ulm and the Multikultur Haus in Neu-Ulm became haunts for radical Islamists: Arabs, German Turks, and converts. As many as twenty of them went to train in IJU camps in Pakistan beginning in 2006.

The lord of this Deutsch Londonistan was one Yehia Yousif, aka Abu Omar, an Egyptian medical student who graduated summa cum laude from the University of Freiburg in 1994.[106] At that time, just when Abu Qatada and company were setting up shop in London, the fledgling physician began to treat souls at the Multikultur Haus in Neu-Ulm. Among Abu Omar's followers were the jihadis who formed the Sauerland Cell. Abu Omar's son Omar trained in Pakistani Kashmir with Lashkar-e-Taiba, the Kashmiri jihadi group later to become notorious worldwide for its 2008 attack on Mumbai. After training as well in Indonesia, Omar Yousif was arrested in Germany in December 2004.[107] His father's Multikultur Haus in Neu-Ulm attracted the likes of Reda Seyam, a suspect in the Bali bombings, and Mamdouh Salim, an al Qaeda moneyman.[108] Abu Omar, much like some lords of Londonistan, posed as an informant, but he dropped out of sight when the authorities learned he was feeding them disinformation.[109]

Daniel Martin Schneider allegedly met fellow convert and Sauerland conspirator Fritz Gelowicz while studying with Abu Omar in Neu-Ulm (both converts were discussed in the previous chapter). The man who recruited Gelowicz was another Abu Omar pupil, known as "Tolga D." On August 14, 2007, Pakistan deported Tolga Dürbin to Germany where he was charged with incitement to commit terror, attempting to join a foreign military and recruiting other Germans to join the jihad.[110] Another Sauerland conspirator, Adem Yilmaz, was also a disciple of the Egyptian doctor. German investigators connected Cüneyt Ciftci directly to Yilmaz.[111]

The Multikultur Haus denied involvement with terrorism, and it claimed that none of those implicated were members during the previous three years.[112] When Bavarian authorities nonetheless closed the center at the end of 2005, the investigators reportedly found literature urging the murder of Christians and Jews. They also claimed that radical

"preachers of hate" raised funds and recruited for jihad there.[113] Simultaneously with the closure of the Multikultur Haus, the association that
ran it was likewise banned. But hardliners continue to meet in the Islamic
Information Center (IIZ) in Ulm. The IIZ's journal, *Denk mal Islamisch*
(*Think Islamic*), was geared to converts. After the events of the summer of
2007, the IIZ shut its doors in October, apparently anticipating closure
by the Bavarian Ministry of Interior.[114]

RETALIATORY JIHAD

Germany's young Turks, converts, and other sympathizers may be forming a strategic reserve for al Qaeda and the Taliban. Those organizations
regard Germany as a weak link in NATO's Afghanistan deployment,
much as Spain was for the Iraq War coalition. The 2003 Madrid train
bombings delivered a strategic coup that led to Spain's pullout.[115] In the
run-up to Germany's general election in September 2009 al Qaeda and
the IJU produced numerous videos in German and Turkish shown on
websites used by al Qaeda. On one, a German Moroccan, dressed in a
dark suit and a blue tie, warned: "If the German people do not use their
chance to select parties that will withdraw their soldiers from Afghanistan, then there will be a terrible awakening after the election."[116] There
was no such "awakening," and the taunt appeared bombastic: while most
Germans oppose the Afghan deployment, only one party, The Left, had
come out in blanket opposition to it, and that party's chances of entering
a new government were remote. Yet German and American authorities
did not consider the threats empty. Airports, train stations, and Jewish
institutions across Germany were put under armed patrol in the days
before the election.[117] The State Department website alerted U.S. citizens in Germany to "maintain a heightened situational awareness and a
low profile."[118]

   A report leaked from the Federal Criminal Police (BKA) observed
that "the many messages addressed directly at Germany are a new development. After the US, Germany is only the second country whose population is being addressed so directly, and in the language of the country,
by al-Qaida and its allied organizations."[119] Included in the September
2009 video collection was a twelve-minute film from the campfire of
the Deutsche Taliban Mujahidin, the group to which Eric Breininger

belonged. The video was produced by the IJU and supplemented its Turkish-language recruitment tapes.[120]

Germany had joined the United States as a target of what we might call strategic jihad, jihad with specific battlefield objectives, terror attacks linked to the Afghan/Pakistani war, retaliatory jihad to punish war enemies. Examples include the 2009 Fort Hood massacre and the 2010 Times Square bomb plot as well as other planned assaults on the United States in retaliation for the Afghan war.[121] They appear to be modeled on the jihadis' most successful attack from a strategic standpoint—the Madrid bombings. If that is the case, Germany looms as a particularly vulnerable target. It is the most fragile NATO ally, one with a large alienated Muslim second generation that is particularly susceptible to the Taliban and al Qaeda's Turkic allies in a country deeply divided not only over immigration and terrorism but even over its own *raison d'être*. If France is the past of European jihad, and Britain its present, Germany could be its future.

PART FIVE

FINALE

FIGURES IN
THE CARPET

I f Northwest Europe, host Europe, finds itself with something like
a Muslim internal colony, that adjunct—we have seen—has not
been the result of any considered policy, still less of popular consent, but of a spontaneous market-driven process, characterized by client
politics and chain migration. "Immigration channels" carried Muslim
families from specific sender countries, regions, and villages to specific
host countries, cities, and neighborhoods.

Neither the hosts nor the visitors envisioned immigrants integrating
into the social ensemble—both groups nursed illusions of transience,
"myths of return." These often stamped themselves on European Muslim settlement—in the form of enclaves, poor performances in school
and in the job market, and of other strains of segregation that were
imposed or self-imposed.

Immigration typically moves families, not isolated individuals. Families characteristically carry attachments—customs, traditions, values,
and creeds—and in the case of Europe's Muslim immigration, these
have been robust. If we bear in mind that in a relatively accommodating American society the assimilation process often extends into
and beyond the third generation, as Nathan Glazer and Daniel Moynihan showed in their classic study *Beyond the Melting Pot*, it should come
as no surprise that Muslim immigration adjustment in Europe, in its
context of deep cultural—really, civilizational—division, reaches into
postmigrant generations.[1]

Though the arrival and settlement of Muslims created hostility and segregation, presenting a challenge to *social cohesion*, the hazard these newcomers could pose to *national security* did not materialize fully until the second generation. The national security threat emerged in the form of restive postmigrant "groups of guys" like the Mullah Boys on Beeston Hill.

The postmigrant alone faced the challenge of assimilation. His migrant parents nursed the illusion of return when not importing village and clan customs into the urban setting. So it was the son, "the marginal man," not the father, the patriarch, on whom fell the burden of socializing to an alien culture and an often-hostile society—an onus hardly allayed by disappointing economic prospects, a "second-generation decline," a decline even from the father's own grueling material circumstances. Far from a welcoming environment, what the new home offered so often was a youth of drug addiction and gang violence and an adulthood driving cabs or bagging groceries.

The family hearth threw no light on these Western ordeals. If a culture is, as Clifford Geertz teaches, "a set of control mechanisms—plans, recipes, instructions . . . programs . . . for the governing of behavior," the clan, the tribal, cultures brought from Anatolia and Mirpur, from Rif and Silyet, offered no algorithms for the algebra of the streets of Lyon, Duisberg, Rotterdam, or Leeds.[2]

What sort of opportunity did the postmigrant Muslim have to protest his situation or even to find company in misery? The multiculturalist Left encouraged the establishment to frame policy, and minorities to protest, on behalf not of a broad class but of a narrow identity. Thus, not only the Outside—the "single narrative"—but the Inside—the bureaucrat, the funder—taught Muslims to define themselves in ethnic or religious and not socioeconomic terms. Identity politics, in the name of diversity, divided the constituency of the Left even before the fall of communism, a by-product of globalization, breathed a curse on class-based politics.

This twin process of diversification and globalization undermined European national identity even as it animated and aggrandized an infatuation with Muslim identity. To properly appreciate this development, we must view it in a wider historical frame via Ibn Khaldun's *asabiyya*. This concept, developed by the fourteenth-century Arab philosopher, can be translated as solidarity, fellowship, group-feeling, fighting spirit, or identity. According to that pioneering sociologist and historian, asabiyya ('asaba, to bind; 'asab, a nerve, ligament, or sinew—cf. the Latin *religio*) held societies together with a tensile strength, a cohesive force. In tribal communities, the Muslim scholar sustained, asabiyya is strong, resisting conquest or outside control. In cities asabiyya is weak. Hence, civilizations inexorably decline, riddled by the luxury of urban life, to be conquered by outsiders who enjoy the dynamic cohesion, the asabiyya, of the tribe.

To apply the idea to present-day Europe, we could also translate asabiyya as nationalism and regard nationalism as a form of asabiyya whose rise and decline shapes Islamic identity in contemporary Europe.

Hans Kohn's magisterial *The Idea of Nationalism* (1943) traced the roots of the nationalist idea deep into the past but saw it budding in the European Enlightenment and found its first full flowering in the French Revolution.[3] Over time, sundry European conditions—markets, cities, the bureaucratic state, the rise of the middle class, individual liberty, democracy, historical consciousness, the rule of law, the breakup of Christendom and the establishment of Westphalian sovereignty, the secular utilitarianism and scientific spirit of the Enlightenment, the printing press, the ascendancy of the vernacular, a reading public, and the emergence of public opinion—converged, Kohn argued, to produce the idea of the nation, transforming a simple, natural, and vegetative group-feeling about home—territory, language, ancestry—into a highly complex, artificial, and abstract consciousness, or "an imagined community" in Benedict Anderson's rich phrase.[4] In that way, the national idea, to use Friedrich Nietzsche's formulations, linked "love of those nearby" (*Nachstenliebe*) with "love of those far away" (*Fernstenliebe*).[5]

At the end of the eighteenth century in the West, "nationalism began to supply that emotional warmth and intimacy of union which religion had provided."[6] In the modern period, as opposed to our postmodernity, the state was sacralized, the nation became the object of supreme loyalty, the axis of group consciousness and the expression of the we-group, "creating homogeneity within the group, a conformity and like-mindedness"—its own form of asabiyya—that could "lead to and facilitate concerted common action."[7]

But, writing under the lengthening shadow of Nazism, Kohn found that what once "had increased individual liberty and happiness" now "undermines them."[8] The nationalist idea had given us world war, Nazism, imperialism, ethnocentrism, and a revulsion in which the nationalist idea waned as a unifying and mobilizing principle in European states.

The decline of European nationalism has been accompanied by segmentation and globalization. By "segmentation," I mean the habit of social- and self-definition, in terms of both ascribed and acquired characteristics—political, partisan, and ideological as well as racial, ethnic, sexual, and religious—on which we bestow the honorific "diversity," which, Christian Joppke remarks, has become "the master rhetoric in all western states."[9] In the twenty-first century, the internal diversity of society is not only considered legitimate but inviolate. By "globalization," I mean the processes of our time by which regional and national economies, societies, and cultures have become integrated through a global network of communication, technology, finance and trade, which transcends and depreciates national boundaries.

Mass immigration is at once a rigorous form of globalization and a relentless instance of segmentation. Taken together, globalization, segmentation, and the revolt against nationalism drained from European states, even as Ibn Khaldun might have anticipated, much of their *amour propre*, their sense of identity, of a we-group, their asabiyya. The state was desacralized and the national idea became a kind of dark energy, not a pole of attraction but of revulsion and repulsion, no longer an "integrating" factor but a disintegrating one. Under these Inside circumstances, the host country could not be counted on as a source of identity for the postmigrant Muslim. Sometimes he turned instead to the Outside, to what, from the national standpoint, appeared as a subnational or segmented identity. From the adopted standpoint of the *ummah*, it was the national that appeared as the segmented, subordinate identity.

Nationalism and asabiyya alike are historical phenomena that appear and disappear, rise and fall; they adhere to certain groups under certain conditions and desert them when those conditions disappear. The nationalism attached to Germany, France, and Britain in the nineteenth century and the first half of the twentieth century, the asabiyya, or "fighting spirit" that led to two world wars on the European continent is—"thankfully" as we say—a thing of the past. But should Europe be unreservedly grateful? Not necessarily, because it could be argued that the flagging of nationalism encouraged the emergence of parallel societies or enclaves with their own "fighting spirit" in places like Beeston.

Before mass immigration and the rise of identity politics, the countries of Northwest Europe were comparatively homogeneous. Indeed, as Joppke points out, the intense "particularisms of nineteenth century nations rested on the enforced sameness of individuals and groups that constituted them." The military uniform constituted the prime symbol of "that sameness of the parts and distinctiveness of the whole that marked the classic nation state."[10]

Today European nations rest, to the contrary, on highly heterogeneous societies in which "individual and group participation is protected under the flag of 'diversity.'" Georg Simmel "crisply articulated" the social logic and implications of this disjunction: "the elements of a distinctive social circle are undifferentiated, and the elements of a circle that is not differentiated are not distinctive." With the help of Simmel's formula, Joppke argues that building a European nation in the twenty-first century cannot reproduce "nineteenth century nation building." All this goes to explain why European governments "find it ever more difficult to instill national particularism through their immigrant and national minority integration policies," relying instead on generic, one-size-fits-all "repetitions of the self-same creed of liberal democracies."[11]

In the past, relatively homogeneous societies, a single identity, and vying European countries; today heterogeneous societies, "diverse" identities in a peaceful European Union. The old nationalism, in Anthony Smith's words, required, if not that members of a nation should be identical, "that they should feel an intense bond of solidarity to the nation and other members of their nation."[12] Citizens of Western states increasingly define themselves through diverse subnational identities—political, partisan, ideological, regional, ethnic, sexual, and religious—which saps the power and transcendence of the national identity. That identity is vitiated from the inside by diversity and from the outside by globalization, fostering, in turn, subnational and transnational identities. This withering away of national identity, at least among the dominant classes, is most pronounced in Western Europe.

The Muslim postmigrant "marginal man" often finds himself suspended between two cultures, neither of which offers him secure footing. He is apt to reject his parents' folk Islam because, like most immigrant offspring, he shuns the old-fashioned ways of the home country. The new country, for the reasons we have charted (ethnocentrism, diversification, globalization, loss of asabiyya, and so on), offers him a *de jure* assimilation (France), a *de facto* segregation (Germany), or a multicultural identity (United Kingdom). Of these poor prospects, the latter, the one a Muslim may find most comfortable, can be the most destructive for the nation. Fond Britain insisted that he be first and last a Muslim, and thereby lit a slow fuse.

The postmigrant Muslim extremist opts for an identity he chooses, not one he inherits. He adopts his own myth of return, to a golden age of Islamic intensity and purity. His anger finds a narrative that depicts his plight as Muslim oppression and channels that anger into jihad. The angry Muslim may riot or join a gang; he is transformed into a terrorist only when he is armed with an ideology, a narrative, only when the Inside finds and embraces the Outside. That narrative awaits him not only in the mosque or in the Islamic center but also in the university prayer room, the bookstore, the gym, and the cellblock. It appeals, as we have seen, to convict, convert, and community organizer.

To understand why Muslim anger played itself out as riots in Paris but in terrorist bombings in London we looked at how France and Britain handled their angry Muslims, such as Khaled Kelkal in Lyon and Mohammed Sidique Khan in Leeds. As of this writing, France has faced terror and turned it away. Armed with custom-made antiterrorist courts, police, and judge-prosecutors, an inquisitorial trial system, and a public not allergic to government surveillance, French authorities have been able to avert the merger of alienated postmigrants with alien Outsiders, of postmigrant anger with the single narrative, the eruption of "two, three, many" Kelkals.[13] By and large, Muslim anger in France did not embrace the radical Islamic narrative. There was thymotic anger—a thirst for identity and a quest for recognition—but no "French Intifada." Paris, in contrast to London, did not undergo a clash of civilizations and did not experience mass murder. Its immigrant riots were about police brutality and joblessness, not Islam and jihad. The rioters asserted a right to be French, to enjoy the opportunities and protections of other Frenchmen; they marched under today's Tricolour and not the Crescent banner of a Muslim golden age.

Trouble and tumult in France, but in Britain conspiracy and calamity—the convergence of rage and revelation. In both countries the Outside knocked on the door—in the form of Saudi pietists, Afghan veterans, jihadi videos, Internet chat rooms, "big brothers," and "bearded ones." But Britain extended the carpet of welcome—overlaid by British traditions, by its identity politics, and by a "covenant of security." What was a dangerous infection became in Britain "dire convergence." The *al-wala' wa'l-bara'* doctrine from Saudi texts, holding Muslims to be a superior breed, joined with their straitened British circumstances, to generate not merely a perception of injustice but a vocation, even among the best and the brightest, for murderous revenge.

In France as well as Britain, Muslim postmigrants experienced the unwanted status of their parents, the decline of the second generation, and the contagion from the Outside. But in France Muslim immigrant communities were less insular.[14] Public policy in the United Kingdom, unlike France, honored and deepened the myth of return through a multiculturalism and an identity politics that nursed a pluralism of ethnic and religious enclaves inside Britain. Again, in both cases the principal sender countries host jihad movements, but the Algerian government suppresses while the Pakistani government encourages those movements.

Both internal history (France's conversion of "peasants into citizens" versus British pluralist confederation) and imperial experience (direct French versus indirect British colonial rule) shaped the legal, political, and cultural regimes—the French melting pot and British communalism— that confronted the challenge of radical Islam in each country. Britain's celebration of difference, its prizing of minority identities, has little parallel in France's political culture that stresses assimilation, even if the actual outcome hardly measures up to the model. Moreover, to its combustible amalgam of Pakistani provenance, an insular culture, identity politics, lenient courts, and shortsighted policy, British intervention in Iraq supplied the torch to ignite its explosive amalgam. The French stayed out of Iraq and away from the charge of occupying a Muslim land.

Germany (not to mention Belgium, Denmark, and the Netherlands) shows that the danger of second-generation radicalization is not confined to France and Britain. Germany lands somewhere between Britain and France in the indices just advanced. That most of its postmigrant Muslims are ethnic Turks certainly no longer offers reassurance. In the cultural realm, Germany appears torn by opposing forces—one, most prevalent in universities and law courts, is centrifugal and multicultural; the other marches under the banner of *leitkultur*. The German courts, like the British, often appear to favor minority rights above state interests, but on the other hand the security forces were quick to discourage in Ulm and Neu-Ulm the building of a Londonistan. Nonetheless, Germany is clearly a jihadi target and will remain so at least as long as its troops remain in Afghanistan. A full analysis of that situation, including the progress of political Islam in Turkey itself, is beyond our reach here, but there is some reason to fear a German revolt of the second generation.

—————————

We have tried to explore the multiple dimensions of European jihad—geographic, temporal, economic, political, and cultural. If there is a "take-away" from this lengthy investigation, it might be invested in developing, so to speak, a theory of relativity in antiterrorism. What you can do depends on where you are. And knowing where you are will almost invariably require the recognition and appreciation of heterogeneity. That is why in the User's Guide we inspected varieties of Islam: folk and fundamentalist; Islamist, Salafist and jihadis; missionary, political, and jihadi Islamists; and national, global, and takfiri jihadi.

What we might call "strategic heterogeneity" would seek to isolate our main enemy, neutralize other enemies, win over neutrals, and broaden the number and deepen the conviction of our friends. In his "axis of evil speech" anticipating his war in Iraq, President George W. Bush embraced the very opposite: strategic homogeneity—"with us or against us." In his second inaugural address, President Bush stated that it was "the policy of the United States to seek and support the growth of democratic movements and institutions in every nation and culture, with the ultimate goal of ending tyranny in our world." In the second half of that second Bush administration, wiser strategic heads prevailed.

Or in Plato's argot, the *nous,* the brain, took over from the *thymos.* The *thymos* may be heroic, but it can "utterly destroy the city." Untamed dogs cannot distinguish "stranger from friend."[15] They snap at all alike. Pundit, president, and vice president conjured up a collaborative relationship between Saddam Hussein and Osama bin Laden so as to pursue strategic homogeneity.[16] Arsonists in the ghetto incinerate even their neighbors' automobiles. Thymotic foreign policy turns friends into neutrals, neutrals to enemies, and short wars into long wars or even defeats.

Homogeneity's first cousin is analogy. What we are up against today, we are told, is "Islamofascism" or the latest version of "totalitarianism."[17] Such exercises are seldom entirely without profit:"Men more frequently require to be reminded than informed." But analogies, as Dr. Samuel

Johnson has also pointed out, "walk on one leg." They may offer support for our impulses, but they do not take us very far and are perfectly capable of pushing us into the abyss. Each historical situation is novel; that's what makes it a historical situation. During the Vietnam War, Hannah Arendt, the author of *The Origins of Totalitarianism,* noted that government spokesmen frequently had recourse to phrases like "monolithic communism" and "a second Munich." She inferred from this habit that the officials suffered from an inability "to confront reality on its own terms because they had always some parallels in mind that 'helped' them to understand those terms."[18]

Broad abstraction can present a second hazard to strategic heterogeneity and to concrete analysis. Here the latter has demanded investigation and depiction in individual national settings, bearing in mind the variety of Islams and Islamisms, their connection, or absence of it, to terrorism, examination of the demographic, geographic, ethnographic and institutional dimensions of immigration and the clarity and depth offered by studying radicalization in the particular instance as well as the general case.

Nuance, specificity, and complexity rank as outsiders in a political culture that rewards partisanship, a media that reduces complex stories to "sound bites," an academy that merchandizes what it calls "theory," agenda-driven foundations and a think-tank world where policy often precedes, or even precludes, research. So take away, please, dear reader, a mind for patient and concrete analysis as a condition for policy and action.

ACKNOWLEDGMENTS

My gratitude goes first to Dr. James Katz of the George Washington University Medical Center who was able to diagnose and begin to treat the mysterious illness that had made this book for many years a labor of Sisyphus.

Steven Brooke, my erstwhile research assistant and colleague, made the Outside chapter possible, contributed signally to the User's Guide, and has remained a perpetual resource and light. Kent Shreeve's astute, meticulous and comprehensive comments straightened not only crooked passages but also entire structures.

I owe a major debt of gratitude to Jean-François Clair, the long-time deputy director of France's Direction de la Surveillance du Territoire. Alain Grignard of the Belgian Federal Police spent the better part of two days briefing me on the Brussels scene. Armando Spataro, the prosecutor attached to the court of Milan, took a day out of his busy schedule to brief me on Islamic terrorism in Italy. Lord Carlile, the British antiterror ombudsman, was also exceptionally generous with his time. I want to thank Marianne van Leeuwen of the Dutch AIVD (Algemene Inlichtingen- en Veiligheidsdienst) and Thelma Gillen and her colleagues at JTAC (The Joint Terrorism Analysis Center) in London, Larry Sanchez at the FBI–New York Police Department *Joint Terrorism Task Force* (FBI-NYPD *JTTF*) and their counterparts in Danish, German, and Spanish intelligence organizations as well as Robert Lambert and Andy Hayman of Scotland Yard. In Madrid, Ricardo Ruiz introduced me to many helpful sources. Guido Steinberg, Gilles Kepel, Olivier Roy, Jocelyne Cesari, Alison Pargeter, Michael Taarnby, Michael Whine, and Lawrence Wright were especially generous and helpful.

John Nathan's counsel and encouragement were sustaining. Joshua Kornberg and Edmund Zagorin, two interns at the Nixon Center (now the Center for the National Interest) extended editorial assistance beyond any reasonable call of duty. The late Samuel Huntington, whose rich and complex *Clash of Civilizations* has regularly been reduced to a shibboleth, helped me through the years not only with his capacious and nuanced mind and analytical method but also with his personal friendship and professional support. The Smith Richardson Foundation and the Center for the National Interest provided patient patronage. Laura Mooney at the Brookings Institution's library went to extraordinary lengths to corral needed books and articles from around the world. My semester as a Bosch fellow at the American Academy in Berlin, with support from the German Marshall Fund, started me on this long adventure.

Georges Chebib and the Belgian Lebanese community lent me hospitality, information, and great goodwill. Shiv Malik of the BBC provided me with an introduction to Beeston Hill, and Jason Burke of the *Observer*, like Shiv, read and commented on certain chapters and assisted me in securing documents. Marc Sageman also helped in that respect. Patrick Chamorel provided helpful contacts in France and read over the French chapters. Sebastian Rotella provided information and perspective on several occasions. Peter Skerry provided helpful bibliographical hints and other suggestions; other encouraging manuscript readers included John Newell; Leslie Hunter; my brother, Sam; and my wife, Katherine (Kate). Oxford's patient David McBride, my editor, annotated the margin of my draft manuscript with helpful observations, procured two splendid outside readers whose comments were tremendously useful, and offered a very constructive revision agenda. Early on, I was the fortunate beneficiary of the late Saki Badawi's insight and wisdom. Other Muslim colleagues and friends who also assisted importantly at various stages were Ahmad Shazaad, Aminul Hoque, Kamal El-Helbawi, Tauofik Cheddadi, Yahya Birt, Intissar Ghannouchi, and Tariq Abbas.

Over the years a battalion of interns hunted for information in search engines. In these ranks, Noura Hemady heads the list of those owed profound thanks for her assistance on the Khaled Kelkal chapter along with Mandy Misko and Carl Bergquist, who located source German chapters. Christina Madden, Jeremy Brown, Anne Trinquet, and Lacey Stewart found French sources. Kristen Gehringer, Samantha Holcombe,

Amanda Testani, and Samara Gottlieb assisted on the British chapters. Angie Kaufman proofread and with Njaal Frilseth diligently worked on the often frustrating task of securing photo permissions. Ghassan Schbley helped with Arabic translations. Other especially helpful interns were Liane Roach, James Murphy, Ann Strachan, Lauren Alexandra Smulcer, Devin Fernandes, Thomas West, Chris Pope, Whitney Shaffer, Shane Lauth, Michael Burge, and Anne Hagood.

My sons, Sam and Ben, suffered without complaint the emotional and financial privations this project proved to entail as did, above all, their mother, who remained an unfailing source of wisdom, insight, support, cheer, comfort and love.

NOTES

Prologue

1. Alfred Lord Tennyson, "Ulysses."
2. Raymond Aron, *The Imperial Republic: The United States and World, 1945–1973* (New Brunswick, NJ: Transaction, 2009), 309. (Originally published by Prentice Hall, 1974.)

Chapter 1

1. There have been numerous allegations that the GIA was infiltrated by the Algerian secret services that staged the attacks on France with the aim of shoring up French support for the military government. See, for example, Lounis Aggoun and Jean-Baptiste Rivoire, *Françalgérie, Crimes et Mensonges d'Etats* [*Franco-Algeria, Crimes and Lies of the States*] (Paris: La Découverte, 2004); see also Naima Bouteldga, "Who Really Bombed Paris?" *Guardian*, September 8, 2005.

2. Gilles Kepel, *Jihad: The Trail of Political Islam* (Cambridge, MA: Harvard University Press, 2002), 254–255.

3. See Brynjar Lia and Ashild Kjok, *Islamist Insurgencies, Diasporic Support Networks, and Their Host States* (Kjeller, Norway: FFI, 2001), 19–21.

4. See, Jean-Louis Bruguière, "Terrorism: Threat and Responses," Occasional Paper Series, No. 31, se2.isn.ch/serviceengine/Files/ESDP/7380/ . . . /doc_7398_290_en.pdf, accessed June 30, 2010.

5. Alison Pargeter, *The New Frontiers of Jihad* (London: I. B. Tauris, 2008), 83.

6. See Lia and Kjok, *Islamist Insurgencies*, 31–32.

7. Personal interview with Jean-François Clair, March 20, 2007.

8. The move to the province was a kind of strategic retreat insofar as Kelkal's "group of young *beurs* [Arabs] in the Lyon region was 'much less robust and professional'" than the militants in Paris. Marie-Amélie Lombard, "Les audiences s'ouvrent cet après-midi; Le box bien garni au procès Chalabi," *Le Figaro*, September 1, 1998.

9. Kelkal qualifies as a "second-generation" postmigrant because his parents were first generation and he was socialized in France.

10. Marlise Simon, "Dead Bomb Suspect's Ties Still a Mystery in France," *New York Times*, October 1, 1995; Dietmar Loch, "Boyhood of a Terror Suspect," *Guardian* (London), October 11, 1995; Daniel Singer, "Battle of Algiers on Paris Metro," *The Nation*, November 6, 1995.

11. Simons, "Dead Bomb Suspect's Ties Still a Mystery in France"; Alison Pargeter, *The New Frontiers of Jihad: Radical Islam in Europe* (Philadelphia: University of Pennsylvania Press, 2008), 89; Frank Viviano, "Killing Exposes France's Racial Divide," *San Francisco Chronicle,* October 27, 1995.

12. Dietmar Loch, *Jugendliche maghrebinischer Herkundft swischen Stadtpolitik und Lebenswelt [North African Youth Between Urban Policy and Life Circumstances]* (Wiesbaden, Germany: VS Verlag, 2002).

13. Dietmar Loch, "Moi, Khaled Kelkal," *Le Monde*, October 7, 1995. When Kelkal is quoted here, it is from the French version of the interview.

14. Bernard Philippe, "L'itinéraire bien ordinaire de Khaled Kelkal, terroriste presume," *Le Monde*, September 19, 1995.

15. Pargeter, *New Frontiers of Jihad*, 89.

16. Loch, "Boyhood of a Terror Suspect"; Milton Viorst, "The Muslims of France," *Foreign Affairs* (September/October, 1996).

17. "Khaled Kelkal, les rodéos et le Coran," *Le Nouvel Observateur*, September 14, 1995.

18. Loch, "Moi, Khaled Kelkal."

19. See Gattegna Herve and Inciyan Erich, "Depuis 1994, La frontière entre militants islamistes et delinquents est devenue incertaine et permeable," *Le Monde*, April 4, 1996. For subsequent analysis of the connection between Islamist radicalization and French prisons, see Farhad Khosrokhavar, *L'islam dans les prisons* (Paris: Balland, 2004); Herve and Erich, "Depuis 1994, La frontière;" "Islamist Extremism in Europe," Hearing Before the Subcommittee on European Affairs of the Committee on Foreign Relations, United States Senate, 106th Congress, Second Session, April 5, 2006.

20. Kepel, *Jihad*, 310; Loch, "Boyhood of a Terror Suspect."

21. Loch, "Moi, Khaled Kelkal."

22. Xavier Terisien, *Les Frères Musulmanes* (Paris: Fayard, 2005), 255–256, 258; see also Samir Amghar, "Les trois âges du discours des frères musulmans en Europe" and "Les Frères musulmans francophone: vers un islamisme de la minorité," *Islamismes d'Occident: perspectives et enjeux,* ed. Samir Amghar (Paris: Lignes de Repères, 2006).

23. See Terisien, *Les Frères Muselmanes*, 257; see also Samir Amghar, "Les mutations de l'islamisme en France," *La vie des idees* [Online], January 10, 2007, www.laviedesidees.fr/Les-mutations-de-l-islamisme-en.html, accessed January 31, 2007; Patrick Haenni and Sami Amghar, "The Myth of Muslim Conquest," *Le Monde Diplomatique* [Online], January 13, 2010, http://mondediplo.com/2010/01/06islam, accessed January 14, 2010.

24. Terisien, *Les Frères Muselmanes*, 257.

25. Jean-Marie Pontaut, "Itinéraire d'un terroriste," *L'Express*, September 26, 1996.

26. Ibid.

27. Khosrokhavar, *L'Islam dans les prisons.*

28. Loch, "Moi, Khaled Kelkal."

29. Ibid.

30. Ibid.

31. "Kelkal: les réseaux apparaissent," *Le Point*, October 7, 1995; Pontaut, "Itinéraire d'un terroriste."

32. Gilles Kepel, "*Foi et Pratique:* Tablighi Jama'at in France," in *Travellers in Faith: Studies of the Tablighi Jama'at as a Transnational Islamic Movement for Faith Renewal*, ed. Muhammad Khalid Masud (Boston: Brill, 2000), 188.

33. DST, "Processus d'Enrolement des Jeunes Musulmans dans le Jihad," Spring 2003.

34. Interview with Jean-François Clair, deputy director of Direction de la Surveillance du Territoire, December 12, 2002.

35. DST, "Processus d'Enrolement."

36. "La deuxième vie de Khaled Kelkal," *Le Monde*, January 17, 1996; Kathryn Hone, "France Fears More Kelkals from the Ghetto," *The Irish Times* (Ireland), October 4, 1995.

37. Andrea Elliott, "Where Boys Grow Up to Be Jihadists," *New York Times*, November 25, 2007.

38. "La deuxième vie de Khaled Kelkal."

39. Hone, "France Fears More Kelkals"; Pargeter, *The New Frontiers of Jihad*.

40. Inciyan Erich, "L'enquête sur les attentats de l'été 1995 a beaucoup progressé," *Le Monde*, July 11, 1996.

41. "Attentats de 1995: chronologie," *Le Nouvel Observateur*, June 23, 2008.

42. Patrica Tourancheau, "Ce 25 juillet-là, huit morts à la stations Saint-Michel; Terrorisme," *Libération*, October 1, 2002. The three bombings were the GIA's protest against the "charade" referendum approving a new Algerian constitution, but they took place in France to protest a trial for eight Frenchmen of North African origin that were members of a France-based terror cell. They were accused of attacks in Morocco that included desecration of a Jewish cemetery in Casablanca and the killing of two Spanish tourists in a Marrakesh hotel. (Craig R. Whitney, "Oct. 15–21: Commuter Train Bombed; Algeria's Civil War Brings New Terror to France," *New York Times*, October 22, 1995; Roger Cohen, "Islam Radicals Are Sentenced in France," *New York Times*, January 11, 1997.)

43. Stéphane Marchand, "Près de six mois après l'attentat dans le RER parisien (4 morts et 90 blessés); Port-Royal: la longue traque policière," *Le Figaro*, May 20, 1997.

44. Simons, "Dead Bomb Suspect's Ties."

45. "Kelkal: les réseaux apparaissent."

46. The video was shown in France on channel M6 during October; see Jonathan Steele, "Death on the Rue," *The Guardian* (UK), October 16, 1995; Eric Collier and Pereira Acacio, "Khaled Kelkal, un homme aux abois," *Le Monde*, October 3, 1995.

47. "Slaying of Suspect Sets off French Riot," *New York Times*, October 2, 1995.

48. Pereira Acacio, "Les trois principaux prévenus du procès," *Le Monde*, June 1, 1999.

49. Robert S. Leiken, *Bearers of Global Jihad? Immigration and National Security After 9/11* (Washington, DC: Nixon Center, 2004), 82.

50. Interview with Jean-François Clair, deputy director of Direction de la Surveillance du Territoire, December 12, 2002.

51. "Paris Bomb Suspect Goes to Trial," BBC News [Online], February 27, 2006, http://news.bbc.co.uk/2/hi/europe/4755582.stm, accessed March 10, 2007.

52. "Algerian Gets 10 Years in 1995 Métro Bombings," *New York Times*, March 30, 2006.

Chapter 2

1. Colin Nickerson, "Youth's Poverty, Despair Fuel Violent Unrest in France," *The Boston Globe*, November 6, 2005; Claude Imbert, "Le bucher d'une politique," *Le Point*, November 10, 2005; Ivan Rioufol, "Cités: les non-dits d'une rébellion," *Le Figaro*, November 4, 2005; Eric Leser, "Banlieues: les médias américains sans complaisance," *Le Monde*, November 15, 2005; Arezki Aït-Larbi and Thierry Oberlé, "Les troubles vus du Maghreb," *Le Figaro*, November 14, 2005; "Comment les expatriés vivent les emeutes," *Le Monde*, November 9, 2005; "Islamistes jettent de l'huile sur le feu sur le net," *Echos du net*, November 9, 2005; "Is Paris Burning? The French 'Intifada'" [Online], August 11, 2005, http://journal-de-bord.blogspot.com/2005/11/is-paris-burning-french-intifada.html, accessed August 31, 2006; John Lichfield, "In the Banlieues—One Year On," *The Independent* (UK) October 26, 2006; "Europe's Muslims: A Year After the Riots, Their Alienation Is Growing," *The Washington Post*, October 25, 2006; Phyllis Chesler, "France's Intifada," *FrontPage Magazine*, November 7, 2005; Michael Gurfinkle, "France Facing

'Horrendous' Balance," *New York Sun,* November 8, 2005; "France's Permanent Intifada," *New York Sun,* October 27, 2006; "French Interior Minister Cancels Trip to Tackle Spreading Paris Riots," *Agence France Press,* November 2, 2003.

2. Daniel Pipes, "Reflections on the Revolution in France," *New York Sun,* November 8, 2005.

3. Ron Liddle, "The Crescent of Fear," *The Spectator* (UK), November 14, 2005; Filip van Laenen, "A Civil War Underway in Old Europe," *The Brussels Journal* [Online], October 31, 2005, http://www.brusselsjournal.com/node/415, accessed October 26, 2006.

4. Piotr Smolar, "Interview with Pascal Mailhos," *Le Monde,* November 24, 2005.

5. Interview with Bruno Laffargue, director of Renseignements Generaux for Île de France, March 30, 2006.

6. Cécilia Gabizon, "L'islam ne joue pas un rôle déterminant dans la propagation des troubles," *Le Figaro,* November 5, 2005.

7. Olivia Recasens, Christophe Labbé, and Jean-Michel Décugis, "UOIF; La fatwa anti-casseurs," *Le Point,* November 16, 2005.

8. Tariq Ramadan, "Nos Ghettos vus d'Angleterre," *Le Monde,* November 8, 2005.

9. Jennifer Joan Lee, "Paris Police Fear Rioters' Heavy Arms," *Washington Times,* November 10, 2005.

10. "Fuck the Police" is the title of a very well-known song by the rap group NWA (an abbreviation for "niggas with attitudes"), perhaps another indication that an adversarial global underclass culture, rather than Islamism, shaped the attitude of rioters.

11. The analogy to the appeasement of Nazism was the keynote of a spate of books, including Bruce Bawer, *While Europe Slept* (New York: Doubleday, 2006); Bat Ye'or, *Eurabia: The Euro-Arab Axis* (Cranbury, UK: Associated University Press, 2005); Melanie Phillips, *Londonistan* (New York: Encounter Books, 2006); Norman Podhoretz, *World War IV: The Long Struggle Against Islamofascism* (New York: Doubleday, 2007).

12. See Robert S. Leiken, "Europe's Angry Muslims," *Foreign Affairs,* June 2005.

13. Rapport sur les émeutes, "Renseignements généraux." December 6, 2005, 18

14. Mark Steyn, "Wake Up, Europe, You've a War on Your Hands," *Chicago Sun-Times,* November 6, 2005.

15. "Intifada in France," *The New York Sun,* November 4, 2005.

16. Nidra Poller, "Intifada a la française," *National Post,* November 8, 2005.

17. Jonathan Laurence and Justin Vaisse, *Integrating Islam: Political and Religious Challenges in Contemporary France* (Washington, DC: Brookings Institution, 2006), 230.

18. Ibid., 226.

19. Cecilia Gabizon, "Les actes racistes aux trois quarts antisémites," *Le Figaro* (France), April 2, 2004.

20. Marie-Estelle Pech and Jean Valbay, "Sarah, victime d'une tournante, harcelée pour avoir parlé," *Le Figaro,* January 15, 2003.

21. Emmanuel Brenner, *Les territoires perdus de la République: Antisémitisme, racisme et sexisme en milieu scolaire* (Paris: Mille et Une Nuits, 2002).

22. Christopher Caldwell, *Reflections on the Revolution in Europe* (New York: Doubleday, 2009), 233.

23. Surah 33:53 and Surah 33:59, respectively. Also "And say to the believing women that they should lower their gaze and guard their modesty; and that they should not display their beauty and ornaments except what must ordinarily appear thereof; that they should draw their veils over their bosoms and not display their beauty except to their husbands" (Quran 24:30–31).

24. Jytte Klaussen, *The Islamic Challenge* (Oxford: Oxford University Press, 2005), 172.

25. See Jocelyne Cesari, *Musulmans et republicans: Les jeunes, l'islam y la France* (Brussels: Editions Complexe, 1988).

26. John R. Bowen, *Why the French Don't Like Headscarves: Islam, the State and Public Space* (Princeton: Princeton University Press, 2007), 83.

27. Ibid., 100.

28. Yamin Makri, "Les 'Nouveau Notables' de la Republique," Oumma.com [Online], April 25, 2005, http://oumma.com/article.php3?id_article=1485&var_recherche=Yamin+Makri+25+Avril, accessed November 16, 2005; Xavier Ternisien, "Associations of Young Muslims Distance Themselves from Tariq Ramadan," *Le Monde*, May 27, 2005.

29. Bowen, *Why the French Don't Like Headscarves*.

30. Magali Faure and Philip Gouge, "Headscarf Row Erupts in France," *BBC News*, April 25, 2003.

31. Bowen, *Why the French Don't Like Headscarves*; Paul Webster, "French Muslims Angry at Veil Move," *The Guardian* (UK), April 22, 2003.

32. "Daniel Cohn-Bendit estime que la laïcité est menacée en France," *Le Monde*, November 27, 2003, cited in Bowen, *Why the French Don't Like Headscarves*, 104.

33. Bowen, *Why the French Don't Like Headscarves*, 98.

34. Ibid., 108.

35. Ibid., 110.

36. Ibid.

37. Ibid., 125.

38. Gros Marie-Joâlle, "Deux soeurs voilées divisent un lycée," *Liberation*, September 22, 2003, cited in Bowen, *Why the French Don't Like Headscarves*, 110.

39. Klaussen, *The Islamic Challenge*, 175.

40. Jean Pierre Obin, "Les signes et manifestations d'appartenance religieuse dans les établissements scolaires" (Ministère de l'éducation nationale, de l'enseignement supérieur et de la recherché, June 2004), 22.

41. Benjamin Peyral, "La loi sur le voile" *La Croix,* March 5, 2004, 9.

42. Obin, "Les signes," 5.

43. Ibid., 12.

44. Bernard Stasi, "Commission de Reflexion sur l'Application du Principe de Laïcité dans la Republique," December 11, 2003, 47.

45. Obin, "Les signes," 20.

46. Ibid.

47. Ibid.

48. Ibid.

49. Ibid., 13.

50. Ibid., 26.

51. Ibid., 27.

52. Ibid., 28.

53. Ibid.

54. Ibid.

55. Ibid., 25.

56. Ibid., 25.

57. Ibid., 11.

58. Ibid., 31; see also 20, 27, 33.

59. Ibid., 31, 32.

60. Ibid., 15.

61. Olivier Guitta, "The Islamization of French Schools," *Weekly Standard,* May 9, 2005.

62. Obin, "Les signes," 5–6.

63. Bowen, *Why the French Don't Like Headscarves*, 121.

64. Mireille Silcoff, "Barricaded in Paris," *National Post*, Canada, November 19, 2005.

65. Steyn, "Wake Up, Europe."

66. Dan Darling, "The French Riots," windsofchange.net [Online], November 8, 2005, http://www.windsofchange.net/archives/007716.php, accessed July 22, 2006.

67. Charles Bremner, "Colour-Blind Policy Has Fed Muslim Radicalism," *London Times*, November 7, 2005.

68. "Leur congres a réuni deux fois plus de participants qu'en 2003," *Le Figaro*, April 12, 2004.

69. "L'UOIF craint une 'laïcité d'exclusion,'" *La Nouvelle Observeur*, April 13, 2004.

70. "Letter de l'UOIF aux musulmans de France concernant l'application de la loi du 15 Mars 2004 à la rentrée scolaire de Septembre 2004," UOIF [Online], June 29, 2004, http://www.aidh.org/laic/chrono-04.htm, accessed September 21, 2005.

71. "Fouad Alaoui (UOIF): il faut adapter la lecture de l'islam en France (TROIS QUESTIONS)," *Agence France Press*, March 23, 2005.

72. Bowen, *Why the French Don't Like Headscarves*.

73. Mansour Benjedid, "Un non européen aux 'Beni oui-ouif'!" Oumma.com [Online], May 27, 2005, http://oumma.com/article.php3?id_article=1543&var_recherche=UOIF+%27oui%27, accessed September 27, 2005.

74. Cécilia Gabizon, "Les profs soulagés, les parents rassurés; 'Le plus dur est passé,'" *Le Figaro*, June 2, 2005.

75. "Letter de l'UOIF."

76. Gabizon, "Les profs soulagés."

77. "Le communiqué des ravisseurs," *Le Télégramme*, August 30, 2004.

78. Sebastian Rotella and Louise Roug, "French Journalists Freed After 4 Months of Captivity in Iraq," *Los Angeles Times* [Online], December 20, 2004, http://articles.latimes.com/2004/dec/22/world/fg-hostages22, accessed March 22, 2010; Gilles Kepel, "French Lessons in Londonistan," *National Interest*, (March–April 2010), 50; Laurence and Vaisse, *Integrating Islam*, 171.

79. Christian Joppke, "Limits of Integration Policy: Britain and Her Muslims," *Journal of Ethnic and Migration Studies* 35, no. 3 (March 2009): 52.

80. Laurence and Vaisse, *Integrating Islam*, 172.

81. Ibid., 226.

82. Sophie Roquelle, "Du train de la peur au train fantôme; Comment 'l'agression antisémite du RER D' est devenue, deux jours durant, une affair d'État," *Le Figaro*, July 14, 2004.

83. Jean Chichizola, "La fausse affaire du RER D indigne des responsables musulmans; Mythomanie le gouvernement sous le feu de la critique pour sa gestion de l'agression imaginaire," *Le Figaro*, July 15, 2004.

84. Jonathan Laurence and Justin Vaisse, "Understanding Urban Riots in France," *New Europe Review*, December 1, 2005.

85. Laurence and Vaisse, *Integrating Islam*, 229.

86. Pascale Robert-Diard, "Quatre mois de sursis et obligation de soins pour Marie Leblanc, fausse victime d'une agression dans le RER," *Le Monde*, July 28, 2004.

87. Walter Lippmann and Charles Merz, "A Test of the News," *New Republic*, August 4, 1920.

88. Ibid., 3.

89. See Peter Braestrup, *The Big Story: How the American Press and Television Reported and Interpreted the Crisis of Tet 1968 in Vietnam and Washington* (Garden City, NY: Anchor Press, 1978); Robert S. Leiken, *Why Nicaragua Vanished: A Story of Reporters and Revolutionaries* (Lanham, MD: Rowman and Littlefield, 2003).

90. Rioufol, "Cités."

91. Melanie Phillips, "Why France is burning," *Daily Mail,* (UK) November 7, 2005; Charles Krauthammer, "What the Uprising Generation Wants," *Time,* November 13, 2005; Phyllis Chesler, "France's Intifada," FrontPage.com, November 7, 2005.

92. "Europe Watches French Riots with Apprehension," *Agence France Presse,* November 8, 2005; Dan Stanca, "Global Islamist Offensive," *Romania Libera,* November 11, 2005.

93. "Europe Watches French Riots."

94. "The Paris Intifada," *Jerusalem Post,* November 8, 2005.

95. Ibid.

96. "The French Riots," *Washington Times,* November 10, 2005. For an analysis of the reporting of the Tet offensive, see Braestrup, *The Big Story.* For an analysis of the Nicaraguan reporting and post-Vietnam stereotypes, see Leiken, *Why Nicaragua Vanished.*

Chapter 3

1. "After the Riots," *The Economist,* December 17, 2005; figures provided by Luc Bronner and Pascal Ceaux, "Le bilan chiffré de la crise des banlieues," *Le Monde,* December 2, 2005.

2. Hugues Lagrange and Marco Oberti, *Émeutes Urbaines et Protestations: Une Singularité Français* (Paris: Presse de Sciences-Po, 2006), 26.

3. "If the difficulties of finding employment are very prominent for the youth of the *banlieue,* in the course of the last three decades, for them, the phases of increased unemployment do not appear to be specific causes for the protests. A cursory review of the riots of the urban youth suggests that there is no relation between the amplification of unemployment at the precise chronology of the explosion of disorder initiated by the youth of the poor neighborhoods." Hugues Lagrange, "La structure et l'accident," in Lagrange and Oberti, *Émeutes Urbaines et Protestations,* 106.

4. Marc Pivois, "Le Petite Carot and le Baton de Sarkozy a La Courneuve," *Liberation* (France), June 30, 2005.

5. Gérard Davet, "Nicolas Sarkozy cherche la bonne formule pour son retour sur la 'dalle' d'Argenteuil," *Le Monde,* February 14, 2007.

6. Ibid.

7. Amir Taheri, "Why Paris Is Burning," *New York Post,* November 4, 2005.

8. John Lichfield, "In the Banlieues—One Year On," *The Independent,* October 26, 2006.

9. Ibid.; "Les Circonstances de la Mort des Adolescents Restent Floues," *Le Monde,* November 4, 2005.

10. Fabien Jobard, "Sociologie Politique de la 'racaille,'" in Lagrange and Oberti, *Émeutes Urbaines et Protestations,* , 61.

11. "Soul-Searching Grips France as Riots Spread Further," *Agence France Presse,* November 4, 2005.

12. For claimed instances of high-tech coordination, see Thomas Crampton, "Blogs and Text Messages Spread Call to Violence," *International Herald Tribune,* November 9, 2005.

13. Interview with Henri Rey, "La Banlieue Nord de Paris Cumule Tous les Désavantages," *Le Temps* (France), November 4, 2005.

14. "Les Emeutes Restent Intenses en Île-de-France," *Le Monde,* November 6, 2005; Crampton, "Blogs and Text Messages"; "Evry: Une Fabrique de Cocktails Molotov," *Le Nouvel Observateur* (France), November 6, 2005; Patricia To100rancheau, "Les Emeutes, Aubaines Policiers," *Liberation* (France), November 16, 2005.

15. Jean-Marc Leclerc, "Des émeutiers violents, mais bien insérés," *Le Figaro*, May 19, 2006; cited in Mitchell Cohen, "French Crisis, Left Crisis," *Dissent* (Summer 2006).

16. "Les renseignements généraux s'inquètent du climat régnant dans les banlieues françaises," *Le Monde*, October 23, 2006.

17. According to the Immigration Act of 1998 these second-generation immigrants, born of foreign-national parents, automatically receive French citizenship upon reaching adulthood. They have to be a resident of France when they turn eighteen and must have lived in France for a total of five years after their eleventh birthday. Second-generation immigrants have the option of refusing their French citizenship and can do so up until the age of nineteen. Citizenship and Immigration Policy, official website of the French Prime Minister and Government [Online], http://www.archives.premier-ministre.gouv.fr/jospin_version3/en/ie4/contenu/29905.html, accessed December 15, 2005.

18. Alec Hargreaves, *Immigration and Identity in Beur Fiction: Voices from the North African Immigrant Community* (Oxford, UK: Berg, 1997), 14.

19. Daniel Williams, "In France, Anthems of Alienation," *Washington Post*, November 24, 2005.

20. French Employment Agency ARDA, "Les Oubliés de L'égalité des Chances" [Online], May 2004, http://www.institutmontaigne.org/site/page.php?page_id=72, accessed June 1, 2009.

21. Lichfield, "In the Banlieues."

22. Milton M. Gordon, *Assimilation in American Life: The Role of Race, Religion and National Origins* (New York: Oxford University Press, 1964), 36.

23. I am speaking in general terms. It is not hard to find rebellion among first-generation immigrants. We need look no further than the United States a century ago, to the Italian anarchists and the large German and Russian components of the early U.S. Communist Party.

24. Richard Rodriguez, *Hunger of Memory: The Education of Richard Rodriguez* (Boston: D. R. Godine, 1982).

25. Jean Pierre Obin, "Les signes et manifestations d'appartenance religieuse dans les établissements scolaires" (Ministère de l'éducation nationale, de l'enseignement supérieur et de la recherché, June 2004), 15.

26. John Carreyrou, "Culture Clash: Muslim Groups May Gain Strength From French Riots—Islamists Try to Mediate Peace But Encourage Isolation from Secular Society—A Minister 'Plays Rambo,'" *Wall Street Journal*, November 7, 2005.

27. David A. Bell, "The Shorn Identity," *New Republic*, December 5, 2005.

28. Roger Scruton, *The West and the Rest: Globalization and the Terrorist West* (Birbeck College, UK: Intercollegiate Studies Institute, 2002), 129.

29. Jonathan Laurence and Justin Vaisse, "Understanding Urban Riots in France," *New Europe Review*, December 1, 2005.

30. John Carreyrou, "The Shame of the Cités: French Unrest Finds a Home in Projects—Racial Tension, Joblessness Wrack Suburban Area; Mr. Bernard's 4 Decades," *Wall Street Journal*, November 14, 2005.

31. *Le Parisien*, November 23, 2005.

32. Laurent Mucchielli, "Introduction générale: Les émeutes de novembre 2005: les raisons de la colère," in *Quand les banlieues brûlent. . . Retour sur les émeutes de novembre 2005*, ed. Véronique Le Goaziou and Laurent Mucchielli (Paris: La Découverte, 2006), 29.

33. Éric Marlière, "Les habitants des quartiers: adversaires ou solidaires des émeutiers?" in Le Goaziou and Mucchielli, *Quand les banlieues brûlent*, 78.

34. David Lepoutre, *Coeur de Banlieue* (Paris: Odile Jacob, 1997), 39–40; Benedict Anderson, *Imagined Communities* (London: Verso, 1983).

35. "Axel Honneth: Le CPE 'bat en brèche les attentes de reconnaissance du tra vailleur,'" *Le Monde*, April 1, 2006.

36. Friedrich Engels, "Introduction" to Karl Marx, *The Class Struggles in France*, 1895, http://www.marxists.org/archive/marx/works/1895/03/06.htm, accessed July 20, 2011.

37. See, for example, Christopher Caldwell, "The Decline of France: And the rise of an Islamist-leftist alliance," *Weekly Standard*, December 8, 2003; David Horowitz, *Unholy Alliance* (New York: Regnery, 2004).

38. "La France Face a ses Musulmanes: Emeutes, Jihadisme et Depolitisation," International Crisis Group (Paris, 2006).

39. It is true that you can readily find Wahhabi literature in the banlieue, for the same reason that Chairman Mao's *Little Red Book* and *The Collected Works of Kim Il Sung* populated bookshelves in shantytowns from Managua to Manila a generation ago. The Saudis have taken a leaf from the Marxists: "All our books are Salafist," says one young resident. "But that's because they're free. No one reads them."

Rachid Ech Chetouani, the ex-rapper turned entrepreneur, prays five times a day and fasts during Ramadan, but he parties the rest of the year. He told me the Salafists had worn out their welcome in many quartiers. "They came here about five years ago. They'd preach for two hours nonstop telling us to pray, to be pious, not to drink, not to hang out. . . . Work? They told us that if we prayed, Allah would find us work."

40. Gilles Kepel, *The War for Muslim Minds* (Cambridge: Belknap Press, 2004), 251.

41. "La France Face a ses Musulmanes."

42. The survey by the Pew Global Attitudes Project, a project of the Pew Research Center, was conducted in thirteen countries from March 31 to May 14 of 2006. It included "special oversamples" of Muslim minorities living in Britain, France, Germany, and Spain. Its results were conveyed in two reports: *The Great Divide: How Westerners and Muslims View Each Other*, published June 22, 2006, and *Muslims in Europe,* published July 6, 2006.

43. Pew Global Attitudes Project, *Muslims in Europe* (Washington, DC: Pew Research Center, 2006), 3.

44. Ibid., 29.

45. Ibid., 8.

46. Pew Global Attitudes Project, *The Great Divide: How Westerners and Muslims View Each Other* (Washington, DC: Pew Research Center, 2006), 49.

47. Pew Global Attitudes Project, *Muslims in Europe,* 28.

48. Pew Global Attitudes Project, *The Great Divide*, 3.

49. Ibid., 43–44.

50. Walter Lippmann, *Public Opinion* (New York: Free Press, 1965), 98, 125; see Leiken, *Why Nicaragua Vanished,* chapter 12.

51. Pew Global Attitudes Project, *The Great Divide*, 45

Chapter 4

1. Roger Ballard, "Popular Islam in Northern Pakistan and Its Reconstruction in Urban Britain." In *Sufism in the West*, ed. Jamal Malik and John Hinnells (London: Routledge, 2006), 160.

2. Olivier Roy, *Globalized Islam* (New York: Columbia University Press, 2004).

3. *Understanding Islamism* (Washington, DC: International Crisis Group), Middle East Report no. 37 (March 2, 2005), 4.

4. Gilles Kepel, *Islam and the West* (Cambridge, MA: Harvard University Press, 2004), 253.

5. See Johannes J. G. Jansen, *The Neglected Duty* (New York: Macmillan, 1986), the translation of the early treatise of the Egyptian jihadi chieftain Abd al Salam Faraj.

6. Gilles Kepel, "French Lessons in Londonistan," *National Interest* (March–April 2010): 47n3.

7. *Understanding Islamism*, i–ii.

8. See Robert S. Leiken and Steven Brooke, "The Moderate Muslim Brotherhood," *Foreign Affairs,* March/April 2007.

9. *Sahih Bokhari, Volume 3, Book 48, Number 819.*

10. Roy, *Globalized Islam,* 233.

11. Also worth mentioning in passing are political Salafists who wish to bring the Salafi creed to the political arena, which they view as crucial because it is the domain of social justice and grounds the alleged sovereign right of God to legislate. An important influence on the "politicos" was the Muslim Brotherhood sojourn in Saudi Arabia when they fled repression by the Egyptian nationalist military government. Thus the political Salafis resemble political Islamists, whose heritage stems from Roy's "old Salafists." But, as Quintan Wiktorowicz points out, "the Brotherhood tended to follow rational thinking, a perspective inherently inimitable to the Salafi approach" (Wiktorowicz, "Anatomy of the Salafi Movement," *Studies in Conflict and Terrorism* 29 [2006]: 222). One of the young Saudis who once shared the point of view of the political Salafists was Osama bin Laden. Unlike the jihadis, the politicos stop short of promoting revolution, but they are very critical of incumbent regimes, unlike the pietists.

12. See Wiktorowicz, "Anatomy of the Salafi Movement," 219; see also *Saudi Arabia Backgrounder: Who Are the Islamists?* (Washington, DC: International Crisis Group), Middle East Report no. 31, September 21, 2004.

13. Wiktorowicz, "Anatomy of the Salafi Movement," 225.

14. Ibid.

15. See Steven Brooke, "Tensions Over the Near and Far Enemy in Jihadist Thought," in Assaf Moghadam and Brian Fishman, eds., *Self-Inflicted Wounds: Debates and Divisions Within al-Qa'ida and Its Periphery* (West Point: Combating Terrorism Center, 2010); see also Steven Brooke, "Jihadist Strategic Debates Before 9/11," *Studies in Conflict and Terrorism* 31, 3 (Spring 2008).

16. The reprobate may have sinned out of ignorance (having accepted bad advice) or coercion (fear of death). Or he or she may transgress for extraneous reasons (such as concupiscence or greed) but not out of disbelief. According to Salafist jihadis like bin Laden, in these cases the offender is certainly a sinner and will not, absent repentance, be part of the "saved sect," but if he retains his belief in Allah he is not an apostate. See Wiktorowicz, "Anatomy of the Salafi Movement," 230.

17. Ibid.

18. Bin Laden and other critics of the GIA ostracized the group with the label "takfiri." Considering him insufficiently bloodthirsty, "takfiris" tried to assassinate bin Laden in Sudan in the mid-1990s. Secular governments in the Arab world, which are frequently despotic, apply the term "takfiri" to all jihadis, thereby to stigmatize all armed opposition to their rule.

19. Lorenzo Vidino catalogs three types of European jihadis: "imports," "homegrown," and also what he calls "homebrewed." He means by the latter those jihadis radicalized in Europe but not born there. One of our lords of Londonistan, Abu Hamza al Masri, could be cited as an example of the latter along with "the underwear bomber," Umar Farouk Abdulmutallab. But the term "homebrewed" is confusing (alcohol hardly being a Muslim radical beverage) and this third type is a rarity (see Lorenzo Vidino, *Al Qaeda in Europe* [New York: Prometheus, 2006]).

20. See Jocelyne Cesari, *When Islam and Democracy Meet: Muslims in Europe and in the United States* (New York: Palgrave Macmillan, 2004), 141–144; Ian Johnson, "The

Brotherhood's Westward Expansion," *Current Trends in Islamist Ideology* (February 2008); and Johnson, *A Mosque in Munich* (New York: Houghton Mifflin Harcourt, 2010).

21. Jason Burke, "Omar Was a Normal British Teenager," *The Observer* (London), January 20, 2008; D. Gambetta and S. Hertog, "Engineers of Jihad," Oxford Department of Sociology Working Papers [Online], 2007, www.nuff.ox.ac.uk/users/gambettaEngineers%20of%20Jihad.pdf, accessed August 4, 2008.

22. Gilles Kepel, *Jihad: The Trail of Political Islam* (Cambridge, MA: Harvard University Press, 2002), 67.

23. See Edwin Bakker, *Jihadi Terrorists in Europe* (Clingendael, NL: Netherlands Institute of International Relations, December 2006), Clingendael Security Paper No. 2.

24. Robert S. Leiken and Steven Brooke, "The Quantitative Analysis of Terrorism and Immigration: An Initial Exploration," *Terrorism and Political Violence* 18, 4 (Winter 2006). More than 40 percent of the 373 *mujahideen* were Western nationals. Fewer than half were born in the Middle East. By the same token, we found twice as many Frenchmen as Saudis and more Britons than Sudanese, Yemenis, Emiratis, Lebanese, or Libyans. Had this study been conducted today, the proportion of Britons would be much higher.

25. Bakker, *Jihadi Terrorists in Europe*, 38.

26. Alison Pargeter discusses first-generation extremists in depth in Pargeter, *The New Frontiers of Jihad* (London: I. B. Tauris, 2008).

27. Michael J. Piore, *Birds of Passage: Migration, Labor and Industrial Societies* (Cambridge: Cambridge University Press, 1979), 107; see also Herbert J. Gans, *The Urban Villagers* (New York: Free Press of Glencoe), 1963.

28. Herbert Gans, "The Second Generation Decline: Scenarios for the Economic and Ethnic Futures of Post-1965 American Immigrants," *Ethnic and Racial Studies* (April 1992); Alejandro Portes and Min Zhou, "The New Second Generation: Segmented Assimilation and Its Variants," *Annals of American Academy of Political and Social Sciences* (November 1993); Alejandro Portes et al., *The New Second Generation* (New York: Russell Sage Foundation, 1996). Recent studies of the American phenomenon include Rubén G. Rumbaut and Alejandro Portes, eds., *Ethnicities: Children of Immigrants in America* (Berkeley: University of California Press, 2001); Roger Waldinger, ed., *Strangers at the Gates: New Immigrants in Urban America* (Berkeley: University of California Press, 2001); Alejandro Portes and Ruben G. Rumbaut *Legacies: The Story of the Immigrant Second Generation* (Berkeley: University of California Press, 2001).

29. For an account of these concepts, see Robert S. Leiken, *Why Nicaragua Vanished: Reporters and Revolutionaries* (Lanham, MD: Rowman & Littlefield, 2003), 271–275.

30. Malcolm Cross, "Migrants and New Minorities in Europe," in *Immigration in Western States*, ed. Hans Entzinger and Jack Carter (Greenwich, CT: JAI Press, 1989), 158; see also Daniel Bell, *The Coming of Post Industrial Society* (New York: Basic Books, 1973).

31. Aristide R. Zolberg, "Preface," in *Minorities in European Cities: The Dynamics of Social Integration and Social Exclusion at the Neighborhood Level*, ed. Marco Martiniello and Sophie Body-Gendrot (New York: St. Martin's Press, 2000), xvi.

32. For an example that is particularly pertinent to our story, see Virinder S. Kalra, *From Textile Mills to Taxi Ranks: Experiences of Migration, Labour and Social Change* (Burlington, VT: Ashgate, 2000).

33. Alec G. Hargreaves, *Immigration, 'Race', and Ethnicity in Contemporary France* (London: Routledge, 1995).

34. Patrick Simon, "France and the Unknown Second Generation," *International Migration Review* 37 (2003): 1091–1120.

35. Brigitte Maréchal, Stefano Allievi, Felice Dassetto, and Jørgen Nielsen, *Muslims in the Enlarged Europe* (Leiden: Brill, 2003), 421.

36. Marlise Simons, "Dead Bomb Suspect's Ties Still a Mystery in France," *New York Times*, October 1, 1995; Pargeter, *New Frontiers,* 89; Frank Viviano, "Killing Exposes France's Racial Divide," *San Francisco Chronicle,* October 27, 1995.

37. Simon, "France and the Unknown Second Generation," 1091–1120.

38. Ibid.

39. National Youth Employment Council, "Unqualified, Untrained, and Unemployed," London 1974.

40. Tariq Modood, Richard Berthoud, Jane Lakey, James Nazroo, Patten Smith, Satnam Virdee, and Sharon Beishon, *Ethnic Minorities in Britain: Diversity and Disadvantage*, Policy Studies Institute Report (1997): 843.

41. This was the case in 1984 and had not changed significantly by 1997. See Esra Erdem, "Minority Employment Patterns in the 1990s Germany" [Online], May 20–22, 2000, http://www.lse.ac.uk/collections/EPIC/documents/ICErdem.pdf, table 7.

42. Wolfgang Siefert, "Social and Economic Integration of Foreigners in Germany," in *Paths to Inclusion: The Integration of Migrants in the United States and Germany*, ed. Peter H. Schuck and Rainer Münz (New York: Berghahn, 1998), 91–95. For example, in 1994 over half of the second-generation youth was employed in some kind of manufacturing job. Brigitte Maréchal, "The Economic Dimension," in *Muslims in the Enlarged Europe*, ed. Brigitte Maréchal, Stefano Allievi, Felice Dassetto, and Jørgen Nielsen (Leiden: Brill, 2003), 420–421.

43. Philip Lewis, *Islamic Britain. Religion, Politics and Identity among British Muslims: Bradford in the 1990s* (London: Tauris, 1994), 25.

44. See Jytte Klausen, *The Islamic Challenge: Politics and Religion in Western Europe* (London: Oxford University Press, 2005).

45. Alejandro Portes and Min Zhou, "The New Second Generation: Segmented Assimilation and Its Variants," *Annals of the American Academy of Political and Social Science* 530 (November 1993): 82.

46. Burke, "Omar Was a Normal British Teenager."

47. Of the 373 jihadis surveyed in 2005, fully 9 percent were converts. See Leiken and Brooke, "Quantitative Analysis," and chapter 12 in this book.

Chapter 5

1. Gilles Kepel, *Jihad: The Trail of Political Islam* (Cambridge: Harvard University Press, 2002), 37–39. See also the terminology used by the militants interviewed in Saad Eddin Ibrahim, "Anatomy of Egypt's Militant Islamic Groups: Methodological Notes and Preliminary Findings," *International Journal of Middle East Studies* 12:4, (December 1980). On Khomeini, see Ervand Abrahamian, *Khomeinism: Essays on the Islamic Republic* (Berkeley: University of California Press, 1993), 41.

2. François Burgat, *Face to Face with Political Islam* (London: I. B. Tauris, 2003), 44.

3. Alison Pargeter, *The New Frontiers of Jihad* (London: I. B. Tauris, 2008), 113. Lewis goes further, contending that "the Muslim fundamentalists . . . do not differ from the mainstream on questions of theology and the interpretation of scripture" (Bernard Lewis, *The Crisis of Islam: Holy War and Unholy Terror* [New York: Random House, 2004], 24, see also 146.) But there appear to be many disparities between folk and fundamentalist Islam in interpreting scripture, if less on the tendency to invoke it.

4. Max Weber, *Wirtschaft und Gesselschaft* (Tübingen: Mohr, 1976), 311, cited in Christian Joppke, "Limits of Integration Policy: Britain and Her Muslims," *Journal of Ethnic and Migration Studies* 35, no. 3 (March 2009): 7. See also Weber, *Economy and Society* (Berkeley: University of California Press, 1978), 574, 1185.

5. Unfortunately, the terms "Wahhabist" and "Wahhabi" have ceased to become descriptive and are now in the main simply perjorative. They have lost much of their analytical and discretionary significance from overuse. For the best account of Wahhabism, see David Commins, *The Wahhabi Mission and Saudi Arabia* (London: I. B. Tauris, 2006). See also Khaled Abou El Fadl, *The Great Theft: Wrestling Islam from the Extremists* (San Francisco: Harper, 2005), chapter 3; and Natana J. DeLong-Bas, *Wahhabi Islam: From Revival and Reform to Global Jihad* (New York: Oxford University Press, 2004), a revisionist history that places great weight on understanding Wahhabism in its historical context as an attempt to reform an outdated and cluttered practice of Islam.

6. Barbara Daly Metcalf, *Islamic Revival in British India: Deoband, 1860–1900* (Princeton: Princeton University Press, 1982), 181.

7. In particular those of the *Hanifi*, the first of the four orthodox schools of Sunni legal scholarship. Metcalf, *Islamic Revival*, 140–141.

8. Ibid., 255.

9. Ibid., 94, 95, 99–100, 156.

10. Ibid., 168, 156.

11. Wilfred Cantwell Smith, *Modern Islam in India* (London: Victor Gollancz, 1946), 295.

12. Metcalf, *Islamic Revival*, 359.

13. Ibid., 266.

14. Philip Lewis, *Islamic Britain: Religion, Politics and Identity among British Muslims: Bradford in the 1990s* (London: Tauris, 1994), 79.

15. Walter Ong, *Orality and Literacy* (London: Routledge, 1988), 74.

16. Ziya-ul-Hasan Faruqi, *The Deoband School and the Demand for Pakistan* (Bombay: Asia Publishing House, 1963), 21.

17. Metcalf, *Islamic Revival*, 87, 267; Faruqi, *Deoband School*.

18. A. Z. M Shamsul Alam, *The Message of Tableegh and Dawai* (Daka: Bangladesh, 1985), 648; cited in Yoginder Sikand, *The Origins and Development of Tablighi-Jama'at* (New Delhi: Orient Longman, 2002), 7.

19. Seyyed Vali Reza Nasr, *Mawdudi and the Making of Islamic Revivalism* (Oxford: Oxford University Press, 1996), 31.

20. Ibid., 40.

21. For Afghani, see Nikki R. Keddie, *An Islamic Response to Imperialism: Political and Religious Writings of Sayyid Jamal ad-Din "al-Afghani"* (Berkeley: University of California Press, 1968); M. A. Zaki Badawi, *The Reformers of Egypt* (London: Croom Helm, 1978); Albert Hourani, *Arabic Thought in the Liberal Age 1798–1939* (London: Oxford University Press, 1970); and Elie Kedourie, *Afghani and Abduh: An Essay on Religious Unbelief and Political Activism in Modern Islam* (London: Frank Cass & Co., 1966).

22. Though Afghani and Abduh were (and still are) considered Salafists, their actual degree of religiosity has been questioned. See Keddie, *Islamic Response*, and Kedourie, *Afghani and Abduh*.

23. Olivier Roy, in *Globalized Islam* (New York: Columbia University Press, 2004), 233, calls it "old Salafism" to differentiate it from contemporary Salafism. Old Salafism meant to compete socially, economically, politically, and ideologically with the West; new Salafism ignores it—or attacks it militarily.

24. *Understanding Islamism* (Brussels: International Crisis Group, March 2, 2005), 9.

25. However, another Afghani disciple, the Syrian Rashid Rida, built an important bridge from that circle to the Wahhabis, thanks in part to a mutual admiration for Ibn Taymiyya, the fourteenth-century herald of all the Salafis. See Charles C. Adams, "Muhammad Abduh and the Transvaal Fatwa," in *The MacDonald Presentation Volume* (Princeton: Princeton University Press, 1933), 13–29; see also Jakob Skovgaard-Petersen, *Defining Islam for the Egyptian State* (Leiden: Brill, 1997), 65–77.

26. For the important Muslim Brotherhood–Sufi connection, see Richard P. Mitchell, *The Society of the Muslim Brothers* (Oxford: Oxford University Press, 1993), 4–5. 14, 300, 326; see also Brynjar Lia, *The Society of the Muslim Brothers in Egypt* (Reading, UK: Garnet: 1998).

27. For a review based on German archival sources of Nazi radio broadcasting to the Middle East, see Jeffrey Herf, *Nazi Propaganda for the Arab World* (New Haven: Yale University Press, 2009).

28. Lia, *Society of the Muslim Brothers*.

29. Hasan al-Banna, *The Concept of Allah in the Islamic Creed*, trans. Sharif Ahmad Khan (New Dehli: Adam Publishers, 2000, rev. ed.), 107.

30. Quoted in Mitchell, *Society of the Muslim Brothers*, 4.

31. Sayyid Qutb, *Social Justice in Islam*, trans. John B. Hardie, rev. trans and introd. Hamid Algar (Oneonta, NY: Islamic Publications International, 2000), 269–270.

32. Sayyid Qutb, *Milestones* (Cedar Rapids, IA: Mother Mosque Foundation, n.d.), 11.

33. See Sayyid Qutb, *Islam and Universal Peace*, trans. Mahmoud Abu Saud et al. (Indianapolis, IN: American Trust Publications, 1977), 10. This is probably the most consistent theme throughout Qutb's work. Qutb, *Milestones*, 25. See also Sayyid Qutb, *In the Shade of the Quran Vol. VIII (Surah al-Tawbah)*, trans. Adil Salahi (Leicester, UK: The Islamic Foundation and Islamonline.net, 2003), 124; Sayyid Qutb, *This Religion of Islam*, trans. "Islamdust" (Palo Alto, CA: Al Manar Press, 1967), 16, 22; Qutb, *Shade of the Quran*, 192–193, 237; Sayed Khatab, "Hakimiyyah and Jahiliyyah in the Thought of Sayyid Qutb," *Middle Eastern Studies* 38:3 (July 2002): 145; and Ahmad S. Moussalli, *Radical Islamic Fundamentalism: The Ideological and Political Discourse of Sayyid Qutb* (Beirut: American University of Beirut Press, 1995), 151.

34. Qutb, *Milestones*, 84.

35. Ibid., 131.

36. Sayyid Qutb, "The America I Have Seen," in *America in an Arab Mirror: Images of America in Arabic Travel Literature*, ed. Kamal Abdel Malik (New York: Palgrave, 2000).

37. Thus, if the student was seeking to flirt with an exotic professor, the overture would redound ruinously on twenty-first-century America.

38. The most complete analysis of this extremely important work is Barbara Zollner, "Prison Talk: The Muslim Brotherhood's Internal Struggle During Gamal Abdel Nasser's Persecution, 1954–1971," *International Journal of Middle Eastern Studies* 39 (2007).

39. Hisham Mubarak, Souhail Shadoud, and Steve Tamari, "What Does the Gama'a Islamiyya Want? An Interview with Tal'at Fu'ad Qasim," *Middle East Report* (January–March 1996): 41.

40. Ayman al-Zawahiri, *Fursan taht rayah al-nabi* [*Knights under the Prophet's banner*], 2001, serialized in *Al-Sharq al-Awsat*, a London-based Arabic daily newspaper.

41. Steven Brooke, "Jihadist Strategic Debates Before 9/11," *Studies in Conflict and Terrorism* 31 (2008).

42. Ayman al-Zawahiri, *Fursan taht rayah al-nabi*.

43. Dr. Naajeh Ibrahim, Asim Abdul Maajid, and Essam ud-Deen Darbaalah, *In Pursuit of Allah's Pleasure* (London: Al Firdous, 1997), 55.

44. For examples of Saudi-funding mosques in Europe, see John Lawton, "Muslims in Europe: The Mosques," *Saudi Aramco World* (January/February 1979): 9–14. More figures are available here: http://www.kingfahdbinabdulaziz.com/main/m450.htm; see also Gilles Kepel, *Les banlieues de l'islam. Naissance d'une religion en France* (Paris: Le Seuil, 1987), 96–99, 215–220; Pargeter, *Frontiers of Jihad*, 34.

45. Olivier Roy, *The Failure of Political Islam* (Cambridge, MA: Harvard University Press, 1996), 112.

46. Mahmoud Abdullah Saleh, "Development of Higher Education in Saudi Arabia," *Higher Education*, 15, no. 1/2 (1986): 22. Though Saleh does not provide a further breakdown

of the foreign students into disciplines, it is a safe assumption that much of this population growth was students studying religion at the two main religious institutions: Islamic University of Medina (est. 1961) and Imam Muhammed Bin Saud Islamic University (est. 1974). In 1981 a third religious institution was created, Umm al Qura University in Mecca. See the chart in Saleh, "Development of Higher Education in Saudi Arabia," 20.

47. Joshua Teitelbaum, *Holier Than Thou: Saudi Arabia's Islamic Opposition* (Washington, DC: Washington Institute for Near East Policy, 2000), 26–30.

48. Abdel Bari Atwan, *The Secret History of Al Qaeda* (London: Saqi Books, 2006), 45. See also Peter Bergen, *The Osama Bin Laden I Know* (New York: Free Press, 2006).

49. Samir Amghar, "Le Salafisme en Europe," *Politique Etrangere* 1 (2006): esp. 71–72.

50. Samuel P. Huntington, "The Clash of Civilizations," *Foreign Affairs* (Summer 1991).

51. BBC Profile, "Abdullah al Faisal" [Online], May 25, 2007, http://news.bbc.co.uk/2/hi/uk_news/6692243.stm, accessed June 20, 2008.

52. Shaykh Muhammad Saeed al-Qahtani, *Al-Wala' wa'l-Bara'* (London: Al-Firdous, 1999).

53. Ibid., I:9.

54. Ibid., III:2.

Chapter 6

1. Gary P. Freeman, "Modes of Immigration Politics in Liberal Democratic States," *International Migration Review* (Winter 1995); Rogers Brubaker, *Citizenship and Nationhood in France and Germany* (Cambridge, MA: Harvard University Press, 1992).

2. Stephen Castles, Heather Booth, and Tina Wallace, *Here for Good: Western Europe's New Ethnic Minorities* (London: Pluto Press, 1984), 28; Klaus J. Bade, *Migration in European History* (Malden, MA: Blackwell, 2003); Gary P. Freeman, *Immigrant Labour and Racial Conflict in Industrial Societies: The French and British Experience 1945–1975* (Princeton, NJ: Princeton University Press, 1979).

3. Two European immigration scholars, Jan Rath and Frank Buijs, stated: "(Muslims) have never before been present on such a large scale as they are now" and "it is clear that we are now dealing with a situation that is historically unique in many respects." Frank Buijs and Jan Rath, *Muslims in Europe: The State of Research* (Amsterdam: IMISCOE, 2006) [Online], http://www.imiscoe.org/publications/workingpapers/documents/MuslimsinEurope-Thestateofresearch.pdf, accessed August 12, 2007, 1–2.

4. Freeman, *Immigrant Labour*, 188.

5. Douglas S. Massey and Joshua S. Reichert, "Guestworker Programs: Evidence from Europe and the United States and Some Implications for U.S. Policy," *Population Research and Policy Review* i: 1 (1982): 3.

6. Michael J. Piore, *Birds of Passage: Migration, Labor and Industrial Societies* (Cambridge: Cambridge University Press, 1979), 34.

7. Freeman, *Immigrant Labour*, 204–205; Piore, *Birds*, 39.

8. Freeman, *Immigrant Labour*, 42.

9. Myron Weiner, *The Global Migration Crisis* (New York: HarperCollins, 1995), 28.

10. Thomas Sowell, *Migrations and Cultures: A World View* (New York: Basic Books, 1996), 145, 162. German immigrants from the Westphalian county of Tecklenburg settled in two adjoining counties of Missouri. Frankfort, Kentucky, was founded by Germans from Frankfurt, but Lorima, Wisconsin, was settled almost exclusively by Prussians from Brandenberg, even as the nearby towns of Hermann and Theresa were settled by Pomeranians (Sowell, *Migrations*, 5–6, 76).

11. Daniel Soyer, *Jewish Immigrant Associations and the American Identity in New York* (Cambridge, MA: Harvard University Press, 1997), 50. See also Robert S. Leiken, *The Melting Border: Mexico and Mexican Communities in the United States* (Washington, DC: Center for Equal Opportunity, 2000). Such migration channels were hardly confined to the New World. Migrants from different Chinese villages settled in corresponding places in Thailand, Indochina, Indonesia, the Philippines, Malaysia, and Singapore as well as in the United States (Sowell, *Migrations*, 177). Likewise, Lebanese immigrants to West Africa settled in different locales according to which part of Lebanon they hailed from, just as they and Syrian migrants did in Colombia. See Louise L'Estrange Fawcett, "Lebanese, Palestinians and Syrians in Colombia," in *The Lebanese in the World*, ed. Albert Hourani and Nadim Shehadi (London: Taurus, 1993), 368.

12. Robert S. Leiken, "The Go-Between for Mexico-U.S. Harmony Along the Border," *Los Angeles Times*, February 25, 2001.

13. Interview with Jose Antonio Lagunas, Community Affairs Consul, New York City, February 2, 2000; interview with Ambassador Jorge Pinto, General Consul of Mexico in New York, New York City, February 2, 2000; "Informe Sobre Migracion: Caracteristicas de la Comunidad Mexican en Nueva York," January 2000, Consulate General of Mexico in New York: Graph, 9.

14. J. Rex and R. Moore, *Race, Community, and Conflict: A Study of Sparkbrook* (London: Oxford University Press for the Institute of Race Relations, 1967), 119–120, cited in Alison Shaw, *Kinship and Continuity: Pakistani Families in Britain* (Amsterdam: Harwood Academic, 2000), 13.

15. Douglas S. Massey and Kristin E. Espinosa, "What's Driving Mexico-U.S. Migration? A Theoretical, Empirical and Policy Analysis," *American Journal of Sociology* 102 (January 1997).

16. Caitlin Killian, *North African Women in France: Gender, Culture, and Identity* (Stanford, CA: Stanford University Press, 2006), 35.

17. Ibid.

18. Shaw, *Kinship and Continuity*, 43, 46–56.

19. Philip Lewis, *Islamic Britain. Religion, Politics and Identity among British Muslims: Bradford in the 1990s* (London: Tauris, 1994), 55.

20. Jørgen S. Neilsen, *Towards a European Islam* (London: Macmillan, 1999), 15–16.

21. Stephen Barton, *What Place for Europe's Muslims: Integration or Segregation: Turks in West Germany: The Bengali Muslims of Bradford* (Birmingham, UK: Centre for the Study of Islam and Christian-Muslim Relations, Selly Oak Colleges, 1982), 12; see also Neilsen, *Towards a European Islam*, 15; Lewis, *Islamic Britain*, 56.

22. Verity Saifullah Khan, "Mirpuri Villagers at Home and in Bradford," in James L. Watson, ed. *Between Two Cultures*, Oxford (Basil Blackwell), 1977, 58.

23. On sending countries, see Priore, *Birds* (London: Cambridge University Press, 1979), 1–3; Philip L. Martin, "Guest Worker Policies: An International Survey," in Weiner, *Migration and Refugee Policies*, ed. Ann Bernstein and Myron (London: Printer, 1999), 45–83.

24. Mark J. Miller, "Policy Ad-Hocracy: The Paucity of Coordinated Perspectives and Policies," *Annals of the American Academy of Political and Social Science* 485 (1986): 64–75.

25. Jonas Widgren, "Sweden," in *International Labor Migration in Europe*, ed. Ronald E. Krane (New York: Praeger, 1979), 19.

26. James Q. Wilson, ed., *The Politics of Regulation* (New York: Harper Press, 1980).

27. Wilson, *Politics of Regulation*; see also Freeman, "Modes of Immigration Politics," 885.

28. Freeman, "Modes of Immigration Politics," 885.

29. Widgren, "Sweden," 19–44; Massey and Reichert, "Guestworker Programs," 3.

30. Freeman, *Immigrant Labour*, 115.

31. Ibid., 118.

32. Alec G. Hargreaves, *Immigration, "Race," and Ethnicity in Contemporary France* (London: Routledge, 1995), 178; Christian Joppke, Immigration and the Nation-State: the United States, Germany and Great Britain (Oxford, England: Oxford University Press, 1999), 66; Stephen Castles and Mark J. Miller, *The Age of Migration* (New York: Guilford Press, 2003), 68–70.

33. Yasemin Nuhoglu Soysal, *Limits of Citizenship* (Chicago: University of Chicago, 1994), 34. James F. Hollifield, "Migration and International Relations: The Liberal Paradox," paper presented at a conference entitled "The Year of the Euro," Nanovic Institute for European Studies, University of Notre Dame, 2002), 14. http://www.nd.edu/~nanovic/events/hollifield.pdf, accessed July 26, 2006.

34. Randall Hansen, *Citizenship and Immigration in Post-war Britain* (Oxford: Oxford University Press, 2000), 16.

35. Ibid., 121.

36. Ibid., 120.

37. Roger Ballard, "Migration and Kinship: The Differential Effect of Marriage Rules on the Processes of Punjabi Migration to Britain," in *South Asians Overseas: Contexts and Communities*, ed. C. Clarke, C. Peach, and S. Vertovek (Cambridge: Cambridge University Press, 1990), 237.

38. Ibid., 237–238.

39. Hansen, *Citizenship and Immigration*, 124

40. Ibid., 123–124.

41. Arnold Rose, *Migrants in Europe* (Minneapolis: University of Minnesota Press, 1969), 72–73.

42. Joppke, *Immigration and the Nation-State*, 103.

43. Freeman, *Immigrant Labour*, 10.

44. Ibid., 38.

45. Christian Joppke, "Asylum and State Sovereignty: A Comparison of the United States, Germany and Britain," *Comparative Political Studies* 30, 3 (1997): 101.

46. Enoch Powell, "Rivers of Blood" speech to the annual general meeting of the West Midlands Area Conservative Political Centre, Birmingham, England [Online], April 20, 1968, http://www.telegraph.co.uk/comment/3643826/Enoch-Powells-Rivers-of-Blood-speech.html, accessed July 17, 2007.

47. Ibid.

48. In his visit to the underworld, the Sybil tells Aeneas War, "fierce war, I see: and the Tiber foaming with much blood" (Virgil, *The Aeneid,* Book Six, 85–86).

49. Powell, "Rivers of Blood" speech; see also Paul Foot, *Rise of Enoch Powell* (Harmondsworth, UK: Penguin, 1969); T. E. Utley, *Enoch Powell: The Man and His Thinking* (London: William Kimber, 1968).

50. Foot, *Rise of Enoch Powell*, 289.

51. Ibid., 117; T. E. Utley, *Enoch Powell*, chapter 1; see also Freeman, *Immigrant Labour*, 285.

52. "How Fall'n, How Changed," *London Times*, February 4, 1970.

53. Dominic Sandbrook, *White Heat: A History of Britain in the Swinging Sixties* (London: Abacus, 2006), 681.

54. Jill Dudley and Paul Harvey, "Control of Immigration Statistics: United Kingdom, 2000," 8 [Online], August 24, 2001, http://www.homeoffice.gov.uk/rds/pdfs/hosb1401.pdf, accessed August 12, 2007.

55. Steve Doughty, "Baby Boom," *The Daily Mail*, May 22, 2009.

56. Jason Burke, "Omar Was a Normal British Teenager," *The Observer* (London), January 20, 2008.

57. Aminul Hoque, *Third Generation Bangladeshis: Identity in Question (A Pilot Study)*, Department of Education, Goldsmiths College (London), Dr. Chris Kearney, July 2005, 5–6.

Chapter 7

1. Tariq Ramadan, *To Be a European Muslim* (Leicester, UK: The Islamic Foundation, 1999).

2. Samir Amghar et al., *European Islam: Challenges for Public Policy and Society* (Brussels: Centre for European Policy Studies, 2007), 5.

3. News reports suggest that 5–7 million Muslims reside in France, with government figures on the higher scale and academics coming in as low as 3.7 million. The variation in estimate of the number of French Muslims is illustrative. In a special 2003 series on "L'Islam en France," the French magazine *L'Express* gave examples of the disparity:

- In 1989, the French historian Bruno Étienne estimated the French Muslim population at 2.5 million.
- A 1993 "Haut Conseil à l'intégration" report gave the number of 3 million.
- In 1994, *Le Monde* estimated the number at 3.7 million, or 6.5 percent of the total French population.
- After September 11, 2001, Interior Minister Nicolas Sarkozy said the number lay between 5 to 6 million.
- Contemporary news accounts range between 5 to 7 million.

Jonathan Laurence and Justin Vaisse report that "France is now home to an estimated 5 million persons of Muslim origin, in a total population of 61 million," or 8.2 percent of the total population. Jonathan Laurence and Justin Vaisse, *Integrating Islam: Political and Religious Challenges in Contemporary France* (Washington, DC: Brookings Institution Press, 2006), 1. Table 1-2 in Laurence and Vaisse conveys various estimates of the Muslim population in France, by date (1989 to 2004) and the methodology employed in each case. That number was much higher than the 3.7 million of a survey directed by Michèle Tribalat of the Institut national d'études démographiques (INED; National Institute of Demographic Studies). Michèle Tribalat, *Faire France: Une enquête sur les immigrés et leurs enfants (Making France: A Study of Immigrants and Their Children)* (Paris: La Découverte/Essais, 1995). Patrick Weil, France's most prominent specialist on immigration policy, cited the figure of 7 million at a meeting on immigration in Europe and the United States convened by the German Marshall Fund and *The American Interest* magazine in Washington, DC, on December 7, 2007. See also "Demographie: le brouillard statistique," *Le Figaro*, January 11, 2003. For approximate percentages of population, see Ceri Peach, "Muslim Population of Europe," in *Muslim Integration* (Washington, DC: CSIS, September 2007); *The World Factbook* (Washington, DC: Central Intelligence Agency, 2008; Field Listings: Religion). The exact calculation of the Muslim population is usually not possible. Religious identity, by law, cannot be employed in French census data or government documents. Accurate sampling is further frustrated by the fact that national origins, frequently employed to determine the extent of Muslim immigration, cannot account for the degree of Islamic observance among those sociologically identified as Muslim.

4. Peter Skerry, "Political Islam in the United States and Europe," in *Political Islam: Challenges for U.S. Policy*, ed. Dick Clark (Washington, DC: The Aspen Institute, 2003), 41; Paul M. Barrett, "American Muslims and the Question of Assimilation," *Muslim Integration* (Washington, DC: CSIS, September 2007), 75, 82; Geneive Abdo, *Mecca and Main Street:*

Muslim Life in America after 9/11 (New York: Oxford University Press, 2006), 64; "Muslim Americans: Middle Class and Mostly Mainstream," Pew Research Center, May 2007.

5. Robert S. Leiken, *Bearers of Global Jihad? Immigration and National Security After 9/11* (Washington, DC: Nixon Center, 2004), 59; Barrett, "American Muslims," 75, 82; Abdo, *Mecca and Main Street*, 64; "Muslim Americans: Middle Class and Mostly Mainstream."

6. Rogers Brubaker offers a most relevant example: "Cultural idioms—ways of thinking and talking about nationhood . . . state centered and assimilationist in France and more ethnocultural and differentialist in Germany [or Britain or the United States]." *Citizenship and Nationhood in France and Germany* (Cambridge, MA: Harvard University Press, 1992), 16. Cultural idioms differ from ideologies, which are "idea systems deployed as self-conscious political arguments by identifiable political actors," in that they are "longer-term, more anonymous and less partisan." Theda Skocpol, "Cultural Idioms and Political Ideologies in the Revolutionary Reconstruction of State Power," *Journal of Modern History* 57 (1985): 86–96.

7. Eugene Weber, *Peasants into Frenchmen: The Modernization of Rural France, 1870–1914* (Stanford, CA: Stanford University Press, 1976), 113.

8. Robert E. Goodin and Philip Pettit, eds., *Contemporary Political Philosophy: An Anthology* (Malden, MA: Blackwell, 2006).

9. Brubaker, *Citizenship and Nationhood*, 5.

10. Ibid., 1.

11. Jeremy Black, *A History of the British Isles,* 2nd ed. (New York: Palgrave Macmillan, 2003), 157, 183.

12. See Linda Colley, *Britons: Forging the Nation 1707–1837* (New Haven, CT: Yale University Press, 1992), 12–17.

13. Krishnan Kumar, *The Making of English National Identity* (New York: Cambridge University Press, 2003), 137–138; Black, *History of the British Isles,* 241.

14. Krishnan Kumar, "Nation and Empire: English and British National Identity in Comparative Perspective," *Theory and Society* 29, 5 (October 2000): 589.

15. Bernard Crick, *National Identities* (Cambridge, UK: Blackwell, 1991), 91.

16. Gilles Kepel, *Allah in the West* (Stanford, CA: Stanford University Press, 1997), 86.

17. Gilles Kepel, "French Lessons in Londonistan," *National Interest* (March 2010).

18. Rudolf von Albertini, *Decolonization* (Garden City, NY: Doubleday, 1971), 266.

19. Christian Joppke, "Limits of Integration Policy: Britain and Her Muslims," *Journal of Ethnic and Migration Studies* 35, 3 (March 2009): 455.

20. Brubaker, *Citizenship and Nationhood*, 6.

21. Ibid., 135. It could be said that when in 2000 Germany made nonethnic German postmigrants eligible to be citizens, due to birthplace as opposed to blood, *jus soli* as opposed to *jus sanguinis* became the basis for the acquisition of citizenship as elsewhere in Europe. Yet the German dispensation was hedged with restrictions. Children of foreigners obtained citizenship only if one parent had acquired permanent residency and had been living in Germany for eight years. These postmigrants must declare by the age of twenty-three that they wish to be Germans and must renunciate their foreign citizenship. Douglas B. Klusmeier and Demitriou Papademetriou, *Immigration Policy in the Federal Republic of Germany* (New York: Berghahn, 2009), 203.

22. Brubaker, *Citizenship and Nationhood*, 14.

23. David A. Bell, "The Shorn Identity," *New Republic* (December 5, 2005).

24. See Gerard Noiriel, *The French Melting Pot: Immigration, Citizenship, and National Identity* (Minneapolis: University of Minnesota Press, 1996).

25. Joel S. Fetzer and J. Christopher Soper, *Muslims and the State in Britain, France, and Germany* (Cambridge: Cambridge University Press, 2004), 6.

26. "Veil issue 'a matter for Muslims,'" *BBC News*, October 6, 2006, http://news.bbc.co.uk/2/hi/uk_news/5412742.stm, accessed July 7, 2007.

27. Fetzer and Soper, *Muslims and the State in Britain*, 5.

28. Christian Joppke, *Veil: Mirror of Identity* (Cambridge, UK: Polity, 2009), 62–63.

29. See Amartya Sen, *Reason Before Identity* (Oxford: Oxford University Press, 1999).

30. Joppke, *Veil*, 32.

31. Ibid., 106; see also Joppke, *Immigration and the Nation-State: The United States, Germany and Great Britain* (Oxford: Oxford University Press, 1999), 69–75; Conseil d'Etat, "Analysis of Major Decisions: 8 December 1978, GISTI et Autres," http://www.conseiletat.fr/ce/jurisp/index_ju_la41.shtml, accessed July 27, 2006.

32. Kepel, "French Lessons in Londonistan."

33. Jonathan Evans, "Speech to the Society of Editors in Manchester," *Daily Telegraph* (UK), November 5, 2007.

34. Sean Rayment, "Report Identifies UK Terrorist Enclaves" *Daily Telegraph*, November 9, 2008; see also "Terrorism Threat in UK 'Growing,'" *BBC News*, November 8, 2008 and Stephen Wright, "British Al-Qaeda Enclaves Back Jihad, According to Leaked Government Document" *Daily Mail*, November 9, 2008.

35. Personal communication, May 20, 2010, Washington, DC.

36. Speech delivered by Jonathan Evans to the Worshipful Company of Security Professionals, reprinted in the *Daily Telegraph* (UK), September 17, 2010; see also Duncan Gardham, "Britain Facing a New Wave of Terrorist Attacks, MI5 Warns," *Daily Telegraph* (UK), September 16, 2010.

37. Evans, September 2010 speech.

38. In July 2008 the DST merged with the Direction Centrale des Renseignements Généraux in order to form the Direction Centrale du Renseignement Intérieur.

39. Email communication from Jean-François Clair, November 14, 2008. In 2008 the British MI5 reported that between 2001 and 2008 more than 1,200 terrorist suspects had been arrested and more than 140 charged. U.K. Home Office, "Terrorism and the Law," February 2008, http://www.homeoffice.gov.uk/security/terrorism-and-the-law/, accessed November 10, 2008. The DST's Clair told me that between 2000 and 2008 "more than 800 persons [had] been arrested in France" in connection with terrorism, and of those, more than 160 had been sent to jail (email communication from Jean-François Clair, November 14, 2008). But the proximity of these numbers here says much more about the difficulties of arresting, charging, and convicting terrorists in Britain than about the comparative threats. France is able to do more about a smaller threat; Britain less about a far bigger one.

40. Michael Taarnby, "Jihad in Denmark: An Overview and Analysis of Jihadi Activity in Denmark, 1990–2006," *Danish Institution of International Affairs Working Paper 35*, November 2006.

41. AIVD, *Violent Jihad in the Netherlands: Current Trends in the Islamist Terrorist Threat* (The Hague: Ministry of Interior and Kingdom Relations, 2006), 52–53.

42. *2008 Annual Report on the Protection of the Constitution*, ed. Bundesministerium des Innern [Online], http://www.verfassungsschutz.de/download/SHOW/vsbericht_2008_engl.pdf, accessed June 2, 2009, 197. Briefing with officials of Danish Security and Intelligence Service, Washington, DC, October 28, 2008.

43. Tim Shipman, "CIA Warns Barack Obama That British Terrorists Are the Biggest Threat to the US," *Telegraph* (London), February 7, 2009.

44. Peter R. Neumann, "Europe's Jihadist Dilemma," *Survival* 48, 2 (June 2006): 71.

45. Lorenzo Vidino, *Al Qaeda in Europe* (New York: Prometheus, 2006), 16; and Robert S. Leiken, "Europe's Angry Muslims," *Foreign Affairs*, June 2006, gave the same misleading impression.

Chapter 8

1. Strictly speaking, only two of the bombers were from Beeston itself. Another grew up in neighboring Holbeck, and a fourth lived in the nearby textile town of Huddersfield.

2. "Area Deliver Plan Inner South Leeds Area Profile and Priorities Document, 2004–2005," Inner South Area Committee, Leeds City Council [Online], http://www.leeds.gov.uk/files/2005/week31/inter__e5c32245-fcc5-477c-8eeb-a66f386b78a4_c6b5d79c-ae60-432c-a59e-cf202caa2ddf.pdf, accessed July 28, 2008, 10.

3. Mirpur is the largest city in the Mirpur district, a bit like, *mutatis mutandis,* New York in New York State, and thus its usage is open to confusion. When I speak of Mirpur I usually mean the district unless the city is specified. The city of Mirpur (about 400,000 in 2000) is the largest of Azad Kashmir, the part of Kashmir administered by Pakistan.

4. Madeleine Bunting, "Orphans of Islam," *The Guardian,* July 18, 2005; "UK Announces Opening of Its Honorary Consulate in Pakistani Kashmir," *BBC Monitoring South Asia,* December 5, 2004; Isambard Wilkinson, "British Pakistanis Bring Fish and Chips to Kashmir's 'Beverly Hills,'" *The Daily Telegraph,* December 5, 2005.

5. Roger Ballard, "The South Asian Presence in Britain and Its Transnational Connections," in *Culture and Economy in the Indian Diaspora,* ed. Bhikhu Parekh, Gurharpal Singh, and Steven Vertovec (London: Routledge, 2003), 26.

6. Alison Shaw, *Kinship and Continuity: Pakistani Families in Britain* (Amsterdam: Harwood Academic, 2000), 72.

7. Ballard, "South Asian Presence," 27.

8. Ibid.

9. See Joshua S. Reichert, "The Migrant Syndrome: Seasonal U.S. Wage Labor and Rural Development in Central Mexico," *Human Organization* 40:1 (Spring 1981); Merilee S. Grindle, *Searching for Rural Development: Labor Migration and Employment in Mexico* (Ithaca, NY: Cornell University Press, 1988), 48.

10. Ballard, "South Asian Presence," 28.

11. V. S. Naipaul, *Among the Believers: An Islamic Journey* (New York: Vintage, 1982), 101.

12. Shiv Malik, "My Brother the Bomber," *Prospect,* May 31, 2007.

13. A bill was introduced into the Commons in 1841 containing a clause to outlaw back-to-backs. Following sustained opposition by builders (and indeed the Town Clerk of Leeds) on the grounds that rents would have to rise and would be unaffordable to many working-class people, driving them into lodging houses, the bill was dropped in 1842. "Between 1886 and 1914 there were 57,029 new houses built in Leeds, two-thirds being back-to-backs" (David Thornton, *Leeds: The Story of a City* [Ayrshire, Scotland: Fort Publishing, 2002], 161).

14. George Orwell, *The Road to Wigan Pier* (New York: Harcourt, 1958), 56.

15. Electronic communications with Val Smith, Communications Manager, and James Kilroy, Project Officer of the Regeneration Project, September 23, 2008.

16. Thornton, *Leeds,* 160.

17. Orwell, *Road to Wigan Pier,* 57.

18. Ibid.

19. Ibid., 58.

20. *Strategy for Back-to-Back Housing in West Yorkshire,* final draft, September 17, www.bradford.gov.uk/NR/. . ./WYBTBHousingStrategyFinal021109.pdf2009, accessed October 21, 2009.

21. Steven Burt and Kevin Grady, *The Illustrated History of Leeds* (Derby: Breedon Books, 1994), 24.

22. *The Journeys of Celia Fiennes*, ed. C. Morris, 1949:219, cited in Burt and Grady, *History of Leeds*, 31.

23. Mike Lewis, *The Urban Geography of Leeds*, http://www.brixworth.demon.co.uk/leeds/leeds2.htm, accessed August 9, 2008.

24. Ibid.

25. Ibid.

26. "Inner South Leeds Profile Document"; see Burt and Grady, *History of Leeds*, chapter 5.

27. Employment in British industry was to fall from 11.5 million in 1964 to 7 million in 1984. In these same years, the manufacturing labor force plunged from 8.7 to 5.43 million. R. L. Martin and Bob Rowthorn, *The Geography of De-Industrialization* (London: Macmillan, 1986), 2.

28. The clothing industry employed more than one in four working people in the city and almost one in two working women. Katrina Honeyman, *Well Suited: A History of the Leeds Clothing Industry 1850–1990* (Oxford: Oxford University Press, 2000), 9.

29. Ibid., 100.

30. Verity Saifullah Khan, "The Pakistanis: Mirpuri Villagers at Home and in Bradford," in *Between Two Cultures*, ed. James L. Watson (Oxford: Basil Blackwell, 1977), 72.

31. Ibid.

32. Honeyman, *Well Suited*, 100.

33. See, for example, Ernest Barker, *Ideas and Ideals of the British Empire* (New York: Macmillan, 1941); see also Bernard Crick, *National Identities* (Cambridge: Blackwell, 1991), 92; Christian Joppke, *Immigration and the Nation-State: The United States, Germany, and Great Britain* (Oxford: Oxford University Press, 1999), 224.

34. Honeyman, *Well Suited*, 101.

35. The Teddy Boy craze, typified by the clothing of Edwardian dandies, started in the 1950s and spread rapidly across the country, reaching an apex with the Beatles.

36. Honeyman, *Well Suited*, 101.

37. By 1975 Britain's share of world exports of textile machinery had dwindled from 30 percent in 1954 to 11 percent, and foreign firms supplied two-thirds of the textile machinery that was newly installed in Britain in 1975–1976. See John Singleton, *The World Textile Industry* (London: Routledge, 1997), 82. Textile production itself was being outsourced to Asia, to be followed shortly thereafter by jobs in foundries and engineering plants. Production in U.K. textile activities fell by some 37 percent between 1973 and 1983; see Geoffrey Underhill, *Industrial Crisis and the Global Economy: Politics, Global Trade, and the Textile Industry in Advanced Economies* (London: Macmillan, 1998).

38. Peter Baker, "Restructuring the Textiles and Clothing Industries," in *The British Economy in Transition: From the Old to the New?* ed. Royce Turner (London: Routledge, 1995), 72.

39. In Bradford, employment in textile factories fell from 70,000 to 7,000 from the mid-1960s to 2001; in the same period it shriveled in nearby Oldham from nearly 20,000 to just over 3,000 (Eric Seward, "Racial Conflict in British Cities," in *Racism in Metropolitan Areas*, ed. Rix Pinxten and Ellen Preckler [New York: Berghahn, 2006], 24). See also Virinder S. Kalra, *From Textile Mills to Taxi Ranks: Experiences of Migration, Labour and Social Change* (Burlington, VT: Ashgate, 2000), 132–133; Martin and Rowthorn, *Geography of De-Industrialization*, 1986.

40. Khan, "Pakistanis," 59.

41. Pnina Werbner, *The Migration Process: Capital, Gifts and Offerings among British Pakistanis* (New York: St Martin's, 1990).

42. Khan, "Pakistanis," 59.

43. Shaw, *Kinship and Continuity*, 19; see also B. Dahya, "Pakistanis in England," in *New Community* 2:1 (1972); Khan, "Pakistanis"; Muhammad Anwar, *The Myth of Return: Pakistanis in Britain* (London: Heinemann, 1979).

44. Shaw, *Kinship and Continuity*, 21.

45. Anwar, *Myth of Return,* 23.

46. Ballard, "South Asian Presence," 213; Anwar, *Myth of Return*, 22.

47. The Punjab connection to England has a similar martial source. During the Raj the Punjab was the key recruiting ground for the Imperial Army. Nearly half of the Indian military came from the Punjab, which, for example, during World War I, with a population of 20,000,000 provided 350,000 soldiers. Bengal with a population of 45,000,000 supplied only 7,000. See Kingsley Davies, *The Population of India and Pakistan* (Princeton, NJ: Princeton University Press, 1951), 181. Cf. Anwar, *Myth of Return,* 21. After Partition, the Pakistan military was likewise recruited mainly from the Punjab. See Khan, "Pakistanis," 65.

48. Badr Dahya, "The Nature of Pakistani Ethnicity in Industrial Cities in Britain," in *Urban Ethnicity*, ed. A. Cohen (London: Routledge, 1974), 84; Ballard, "South Asian Presence," 214; Anwar, *Myth of Return,* 22.

49. Anwar, *Myth of Return,* 22; Ballard, "South Asian Presence," 215.

50. Shaw, *Kinship and Continuity*, 26. Shaw also notes that Nair judges that the Punjab's unsettled political history has made Punjabis "one of the least 'rooted' people in India." K. Nair, *Blossoms in the Dust* (London: Duckworth, 1979), 112.

51. Shaw, *Kinship and Continuity*, 30.

52. Khan, "Pakistanis," 67; Anwar, *Myth of Return*, 23.

53. Ballard, "South Asian Presence," 214–215.

54. Anwar, *Myth of Return,* 24.

55. Shaw, *Kinship and Continuity*, 31, 38.

56. Douglas S. Massey, Rafael Alarcon, Jorge Durand, and Humberto González, *Return to Aztlan: The Social Process of International Migration from Western Mexico* (Berkeley: University of California Press, 1987), 219; see also Grindle, *Searching for Rural Development*.

57. Shaw, *Kinship and Continuity*, 290.

58. Khan, "Pakistanis," 71.

59. Ibid., 69.

60. See Robert S. Leiken, "The Go-Between for Mexico-U.S. Harmony along the Border," *Los Angeles Times,* February 25, 2001, and "Border Colleagues," *Washington Post Outlook*, September 2, 2001.

61. Shaw, *Kinship and Continuity*, 100.

62. Roger Ballard, "Migration and Kinship: The Differential Effect of Marriage Rules on the Processes of Punjabi Migration to Britain," in *South Asians Overseas: Contexts and Communities,* ed. C. Clarke, C. Peach, and S. Vertovek (Cambridge: Cambridge University Press, 1990).

63. Shaw, *Kinship and Continuity*, 100.

64. Ballard, "Migration and Kinship."

65. His family did insist that a second postmortem be conducted by Scotland Yard to ascertain his cause of death. Joshua Rozenberg, "Relatives of Tube Bomber Want Another Post-Mortem," *Daily Telegraph* [Online], October 29, 2005, http://www.telegraph.co.uk/news/uknews/1501741/Relatives-of-Tube-bomber-want-another-post-mortem.html,accessed March 23, 2007.

66. Andrew Alderson and Massoud Ansari, "British Bomber's Dad Breaks His Silence: Shehzad Tanweer Buried in Pakistani Graveyard," *Edmonton Journal* (Alberta), October 30, 2005.

67. Rebecca Camber, "Relatives of July 7 Bomber Hold Party at His Grave to 'Celebrate His Life,'" *Daily Mail*, July 8, 2008.

68. Thomas Gray, "Elegy Written in a Country Churchyard," 1751.

69. Khan, "Pakistanis," 77.

70. Shaw, *Kinship and Continuity*, 82.

71. Malik, "My Brother the Bomber."

72. Shaw, *Kinship and Continuity*, 82.

73. Ibid., 87.

74. Werbner, *Migration Process*, 150.

75. Ibid., 232.

76. Ibid.

77. Shaw, *Kinship and Continuity*, 260.

78. Werbner, *Migration Process*, 232.

79. Khan, "Pakistanis," 76.

80. Werbner, *Migration Process*, 101.

81. Shaw, *Kinship and Continuity*.

82. Ibid.

83. Ibid., 66.

84. Ibid., 292.

85. Werbner, *Migration Process*, 120.

86. Max Weber, *The Protestant Ethic and the Spirit of Capitalism*, chapter 5, "Asceticism and the Spirit of Capitalism" (New York: Penguin Books, 2002).

87. Ibid., chapter 5.

88. Ibid.

89. "Three Are Charged over July 7 Bombings," *Times Online* (London), April 5, 2007, http://www.timesonline.co.uk/tol/news/uk/article1618730.ece, accessed July 20, 2008.

90. Robert S. Leiken, "Nicaragua's Untold Stories," *The New Republic* (October 1984).

91. Unpublished manuscript of Shiv Malik, *The Messenger*.

92. Malik, "My Brother the Bomber."

93. "Area Deliver Plan Inner South Leeds Area Profile."

Chapter 9

1. Amanda White, ed., *Social Focus in Brief: Ethnicity* (London: Office of National Statistics, December 2002), 9.

2. For those aged sixteen to twenty-four, 18 percent of Muslims were unemployed. By comparison, 10 percent of Sikhs and 7 percent of Hindus in that age group were unemployed. Nationally, 7 percent of people in the age range of sixteen to twenty-four were unemployed. In the twenty-five and above age group, Muslims again, at 14 percent, had the highest unemployment by a large margin. The unemployment rate for Sikhs was 6 percent and for Hindus it was 5 percent. James A. Beckford, Richard Gale, David Owen, Ceri Peach, and Paul Weller, *Review of the Evidence Base on Faith Communities* (London: University of Warwick, April 2006), 32, 16.

3. Ibid., 18, 34.

4. Ibid., 16, 34. Twenty-nine percent of Muslim women were employed versus 62 percent of Hindu and Sikh women and 59 percent of all British women.

5. Ibid., 19.

6. White, *Social Focus*, 9, 10.

7. Malcolm Harrison and Deborah Phillips, *Housing and Black and Minority Ethnic Communities* (London: Office of the Deputy Prime Minister, May 2003), 20.

8. Beckford et al., *Review of the Evidence,* 36.

9. Office of the Mayor of London, *Muslims in London* (London: Greater London Authority, October 2006), 41.

10. Ibid., 45; In 2000, only 29 percent of Pakistanis and Bangladeshis gained five or more grades of C and higher on their General Certificate of Secondary Education (GCSE) exams. This was the lowest of any ethnic group and well below the national average of 49 percent. EU Accession Monitoring Program, *The Situation of Muslims in the UK* (Budapest: Open Society Institute, 2002), 32.

11. Phillip Lewis, *Islamic Britain. Religion, Politics and Identity among British Muslims: Bradford in the 1990s* (London: Tauris, 1994), 174.

12. Harrison and Phillips, *Housing,* 22. The 2006 British government survey also found Muslims had the highest percentage of residents in the worst housing: 33 percent of Muslims were in the lowest decile (tenth) and 22 percent of Muslims were in the second worst decile. In contrast, only 7 percent of Hindus and 11 percent of Sikhs were in the worst decile, 13 percent of Hindus were in the next lowest with 15 percent of Sikhs. Beckford et al., *Review of the Evidence,* 46.

13. Housing deprivation is defined as when there are fewer bedrooms than household members. Nationally, 15 percent of general households experienced housing deprivation, along with 40 percent of the Muslim population, 25 percent of Hindus, and 22 percent of Sikhs (ibid., 40).

14. ibid., 19–20. Pakistani and Bangladeshi houses had the least amount of space per person, at twenty-two square meters per person. Indians had an average of thirty-five square meters per person, and whites had an average of forty-five square meters per person (ibid., 65). Muslims were least likely to live in owner-occupied housing at only 52 percent, whereas 82 percent of Sikhs and 74 percent of Hindus lived in owner-occupied houses. Nationally, 69 percent of people lived in owner-occupied houses (ibid., 36). Twenty-eight percent of Muslims lived in public housing compared to 8 percent of Sikhs and Hindus (ibid., 64).

15. Jane Lakey and Tariq Modood, *Ethnic Minorities in Britain: Diversity and Disadvantage* (London: Policy Institute, 1997).

16. Beckford et al., *Review of the Evidence,* 49.

17. Ibid., 41.

18. Ibid., 39.

19. Ten weeks after the London bombing, Trevor Phillips, then the director of the prestigious Committee on Racial Equality, a cornerstone of British multiculturalism, denounced proliferating "ghetto communities" and "color coded schools and universities" and "a society . . . almost without noticing it . . . becoming more divided by race and religion . . . sleepwalking into apartheid" (Trevor Phillips, "After 7/7: Sleepwalking to Segregation," Remarks at Manchester Council for Community Relations, September 22, 2005).

20. See Lakey and Modood, *Ethnic Minorities in Britain;* C. Brown, *Black and White Britain: The Third PSI Survey* (Aldershot, UK: Gower, 1984); D. J. Smith, *The Facts of Racial Disadvantage* (London: Political and Economic Planning, 1976); W. W. Daniel, *Racial Discrimination in England* (Harmondsworth, UK, 1968).

21. Roger Ballard, "Migration and Kinship: The Differential Effect of Marriage Rules on the Processes of Punjabi Migration to Britain," in Clarke, C. Peach, C. and Vertovek, *South Asians Overseas,* Cambridge 1990, 220, 223.

22. Ibid., 220.

23. Ibid., 227.

24. Ibid., 228.

25. Ibid.

26. Jerrold Green, quoted in Martin Kramer, *Ivory Towers on Sand: The Failure of Middle Eastern Studies in America* (Washington, DC: Washington Institute for Near East Policy, 2001), 79.

27. Stanley Kurtz, "Marriage and the Terror War, II," *National Review Online,* February 16, 2007.

28. Ballard, "Migration and Kinship," 228–229.

29. Kurtz, "Marriage." Kurtz sees the "need to consider the possibility that cultural differences might have played a significant role in the divergent economic histories of Muslim Mirpur, on the one hand, and Sikh–Hindu Jullundur, on the other." He notes that Ballard himself "highlights the inhibiting effects that Mirpuri notions of honor have on land sales, as well as the negative economic effects of the flight of Mirpur's overwhelmingly Sikh and Hindu middle class during the partition of India and Pakistan."

30. Ballard, "Migration and Kinship," 219–249.

31. There are two forms of cousin marriage: cross-cousin and parallel-cousin. In cross-cousin marriages, unions take place between the children of a pair of siblings of the opposite sex. For example, a father's son marries the father's sister's daughter. The vast majority of consanguineous unions are cross-cousin marriages. In parallel-cousin marriages, unions take place between the children of siblings of the same sex. This also takes two forms: matrilineal and patrilineal cousin marriages. Patrilineal cousin marriage is far more prevalent in Islamic societies than matrilineal cousin marriage, which is rarely practiced.

32. Ballard, "Migration and Kinship," 229.

33. See K. M. Kapadia, *Marriage and the Family in India* (Calcutta: Oxford University Press, 1958). In the south of India, cousin marriage among Hindus is more common. See Edward Westermarck, *The History of Human Marriage* (London: Macmillan, 1921), 71; Alison Shaw, *Negotiating Risk: British Pakistani Experiences of Genetics* (London: Berghahn, 2009), 51.

34. Ballard, "Migration and Kinship."

35. First cousin marriages are the most common, accounting for almost 30 percent of all marriages in, for example, Jordan, Iraq, Kuwait, and Saudi Arabia. Rates in North African countries such as Algeria and Morocco and in Turkey are lower—about 25 percent. See also Hanan Hamamy, "Genetic Disorders in the Arab World," *British Medical Journal* (October 2006): 333, 831–834.

36. S. A. Shami, J. C. Grant, and A. H. Bittles, "Consanguineous Marriage within Social/Occupational Class Boundaries in Pakistan," *Journal of Biosocial Science* 26:1 (January 1994): 91–96.

37. A. H. Bittles, "A Background Summary of Consanguineous Marriage," Centre for Human Genetics, Edith Cowan University, Perth, Australia, May 2001.

38. R. Hussain cites a *hadith* that "discouraged marriages to cousins who, because of the closeness of the relationship, were almost like siblings," though its social and economic rationale served to "ensure wider marriage alliances which would facilitate the spread of Islam through Arabia" ("Community Perceptions of Reasons for Preference for Consanguineous Marriages in Pakistan," *Journal of Biosocial Science* 31: 453). See Robert F. Murphy and Leonard Kasdan, "The Structure of Parallel Cousin Marriage," *American Anthropologist* 61:1 (February 1959): 17–29; Andrey Korotayev, "Parallel-Cousin (FBD) Marriage, Islamization, and Arabization," *Ethnology* 39:4, Special Issue: Comparative Research and Cultural Units (Autumn 2000): 395–407; Fredrik Barth, "Father's Brother's Daughter Marriage in Kurdistan," *Southwestern Journal of Anthropology* 10:2 (Summer 1954): 164–171.

The phenomenon of cousin marriage has aroused much speculation. Shiv Malik offers an economic explanation:

In Mirpur, as in many poor parts of the world, the basic structures of life-justice, security and social support are organised by the local tribe and not by a central state. One consequence is that people can't just marry whom they want. If they did, then over time tribal lands would be broken up by the rules of inheritance, and the economic base of the tribe . . . . would be destroyed. On the other hand, marriage with patrilateral cousins would guarantee that property would pass from tribal control and hence progressively diminish the tribe's land.

In a similar vein, to explain cousin marriage in her most recent book, Alison Shaw cites Germain Tillon's speculation that cousin marriage accompanied the transition from hunter-gathering to settled agricultural societies. See Shaw, *Negotiating Risk,* 66; Germain Tillon, *Republic of Cousins* (London: Zed Press, 1983), 14. Marriage between cousins then ensured high birth rates and protected the integrity of tribal land. Yet if tribal property were the basis for cousin marriage, it is not clear why all Punjabis have not followed suit or what accounts for the discrepancies in South Asia and worldwide between Muslim and non-Muslim communities.

Was the adoption of the practice a response to the Qur'an's departure from patriarchal traditions, allowing daughters to inherit property (4:7, 11–2, 176)? If so, it would not take us far in explaining practices in the modern Punjab. An extensive in-depth study of attitudes among married Pakistani women found that "given their subordinate position, not only are women unlikely to inherit but, more importantly, very few women are inclined to assert their legal rights of inheritance." See Hussain, "Community Perceptions," 449–461.

Did cousin marriage spread with the Umayyid Caliphate? Andrey Korotayev attributes the presence of cousin marriage in Muslim countries to Umayyid rulers compelling Islamized non-Arab groups to adopt Arab customs and traditions. Cousin marriage was to ensure the continuance of Arab culture for generations to come. Thus, according to Korotayev there remains a strong correlation between the area once ruled by the Umayyads and populations that practice patrilineal parallel cousin marriage (Andrey Korotayev, "Parallel-Cousin (FBD) Marriage," 402). As against this theory is the view that the practice of cousin marriage among Pakistanis appears to date only to the adoption of Islam in the sixteenth and seventeenth centuries (A. Darr and B. Modell, "The Frequency of Consanguineous Marriage among British Pakistanis," *Journal of Medical Genetics,* Vol. 25: 189). But recent fossil evidence appears to suggest that cousin marriage was actually the norm among the first humans to arrive in the Indian subcontinent 60,000 years ago in Neolithic times. Spencer Wells and Ramasamy Pitchappan have found an ancient DNA marker in the blood of Piramal Kallars in south India (Spencer Wells, *Deep Ancestry: Inside the Genographic Project* [National Geographic Society, 2006]: 114-117; Pitchappan et al., "Sociobiology and HLA Genetic Polymorphism in Hill Tribes," *Human Biology* 69 [1997]: 59–74). The Piramala Kallars are the oldest human inhabitants of the subcontinent and they married their cousins according to mitochondrial polymorphic marker analysis. If that is the case, Mirpuri cousin marriage predates "the Republic of Cousins, the biblical taboo against incest (with siblings and parents), the Umayyad caliphate and the Mogul conquest." See also Robert F. Murphy and Leonard Kasdan, "The Structure of Parallel Cousin Marriage," *American Anthropologist* 61:1 (February 1959): 17–29; Fredrik Barth, "Father's Brother's Daughter Marriage in Kurdistan," *Southwestern Journal of Anthropology* 10:2 (Summer 1954): 164–171.

39. See Jared Diamond, *Guns, Germs and Steel* (New York: Norton, 1997); Numa Denis Fustel de Coulanges, *The Ancient City* (Garden City: Doubleday, 1965); Henry Summer Maine, *Ancient Law* (Boston: Beacon Press, 1963); Elman R. Service, *Primitive Social Organization* (New York: Random House, 1973); Morton Fried, *The Evolution of Political Society* (New York: Random House, 1967)

40. Hussain, "Community Perceptions," 449–461. Ballard points to another concern: cousin marriage is "not only a highly effective means of reinforcing biraderi solidarity, but also of ensuring that daughters will not be mistreated by their in-laws" (Ballard, "The Impact of Kinship on the Economic Dynamics of Transnational Networks: Reflections on some South Asian Developments," Center for Applied Asian Studies, 2007).

41. Shaw, *Kinship and Continuity,* 154.

42. Ballard, "Migration and Kinship," 231. Although the retention of property ranks as one of the most advantageous aspects of cousin marriage, Pakistanis, particularly in Britain, view such an arrangement "as a means of sustaining kinship links that would otherwise be broken" (Shaw, *Negotiating Risk,* 70) often as a result of immigration. As parents remain heavily involved in spouse selection, consanguineous marriages offer the "best opportunity for compatibility between the husband and wife" (Hussain, "Community Perceptions," 455). Partisans of cousin marriages also believe that marriage to relatives allows for "the presence of common relatives who can intercede with both spouses in times of marital conflict" (Hussain, "Community Perceptions," 456).

43. Saifullah Khan arrived at the same approximation, as did Pnina Werbner. See Verity Saifullah Khan, "The Pakistanis: Mirpuri Villagers at Home and in Bradford," in *Between Two Cultures,* ed. James L. Watson (Oxford: Basil Blackwell, 1977), 61; Werbner, *The Migration Process: Capital, Gifts and Offerings among British Pakistanis* (New York: St Martin's, 1990), 231, 242. In Urdu and Punjabi, Shaw notes, "Your cousin is your 'aunt (or uncle)-born sister (or brother),' and separate terms denote which aunt or uncle; for example, mother's brother, or father's older brother, etc.; there are no single words for 'aunt', 'uncle' or 'cousin'" (Shaw, *Kinship and Continuity,* 95).

44. Ballard, "Impact of Kinship"; see also Ballard, "Migration and Kinship," 231. Among British Pakistanis, the persistence of consanguinity has been linked to genetic disorders. Consanguineous marriages increase the offspring's risk for inheriting diseases linked with recessive genes and can lead to an increase in congenital malformations (B. Modell, "Social and Genetic Implications of Customary Consanguineous Marriage among British Pakistanis. Report of a meeting held at the Ciba Foundation on 15 January 1991," *Journal of Medical Genetics* 28: 721), as children inherit a copy of a recessive allele from each parent (A. D. J. Overall, M. Ahmad, M. G. Thomas, and R. A. Nichols, "An Analysis of Consanguinity and Social Structure Within the UK Asian Population Using Microsatellite Data," *Annals of Human Genetics* 67: 526). At nineteen deaths per one thousand births (Modell, "Social and Genetic Implications," 720), perinatal mortality among British Pakistanis is relatively high compared with other ethnic groups, due in part to genetic problems caused by consanguineous marriage. Moreover, first cousin couples have a 5 percent risk of neonatal childhood death, stillbirth, or congenital malfunction (Ibid.). Disorders common in children born to consanguineous couples include cystic fibrosis, hemoglobinopathies, glucose-6-phosphate dehydrogenase deficiency, and several metabolic disorders (Lihadh al-Gazali | Hanan Hamamy | Shaikha al-Arrayad, "Genetic Disorders in the Arab World," *British Medical Journal* 333: 831; Darr and Modell, "Frequency of Consanguineous Marriage," 186). Moreover, the number of children born with Down's syndrome is relatively higher in societies that practice consanguineous marriages than the usual figure for industrialized countries, perhaps due to a higher proportion of births to older mothers (al-Gazali et al., "Genetic Disorders," 831).

45. Ballard, "Migration and Kinship," 231.

46. Shaw, *Kinship and Continuity,* 94.

47. Stanley Kurtz, "Assimilation Studies, Part II," *National Review Online,* March 22, 2007.

48. Ballard, "Migration and Kinship."

49. Muhammad Anwar, *The Myth of Return: Pakistanis in Britain* (London: Heinemann Educational, 1979), 39.

50. Ibid., 39–40.

51. Lewis, *Islamic Britain,* 203.

52. Christian Joppke, *Immigration and the Nation-State: The United States, Germany, and Great Britain* (New York: Oxford University Press, 1999), 245; D. Coleman and J. Salt,

Ethnicity in the 1991 Census, Volume One: Demographic Characteristics of the Ethnic Minority Populations (London: Office for National Statistics, 1996), 246.

53. Barbara D. Metcalf, "'Remaking Ourselves,'" in *Accounting for Fundamentalisms: The Dynamic Character of Movements*, ed. Martin E. Marty and R. Scott Appleby (Chicago: University of Chicago Press, 1994), 721, quoted in Peter Mandaville, *Transnational Muslim Politics: Reimagining the Umma* (London: Routledge, 2001), 146.

54. Lewis, *Islamic Britain*, 143.

55. Ibid., 6, 63.

56. Darr and Modell, "Frequency of Consanguineous Marriages," 186, 187. See also Alison Shaw, "Kinship, Cultural Preference and Immigration: Consanguineous Marriage among British Pakistanis," *Journal of the Royal Anthropological Institute* 7:2 (June 2001).

57. Werbner, *Migration Process,* 84.

58. Shaw, *Kinship and Continuity*, 138.

59. Ibid., 227.

60. Ballard, "Migration and Kinship."

61. Ibid.

62. Ibid.

63. Kurtz, "Marriage"; Kurtz, "Assimilation Studies."

Chapter 10

1. See chapter 4; Omar Nasiri, *Inside the Jihad* (New York: Basic Books, 2006), 296.

2. UN Security Council Official Records, *Pursuant to Resolution 1267 (1999) concerning Al-Qaida and the Taliban and Associated Individuals and Entities.* [Online] October 17, 2001. Available: http://www.un.org/sc/committees/1267/NSQI03101E.shtml. [October 26, 2005].

3. Christian Joppke, "Immigration Challenges to the Nation-State," in *Challenge to the Nation-State*, ed. Christian Joppke (Oxford: Oxford University Press, 1999), 233.

4. Ibid., 254.

5. Ibid. Straw, also a former Labor Home Secretary (and a Foreign Secretary), would later follow in Jenkins's footsteps when, as deputy leader of the House of Commons and Lord Privy Seal, he raised a storm of controversy by acknowledging that women wearing the *niqab*, the full-face Muslim veil, to interviews with him in his office made him feel "uncomfortable about talking to someone 'face-to-face' who [*sic*] I could not see." "Jack Straw on the Veil," *BBC News* [Online], October 6, 2006, http://news.bbc.co.uk/2/hi/uk_news/politics/5413470.stm, accessed December 18, 2009.

6. *Trends*, 3/2, 1989: 8, quoted in Phillip Lewis, *Islamic Britain. Religion, Politics and Identity among British Muslims: Bradford in the 1990s* (London: Tauris, 1994), 176.

7. Elizabeth Scantlebury, "Muslims in Manchester: The Depiction of a Religious Community," *New Community* 21:3 (July 1995): 430–431; see also Peter Mandaville, *Transnational Muslim Politics: Reimagining the Umma* (London: Routledge, 2001), 123–124.

8. Lewis, *Islamic Britain*, 141.

9. Mandaville, *Transnational Muslim Politics*, 124.

10. Lewis, *Islamic Britain*, 181.

11. Ibid., 178.

12. Scantlebury, "Muslims in Manchester," 430.

13. See *Studies into Violent Radicalisation; Lot 2, The Beliefs, Ideologies and Narratives* (Brussels: Change Institute for the European Commission, 2008), 61–62.

14. Walthamstow would become notorious nearly two decades later as the hometown of those who plotted to crash transatlantic jetliners in the "Second September 11."

15. Quintan Wiktorowicz, *Radical Islam Rising: Muslim Extremism in the West* (New York: Rowman and Littlefield, 2005), 7.

16. Suha Taji-Farouki, *A Fundamental Quest: Hizb al-Tahrir and the Search for the Islamic Caliphate* (London: Grey Seal, 1996), 171.

17. Ibid., 1.

18. Sadek Hamid, "Islamic Political Radicalism in Britain: The Case of Hizb ut-Tahrir," in *Islamic Political Radicalism: A European Perspective*, ed. Tahir Abbas (Edinburgh: Edinburgh University Press, 2007), 147.

19. Ibid.

20. Zeno Baran, *Hizb ut-Tahrir: Islam's Political Insurgency* (Washington, DC: Nixon Center, 2004), 24.

21. Ibid., 24–25.

22. Taji-Farouki, *Fundamental Quest*, 171.

23. Baran, *Hizb ut-Tahrir*, 21.

24. Taji-Farouki, *Fundamental Quest*, 16–18, 171–172.

25. Wiktorowicz, *Radical Islam Rising*, 8.

26. Ed Husain, *The Islamist: Why I Joined Radical Islam in Britain, What I Saw Inside and Why I Left* (New York: Penguin, 2007), 117.

27. Husain, *Islamist*, 82.

28. Wiktorowicz, *Radical Islam Rising*, 9.

29. Ibid., 21–24.

30. Conversation with Maajid Nawas, Washington, DC, September 10, 2009.

31. Husain, *Islamist*, 74.

32. Ibid.

33. Ibid., 79–80M; *Studies into Violent Radicalisation*, 63.

34. Husain, *Islamist*, 71.

35. Ibid., 73.

36. *Studies into Violent Radicalisation*, 61–62.

37. Jonathan Birt, "Terrorism and Islam: The British Muslim Experience," in *Bloody Terrorists*, ed. Ziauddin Sardar (unpublished manuscript). See also Johannes Jansen, *The Dual Nature of Islamic Fundamentalism* (Ithaca, NY: Cornell University Press, 1997), chapter 1.

38. The salience of cultural issues is also the central finding of the best introduction to the European jihadi mind: Farhad Khosrokhavar's extensive 2004–2005 interviews of jihadis in French prisons. Of the 160 interviews conducted in three prisons chosen for their high percentage of Muslim inmates, twenty of the subjects had been convicted of criminal association with terrorists. From this group, Khosrokhavar was able to interview fifteen and to obtain significant information from ten. Next to the usual political grievances—Israel, Bosnia, Afghanistan, Chechnya, Iraq—stood out "those of a cultural nature[:] . . . the menace of the Western model of sexuality to relations between men and women, as well as consumerism that includes alcohol, drugs, and sexual perversions among which Islamists place homosexuality" (Farhad Khosrokhavar, *Quand Al-Qaïda Parle: Témoignages derrière les barreaux* [Paris: Grasset & Fasquelle, 2006], 23). The interviewees universally assailed "the depravation of the West, with the disintegration of the family, alcoholism, and lack of clear and traditional gender roles extending to homosexuality. . . . [A]rrogance and hypocrisy are central aspects of Islamist views of the West" (ibid., 382).

One militant insisted that "the emancipation of women, homosexuality, license and debauchery, AIDS and genetic manipulations demonstrate the same agenda: the diabolical character of the West and its destructive character for Islam. Therefore the necessity of an unmerciful struggle and the legitimacy of people like [bin] Laden" (ibid., 87). Another explained, "Islam teaches me to control my bestial instincts: on the bus, the metro, I start to want a woman, but I resist, it is forbidden by Islam" (ibid., 33). Asked the question, "What bothers you about Western modernity?" another jihadi answered, "To start, homosexuality. . . . Homosexuality must be forbidden. It is a sickness. . . . It is a sin and a mortal sin. Alcohol also. The Prophet banned alcohol. It is necessary to ban it and to explain to these people that it is bad. Not only for Muslims, but for the whole world, without exception. God's commandments were not for a particular group, but for all of humanity" (ibid., 72–73).

Echoing another theme of Londonistan, a jailed jihadi declares: "This secular culture is founded on hypocrisy. . . . They say they are tolerant but when a girl doesn't follow the dominant model, they become intolerant. . . . They are tolerant of homosexuality, of all sexual idiosyncrasies, but they are intolerant when you . . . want to uphold a sense of family, the law, religion, and marriage. It is a way of life that is different in its nature than that commanded by Islam" (ibid., 177).

39. Birt, "Terrorism and Islam."

40. "Profile: Abu Qatada," *BBC News* [Online], February 2007, http://news.bbc.co.uk/go/pr/fr/-/2/hi/uk_news/4141594.stm, accessed August 18, 2009.

41. Brynjar Lia, *Architect of Global Jihad: The Life of Al-Qaida Strategist Abu Mus'ab al-Suri* (London: Hurst & Company, 2008), 3.

42. Quintan Wiktorowicz and John Kaltner, "Killing in the Name of Islam: Al-Qaeda's Justification for September 11," *Middle East Policy Council Journal* X:2 [Online], Summer 2003, http://www.mepc.org/journal_vol10/0306_wiktorowiczkaltner.asp, accessed August 9, 2007.

43. Lia, *Architect of Global Jihad*, 184–185.

44. Omar Nasiri, *Inside the Jihad* (New York: Basic Books, 2006), 267; Lia, *Architect of Global Jihad*, 185.

45. See Mamoun Fandy, *Saudi Arabia and the Politics of Dissent* (New York: Palgrave, 2001). Many of the letters are available online in the Harmony database at http://ctc.usma.edu/harmony/harmony_docs.asp.

46. Lia, *Architect of Global Jihad*, 121.

47. Ibid., 150; see also Sean O'Neal and Daniel McGrory, *The Suicide Factory: Abu Hamza and the Finsbury Park Mosque* (London: HarperPerennial, 2006), 73.

48. Lia, *Architect of Global Jihad*, 121.

49. Ibid., 185; see also Nasir, *Inside the Jihad*, 267.

50. Kathy Evans, "Radical Time Bomb Under British Islam," *Guardian*, February 7, 1994. Cited in Alison Pargeter, *The New Frontiers of Jihad: Radical Islam in Europe* (Philadelphia: University of Philadelphia Press, 2008), 103.

51. Lia, *Architect of Global Jihad*, 185–187.

52. Ibid.

53. Terry McDermott, *Perfect Soldiers* (New York: HarperCollins, 2005), 82.

54. Mark Honigsbaum and Alan Travis, "Al-Qaida's 'Spiritual Ambassador' Faces Return to Jordan," *The Guardian* [Online], August 12, 2005, http://www.guardian.co.uk/uk_news/story/0,1547507,00.html, accessed August 28, 2008.

55. Mark Hosenball, "Terror Watch: Terror Threat?" *Newsweek* [Online], March 9, 2005, http://www.newsweek.com/id/48929, accessed May 13, 2006.

56. Lorenzo Vidino and Steven Emerson, *Al Qaeda in Europe* (Amherst, NY: Prometheus, 2006), 300.

57. Honigsbaum and Travis, "Al-Qaida's 'Spiritual Ambassador.'"

58. Nasiri, *Inside the Jihad*, 273, 281; "Profile: Abu Qatada [BBC];" "Investigating Al-Qaeda," *BBC News* [Online], 2003, http://news.bbc.co.uk/2/shared/spl/hi/world/02/

september_11/investigating_al_qaeda/html/people/other_suspects.stm, accessed January 31, 2009.

59. "Qatada's Key UK al Qaeda Role,'" *BBC News* [Online], March 23, 2004, http://news.bbc.co.uk/2/hi/uk_news/politics/3562695.stm, accessed March 6, 2007.

60. "Cleric Loses Deportation Appeal," *BBC News* [Online], February 26, 2007, http://news.bbc.co.uk/2/hi/uk_news/6396447.stm, accessed August 5, 2008.

61. James Brandon, *Unlocking al Qaeda* (London: Quilliam Foundation, 2009), 92–96; see also "Profile: Abu Qatada" [BBC]; Vidino and Emerson, *Al Qaeda in Europe*, 115; Honigsbaum and Travis, "Al-Qaida's 'Spiritual Ambassador'"; "Profile: Abu Qatada," *Cooperative Research History Commons* [Online], http://www.cooperativeresearch.org/entity.jsp?entity=abu_qatada, accessed July 13, 2008.

62. O'Neal and McGrory, *Suicide Factory*.

63. "Hamza's Ex-Wife Life Threatened," *BBC News* [Online], February 8, 2006, http://news.bbc.co.uk/go/pr/fr/-/2/hi/uk_news/4694218.stm, accessed October 8, 2007.

64. "Abu Hamza Arrested in London on Terrorism Charges Filed in the United States," U.S. Department of Justice [Online], May 27, 2004, http://www.justice.gov/opa/pr/2004/May/04_crm_371.htm, accessed October 2, 2005.

65. O'Neal and McGrory, *Suicide Factory*, 16.

66. Ibid., 22–27.

67. Nagra Plunkett, "'Terrorist' Preacher Was a Quiet Boy—Mother," *Jamaica Gleaner*, August 27, 2006.

68. Cahal Milmo, "The Imam Who Twisted His Faith to Preach Race Hatred, Murder and Violence," *The Independent,* February 25, 2003.

69. *Studies into Violent Radicalisation,* 62.

70. El Faisal's videos can be found at http://video.yahoo.com/playlist/101817946, accessed June 2, 2009.

71. O'Neal and McGrory, *Suicide Factory*, 272.

72. "Judgment in Appeal of Crown v. El Faisal, Supreme Court of Judicature, Court of Appeal" [Online], March 4, 2004, http://nefafoundation.org/miscellaneous/FeaturedDocs/RoyalCourtsofJustice_AlFaisal.pdf, accessed January 12, 2010.

73. Alan Cowell, "Britain Deports Muslim Preacher Linked to Bombings," *New York Times*, May 25, 2007.

74. Alan Cowell, "Kenya Seeks to Deport Muslim Cleric to Jamaica," *New York Times,* January 4, 2010.

75. *Report of the Official Account of the Bombings in London on July 7, 2005 [Online],* May 11, 2006, www.official-documents.gov.uk/document/. . ./1087.asp, accessed August 4, 2006; Farah Stockman and Donovan Slack, "For Jamaican Native, Life Path Led from Success to Extremism," *Boston Globe,* July 22, 2005; Shiv Malik, "My Brother the Bomber," *Prospect,* May 31, 2007.

76. See Robert Leiken, "London Breeding Islamic Terrorists," *CNN,* January 6, 2010; Scott Shane and Souad Mekhennet, "Imam's Path from Condemning Terror to Preaching Jihad," *New York Times,* May 8, 2010; John F. Burns, "Terror Inquiry Looks at Suspect's Time in Britain," *New York Times,* December 30, 2009; Chris Irvine, "Al-Qaeda 'Groomed Abdulmutallab in London,'" *London Times,* December 30, 2009.

77. Wiktorowicz, *Radical Islam Rising*, 9.

78. Omar Bakri Muhammed, *The British Plan Upon Islam and Muslims: A Continuation of the Crusader Wars* (London: Ad-Dawah, 2004), 91.

79. Husain, *Islamist,* 115.

80. "Cleric Bakri Barred from Britain," *BBC News* [Online], August 12, 2005, http://news.bbc.co.uk/2/hi/uk_news/4144792.stm, accessed May 15, 2008; James Slack, "Islamist Group

That Planned Wootton Bassett Hate March Is Finally Banned but Will They Just Find a new Front?" *Daily Mail,* January 13, 2010, http://www.dailymail.co.uk/news/article-1242530/ Islam4UK-group-planned-Wootton-Bassett-hate-march-banned-Alan-Johnson.html, accessed January 15, 2010.

81. Baran, *Hizb ut-Tahrir,* 22.

82. Sean O'Neill, "Keeping Faith with a Circle of Awareness," *The Guardian,* August 2, 1989.

83. Kathy Evans, "Radical Time Bomb Under British Islam," *The Guardian,* February 7, 1994.

84. Ibid.

85. Ibid.

86. Muhammed, *British Plan Upon Islam and Muslims,* 78–79.

87. Ibid., 84–85.

88. Ibid.

89. Pnina Werbner, "The Making of Muslim Dissent: Hybridized Discourses, Lay Preachers, and Radical Rhetoric among British Pakistanis," *American Ethnologist* 23:1 (February 1996): 115.

90. Wiktorowicz, *Radical Islam Rising,* 93.

91. Ibid., 23, 92.

92. Husain, *Islamist,* 140.

93. Taji-Farouki, "Islamists and the Threat of Jihad," 31–32; Baran, *Hizb ut-Tahrir,* 54; see also Vikram Dodd, "Jews Fear Rise of the Muslim 'Underground,'" *Guardian* (London), February 18, 1996; Michael Whine, "Islamist Recruitment and Antisemitism on British Campuses" (London: RUSI Homeland Security & Resilience Department Workshop, 2006).

94. Husain, *Islamist,* 100.

95. Wiktorowicz, *Radical Islam Rising,* 10.

96. Lewis Rambo, *Understanding Religious Conversion* (New Haven, CT: Yale University Press, 1995), 103–104.

97. Wiktorowicz, *Radical Islam Rising,* 48.

98. Ibid., 47–50.

99. Ibid., 107, figure 2.3; 118.

100. Kylie Connor, "'Islamism' in the West? The Life-Span of the Al-Muhajiroun in the United Kingdom," *Journal of Muslim Minority Affairs* 25:1 (April 2005): 124.

101. Wiktorowicz, *Radical Islam Rising,* 118.

102. Connor, "'Islamism' in the West?" 122–123.

103. Olivier Roy, *Globalized Islam* (New York: Columbia University Press, 2005), 324.

104. Ibid., 324.

105. Ibid., 324.

106. Ibid.

107. Alison Pargeter, *The New Frontiers of Jihad* (London: I. B. Tauris, 2008), 144.

108. Ibid., 113. Lewis himself goes further, contending that "the Muslim fundamentalists . . . do not differ from the mainstream on questions of theology and the interpretation of scripture" (Bernard Lewis, *The Crisis of Islam: Holy War and Unholy Terror* [New York: Random House, 2004], 24, see also 146). But there appear to be many disparities between folk and fundamentalist Islam in interpreting scripture, if less on the tendency to invoke it.

109. Pargeter is correct with regards to what we can call the first, pre-9/11 wave of European jihadis, Outsiders. But Pargeter wishes to turn the second wave, the postmigrants, into Outsiders too. Here, the facts broadly support Roy's Insider thesis. Pargeter's "Outsider" and Roy's "Insider" theses obscure the heterogeneity of Europe's angry Muslims. In Pargeter's own words, "From veterans of the war in Afghanistan, to members of Middle

Eastern insurgent groups, to second generation insurgents and European converts, these radicals have all contributed to the image of Europe as a breeding ground for religiously inspired political violence" (Pargeter, *New Frontiers of Jihad*, 1). Like Pargeter, Roy's incidental recognition of the twofold (Outsider-Insider; Eastern-Western) character of the European radicalization process stands out against his own (Insider) thesis: "There is a general pattern of radicalization in Europe. A politicized middleman from the Middle East (usually with an 'Afghan' background) contacts a group of local friends, often involved in petty delinquency or drug abuse, whose ethnic origin is less relevant than their sense of isolation and uprootedness, and who find in radical Islam a positive protest identity" (Roy, *Globalized Islam,* 315). Without either of them explicitly saying so, both acknowledge the *dual,* heterogeneous character of radical Islam in Europe: Inside and Outside, Western and Eastern.

110. Abu Hamza al-Masri, *The Khawaarij and Jihad,* cited in Vidino and Emerson, *Al Qaeda in Europe,* 138. *Al-Ansar* was also produced in Sweden for some time.

111. Lia, *Architect of Global Jihad,* 188; Gilles Kepel, *Jihad: The Trail of Political Islam* (Cambridge, MA: Harvard University Press, 2002), 270.

112. Nasiri, *Inside the Jihad,* 272; Kepel, *Jihad,* 271; James Phillips, "The Rising Threat of Revolutionary Islam in Algeria," *The Heritage Foundation,* Backgrounder 1060, November 9, 1995. Defectors from the GIA eventually formed the Salafist Group for Preaching and Combat (Groupe Salafiste pour la Predication et le Combat, or GSPC), which condemned the wholesale slaughter of civilians by the GIA and pledged to continue the armed jihad against the "infidel" Algerian government without harming civilians. The GSPC completely replaced the GIA in Europe, where it had the opportunity to interact with other networks of radicals, particularly al Qaeda, to the point where the distinction between the GSPC and al Qaeda became fuzzy, especially in Europe. Later, the GSPC became al Qaeda in the Maghreb.

113. http://www.historycommons.org, accessed January 4, 2010.

114. Nasiri, *Inside the Jihad,* 275.

115. Ibid., 295.

116. O'Neal and McGrory, *Suicide Factory,* 39–40.

117. Ibid., 37.

118. Ibid., 38.

119. Exhibit no. MA/13, June 19, 2005, 55.

120. Ibid., 68.

121. O'Neal and McGrory, *Suicide Factory,* 41.

122. Ibid., 42.

123. Ibid.

124. Ibid.

125. Ibid., 43.

126. Exhibit no. MA/13, June 19, 2005, 2.

127. Abu Hamza, "The Hypocrites" [Online], http://ilaljibal.com/downloads/audio/lectures/Abu%20Hamza%20al-Masri/The%20Hypocrites/thehypocrites1.mp3, accessed June 13, 2009.

128. Sheik Abdullah el Faisal, *The Devil's Deception of the Saudi Salafis* [Online], 1996, http://www.youtube.com/watch?V=QZ_7BTA6MxM, accessed September 6, 2009.

129. From Abu Qatada's "Iman Series" of videotapes, cited in Raffaello Pantucci, "Abu Qatada's Comfortable British Jihad," *Terrorism Monitor* 6:14 (July 10, 2008).

130. Salafimanaj.com Research Team, "A Critical Study of the Multiple Identities and Disguises of 'al Muhajiroun, London'"; see also Anthony McRoy, *From Rushdie to 7/7: The Radicalisation of Islam in Britain* (London: Social Affairs Unit, 2006), 201.

131. El Faisal, *Devil's Deception of the Saudi Salafis.*

132. Ibid.

133. Milmo, "Imam Who Twisted His Faith."

134. El Faisal, *Devil's Deception of the Saudi Salafis.*

135. "Qatada's Key UK al Qaeda Role," *BBC News* [Online], March 23, 2004, http://news.bbc.co.uk/2/hi/uk_news/politics/3562695.stm, accessed March 30, 2006; Lia, *Architect of Global Jihad*, 185; "Investigating Al Qaeda," *BBC News* [Online], http://news.bbc.co.uk/2/shared/spl/hi/world/02/september_11/investigating_al_qaeda/html/people/other_suspects.stm, accessed June 4, 2007; Mark Hosenball, "Terror Watch: Terror Threat?" *Newsweek* [Online], March 9, 2005, http://www.newsweek.com/id/48929, accessed July 1, 2007.

136. "Qatada's Key UK al Qaeda Role."

137. Vidino and Emerson, *Al Qaeda in Europe*, 192.

138. O'Neal and McGrory, *Suicide Factory*, 73.

139. Vidino and Emerson, *Al Qaeda in Europe*, 192.

140. El Faisal, *Devil's Deception of the Saudi Salafis.*

141. Hamza, "Hypocrites."

142. Richard Watson, "The One True God, Allah: The Rise of the British Jihad," *Granta* 103 (2008).

143. Abul Taher, "A Growing Number of Students Are Being Recruited on British Campuses by Islamic Extremists—and End Up on the World's Frontlines," *The Guardian,* May 16, 2000.

144. Watson, "One True God, Allah."

145. Ibid.

146. Ibid.; see also Paul Lewis, "Banned Group Tried to Rent Hall Near Suspects' Homes," *The Guardian*, August 16, 2008; Adrian Morgan, "UK: How Britain Encouraged Islamic Radicalism," *Spero News*, May 11, 2007; Adrian Morgan, "UK: How Britain Encouraged Terrorism—Part Two," *Spero News*, May 13, 2007.

147. Watson, "One True God, Allah," 65–66.

148. Daniel McGrory, Nicola Woolcock, Michael Evans, Sean O'Neill, and Zahid Hussain, "Meeting of Murderous Minds on the Backstreets of Lahore," *Times Online*, May 1, 2007, http://www.timesonline.co.uk/tol/news/uk/crime/article1728929.ece, accessed June 12, 2007.

149. Jonathan Calvert and Claudio Franco, "July 7 Ringleader Linked to Tel Aviv Suicide Bombers," *Sunday Times,* July 9, 2006.

150. Philippe Naughton, "Five Given Life for Fertilizer Bomb Terror Plot," *Times* (UK), April 20, 2007.

151. Crevice trial clips [Online], http://www.historycommons.org/searchResults.jsp?searchtext=al-muhajiroun&events=on&entities=on&articles=on&topics=on&timelines=on&projects=on&titles=on&descriptions=on&dosearch=on&search=Go, accessed July 20, 2008.

152. Ian Cobain and Richard Norton-Taylor, "Because British Soldiers are Killing Muslims," *Guardian* (UK), April 30, 2007.

153. Crevice trial transcript, September 14, 2006.

154. Ibid.

155. Justine Smith and Alex Williams, "Bomb-Plot Son Brainwashed, Say Family," *Daily Mirror,* April 1, 2004.

156. Watson, "The One True God, Allah;" Crevice trial transcript.

157. O'Neal and McGrory, *Suicide Factory*, 55–56.

158. "Muslim Cleric Guilty of Soliciting Murder," Guardian, February 4, 2003.

159. Alan Cowell, "Kenya Seeks to Deport Muslim Cleric to Jamaica," *New York Times,* January 4, 2010.

160. O'Neal and McGrory, *Suicide Factory*, 189.

161. Ibid., 193.

162. Ibid., 86.

163. Interview with Jean-François Clair, Deputy Director of Direction de la Surveillance du Territoire (DST), December 12, 2002; Chris Hedges, "A Powerful Combatant in France's War on Terror," *New York Times*, November 24, 2001.

164. O'Neal and McGrory, *Suicide Factory*, 45.

165. Ibid., 46.

166. Ibid., 88, Wiktorowicz, *Radical Rising Islam*, 3.

167. O'Neal and McGrory, *Suicide Factory*, 86.

168. Daniel McGrory, "A Haven for Faithful Hijacked by Extremists," *Times Online* [Online], January 21, 2003, http://www.timesonline.co.uk/tol/news/uk/article1070199.ece?token=null&offset=0&page=1, accessed December 30, 2004.

169. O'Neal and McGrory, *Suicide Factory*, 98–100.

170. Ibid., 100.

171. Ibid., 97.

172. "Stevens: Bombers 'Almost Certainly' British," *Daily Mail*, July 10, 2005; Brendan Bourne, "Up to 200 Al-Qaeda Terrorists in Britain," *Sunday Times*, March 6, 2005. A few weeks later, the terrorism specialist Peter Bergen told the U.S. House of Representatives Committee on International Relations that British authorities believed "that between three and six hundred British citizens were trained in al-Qaeda and Taliban camps in Afghanistan. And several hundred men are believed to have fought in Kashmir and returned to Britain in the 1990s. In March, Sir Ian Blair, the present Metropolitan Police Commissioner, told a radio interviewer 'I agree with the Prime Minister's assessment . . . that there are hundreds of people who came back from the [Afghan training] camps and are now in the United Kingdom, and that is a very dangerous issue'" (Peter Bergen, Testimony on "Islamic Extremism in Europe," U.S. House of Representatives, Committee on International Affairs, April 27, 2005).

173. Marie Colvin and Dipesh Gadher, "Britain's Islamic Army," *Sunday Times,* January 17, 1999.

174. McRoy, *From Rushdie to 7/7*, 40.

175. O'Neal and McGrory, *Suicide Factory*, 101.

176. Ibid., 102.

177. Personal interview at a conference on terrorism organized by the NYU Center for Law and Security, May 27, 2005; O'Neal and McGrory, *Suicide Factory*, 116.

178. Al-Muhajiroun's website [Online], http://www.muhajiroun.com, accessed May 5, 2005.

179. According to Islamic scholars, such an arrangement, rather like a treaty, could only be authorized by an Islamic state, not by a group or individual. See Muhammad Afifi al-Akiti, *Defending the Transgressed* (Birmingham, UK: Aqsa Press, 2005), 13. An appropriate corresponding body would also have to authorize such an agreement, in Britain's case, it would be Parliament.

180. Crispin Black, *The London Bombs—What Went Wrong?* (London: Gibson Square, 2005), 31–32.

181. Michael Clarke, "The Contract with Muslims Must Not Be Torn Up," *Guardian*, August 26, 2005.

182. O'Neal and McGrory, *Suicide Factory*, 38.

183. Exhibit no. MA/13, June 19, 2005, 9.

184. Ibid., 11–12.

185. Ibid., 29.

186. "Tottenham Ayatollah," Channel Four, 1997; "Tottenham Ayatollah Revisited" [Online], February 28, 2008, http://quicksilverscreen.com/watch?video=34924, accessed June 1, 2008.

187. Clarke, "Contract with Muslims."

188. "Report into the London Terrorist Attacks on 7 July 2005" (London: Intelligence and Security Committee of the House of Commons, 2006), paragraph 92.

189. Presentation by Peter Clarke, "Transatlantic Dilemmas: Coordination and Strategy," at the conference "Prosecuting Terrorism: The Global Challenge," May 26, 2005.

Chapter 11

1. Paul Tumelty, "Reassessing the July 21 London Bombings," *Terrorism Monitor* 3, 17 (September 8, 2005).

2. Report of the Official Account of the Bombings in London on 7th July 2005, HC 1087, Session 2005–2006, May 11, 2006.

3. Shiv Malik, "My Brother the Bomber," *Prospect*, May 31, 2007.

4. Jane Perlez, "3 Are Charged with Aiding London Transit Attack," *New York Times,* April 6, 2007; on the rule of Scotland Yard's counter-terrorism unit the Murdoch media hacking scandal, an affair which came to light as this book went to press, see Don Van Natta Jr., "Stain From Tabloids Rubs Off On A Cozy Scotland Yard," *New York Times,* July 16, 2011.

5. Rachel Williams, "Judge Says Muslim Men Betrayed UK," *Guardian,* April 30, 2009; Cahal Milmo, "Close Friends of 7/7 Bombers Cleared of Scouting Attacks," *Independent,* April 29, 2009.

6. Carrick Mollenkamp, "How a Teacher's Aide Evolved into a Terrorist Bomber," *Pittsburgh Post Gazette,* July 25, 2005.

7. Kevin Cullen, "Bomb Suspect Hid Turmoil," *Boston Globe,* July 15, 2005.

8. Ian Herbert, "Revealed: How Suicide Bomber Used to Work for the Government," *Independent,* March 11, 2006.

9. Ibid.

10. Tom Hundley, "Attacks Spur Identity Crisis for Britain," *Chicago Tribune,* December 16, 2005.

11. Sandra Laville et al., "'Father Figure' Inspired Young Bombers," *Guardian,* July 15, 2005.

12. "Biography of a Bomber," BBC, Radio 4 FM, November 17, 2005. The correspondent for the program, Nasreen Suleaman, furnished me with the script from which I am quoting. There is no other record for the program.

13. Ibid.

14. Ibid.

15. Ibid.

16. "Profile, Mohammed Sidique Kahn," BBC, April 30, 2007.

17. "Biography of a Bomber," BBC.

18. Interview with Nazreen Suleaman, April 3, 2006.

19. "Biography of a Bomber," BBC.

20. Ibid.

21. Herbert, "Revealed."

22. "Biography of a Bomber," BBC.

23. *Could 7/7 Have Been Prevented? Review of the Intelligence on the London Terrorist Attacks on 7 July 2005,* presented to Parliament by the Prime Minister, May 2009.

24. "Profile, Mohammed Sidique Kahn."

25. Home Office, *Report of the Official Account of the Bombings in London on 7th July 2005,* (London 2006), 13.

26. "Biography of a Bomber," BBC.

27. "Profile, Mohammed Sidique Kahn."

28. Kenan Malik, *From Fatwa to Jihad* (London: Atlantic Books, 2009), 98.

29. Malik, "My Brother the Bomber."

30. Christopher Caldwell, *Reflections on the Revolution in Europe* (New York: Doubleday, 2009), 176.

31. A Mullah is an educated Muslim, trained in theology.

32. Mollenkamp, "How a Teacher's Aide."

33. Malik, "My Brother the Bomber."

34. Alan Hamilton and Stewart Tendler, "They Aroused No Suspicion," *London Times,* May 12, 2006.

35. Andrew Norfolk, "Iqra: The Backstreet Bookshop That Taught Frontline War," *London Times,* April 29, 2009.

36. David Leppard and Jonathan Calvert, "Focus Special: The Web of Terror," *Sunday Times,* July 17, 2005.

37. Ali Hussain, "Undercover on Planet Beeston," *London Times,* July 5, 2006.

38. It is nonetheless the case that quite a few jihadis passed through TJ in their radicalization process, such as several of the 9/11 Hamburg Cell, Richard Reid (the shoe bomber), and the Glasgow bombers and several of Germany's Angry Young Turks we will meet in chapter 13. The Taliban arose out of Deobandi madrasahs in Pakistan.

39. Philip Lewis, *Islamic Britain. Religion, Politics and Identity among British Muslims: Bradford in the 1990s* (London: Tauris, 1994), 186.

40. Mollenkamp, "How a Teacher's Aide."

41. Malik, "My Brother the Bomber."

42. Ibid.

43. Norfolk, "Iqra"; "Muslim Groups Infiltrated by 7/7 Bombers Had Huge Govt Grants," *Daily Mail,* September 8, 2006.

44. Jonathan Petre, Nick Britten, and Paul Stokes, "Bomb Experts Search Youth Centre Where Terrorists Hatched Their Plot," *Telegraph,* July 15, 2005; "Profile: Hilary Benn," BBC News, June 24, 2007.

45. Herbert, "Revealed."

46. Malik, "My Brother the Bomber."

47. Samuel P. Huntington, *The Clash of Civilizations* (New York: Simon and Schuster, 1996), 161.

48. Sharon Churcher, "Suicide Bomber Cried for Sept 11 Victims," *Daily Telegraph* (Australia), July 18, 2005.

49. "Muslim Groups Infiltrated," *Daily Mail.*

50. Telephone conversation with Shiv Malik, July 30, 2009.

51. http://www.youtube.com/watch?v=QDl_Cf8LEkk.

52. Norfolk, "Iqra."

53. Ibid.

54. Ibid.; Ed Vulliamy, "IT Expert: I Worked with 7/7 Bombers and Warned Police," *Guardian,* June 24, 2006.

55. Muhammad Saeed al-Qahtani, *Al-Wala' wa'l-Bara'* (London: Al-Firdous, 1993), part I.

56. Ibid., I:1.

57. Ibid., I:1. '*Bara*', which signifies "to be free from" or "separation," or even "innocence," was often translated in jihadist circles as "hatred" or "enmity." Thus, *Al-Wala' wa'l-Bara'* can mean "love and hate."

58. Ibid.

59. Ibid.

60. Ibid.

61. Ibid.

62. Ibid.

63. Ibid.

64. "Biography of a Bomber," BBC. An HND is roughly the equivalent of two years of undergraduate education and can be used to gain entrance to a British university. See also Herbert, "Revealed."

65. Malik, "My Brother the Bomber."

66. Ibid.

67. Alison Shaw, *Kinship and Continuity: Pakistani Families in Britain* (Amsterdam: Harwood Academic, 2000), 189–190.

68. Robert Park, "Migration and the Marginal Man," in Richard Sennett (ed.) *The Classic Essays on the Culture of Cities*, (Appleton-Century-Crofts, New York, 1969); see also Park, "Cultural Conflict and the Marginal Man," in Everett V. Stonequist, ed., *The Marginal Man* (New York: Charles Scribner's Sons, 1937).

69. Malik, "My Brother the Bomber."

70. Shaw, *Kinship and Continuity,* 189–190.

71. Stanley Kurtz, "Marriage and the Terror War, II," *National Review Online,* February 15, 2007.

72. Olivier Roy, *Globalized Islam* (New York: Columbia University Press, 2004), 312; Roger Ballard, "Migration and kinship."

73. Ibid., 311.

74. Roy, *Globalized Islam,* 310.

75. Malik, "My Brother the Bomber."

76. Al-Qahtani, *Al-Wala' wa'l-Bara'.*

77. Ibid.

78. Ibid.

79. Interview with Nazreen Suleaman, April 3, 2006.

80. Ian Herbert and Kim Sengupta, "The Jihadist Who Needed No Brainwashing to Blow Up Aldgate Train," *Independent,* September 10, 2005; interview with Nazreen Suleaman, April 3, 2006.

81. Herbert and Sengupta, "Jihadist Who Needed No Brainwashing."

82. "Life Sentences for Teen Killers," BBC News, March 4, 2005; Herbert and Sengupta, "Jihadist Who Needed No Brainwashing."

83. David Bruce, "Beeston's Tyrone Clarke: Murder Suspect Spotted in Pakistan," *Beeston Today,* June 24, 2008.

84. Ibid.

85. David McNab, "Where the New Kid Is Old Hat," *London Times Educational Supplement,* April 26, 2002.

86. http://www.youtube.com/watch?v=QDl_Cf8LEkk.

87. Sean O'Neill, "I Pray for 7/7 Bomber, My Husband," *Times Online* [Online], July 27, 2007, http://www.timesonline.co.uk/tol/news/uk/crime/article2148288.ece, accessed July 31, 2007.

88. Sky News exclusive interview with Hasina Patel, the widow of Mohammed Sidique Khan, July 27, 2007, http://news.sky.com/skynews/article/0,30100-1277316,00.html, accessed July 31, 2007.

89. Jonathan Calvert and Claudio Franco, "July 7 Ringleader Linked to Tel Aviv Suicide Bombers," *Sunday Times,* July 9, 2006.

90. Mushtak Parker, "Take Care of Mom, UK Ringleader Told Daughter," *Arab News,* April 25, 2008.

91. David Brown, "Court Sees 7/7 Bomber Grooming Baby Daughter for Terror," *London Times*, April 25, 2008.

92. Ibid.

93. Ibid.

94. "Cleric Bakri Barred from Britain," BBC, August 12, 2005.

95. Dominic Casciani and Sharif Sakr, "The Battle for the Mosque," BBC, February 7, 2006.

96. Brian Bennett and Douglas Waller, "Thwarting the Airline Plot," *Time*, August 10, 2006; Don Van Natta Jr., Elaine Sciolino, and Stephen Grey, "Details Emerge in British Terror Case," *New York Times*, August 28, 2006.

97. Neville Dean and David Barrett, "Young Mother among 11 Charged over Terror Plot," *Daily Post* (Liverpool), August 22, 2006; Van Natta Jr. et al., "Details Emerge."

98. Jamie Doward, "Top British Terror Suspect Escapes," *Observer* (UK), December 16, 2007.

99. Eliza Manningham-Buller, "Speech on the Terrorist Threat Facing the UK, November 9, 2006," *Times of London* [Online], November 10 2006, http://www.timesonline.co.uk/article/0,2-2447690,00.html, accessed November 10, 2007.

100. Sean Rayment, "Report Identifies UK Terrorist Enclaves," *Daily Telegraph*, November 9, 2008.

101. Ibid.

102. Michael Evans, "MI5's Spymaster Jonathan Evans Comes Out of the Shadows," *Times* (London), January 7, 2009.

103. Personal conversation, May 20, 2010, Washington, DC.

104. "History of the Metropolitan Police: Brixton Riots 1981," *Metropolitan Police* [Online], http://www.met.police.uk/history/brixton_riots.htm, accessed September 2, 2005.

105. Malik, *From Fatwa to Jihad*, 56.

106. Ibid., 57.

107. Ibid., 113.

108. Ibid., 59.

109. Gilles Kepel, *Allah in the West* (Stanford, CA: Stanford University Press, 1997), 150.

110. Mustafa Yusuf McDermott and Muhammad Manazir Ahsan, *The Muslim Guide: for Teachers, Employers, Community and Social Administrators in Britain* (Leicester, UK: Islamic Foundation, 1980) [Online], http://catalogue.nla.gov.au/Record/499632, accessed July 1, 2009; Kepel, *Allah in the West*, 122.

Chapter 12

1. Hubert Gude and Axel Spilcker, "Unbekannt Verschunden," *Focus Online,* March 22, 2008; "Interview with Wolfgang Schäuble," *Frankfurter Allgemeine Sonntagszeitung*, September 16, 2007.

2. "Germany Warns of Left-Wing Terrorism at G8 Summit," *Reuters* [Online], January 12, 2007, http://www.reuters.com/article/latestCrisis/idUSL12310888, accessed June 4, 2008.

3. Dirk Laabs, "Man Convicted of Role in 9/11 Terror," *Los Angeles Times*, February 20, 2003; Terry McDermott, "How Terrorists Hatched a Simple Plan to Use Planes as Bombs," *Los Angeles Times*, September 1, 2002; personal interview with Udo Steinbach, Director Deutsches Orient-Institut, Hamburg, March 27, 2003 (hereafter referred to as Steinbach interview).

4. Personal interview with Ranier Münz, Humboldt University, Berlin, December 16, 2002 (hereafter referred to as Münz interview).

5. Richard Bernstein, "German Police Raid an Islamic Militant Group," *New York Times,* April 11, 2003.

6. Robert S. Leiken, "The Menace in Europe's Midst," *Current History* 108 (April 2009): 717.

7. See Robert S. Leiken and Steven Brooke, "Who Is Abu Zarqawi?" *Weekly Standard,* May 24, 2004.

8. Interview with Gunter Krause, spokesperon for interior ministry, Berlin, April 12, 2003 (hereafter referred to as Krause interview).

9. Krause Interview; Stefan Theil and Michael Isikoff, "A Missing Diplomat," *Newsweek,* April 14, 2003.

10. "Tunisian Held in Germany in Scam to Finance al-Qaeda," *Agence France-Presse,* June 1, 2003; Theil and Isikoff, "Missing Diplomat."

11. Krause interview; "Tunisian Held in Germany"; Desmond Butler, "Saudis Withdraw Berlin Diplomat," *New York Times,* April 25, 2003; David Crawford, "Germans Investigate Saudi Official—Probe of Islamic Extremism; Uncovers Possible Links Between Diplomat, Terror," *Wall Street Journal,* April 22, 2003.

12. Krause interview.

13. Butler, "Saudis Withdraw Berlin Diplomat"; Crawford, "Germans Investigate Saudi Official."

14. David Crawford, "How a Diplomat from Saudi Arabia Spread His Faith," *Wall Street Journal,* September 10, 2003. Interviews with Ernst Urlau, Ministerialdirector Bundesnachrichtendienst, Koordiniergung der Nachrictendeienste des Bundes, May 28, 2003, Heiner Wegesin Chief of Brandenburg Verfassungsschut, Potsdam, April 3, 2003;

15. Interviews with Ernst Urlau, and Heiner Wegesin, David Crawford, "Germans Investigate Saudi Official."

16. David Crawford, "How a Diplomat from Saudi Arabia Spread His Faith."

17. Michael Isikoff and Stefan Theil, "Saudi Government: Bin Laden Loyalists: How High Do They Go?" Newsweek May 5, 2004; Neil Mackay, "Revealed: Saudi's New Links to 9/11; US Suspects Diplomat of al-Qaeda Connection," *Sunday Herald,* Aug. 3, 2003.

18. Crawford, "How a Diplomat from Saudi Arabia Spread His Faith."

19. Richard Bernstein, "German Police Raid an Islamic Militant Group," *NYT,* April 11, 2003; Interviews with Jürgen Hohnen, Chief of Potsdam State Police, Ministry of Interior March 28, 2003, Ernst Urlau, Ministerialdirector Bundesnachrichtendienst, Koordiniergung der Nachrictendeienste des Bundes, May 28, 2003; Heiner Wegesin Chief of Brandenburg Verfassungsschut, Potsdam, April 3, 2003; William Boston, "Germany's Center-Left Coalition Agrees on New Security Measures," *Wall Street Journal,* October 29, 2001; David Crawford. "Europe Eases Limits on Police, Intelligence Services, " *Wall Street Journal,* December 17, 2003.

20. AFP, "Zeuge: 'Kofferbomber' erwogen Anschlag auf WM Stadion" [Online], January 10, 2008, http://www.faz.net/s/RubF359F74E867B46C1A180E8E1E1197DEE/Doc~E68 902426AA1C46ABBB37A1139AA70BC8~ATpl~Ecommon~Scontent.html, accessed May 12, 2007.

21. Daryl Lindsey, "A Terrorist Gets the Judicial Middle Finger," *Der Spiegel Online,* December 10, 2008.

22. Fabian Löhe, "Wir lassen Blut aus euren Gesichtern fließen," *Focus Online,* August 1, 2007.

23. Löhe, "Wir lassen Blut"; Andreas Ulrich, "Failed Bomb Plot Seen as Al-Qaida Initiation Test," *Der Spiegel Online,* April 9, 2007.

24. Ulrich, "Failed Bomb Plot."

25. Friederike von Tiesenhausen Cave and Frances Williams, "Schauble Warns of Raised Terror Threat in Germany," *Financial Times,* June 23, 2007.

26. "Stimmung wie vor dem 11. September," faz.net [Online], June 22, 2007, http://www.faz.net/s/Rub594835B672714A1DB1A121534F010EE1/Doc~E4DC6D6BB366E4C8DBEDA5BE10A060E12~ATpl~Ecommon~Scontent.html, accessed June 12, 2008.

27. Löhe, "Wir lassen Blut."

28. "Interview with Wolfgang Schäuble."

29. Interview with Ralf Stegner, "Schäubles Kalkül ist schäbig," *Tageszeitung*, August 29, 2007.

30. For other historical analogies drawn, see Mark Landler, "Germans Weigh Civil Rights and Public Safety," *New York Times*, July 13, 2007.

31. Tiesenhausen Cave and Williams, "Schauble warns of raised terror threat."

32. "Schäuble in Trouble," *Der Spiegel* [Online], July 16, 2007, http://www.spiegel.de/international/germany/0,1518,494635,00.html, accessed July 28, 2007.

33. Landler, "Germans Weigh Civil Rights."

34. "Wie Sicher lebe ich Noch in Deutschland?" *Bild.de* [Online], August 20, 2006, http://www.bild.de/BTO/news/aktuell/2006/08/21/terror-kofferbomben-sicherheit-deutschland/hg-1-schaeuble.html, accessed June 12, 2007.

35. Souad Mekhennet, Claudia Sautter, and Michael Hanfeld, *Die Kinder des Dschihad: Die neue Generation des Islamistischen Terrors in Europa* (Piper Verlag, 2007).

36. "Prozess gegen Deutsch-Marokkaner:Vom Philosophen zum Terrorhelfer," *Der Tagespiegel*, July 25, 2007.

37. Ibid.

38. "Timeline: Al-Qaeda," BBC News, September 4, 2006, http://news.bbc.co.uk/2/hi/3618762.stm, accessed March 31, 2008.

39. U.S. State Deparment, "Country Reports on Terrorism, 2008," Chapter 2, Germany, Washington D.C. April 30, 2009.

40. Peter Frey, "Der Hindukusch und Berlin," ZDF German Television [Online], August 17, 2007, http://berlindirekt.zdf.de/ZDFde/inhalt/29/0,1872,5590685,00.html, accessed August 2007.

41. Ibid.

42. Simone Kaiser, Holger Stark, and Marcel Rosenbach, "How the CIA Helped Foil Terror Plot," *Der Spiegel* [Online], September 10, 2007, http://www.spiegel.de/international/germany/0,1518,504837,00.html, accessed September 25, 2007.

43. See Ahmed Rashid, *Jihad: The Rise of Militant Islam in Central Asia* (New Haven: Yale University Press, 2002), chapter 1.

44. Michael Isikoff and Mark Hosenball, "A Sense of Unease; Al Qaeda's Regrouped. But What Does That Mean?" *Newsweek*, July 23, 2007.

45. AFP, "Uzbeksiche Islamisten haben engen Verbindungen zur al Kaida," September 15, 2007, http://www.net-tribune.de/article/150907-158.php, accessed September 24, 2007.

46. David Mchugh, "Germany: Muslim Group Claims Foiled Plot," *USA Today*, September 11, 2007; "Country Reports on Terrorism 2008," US Department of State: Office of the Coordinator for Counterterrorism [Online], April 30, 2009, http://www.state.gov/s/ct/rls/crt/2008/122432.htm, accessed May 21, 2009.

47. Einar Wigen, "Islamic Jihad Union: al-Qaida's Key to the Turkic World?" Norwegian Defence Research Establishment (FFI). http://www.sehadetvakti.com/haber_detay.php?haber_id=1587, accessed February 23, 2009; Guido Steinberg, "The Threat of Jihadist Terrorism in Germany," Instituto Real Elcano, November 6, 2008; Guido Steinberg, "A Turkish al-Qaeda: The Islamic Jihad Union and the Internationalization of Uzbek Jihadism," *Strategic Insights* 7: 3 (July 2008); Ulrich Heyden, "Absuchen der Computer bringt nichts," *Suedkurier* [Online], September 14, 2007, http://www.suedkurier.de/nachrichten/seite3/

art1798,2800338, accessed September 24, 2007. See also Souad Mekhennet and Michael Moss, "Europeans Get Terror Training Inside Pakistan," *New York Times*, September 10, 2007.

48. Craig Whitlock, "Germany Says It Foiled Bomb Plot," *Washington Post,* September 6, 2007.

49. Katherine Shrader, "Official: US Interests in Germany May Be Target," Associated Press, May 12, 2007.

50. Gordon Corera, "Germany Concern over 'Terror Plot,'" BBC News, September 5, 2007; Whitlock, "Germany Says It Foiled Bomb Plot."

51. Markus Wehner, "Sie sind gekommen, um zu töten," *Faz.Net* [Online], February 6, 2009, http://www.faz.net/s/Rub594835B672714A1DB1A121534F010EE1/Doc~E7E9D0 2193F364B35BC2999B751BE8F86~ATpl~Ecommon~Scontent.htm, accessed June 4, 2009; Corera, "Germany Concern."

52. Whitlock, "Germany Says It Foiled Bomb Plot."

53. "10 Hunted in German 'Terror Plot,'" CNN, September 6, 2007. On March 3, 2010, a German state court in Dusseldorf handed down sentences in the trial of the Sauerland plotters on charges of supporting a terrorist organization. The judge gave the longest sentences to the two German converts, Gelowicz and Schneider, who each received twelve-year terms. Yilmaz, a Turkish citizen, received an eleven-year term; Selek, a German ethnic Turk, received five years. All of the men had been charged with supporting a terrorist organization. "You planned a monstrous bloodbath with an untold number of fatalities," Judge Ottmar Breidling told the convicted men. Associated Press and Reuters, May 4, 2010, http://www. guardian.co.uk/world/2010/mar/04/islamic-jihad-union-bomb-plot, accessed May 5, 2010.

54. "Denmark Arrests 'Bomb' Suspects," BBC News, September 5, 2007.

55. "Germany Hunts for 10 Terror Suspects," Associated Press, September 6, 2007.

56. Wigen, "Islamic Jihad Union."

57. "Wir sind und bleiben bedroht," interview with Wolfgang Schäuble, September 16, 2007, *Frankfurter Allgemeine Sonntagszeitung.*

58. Ibid.

59. Katrin Bennhold, "Local Terrorism Suspects Puzzle Germany," *International Herald Tribune*, September 12, 2007.

60. Thomas Hall, "Radikalisierungsprozess in Zeitraffer," *Frankfurter Allgemeine Zeitung*, September 20 and 24, 2007.

61. Ibid.

62. "Terrorverdächtiger Sollte V-Mann werden, "*Die Welt—DPA*, September 22, 2007, http://www.welt.de/politik/article1205801/Terrorverdaechtiger_sollte_V-Mann_werden. html; Hall, "Radikalisierungsprozess in Zeitraffer."

63. Bennhold, "Local Terrorism Suspects."

64. Günther Lachmann, "Terror-Fritz und seine gefährliche Freunde," *Die Welt* [Online], September 8, 2007, http://www.welt.de/politik/article1168633/Terror-Fritz_und_ seine_gefaehrlichen_Freunde.html, accessed September 24, 2007.

65. Bennhold, "Local Terrorism Suspects"; Hall, "Radikalisierungsprozess in Zeitraffer."

66. Eric Breininger, "Mein Weg nach Jannah" [Online], http://www.scribd.com/ doc/31071994/Schaheed-Abdul-Ghaffar-al-Almani-Mein-Weg-Nach-Jannah, accessed May 10, 2010.

67. Thomas Hegghammer, "Preview:Autobiography of a German Jihadist- Comments" [Online], http://www.jihadica.com/preview-autobiography-of-a-german-jihadist/#comments, accessed May 19, 2010.

68. Breininger, "Mein Weg nach Jannah."

69. William James, *The Varieties of Religious Experience* (New York, Modern Library, 1902), 208.

70. Ibid., 223.

71. Ibid., 213.

72. Ibid., 236.

73. Ibid., 259.

74. Ibid., 233.

75. Robert S. Leiken and Steven Brooke, "The Quantitative Analysis of Terrorism and Immigration: An Initial Exploration," *Terrorism and Political Violence* 18: 4 (Winter 2006).

76. Larry Poston, *Islamic Da'wah in the West: Muslim Missionary Activity and the Dynamics of Conversion to Islam* (London: Oxford University Press, 1992); Ali Kose, *Conversion to Islam* (London: Kegan Paul, 1996).

77. Olivier Roy, "Islam in Europe, Clash of Religions or Convergence of Religiosities?" *Eurozine*, May 3, 2007; see also Roy, *Globalized Islam* (New York: Columbia University Press, 2004), 26 and passim.

78. Bennhold, "Local Terrorism Suspects"; Hall, "Radikalisierungsprozess in Zeitraffer."

79. Lewis R. Rambo, *Understanding Religious Conversion* (New Haven, CT: Yale University Press, 1995), 162.

80. Summing up a century of the study of conversions, Lewis Rambo's identified seven stages of the conversion process are *Context, Crisis, Quest, Encounter, Interaction, Commitment,* and *Consequences.* These seven states correspond eerily to the radicalization process as it can be gleaned from public sources (news accounts and court records) and interviews with former radicals and with intelligence officials. See Rambo, *Understanding Religious Conversion.*

81. "Nach Video-Aufruf zum Heiligen Krieg: Schwester des deutschen Islamisten Eric Breininger im ZDF-Interview," Daily Net [Online], May 9, 2008, http://www.dailynet.de/TvMedien/17058.php, accessed May 25, 2009.

82. Breininger, "Mein Weg Nach Jannah," 76.

83. Rambo, *Understanding Religious Conversion,* 108.

84. Abd Samad Moussaoui, *Zacarias, My Brother* (New York: Seven Stories Press, 2003), 91.

85. Ibid., 115.

86. Friedrich Nietzsche, *The Anti-Christ* (Whitefish, MT: Kessenger Publishers, 1895), 60.

87. According to a French intelligence estimate cited by the French newspaper *Le Figaro,* in 2003 there were roughly 40,000 French converts to Islam. According to the U.S. State Department, in 2003 there were roughly 4.5 million Muslims living in France that same year. See "The RG Report on Converts to Islam," *Le Figaro,* August 7, 2003, and Craig S. Smith, "Europe Fears Islamic Converts May Give Cover for Extremism," *New York Times,* July 19, 2004. For the population of French Muslims, see "The International Religious Freedom Report for 2004" issued by the U.S. State Department. Due to the absence of confessional categories in European censuses, this figure is a deduction; however, we found this source to contain the best available statistics, particularly for its attempts to include estimates of both legal and illegal populations. The report is available at http://www.state.gov/g/drl/rls/irf/2003/24357.htm.

88. Kose, *Conversion to Islam,* 19; see also the research by Yahya (formerly Jonathan) Birt, a research fellow at the Islamic Foundation in Nicholas Hellen and Christopher Morgan, "Islamic Britain Lures Top People," *Times (UK),* February 22, 2004, and his subsequent letter to the *Sunday Times* on March 14, 2004. For other European countries, see Jorgen S. Nielsen, *Muslims in Western Europe* (Edinburgh: Edinburgh University Press, 1992), 11, 26, 61.

89. Interview with Jean-François Clair, Paris, April 15, 2003.

Chapter 13

1. Özlem Gezer, Rainer Nübel, Christian Parth, and Georg Wedemeyer, "Der Dschihad-Kämpfer aus Deutschland," *Stern.de* [Online], March 28, 2008, http://www.stern.de/panorama/selbstmordattentaeter-der-dschihad-kaempfer-aus-deutschland-615260.html?nv=ct_mt, accessed June 8, 2009.

2. John Rosenthal, "Germany's Taliban Trail: From Murat Kurnaz to Cüneyt Ciftci," *World Politics Review* [Online], May 14, 2008, http://www.worldpoliticsreview.com/article.aspx?id=2114, accessed June 12, 2010.

3. Matthias Gebauer, "The Smiling Suicide Bomber," *Spiegel Online*, March 27, 2008; Stefan Meining and Ahmet Senyurt, "The Case of the Bavarian Taliban," Hudson Institute, November 11, 2008.

4. Katrin Brettfeld and Peter Wetzels, *Muslime in Deutschland: Integration, Integrationsbarrieren, Relgion und Einstellungen zu Demokratie, Rechtsstaat und politisch-religiös motivierter Gewalt*, Bundesministerium des Innern (Hamburg: Universität Hamburg, 2007), 38–39.

5. "Islam and Identity in Germany," *International Crisis Group, Europe Report 181*, March 2007.

6. See, Stephen Castles and Mark J. Miller, *The Age of Migration* (New York: Guilford, 2003), 68–70; Michael J. Piore, "The Shifting Grounds for Immigration," *Annals of the American Academy of Political and Social Science* 485 (1986): 24, 29.

7. See Gary P. Freeman, *Immigrant Labor and Racial Conflict in Industrial Societies: The French and British Experience 1945–1975* (Princeton: Princeton University Press, 1979), 121–122.

8. Mark J. Miller, "Introduction," *International Migration Review* XX:4 (Winter 1986): 740–757. On Germany's intricate systems, see Stephen Castles, Heather Booth, and Tina Wallace, *Here for Good: Western Europe's New Ethnic Minorities* (London: Pluto Press, 1984), 82–83.

9. Werner Kanein quoted in Christian Joppke, *Immigration and the Nation-State: The United States, Germany and Great Britain* (Oxford: Oxford University Press, 1999), 66.

10. Klaus J. Bade, *Migration in European History* (Malden, MA: Blackwell, 2003), 220.

11. See Leo Lucassen, *The Immigrant Threat: The Integration of Old and New Migrants in Western Europe since 1850* (Chicago: University of Illinois Press, 2005), 149–50.

12. Robert J. Pauly, Jr., *Islam in Europe: Integration or Marginalization?* (London: Ashgate, 2004), 72; see also Yasemin Karakasoglu, "Turkish Cultural Orientations in Germany and the Role of Islam," in *Turkish Culture in Germany Society Today* (London: Berghahn, 1996), 160; Lucassen, *Immigrant Threat*, 157.

13. Gerald Parsons, *The Growth of Religious Diversity: Britain from 1945* (London: Routledge, 1994), 147; see also Madawi Al-Rasheed, "Saudi Religious Transnationalism in London," in *Transnational Connections and the Arab Gulf*, ed. Madawi Al-Rasheed (London: Routledge, 2005), 155.

14. W. Scott Haine, *Culture and Customs of France* (Westport, CT: Greenwood, 2006), 66. Gilles Kepel, *Banieues de Islam* (Paris: Editions du Seuil, 1987): there are sixty-three claims that six hundred mosques were built in France in the 1970s. While figures obviously differ, sources agree as to the sharp rise in construction after the adoption of family reunion policies.

15. Felice Dassetto and Gerd Nonneman, "Islam in Belgium and the Netherlands: Towards a Typology of 'Transplanted Islam,'" in *Muslim Communities in the New Europe*, ed. Gerd Nonneman, Tim Niblok, and Bogdan Szajkowski (Berkshire, UK: Ithaca, 1998), 192. If family reunion was the fundamental factor accounting for the postimmigration surge of mosques in Western Europe, the appearance of purpose-built mosques owed much to the Saudis. The Kingdom's program to build mosques and madrasahs worldwide reaped a windfall from the 1973 Arab oil boycott. Petrodollars found their way back to Europe in the form of "petro-Islam," purpose-built mosques, or "cultural centers" manned by fundamentalist or

even radical imams on the Saudi dole preaching from Wahhabi Qur'ans and prayer books. By 1996 the Saudis had built 1,500 mosques and 210 Islamic centers on five continents and had spent more than $70 million in Europe alone. Ignace Leverrier "L'Arabie Saoudite, le Pelerinage et Iran," *Cemoti* 22 (1996).

16. Joppke, *Immigration and the Nation-State*, 69–70.

17. Ibid., 71–74.

18. Ibid., 75.

19. Ibid., 73.

20. Ibid., 71.

21. James F. Hollifield, *Immigrants, Markets and States:The Political Economy of Post-war Europe* (Cambridge: Harvard University Press, 1993), 231; see also Lucassen, *Immigrant Threat*, 149.

22. Joppke, *Immigration and the Nation-State*, 72.

23. Ibid., 79–80.

24. Christian Joppke, "Immigration Challenges to the Nation-State," in *Challenge to the Nation-State*, ed. Christian Joppke (Oxford: Oxford University Press, 1999), 78, 80.

25. Joppke, *Immigration and the Nation-State*, 81.

26. Ibid., 82; Sabine von Dirke, "Multikulti:The German Debate on Multiculturalism," *German Studies Review* 17:3 (October 1994).

27. For concrete links bridging immigration permissiveness, family reunification, and weakness of national interest as an argument and as a reality, see Joppke, *Challenge to the Nation-State*, 83.

28. Joppke, *Immigration and the Nation-State*, 84.

29. The new law made naturalization somewhat easier for these postmigrants born before 2000, but it remained arduous and uncertain as the experience of Hafiz (Cüneyt Ciftci) below illustrates.

30. "Mehr Muslime als Gedacht in Deutschland," *Focus Online*, June 24, 2009, http://www.focus.de/politik/deutschland/gesellschaft-mehr-muslime-als-gedacht-in-deutschland_aid_410874.html, accessed June 28, 2009.

31. "Turkei: Beziehungen zu Deutschland," *Auswärtiges Amt* [Online], April 2010. http://www.auswaertiges-amt.de/diplo/de/Laenderinformationen/Tuerkei/Bilateral.html, accessed April 20, 2010; Susanne Worbs, "The Second Generation in Germany: Between School and Labor Market," *International Migration Review* (December 2003): 1013.

32. "Turkei: Beziehungen zu Deutschland."

33. See Lucassen, *Immigrant Threat*, 159.

34. Michael Scott Moore, "Muslims in Germany Choose to Be Buried Abroad," *Der Spiegel Online International,* February 21, 2007 http://www.spiegel.de/international/0,1518,462035,00.html, accessed March 3, 2009.

35. See Maurice Crul and Hans Vermeulen, "The Second Generation in Europe," *International Migration Review* (2003): 970; Ali Gitmez and Czarina Wilpert, "A Micro-Society or an Ethnic Community? Social Organization and Ethnicity Amongst Turkish Migrants in Berlin," in *Immigrant Associations in Europe*, ed. John Rex, D. Joly, and C. Wilpert (Gower, UK: Aldershot, 1987), 96. Lucassen considers "the Anatolian image" overdrawn, noting that many immigrants came from Istanbul and other western cities. But he goes on to note that many of the latter "had not been city dwellers for very long, having moved from the countryside to the urban centers" (Lucassen, *Immigrant Threat*, 147).

36. See Gitmez and Wilpert, "A Micro-Society or Ethnic Community?"; Jenny B. White, "Turks in the New Germany," *American Anthropologist* 99:4 (December 1997): 757; Gary Straßburger, "Transnational or Interethnic Marriages of Turkish Migrants: The (In) significance of Religious or Ethnic Affiliations," in *Muslim Networks and Transnational Communities in and Across Europe*, ed. Stefano Allievi and Jørgen Nielsen (Boston: Brill, 2003), 210.

37. Imre Karacs, "Germany's Turkish Children Sink into the Underclass," *Independent* (UK), November 12, 2000.

38. Faruk Sen, "Berlin's Turkish Community," in *The Spirit of the Berlin Republic*, ed. Dieter Dettke (New York: Berghahn, 2003), 132.

39. Gaby Straßburger, "Transnational Ties of the Second Generation: Marriages of Turks in Germany," in *Transnational Social Spaces: Agents, Networks and Institutions*, ed. Thomas Faist and Eyüp Özveren (Aldershot, UK: Ashgate, 2004), 215.

40. Ursula Sautter, "Losers in the Language Gap," *Time,* April 30, 2001.

41. Claudia Diehl and Rainer Schnell, "'Reactive Ethnicity' or 'Assimilation'?" *International Migration Review* (Winter 2006): 809, 802.

42. Emmanuel Todd, *Le destin de assimilation et ségrégation dans les democracies* (Paris: Seuil, 1994), 366–367; see also Lucassen, *Immigrant Threat*, 192.

43. Christopher Caldwell, "Where Every Generation Is First Generation," *New York Times Magazine*, May 27, 2007.

44. Lucassen, *Immigrant Threat*, 166; Diehl and Schnell, "'Reactive Ethnicity,'" 805–806, 810; White, "Turks in the New Germany."

45. Claus Mueller, "Integrating Turkish Communities: A German Dilemma," *Population Research and Policy Review* 25 [Online], December 2006, http://www.springerlink.com. proxygw.wrlc.org/content/0842318k42m7234v/fulltext.pdf, accessed January 26, 2010; see also Sautter, "Losers in the Language Gap."

46. Mueller, "Integrating Turkish Communities." Some earlier research contested the widespread perception of a language deficit: see works cited in Worbs, "Second Generation in Germany," 1016.

47. Lucassen, *Immigrant Threat*, 164.

48. Karacs, "Germany's Turkish Children." But Claudia Diehl and Rainer Schnell dispute so pessimistic a conclusion in "'Reactive Ethnicity'?"

49. Usually after the third school year (when they are about nine years old), children are assigned by most German states to a specific track. *Hauptschule* is the lowest, *Realschule* is in the middle, and the highest track is *Gymnasium*. An additional track, *Sonderschule* (special school), accommodates students with special needs.

50. Gamze Avci, "Comparing Integration Policies and Outcomes: Turks in the Netherlands and Germany," *Turkish Studies* 7:1 (March 2006): 76. Almost a third of Turkish immigrant children are without high school diplomas, and only 14 percent (only half the average of the German population) get their *Abitur,* as the degree from Germany's top-level high schools is called.

51. Karacs, "Germany's Turkish Children."

52. Sautter, "Losers in the Language Gap," 2001.

53. Crul and Vermeulen, "Second Generation in Europe," 979.

54. Ibid., 973.

55. See Worbs, "Second Generation in Germany," 1029, 1030, 1034.

56. Avci, "Comparing Integration Policies," 74, graph on p. 75; Worbs, "Second Generation in Germany," 1028.

57. "Police Crime Statistics 2008: Federal Republic of Germany," Bundeskriminalamt [Online], http://www.bka.de/pks/pks2008ev/pcs_2008.pdf, accessed May 24, 2009.

58. Hans-Jörg Alberecht, "Ethnic Minorities, Crime and Criminal Justice in Germany," *Crime and Justice* 21 [Online], 1997, http://www.jstor.org/pss/1147630, accessed May 24, 2009.

59. Katrin Elger, Ansbert Kneip, and Merlind Theile, "Survey Shows Alarming Lack of Integration in Germany," *Spiegel Online* [Online], January 26, 2009, http://www.spiegel.de/ international/germany/0,1518,603588,00.html, accessed April 26, 2009. The largest groups of

immigrants to Germany hail from Eastern Europe and the former Soviet bloc, and there are also large communities made up of former guest workers and their descendants from Greece, Italy, Portugal, and Spain as well as Africa. Turks are the second largest immigrant group in the country, totaling almost three million people.

60. See Worbs, "Second Generation in Germany," 2003.

61. Lucassen, *Immigrant Threat*, 163.

62. See Diehl and Schnell, " 'Reactive Ethnicity,' " 819, 789.

63. Sautter, "Losers in the Language Gap."

64. Frank Gesemann, "The Integration of Young Muslims in Germany," 2007, http://www.migrationeducation.org/22.1.html?&rid=82&cHash=6af0a6874a, accessed October 24, 2008.

65. German Marshall Fund, *Transatlantic Trends, 2005*: 22, http://www.gmfus.org/trends/doc/2005_german_breakdown.pdf, accessed May 22, 2006; German Marshall Fund, *Transatlantic Trends, 2007*: 11 http://www.gmfus.org/trends/doc/2007_english_key.pdf, accessed May 26, 2008.

66. Elger, Kneip, and Theile, "Survey Shows Alarming Lack of Integration in Germany."

67. Pew Research Center, *Muslims in Europe: Economic Worries Top Concerns about Religious Identity*, http://pewglobal.org/2006/07/06/muslims-in-europe-economic-worries-top-concerns-about-religious-and-cultural-identity, accessed March 2, 2007.

68. Hartwig Pautz, "The Politics of Identity in Germany: The Leitkultur Debate," *Race & Class* 46 (2005).

69. The term "leitkultur" was originally introduced by the German Syrian sociologist Bassam Tibi, who objected to its subsequent appropriation by Christian Democrat politicians. Bassam Tibi, *Europa ohne Identität* (Munich: Bertelsmann, 1998).

70. Stefan Manz, "Constructing a Normative National Identity: The Leitkultur Debate in Germany, 2000/2001," *Journal of Multilingual and Multicultural Development* (September 2004).

71. Dominic Sachsenmaier, "Germany Deadlocked over Immigration Policy," *Yale Global Online Magazine,* http://yaleglobal.yale.edu, accessed May 30, 2008.

72. Von Dirke, "Multikulti," 513–536.

73. "The Über-Citizen and German Kulturkampf," September 2007; IHRC Wembley UK, euro-citizenship.eu/docs/RSCAS, accessed May 2, 2009.

74. Von Dirke, "Multikulti," 513–536.

75. Ibid.

76. Manz, "Constructing a Normative National Identity."

77. Martin Kramer, *Ivory Towers on Sand: The Failure of Middle Eastern Studies in America* (Washington, DC: Washington Institute for Near East Policy, 2001).

78. David Mchugh, "Germany: Muslim Group Claims Foiled Plot," September 11, 2007; U.S. Department of State, "Terrorist Organizations," *Country Reports on Terrorism 2008* [Online], April 30, 2009, http://www.state.gov/s/ct/rls/crt/2008/122449.htm, accessed June 1, 2010.

79. "Konvertiten Datei' – Bosbach: So nicht gesagt," N-TV [Online], September 12, 2007, http://www.n-tv.de/851895.html, accessed September 24, 2007.

80. Thomas M. Sanderson, Daniel Kimmage, and David A. Gordon, "From the Ferghana Valley to South Waziristan, The Evolving Threat of Central Asian Jihadists," CSIS, Washington DC, March 2010.

81. Guido Steinberg, "The Islamic Jihad Union: Willing Terrorists from Germany," http://www.qantara.de, accessed November 22, 2008.

82. Guido Steinberg, "A Turkish al-Qaeda: The Islamic Jihad Union and the Internationalization of Uzbek Jihadism," *Strategic Insights,* July 2008.

83. From September, the IJU started posting an increasing amount of propaganda messages and videos on the Turkish website www.sehadetvakti.com ("Time for Martyrdom"),

which has been online since November 2006. In early September, a "press release" signed by the "political leadership of the IJU" appeared on this website, commenting on the arrest of the Sauerland Cell some days earlier. It stated that the three "brothers" had planned attacks on the U.S. airbase in Ramstein in Germany and on the American and Uzbek consulates. Their goal had been to protest against U.S. and Uzbek policy and to prompt Germany to give up its base in Termez, Uzbekistan. Most interestingly, many of the texts posted on www. sehadetvakti.com (including the interview) are written in faulty Turkish, suggesting that the authors might be Uzbeks or perhaps Turks who have spent most of their lives in Germany.

84. Interview with Wolfgang Schäuble, *Frankfurter Allgemeine Sonntagszeitung*, September 16, 2007.

85. Mark Landler, "Germans Weigh Civil Rights and Public Safety," *New York Times,* July 13, 2007; see Elke Winter and Kristina John, "A New Approach to Citizenship and Integration: Some Facts about Recent Policy Changes in Germany," *Canada-Europe Transatlantic Dialogue* [Online], March 2010, http://www.carleton.ca/europecluster, accessed March 8, 2010.

86. John Rosenthal, *World Politics Review,* 2008, http://www.worldpoliticsreview.com/article.aspx?id=2114, accessed October 4, 2009.

87. Stefan Meining and Ahmet Senyurt, "The Case of the Bavarian Taliban," *Current Trends in Islamist Ideology* 7 (November 2008).

88. Guido Steinberg, "A Turkish al-Qaeda: The Islamic Jihad Union and the Internationalization of Uzbek Jihadism," *Strategic Insights* (July 2008).

89. Cited in Meining and Senyurt, "Case of the Bavarian Taliban."

90. Bassam Tibi, the prominent Syrian-German scholar, notes that "it is important to distinguish between institutional Islamists (such as the Muslim Brotherhood or Milli Görüs) and the jihadists (such as Groupes Islamiques Armées [sic]/GIA)—"Europeanizing Islam, or the Islamization of Europe," in Timothy Byrnes and Peter Katzenstein, eds., *Religion in an Expanding Europe* (Cambridge: Cambridge University Press, 2006), 226.

91. Tibi contends that the differences between the Diyanet and Milli Görüs mosques have "eroded" since the coming to power of the Islamist AKP in Turkey gave it control of the Diyanet ("Islamists Approach Europe," *Middle East Quarterly,* Winter 2009).

92. See, Gökçe Yurdakul, *From Guest Workers into Muslims: The Transformation of Turkish Immigrant Associations in Germany* (Cambridge Scholars Publishing, Newcastle upon Tyne, 2009), chapter 3; Valérie Amiraux, "Turkish Islam in Germany," in *Political Participation and Identities*, ed. W. A. R. Shadid and P. S. van Koningsveld (Kok Pharos.eds.Kampen, NL, 2006).

93. Meining and Senyurt, "Case of the Bavarian Taliban."

94. Ibid.

95. Ibid.

96. Katrin Brettfeld and Peter Wetzels, *Muslime in Deutschland: Integration, Intergrationsbarrieren, Religion und Einstellungen zu Demokratie, Rechtsstaat und politisch-religiös motivierter Gewalt* (Hamburg: Universität Hamburg, 2007), 39.

97. Meining and Senyurt, "Case of the Bavarian Taliban."

98. See, e.g., Omar Nasiri, *Inside the Jihad* (New York: Basic Books, 2006), 111.

99. Interview with New York Police Department Assistant Commissioner Larry Sanchez., New York City, June 13, 2007

100. Claudia Preckel, "Philosophers, Freedom Fighters, Pantomimes: South Asian Muslims in Germany," in *Minorities: Islam and Muslims in Germany,* ed. Ala Al-Hamarneh and Jörn Thielmann, 7 vols. (Leiden: Brill, 2008), 7:319.

101. Meining and Senyurt, "Case of the Bavarian Taliban."

102. Ibid.

103. Ibid.

104. Ibid.

105. Markus Wehner, "Sie sind gekommen, um zu töten," *Faz.Net* [Online], February 6, 2009, http://www.faz.net/s/Rub594835B672714A1DB1A121534F010EE1/Doc~E7E9D 02193F364B35BC2999B751BE8F86~ATpl~Ecommon~Scontent.html, accessed August 4, 2009.

106. Göran Schattauer and Sandra Zistl. "Um Gottes Willen," *Focus* [Online], July 9, 2007, http://www.focus.de/politik/deutschland/terror-um-gottes-willen_aid:225508.html, accessed August 4, 2009.

107. Ronald Sandee, "Al Qaeda and Europe; the Case of the German Pakistani Aleeem Nasir" [Online], June 2, 2009, www.nefafoundation.org, accessed August 1, 2009.

108. "In Ulm und Neu-Ulm herum," Jungle World [Online], September 20, 2007, http://www.jungle-world.com/seiten/2007/38/10637.php, accessed September 25, 2007; Concern Resurfaces Over Islamist Radicals in Germany's South, Deutsche Welle [Online], September 6, 2007, http://www.dw-world.de/dw/article/0,2144,2768038,00.html, accessed September 26, 2007.

109. Markus Wehner, "Sie sind gekommen um zu töten," *Frankfurter Allgemeine Sonntagszeitung,* July 21, 2007.

110. "Deutscher Dschihadist bei Einreise festgenommen", *Die Welt,* August 16, 2007; Rudiger Soldt, "Rieche den Duft des Paradeises," *Frankfurter Allgemeine Zeitung,* August 16, 2007.

111. Meining and Senyurt, "The Case of the Bavarian Taliban."

112. Statement by Islamic Information Center, *Tagespiegel,* September 9, 2007.

113. David Crawford, "Germany Bans Group over Jihad Allegations," *Wall Street Journal,* December 29, 2005; Roland Ströbele, "Southern German Towns Become Hub of Jihadism," *World Politics Review* [Online], September 17, 2007, http://www.worldpoliticsreview.com/ author.aspx, accessed January 15, 2008.

114. "Informationszentrum in Ulm will sich auflösen," *Der Tagespiegel,* October 2, 2007.

115. For recent evidence of al Qaeda's involvement in the Madrid train bombings, see Fernando Reinares, "11-M: la conexion al-Qaeda," *El Pais,* December 17, 2009.

116. Roger Boyes, "Germany on Edge after Fourth Consecutive al-Qaeda Bomb Attack Warning," *Times* (London) [Online], September 21, 2009, http://www.timesonline.co.uk/ tol/news/world/europe/article6841890.ece, accessed September 30, 2009.

117. Einar Koch and Joachim Offermannis, " German Airports Under Armed Guard After Al-Qaeda Threats" [Online], September 24, 2009, http://www.bild.de/BILD/news/ bild-english/world-news/2009/09/24/german-airports-terror-alert/armed-guard-after-al-qaeda-threats-ahead-of-election.html, accessed October 6, 2009; Boyes, "Germany on Edge."

118. Yassin Musharbash, Marel Rosenbach, and Holger Stark, "Al-Qaida Threatens Terror Attacks in Germany after Election," Spiegelonline, September 18, 2009. http://www. spiegel.de/international/germany/0,1518,651811,00.html, accessed October 14, 2009.

119. Musharbash, Rosenbach, and Stark, "Al-Qaida Threatens Terror Attacks."

120. Nick Grace, "Al Qaeda's Final Push before German Elections," *Long War Journal* [Online], September 27, 2009; http://www.longwarjournal.org/threat-matrix/ archives/2009/09/al_qaedas_final_push_before_ge.php, accessed October 10, 2009.

121. Another example is the July 2010 attack by the al Qaeda regional affiliate al-Shabab on Kampala in retaliation for Ugandan participation with the African Unity peacekeeping force in Somalia.

Chapter 14

1. Nathan Glazer and Daniel P. Moynihan, *Beyond the Melting Pot* (Cambridge, MA: MIT Press), 1970.

2. Clifford Geertz, *The Interpretation of Cultures* (New York: Basic Books, 1973), 44.

3. Hans Kohn, *The Idea of Nationalism: A Study in Its Origins and Background* (New York: Macmillan, 1944).

4. Benedict Anderson, *Imagined Communities* (London: Verso, 1983).

5. Friedrich Nietzsche, *Thus Spoke Zarathustra* (New York: Penguin, 1969), 86.

6. Kohn, *Idea of Nationalism*, 188; see also Anthony Smith, *The Ethnic Origin of Nations* (Malden, MA: Blackwell, 1986), 18.

7. Kohn, *Idea of Nationalism*, 11.

8. Ibid., 22.

9. Christian Joppke, *Veil: Mirror of Identity* (Cambridge, UK: Polity, 2009), 120–121.

10. Ibid.

11. Ibid.

12. Anthony Smith, *National Identity* (London: Penguin, 1991), 73.

13. Che Guevara's famous slogan, transmitted in 1966 from the jungles of Bolivia to the Organization of Solidarity with the Peoples of Asia, Africa and Latin America, known as the Tricontinental, in Cuba was "Create two, three, many Vietnams."

14. See chapter 13, and Jonathan Laurence and Justin Vaisse, *Integrating Islam: Political and Religious Challenges in Contemporary France* (Washington, DC: Brookings, 2006), and Emmanuel Todd, *Le destin de assimilation et ségrégation dans les démocraties* (Paris: Seuil, 1994).

15. Plato is unfair to mixed breeds. They can make as good watchdogs as pedigreed canines. The issue is how they are educated.

16. Al Qaeda is the terrorist excrescence of the Islamist revival movement; Saddam's Ba'ath Party was an Arabist secular political party. Until our invasion of Iraq brought them temporarily together, al Qaeda and the Ba'ath Party were inveterate and bitter enemies. For two generations the combat between Islamism and secularism (in the form of Arab nationalism) bloodied Middle East campuses, villages, and slums, including those within Ba'athist Syria and Iraq. To be sure, both groups can be described as totalitarian, with the Ba'ath being indubitably inspired by Hitler and Stalin, and issuing bloodthirsty Syria and in an Iraqi regime that Kenan Makiya argued was totalitarian in *The Republic of Fear* (Berkeley: University of California Press, 1998). And the 9/11 Commission and the Senate Select Committee on the CIA each found that what there was of Saddam's narrow, sporadic "interaction with al Qaida was impelled by mutual antipathy towards the United States and the Saudis" (see Robert S. Leiken, "The Truth about the Saddam–al Qaeda Connection" [Online], November 2004, http://www.inthenationalinterest.com/Articles/November2004/November2004Leiken.html, accessed December 7, 2004).

17. Unsurprisingly, the fascist label enters political discourse more often as a slur than as historical analysis or political science. The Comintern in its radical "third period" tagged their Social Democrat rivals as "Social Fascists." Franklin Delano Roosevelt and his New Deal were branded fascist. More recently the malediction has been applied to conservatives such as Charles de Gaulle, Barry Goldwater, Margaret Thatcher, Ronald Reagan, and George W. Bush. In reprisal, an American neoconservative gained a spot on the best-seller list with the title *Liberal Fascism*.

To be sure, the Nazis ruled and conducted international affairs by terror. The fascists were aggressive and militarist foes of democracy and liberal values. They adulated violence and death, revered charismatic leaders, and singled out Jews for mass murder. Today's Holy Warrior shares with fascism an appalling fetish: not merely a cult of death but of suicide terror—"martyrdom operations" for the former; the cult of heroic death (*Heldentod*, or *kamikaze)*, for the latter.

Like the fascists and the Nazis of yesteryear, jihadis, and here also many Islamist militants, imagine themselves victims, plot revenge against the liberal West and propagate paranoid conspiracy theories. Also, like the Nazis, the jihadis have on their heads the slaughter of countless defenseless civilians and proudly declare their hatred for the Enlightenment. But like all analogies used in historical analysis this one limps. Fascism was shaped by a time and a place and its epoch appears to have ended with World War II. The label disregards the specific Arabic contribution, though Nazi propaganda did reach the Middle East in the form of short-wave radio broadcasts in Arabic, but its influence there was not limited to Islamists.

"Fascism" itself, like Islamism, came in quite different varieties as Walter Laqueur reminds us in his refreshingly temperate and informed analysis of the "Islamofascist" label. "Hitler," Laqueur points out, "would have emphatically rejected the fascist label—Nazism, as he saw it, was a specifically German phenomenon and despite certain ideological communalities and common interests was quite different from Italian fascism." Laqueur concludes that "Islamofascism" and "Islamophobia" are both "imprecise terms we could well do without, but it is doubtful whether they can be removed from our political lexicon" (Walter Laqueur, *The Origins of Fascism: Islamic Fascism, Islamophobia, Antisemitism* [Oxford: Oxford University Press]. Available: http://blog.oup.com/2006/10/the_origins_of_2/, accessed December 2, 2007.

    18. Pankaj Mirsha, "How Should Western Intellectuals Respond to Muslim Scholars?" *New Yorker*, June 7, 2010.

GLOSSARY

Umar Farouk Abdulmutallab: The 2009 underwear bomber.

Abu Hamza al Masri: The one-eyed, hook-handed preacher and "Lord of Londonistan" who presided over London's most prominent radical mosque at Finsbury Park.

Abu Qatada: The "Lord of Londonistan" who was once called "the most significant extremist preacher in the UK."

Abdullah Azzam: The father of the Afghan-Arab jihad.

Al Jihad: A terrorist group run by Ayman Al-Zawahiri, which began as a nationalist jihad group focused on the Egyptian home country, but after its efforts there faltered, the group adopted bin Laden's strategy of global jihad.

al-Muhajiroun: The organization founded by Omar Bakri after he left Hizb ut-Tahrir.

Al-Wala' wa'l-Bara': Loyalty and repudiation; Saudi doctrine enjoining the repudiation of infidels and "hypocrites."

Arab Case: A German court decision that ruled that expelling Palestinian students after the 1972 Munich Olympics violated the Palestinians' constitutional rights.

Asabiyya: A cohesive force, postulated by the fourteenth-century Arab philosopher Ibn Khaldun, which holds societies together.

Omar Bakri: A "Lord of Londonistan" who founded the British branch of Hizb ut-Tahrir and, later, al-Muhajiroun, which sent second-generation British Muslim radicals to Pakistan.

Banlieues: The depressed suburbs on the outskirts of French cities.

Hasan al-Banna: Founder of the Muslim Brotherhood in 1928; he was assassinated in 1949.

Barlevi: A Sufi school of Islam that was opposed by the Deobandis in the mid-nineteenth-century Indian subcontinent.

Bida: Heretical innovations.

Biradiri: "Clan" in Urdu.

Mohammad Bouyeri: The Dutch slayer of Theo van Gogh.

Farouk Butt: The owner of the Stratford Street Mosque, who, along with Hanif Malik, helped to fund Mohammed Sidique Khan's operations.

Caliphate: The traditional Islamic form of government, led by a caliph, either appointed or elected, who is considered the political leader of all Muslims.

CFCM (Conseil Français du Culte Musulman; French Council of the Muslim Faith): A group created in 2003.

Covenant of Security: A doctrine that supposedly allowed extremists to organize and agitate in return for not harming Britain.

CPE (First Employment Contract): A plan devised by Prime Minister de Villepin that was devised to loosen the stratified labor system in France.

Crevice Plot: The first Islamist terror plot (in 2004) against Britain itself.

Cüneyt Ciftci: A German Turk who steered a pickup truck loaded with five tons of explosives into a guard post in Afghanistan.

Da'wa: Propagation of Islam; preaching; literally, an "invitation" to the faith.

Deobandi: A fundamentalist school of Islam that rejected the traditional Barelvi conventions starting in mid-nineteenth-century India.

Desh pardesh: "Home away from home" in Urdu.

Deutsche Taliban Mujahidin: The Jihadi group to which Eric Breininger belonged.

DST (Direction de la Surveillance du Territoire; Territorial Surveillance Directorate): Security bureau of the French national police; merged in 2007 with the RG (see below) to form the DCRI (Direction Centrale du Renseignement Intérieur).

FAF (Fraternité Algérienne en France): An FIS-linked Algerian group in France.

Abdullah el Faisal: Jamaican convert and the "Lord of Londonistan" who mentored Richard Reid, the shoe bomber, and Germaine Lindsay, Sidique Khan's comrade-in-arms.

Far Enemy: The imperialist power, usually the United States, that props up the "apostate" regime in Muslim countries.

Fatwa: Islamic religious decree.

Fiqh: Islamic jurisprudence.

FIS (Front Islamique du Salut; Islamic Salvation Front): A loose confederation of Islamists and Salafists that was widely expected to win the second round of an emergency election in Algeria in January 1992. The Algerian army canceled the election.

Fitna: Discord, specifically among Muslims.

Fundamentalist: A form of Islam that is austere, literal, orthodox, and scriptural.

GI (Gamaa Islamiyya): An Islamist jihadi group founded in opposition to the Egyptian Muslim Brotherhood.

GIA (Groupe Islamique Armé; Armed Islamic Group): An Algerian jihadi group that was implicated in a wave of bombings and assassinations in France during 1995–1996.

Hadith: The collection of sayings and doings of the Prophet.

Hafiz: Someone who has memorized the Qur'an.

Haram: Shame; actions that bring shame because they are forbidden by Islam.

Hijab: Headscarf.

Hijra: The emigration of the Prophet from Mecca to Medina in 622 AD; by extension it refers to any migration from an environment that is threatening to Muslims.

HT (Hizb ut-Tahrir; Party of Liberation): An Islamist cadre organization. Under Omar Bakri's leadership, it became Britain's leading radical Muslim group in the early 1990s.

Ibn Khaldun: The fourteenth-century Islamic philosopher who developed the concept of asabiyya.

IJU (Islamic Jihad Union): An al Qaeda–affiliated group that took responsibility for a March 2008 attack in Afghanistan, which resulted in the deaths of sixty individuals. The IJU split from the IMU in 2002.

Imam: A prayer leader.

IMU (Islamic Movement of Uzbekistan): A jihadi group that until recently focused on the "near enemy."

Indian Case: 1978 German court decision in which it was decided that workers who had stayed in Germany a long time had thereby acquired a constitutionally protected "reliance interest" that overrode the official state policy of zero immigration.

Islamism: Islamism comes in three broad types—missionary, political, or jihadi—each of which seeks to preserve the tradition while borrowing selectively from the West.

Jahiliyya: Ignorance, specifically the period of barbarism that preceded Mohammad's ministry.

Jaish e Mohammed: A mujahideen organization, based in Pakistan, that seeks to separate Kashmir from India.

Jihadis: Militants who reject "man-made" electoral politics and embrace violence.

Jihadism: Muslims who "wish to revolt" by embracing violence against the infidel. An important distinction among jihadis is between nationalists and globalists.

JIMAS (Jamiat Ihyaa Minhaaj Al Sunnah; The Association to Revive the Way of the Messenger): A Salafist group that many British students joined after having studied abroad in Saudi Arabia; a rival of Hizb ut-Tahrir.

Jus sanguinis: Blood lineage.

Jus soli: Territorial birthright.

Kaffir: Infidels.

Khaled Kelkal: An Algerian involved in the 1995 terror bombings in France.

Mohammed Sidique Khan: The leader of the 2005 London bombings.

Omar Khyam: The leader of the plot to bomb London malls and nightclubs in 2004.

Laïcité: The French conception of a secular society, denoting the strict separation of church and state, especially the absence of religious involvement in politics or government.

Lashkar-e-Taiba: The Kashmiri jihadi group notorious worldwide for its 2008 attack on Mumbai.

Leitkultur: The German "leading culture" to which immigrants are expected to conform.

Lena dena: Urdu for a protracted and regular exchange of gifts.

LIFG (Libyan Islamic Fighting Group): A Libyan nationalist jihadi group, formed by Libyan veterans of the Afghan war, which joined with al Qaeda in 2007.

Germaine Lindsay: A Jamaican convert to Islam and one of the Beeston bombers.

Madrasah: A religious school at which the Qur'an is taught.

Hanif Malik: Malik, with the aid of Farouk Butt, presided over a welfare conglomerate on Beeston Hill that embraced the Hamara Centre. He helped finance Mohammed Sidique Khan's operations.

Abdul a la Maududi: The Indian lawyer and journalist who founded the Jama'at-Islami (JI) party in the early 1940s as the only Islamist movement on the subcontinent with an explicit political orientation.

Zacarias Moussaoui: A French citizen who trained for but did not take part in the September 11, 2001, attacks. He is known as the twentieth hijacker.

Mullah: An educated Muslim who is trained in theology.

Mullah Crew/Mullah Boys: A group of young Muslims on Beeston Hill.

Multikultur Haus: A mosque in Ulm Germany that several jihadis frequented.

Muslim Brotherhood (aka Ikhwan): A political Islamic group founded in Egypt after the collapse of Ottoman rule after World War I. It would open branches in other regions and after World War II in Europe.

Omar Nasiri: The Moroccan double agent who attended training camps in Afghanistan. He passed information to the UK and French intelligence services.

Near Enemy: The "apostate" regime in Muslim countries (such as the Egyptian secular regime and the Jordanian royal family).

Niqab: Face cover.

Obin Commission: Government commission that investigated conditions in French schools.

Abu Omar: An Egyptian medical student who graduated summa cum laude from the University of Freiburg in 1994 and became, in Ulm and Neu Ulm, a lord of "Deutsche Londonistan" involved with Multikultur Haus.

Political Islamism: Political Islamists seek the restoration of Islam not through missionary work but through politics.

Postmigrant: A broad term that encompasses the second and third generations of immigrants.

Purdah: A curtain or screen, used mainly on the Indian subcontinent to segregate women; rules regarding female segregation.

Sayyid Qutb: The Egyptian intellectual who inspired Islamist jihadism.

Rachid Ramda: Accused by the French of being the "banker, logistics chief and the mastermind" of the attacks orchestrated by Kelkal.

Richard Reid: The failed shoe bomber.

RG (Direction Centrale des Renseignements Généraux; Central Directorate of General Intelligence; often called Renseignements Généraux): An intelligence service of the French police; the service merged in 2007 with the DST (see above) to form the DCRI (Direction Centrale du Renseignement Intérieur).

Sahwa: Awakening; a movement that formed in Saudi Arabia under the influence of the exiled Muslim Brotherhood.

Salafism: The branch of Islam that relies on Islam's pious patristic ancestors, especially the Prophet and his companions (the Salafs), for strict instructions on how to live a religious life.

Salafist jihadis: Salafists who practice violent jihad.

Salafist pietists: Salafists who practice peaceful methods of propagation, education, and purification to convince followers to embrace literally the teachings of the Salafs.

Salwar kameez: Dress worn by both men and women in South and Central Asia.

Sauerland plot: A jihadi plot to kill at least 150 American soldiers stationed in Germany. The majority of the forty or so implicated in the 2007 Sauerland plot were ethnic Turks.

Ahmed Omar Sayyid Sheik: British Pakistani convicted in Pakistan for his role in the murder of the *Wall Street Journal* reporter Daniel Pearl.

Sharia: Islamic law.

Shia: A faction of Islam that emerged in the seventh century over claims to the succession of the Prophet. This minority tradition believed "Ali," the Prophet's son-in-law, should have been the Prophet's rightful successor.

Shirk: Idolatry; associating unholy things with God; the greatest sin in Islam because it undermines monotheism.

Stasi Commission: A commission under Jacques Chirac that recommended banning the wearing of the headscarf by minors in schools receiving state funds, whether public or private.

Sufi: Folk Islam that is characterized by custom, worship at shrines, reverence of holy men (variously *pirs* or *marabouts*), adornment of gravestones, prayer in brightly decorated mosques, and song and dance in festivals.

Sunni: The "orthodox" branch of Islam that believes that the first four caliphs—Mohammad's successors—rightfully took his place as the religion's leaders. Sunni Islam, the faith that al Qaeda and most European Muslims share, comes in a variety of forms.

Surah: Qur'anic verse.

TJ (Tabligh Jama'at): Founded in India in 1926, Tablighi activists have spread throughout the world to become the most prominent Islamic missionary group. Jihadis have used TJ networks to make contacts, but they abjure the group's apolitical orientation.

Tahhara: Purification.

Takfir: Anathema.

Shehzad Tanweer: One of the four Beeston men who detonated explosives during the July 7, 2005, bombings in the London underground.

Tarbiyaa: Education and training; "culturing."

Tariqa: The path or way or method toward knowledge of God; the province of sheiks.

Tawhid: Monotheism.

'Ulema: Lawyers and scholars of Islam.

Ummah: The worldwide Muslim community.

UMP (Union for a Popular Movement): A center-right political party in France founded in 2002 by Jacques Chirac. The UMP supported the headscarf ban as a way of reinforcing laïcité, neutralizing political opponents, and stigmatizing the Left's embrace of multiculturalism.

UOIF (Union of French Islamic Organizations): A French Muslim umbrella organization led by the Muslim Brotherhood that accepts Muslims' minority status and emphasizes respecting the host society's laws.

Verfassungschutz: The German Office of the Protection of the Constitution.

Le voile: French term for "veil."

Wahhabism: A movement based on the eighteenth-century preaching of Arabian Mohammed ibn Abd-al-Wahhab. His doctrine held that pure Islam had been perverted by the worship of shrines and holy men. Wahhab sustained that the way to reestablish Islam's dominance over its competitors was to cauterize any impurities, violently when necessary. Wahhab joined forces with Mohammed Ibn Saud in wars of conquest that eventually would make the Saudis kings and Wahhabism the creed of their subjects. Today, the term has lost much of its descriptive value and is often used pejoratively.

INDEX

racism
  in court system, 12–13
  as institutionalized, 7, 12–13, 20–21, 27,
    38, 42, 144
  rapper lifestyle *vs.*, 42
  resentment of, 8
radicalization, Islamic, 330
  of Abu Hamza al Masri, 163–64, 171,
    284n18
  asabiyya and, 74, 262, 264, 267,
    327, 330
  conversion as, 234–35, 318n80
  encapsulation for, 169–70, 235
  by FPM, 171, 180–83
  in Germany, 229, 231, 233–34, 238,
    317n53
  by HT, 157
  of Insiders, 90, 187, 207
  Islam and, 10, 78, 159
  of Kelkal, 6–9, 11–12, 14–15, 27, 65,
    196, 254
  of Khan, 27, 62, 73, 80, 150, 176, 190–91,
    198–99, 208–9, 215, 233, 254
  of Mullah Crew, 73, 138, 159, 195
  against near enemy, 160
  by Outsiders, 90, 155
  of postmigrants, 75, 155
  reasons for, 159, 198
  of Reid, 152
  by TJ, 14, 82, 196, 254, 312n38
  Wahhabism and, 223
  by Al-Wala' wa'l-Bara', 90, 201, 232,
    312n57
Raffarin, Jean-Pierre, 24
Ramadan, 27, 32
Ramadan, Tariq, 19, 32, 103
Rambo, Lewis, 234–35, 318n80
Ramda, Rachid, 16, 151, 182, 332
rap, gangsta, 42
Reagan, Ronald, 48
Reid, Richard
  radicalization of, 152, 162, 254
  as shoe bomber, 65, 89, 152, 182, 235, 329,
    333
Reidel, Bruce, 112–13
Renseignements Généraux. *See* Direction
    Centrale du Renseignement Généraux
Ressam, Ahmed, 182
reversion, by postmigrants, xiii, 236

R.G. *See* Direction Centrale du
    Renseignement Généraux
rioting
  in England, 213–14
  in France, 17–18, 30, 34, 37–40, 46, 58,
    109, 278n10, 281n3
  RG report on, 41
  suppression of, 47–48
  as unorganized, 39–40, 46
"Rivers of Blood" (speech), 99, 291n48
Rodriguez, Richard, 43
Romania Libera (newspaper), 34
Romeo and Juliet (Shakespeare), 189
Ronson, Jon, 186
Roy, Olivier, 63, 66, 75, 171, 205, 284n11,
    287n23
Rushdie, Salman, 152, 158
Rushdie Affair, 22, 103, 152–53, 214

Sadat, Anwar, 67, 85–86
Saeed Sheikh, Ahmed Omar, 182, 216
Sahih Bokhari (hadith collection), 66
Sahraoui, Abdelkader, 15
sahwa (Awakening), 87, 333
Said, Edward, 144
Salafism, 333
  as apolitical, 52–53, 66
  apostasy and, 68, 284n16
  in FIS, 329
  as fundamentalism, 63, 83
  jihad for, 66–67, 333
  JIMAS as, 331
  Old Salafism *vs.*, 287n23
  as political, 284n11
  for postmigrants, 53
  revival of, 83
  TJ and, 53
  Wahhabis and, 67
Salafist Group for Preaching and Combat.
    See Groupe Salafiste pour la
    Predication et le Combat
Salafist Pietists, 333
  as apolitical, 53, 88, 177
  music and, 222
  as peaceful, 333
  from Saudi Arabia, 266
  as separatists, 67
Salafs (Prophet's companions), 333
Salim, Mamdouh, 255